Getting the framework right

Policy and re[...]

Paul B. McGuir[...]
John D. Conro[...]
Ganesh B. Tha[...]

The Foundatio[...]

Published with ge[...]
Sustainable Banki[...]

THE FOUNDATION FOR DEVELOPMENT COOPERATION

B.W[...]
Banking[...]

Published by
The Foundation For Development Cooperation Ltd A.C.N. 011 025 997
PO Box 10445 Adelaide Street
Brisbane QLD 4000 Australia

First published 1998

National Library of Australia
Cataloguing-in-Publication entry:

McGuire. Paul (Paul B.). 1962-.
Getting the framework right : policy and regulation for microfinance in Asia.

Bibliography.
ISBN 0 9586728 3 0.

1. Financial institutions - Asia. 2. Banks and banking - Asia. 3. Small business - Asia - Finance. I. Controy, John D. (John David). 1938-. II. Thapa, G. B. (Ganesh B.). III. Foundation for Development Cooperation. IV. Title.

332.1095

Manuscript editor
Barbara Henson

Cover design and production
Peter Evans

Printed by
Merino Lithographics Pty Ltd

The Foundation for Development Cooperation
PO Box 10445 Adelaide Street
Brisbane QLD 4000 Australia
Telephone 61 7 3236 4633
Facsimile 61 7 3236 4696
E-mail fdc@ozemail.com.au

Foreword

This study of the policy and regulatory environment for microfinance in Asia was prepared by The Foundation for Development Cooperation on behalf of the Banking with the Poor (BWTP) Network, a network of more than thirty microfinance institutions (MFIs), commercial banks, central banks and other institutions involved in microfinance from nine countries in Asia.

The study represents the third in a series of major studies of best practice in microfinance prepared by the Foundation for the BWTP Network. It follows the influential publications *Banking with the Poor* (1992) and *Best Practice of Banking with the Poor* (1995). Drawing on the experiences of members of the Network, these publications demonstrated the efficacy of linkages between commercial banks on the one hand, and non-governmental organisations (NGOs) and self-help groups (SHGs) of the poor on the other, as a mechanism for extending financial services to the poor on a sustainable basis. They also outlined a set of best practices that could be adopted by NGOs, SHGs, governments, central banks, commercial banks and donor agencies to encourage such linkages and, more generally, to encourage the development of microfinance on a sustainable basis.

The focus of the current study is more narrowly defined than those of the two preceding volumes. When the Banking with the Poor project commenced in 1991, microfinance was very much on the fringe of the development debate. While a number of major MFIs were already operating very successfully, the role and importance of microfinance was not generally acknowledged by governments and donor agencies. There was a need for careful research to demonstrate that microfinance is indeed able to reach large numbers of poor households on a sustainable basis, as well as to highlight the potential role of microfinance to a much wider audience. *Banking with the Poor* and *Best Practice of Banking with the Poor* played an important role in this process, with particular reference to the Asian region.

These objectives have now largely been achieved. It is now generally accepted by the international development community that microfinance has an important role in poverty reduction. This acceptance is perhaps best demonstrated by the establishment in 1995 of the Consultative Group to Assist the Poorest (CGAP) under the auspices of the World Bank to increase the resources devoted to microfinance, and by the 1997 Microcredit Summit which launched a global movement to reach 100 million of the world's poorest families with microfinance by the year 2005.

Reflecting this increased acceptance, there has been an explosion of information and research on microfinance. Numerous agencies and research bodies, not least the CGAP itself, are promoting detailed studies of key issues related to microfinance, and are producing guidelines and standards to assist MFIs in expanding their outreach to poor clients on a sustainable basis. Given this, there would be limited value in conducting another study which attempted to provide a *tour de horizon* of best practice in microfinance.

For this reason, the BWTP Network decided that it would be appropriate in its research program for 1997 to focus on two specific issues, namely, the policy and regulatory environment for microfinance, and the role of commercial banks. These issues were chosen because they address perceived gaps in the literature, and because they build on the specific character and areas of expertise of the BWTP Network. The study of the role of commercial banks is to be published separately by the Foundation. We are grateful to Ms Ruth Goodwin-Groen for discussions which assisted us to define these two research topics and to design the framework for this report.

This policy study has been financed and conducted by The Foundation for Development Cooperation. The BWTP Network is grateful to FDC Chairman Dr Brian Scott and his board for committing these resources. I am indebted to my colleague, principal author Mr Paul McGuire, and to Mr G. B. Thapa, consultant to Banking with the Poor, for carrying the major burden of travelling and data gathering in the nine Network countries in preparation for this study. We are jointly indebted to our colleagues in the BWTP Network institutions in those countries, and to more than 250 microfinance practitioners, bankers, regulators and policymakers whose names are listed after each of the relevant country studies. The high levels of cooperation and interest shown by people associated with microfinance throughout the region are indicative of the timeliness of this report.

Commencing around the time our fieldwork was completed, in July 1997, there occurred a rolling series of economic disturbances in countries of East Asia, beginning with Thailand. At the time of writing this foreword, the economies of Indonesia, Malaysia and the Philippines, in addition to Thailand, have experienced currency devaluations, a marked reduction in levels of economic activity, and severe pressure on their financial systems and individual financial institutions. It is too early for us to judge what the longer term impacts of such developments will be upon the potential for sustainable microfinance in these and other countries of the region. It will be a tragedy if current events retard the acceptance by formal financial institutions of the potential for profitable engagement with microfinance, or if hasty impulses to re-regulation throw up unintended barriers to microfinance institutions. It is not the bad debts of the poor which have caused financial systems in the region to reel.

As explained in the introduction to the study, an earlier draft of the report was presented to members of the BWTP Network, meeting in Bangkok in November 1997. The BWTP Network issued a statement based on the study which is reprinted as a preface to this volume.

The Bangkok meeting was conducted jointly by The Foundation for Development Cooperation, the BWTP Network and the *Sustainable* Banking with the Poor project of the World Bank. The Foundation and the BWTP Network appreciate the financial support of the World Bank for the conduct of the workshop, as well as contributions from the Ford Foundation, Japan Foundation, Asia Center, and the Australian Agency for International Development.

The publication of this book has been supported by an additional grant from the *Sustainable* Banking with the Poor project of the World Bank. This is acknowledged with thanks.

John D. Conroy
Executive Director
The Foundation for Development Cooperation
BWTP Secretariat

May 1998

Contents

Notes All local currency amounts are converted to US dollars using year average exchange rates for 1996. However, note that the currencies of the four Southeast Asian countries (Indonesia, Malaysia, Philippines and Thailand) have depreciated sharply since mid-1997, reflecting the financial crisis in those countries. For instance, by end-January 1998 the Indonesian rupiah had depreciated by 80.5 per cent against the dollar, and the Thai baht had depreciated 54.2 per cent against the dollar.

Unless indicated otherwise, all dollar amounts in this publication are in US dollars.

Acronyms

General

ADB	Asian Development Bank
APRACA	Asia Pacific Rural and Agricultural Credit Association
AusAID	Australian Agency for International Development
BWTP	Banking with the Poor
CASHPOR	Credit and Savings for the Hardcore Poor
CECI	Canadian Center for International Studies and Cooperation
CIDA	Canadian International Development Agency
CGAP	Consultative Group to Assist the Poorest
FAO	Food and Agriculture Organization
FDC	The Foundation for Development Cooperation
GDP	gross domestic product
GNP	gross national product
GTZ	German agency for technical cooperation
IFAD	International Fund for Agricultural Development
ILO	International Labour Organization
MFI	microfinance institution
NGO	non-governmental organisation
OECF	Overseas Economic Cooperation Fund (Japan)
ROSCA	rotating savings and credit association
SAARC	South Asian Association for Regional Cooperation
SHG	self-help group
UNDP	United Nations Development Programme
UNICEF	United Nations International Children's Emergency Fund
USAID	United States Agency for International Development
WFP	World Food Programme

Bangladesh

ASA	Association for Social Advancement
BRAC	Bangladesh Rural Advancement Committee
BRDB	Bangladesh Rural Development Board
CDF	Credit and Development Forum
HES	household expenditure survey
PKSF	Palli Karma Sahayak Foundation

India

AIAMED	All India Association of Micro Enterprises Development
EFICOR	Evangelical Fellowship of India Commission on Relief

IRDP	Integrated Rural Development Programme
JRY	Jawahar Rozgar Yojana
MYRADA	Mysore Resettlement and Development Agency
NABARD	National Bank for Agriculture and Rural Development
PDS	Public Distribution System
PRADAN	Professional Assistance for Development Action
RMK	Rashtriya Mahila Kosh
SHARE	Society for Helping and Awakening Rural Poor through Education
SIDBI	Small Industries Development Bank of India

Indonesia

BKD	rural credit agencies
BKKBN	National Family Planning Coordination Board
BPDs	provincial government banks
BPRs	rural banks
BRI	Bank Rakyat Indonesia
CUCO	Indonesian Credit Union Coordinating Office
IDT	Inpres Desa Tertinggal, or Presidential Instruction relating to backward villages
KUD	Koperasi Unit Desa
KUK	Kredit Usaha Kecil, small-scale business credits
KUT	farming activities credit
LDKP	rural fund and credit institutions
Perbanas	Association of Indonesian National Private Banks
Perbarindo	Association of Indonesian Rural Banks
P4K	Income Generating Project for Marginal Farmers and Landless
PHBK	project linking banks with self-help groups
SFG	small farmer group

Malaysia

AIM	Amanah Ikhtiar Malaysia
CGC	Credit Guarantee Corporation
KLIBOR	Kuala Lumpur inter-bank offer rate
YPEIM	Foundation for Islamic Economic Development

Nepal

ADB/N	Agricultural Development Bank of Nepal
BNA	basic need approach
CSD	Center for Self-Help Development
ERDB	Eastern Region Development Bank
IBP	Intensive Banking Program
MCPW	Micro Credit Project for Women
MPHBS	Multi-purpose Household Budget Survey

NBL	Nepal Bank Ltd
NEFSCUN	Nepal Federation of Saving and Credit Cooperatives Union
NLSS	Nepal Living Standards Survey
NRB	Nepal Rastra Bank
PCRW	Production Credit for Rural Women
RBB	Rastriya Banijya Bank
RRDBs	regional rural development banks
RSRF	Rural Self-Reliance Fund
SAARC	South Asian Association for Regional Cooperation
SCO	savings and credit organisation
SFDP	Small Farmers Development Program
SPO	Sub-Project Office
VDC	village development committee
WDS	Women Development Section

Pakistan

AKRSP	Aga Khan Rural Support Program
BUSTI	Basic Urban Services for Katchi Abadis
NDFC	National Development Finance Corporation
NWFP	North West Frontier Province
SBFC	Small Business Finance Corporation

Philippines

APPEND	Association of Philippine Partners in Enterprise Development
BAP	Bankers' Association of the Philippines
BPI	Bank of the Philippine Islands
CDA	Cooperative Development Authority
DSMP	Developing Standards for Microfinance Project
LandBank	Land Bank of the Philippines
NATCCO	National Confederation of Cooperatives
NCC	National Credit Council
PCFC	People's Finance and Credit Cooperation
PHILNET	a group of MFIs engaged in Grameen replication
SEC	Securities and Exchange Commission
SRA	Social Reform Agenda

Sri Lanka

CRB	cooperative rural bank
FTCCS	Federation of Thrift and Credit Cooperative Societies
GPU	Gami Pubuduwa Upadeshaka (Hatton National Bank)
JTF	Janasaviya Trust Fund
NDTF	National Development Trust Fund, originally Janasaviya Trust Fund

RRDB	regional rural development bank
SEEDS	Sarvodaya Economic Enterprises Development Services
SFLC	Small Farmers and Landless Credit
TCCSs	thrift and credit cooperative societies

Thailand

BAAC	Bank for Agriculture and Agricultural Cooperatives
CDD	Community Development Department
CODI	Community Organisation Development Institute
GSB	Government Savings Bank
NESDB	National Economic and Social Development Board
UCDO	Urban Community Development Office

Preface

Statement by the Banking with the Poor Network

Preamble

At this Fourth Asia-Pacific Regional Workshop,[1] we have turned our attention to the broad policy and regulatory environment for microfinance in Asia.

Here in Bangkok, representatives from the Banking with the Poor (BWTP) Network, a network of 35 organisations from nine countries of the region, endorse the following statement on the policy and regulatory environment for microfinance in Asia. We commend it to governments, monetary authorities, donor agencies and international financial institutions in the region as the basis for achieving sustainable provision of microfinance services within the broader financial system.

Introduction

The nine countries in the Banking with the Poor (BWTP) Network[2] have a total population of some 1,560 million, or around 27.5 per cent of the world's population. While economic conditions and living standards differ significantly between the countries, around 500 million people in them (one third of the total population) are living in poverty.

Reducing poverty remains the greatest challenge facing governments in the countries in the Network. This requires an integrated policy strategy. Governments should ensure that all policies, including macroeconomic policies, policies for human development, infrastructure policies, policies to support income generation and other policies, are directed firmly and in a coordinated manner to achieving rapid and sustainable reductions in poverty.

Microfinance has an important role in this area. Members of the Network consider that microfinance, along with other supportive activities, is an important ingredient in increasing the productivity of self-employment in the informal sector of the economy. For such 'microentrepreneurs', lack of access to financial services is often a critical constraint to the establishment or expansion of viable microenterprises.

While microfinance has the potential to make an important contribution to poverty reduction in the region, this requires the development of a microfinance

---

1 Held in conjunction with the Asia Regional Conference on *Sustainable* Banking with the Poor. Both meetings were organised jointly by The Foundation for Development Cooperation and the World Bank.

2 Bangladesh, India, Indonesia, Malaysia, Nepal, Pakistan, Philippines, Sri Lanka, Thailand.

sector that is able to reach large numbers of poor people on a sustainable basis. This, in turn, requires increased attention to all aspects of microfinance, including both the internal operations of microfinance institutions (MFIs) and the external policy and regulatory environment in which they operate. This statement on the policy and regulatory environment for microfinance in Asia is based on research conducted by The Foundation for Development Cooperation on behalf of the Network, and discussions at the Fourth Asia-Pacific Regional Workshop on Sustainable Banking with the Poor.

Arrangements for direct support

Members of the Network consider that active support from government and/or donor agencies, including direct financial support, is a necessary catalyst to the establishment of a viable microfinance sector. The research showed that in all countries in the Network where microfinance has achieved significant scale, strong support from governments and/or donor agencies for operating expenses, capacity building and loanable funds has been crucial. While MFIs should strive for self-sufficiency, attaining it takes a considerable period of time, especially if MFIs are targeting the poorest of the poor in an effective manner. To set up their programs, and for a number of years thereafter, MFIs need to be subsidised.

Support for individual microfinance institutions

MFIs in all countries have received considerable support from government and/or donor agencies. In the past, most of this has been in the form of financial assistance direct to individual non-governmental organisations (NGOs) engaged in microfinance. This support has been critical in enabling them to establish, and to increase their outreach and self-sufficiency. NGOs have proven to be particularly effective in the field of microfinance, both as financial intermediaries and as social intermediaries, reflecting their commitment, flexibility, responsiveness, proximity and trust. NGOs have also been very successful in targeting poor women, who are generally the most disadvantaged members of the community, and generally have an excellent record in loan repayment. In some countries, cooperatives have also played an effective role in microfinance.

Nevertheless, the development of microfinance and the success of leading MFIs owes more to the vision of their founders and management than to the criteria used by government and donor agencies for supporting them. Support has been largely ad hoc in nature.

The Guiding Principles for Selecting and Supporting Intermediaries, agreed by major donor agencies in October 1995, provide a number of suggestions as to how support by donors and government can best be directed to maximising outreach and sustainability. Most importantly, governments and donor agencies should only support institutions which demonstrate a capacity to reach poor clients, particularly poor women, on a sustainable basis. Support should be directed to institutions with demonstrated performance or credible plans in areas such as institutional strengths, quality of services and outreach, and financial performance. It is also important that support be transparent, and not be politicised.

The role of second tier microfinance institutions

Most countries included in the study have some form of 'second tier' microfinance institution which channels funds from government and/or donor agencies to individual MFIs.

The Network considers that second tier microfinance institutions can be very effective in supporting MFIs. They are a one-stop funding source, enable easier supervision of partner organisations, and can avoid the delays that often arise when relying on other funding sources. For these reasons, governments and donor agencies should channel their support for microfinance, as much as possible, through efficient and well-managed second tier microfinance institutions.

At the same time, experience points to a number of issues that need to be addressed to ensure that second tier institutions operate on a sound basis. They should:

- Establish and enforce appropriate performance and reporting standards for the MFIs that they fund. This is discussed in more detail in the section on regulation of non-bank MFIs.
- Support MFIs based on the standards they achieve, rather than the model they follow. There is scope for a diversity of models and institutional forms, including financial intermediaries, social intermediaries, and mixed financial/social intermediaries.
- Facilitate training to partner organisations, and enable exchange of best practice between them.
- Avoid unrealistic disbursement targets. Pressure to meet unrealistic targets may cause institutions to lower their standards.
- Not impose interest rate ceilings on their partner organisations or, if they do, they should ensure that ceilings are adequate for partners to operate on a sustainable basis.
- Develop appropriate criteria for the funding of scaling-up, institutional development and equity, as well as for providing loanable funds.
- Operate as independent entities and avoid becoming politicised. This may require appropriate by-laws, and rotating board members through fixed-term memberships.

Support through the banking system

Seven of the nine countries in the Network impose directed credit requirements, whereby banks are required to lend a certain proportion of their loan portfolio to particular sectors. While directed credit schemes which target the poor will cause banks to lend more to poor borrowers than would otherwise be the case, the research found that in some cases they are an inefficient means of reaching the poor, and impose economic costs.

In some countries, the government operates specific microfinance programs in which funds are channelled through the banks. Such programs have generally not been successful. The Network considers that where public funds are available to support microfinance, it is more appropriate to channel them through second tier microfinance institutions and specialist MFIs, rather than through the banking system. Nevertheless, there are some apparent exceptions to the above analysis, with some microfinance programs channelled through banks appearing to have been successful.

In general, however, the most effective way for governments to encourage regulated banks to become involved in microfinance is to ensure an appropriate regulatory and prudential framework, rather than through direct financial support. On the other hand, it should be recognised that a wide variety of institutions, including banks, may engage successfully in microfinance. In those countries with networks of small banks, it may be appropriate to permit small banks with a commitment to microfinance to borrow from second tier institutions.

One important way in which commercial banks can become involved in microfinance is through linkages with NGOs and self-help groups (SHGs). In most countries, there is little positive support for linkages from policymakers. The Network believes that central banks should take a more active role in encouraging linkages, by documenting and publicising successful examples, issuing clear guidelines that banks can follow, providing training to banks, establishing ratings systems for MFIs, and more generally promoting change in the culture of banking.

Programs operated directly by government agencies

The other main category of microfinance programs is those operated directly by government agencies. Such programs have usually not been successful. The Network considers that, in general, governments should abolish direct microfinance programs and channel the funds through well-managed second tier microfinance institutions or MFIs instead. Direct government programs should only be retained where it can be shown through a rigorous evaluation that they are as cost-effective as leading MFIs, taking all direct and indirect subsidies into account.

In a number of countries, governments have forgiven indebtedness for certain categories of small loans under their own programs or by state commercial banks. These episodes have created major problems for MFIs. Governments should avoid debt forgiveness for small loans in future.

Regulation of non-bank microfinance institutions

The broad regulatory framework

In most countries, MFIs are able to obtain registration under the general provisions applying to NGOs and cooperatives. The requirements for registration are generally not onerous.

In some countries, the requirements for registration are not enforced rigorously. This has enabled some unscrupulous operators to set up and take advantage of clients, undermining the efforts of the vast majority of MFIs that are operating legitimately. NGOs engaged in microfinance should be required to be registered, and regulatory agencies should undertake simple monitoring of their activities to reduce the scope for fraud.

On the other hand, in some cases MFIs are subject to unnecessary and burdensome rules and regulations, and the rules are not transparent. The Network is of the view that unnecessary restrictions applying to both NGOs and cooperatives should be removed, and that discretionary powers vested in regulatory agencies should be limited as much as possible.

Interest rates

Only two countries in the Network impose general ceilings on the interest rates that MFIs can charge borrowers. However, this does not mean that in other countries MFIs are always free to determine their own interest rates. In a number of countries, there are ceilings on interest rates under government microfinance programs or as a result of various other actions by government.

These measures generally tend to impede the development of microfinance on a sustainable basis. Countries that impose interest rate ceilings should either remove them or set them at levels that are consistent with the sustainability of efficient, well-managed MFIs. Other countries should examine policies designed to support microfinance, to ensure that such policies do not reduce the margins available to MFIs and make it difficult for them to operate sustainably.

Prudential regulation and supervision

MFIs which do not accept deposits from the general public are not subject to prudential regulation or supervision in any country in the Network. There are also no compulsory reporting requirements designed specifically with the needs of MFIs in mind.

This situation is appropriate. It is generally agreed that where MFIs do not accept deposits from the public, it is unnecessary to subject them to formal prudential regulation and supervision by a government agency. In most countries, there would also be significant practical difficulties in subjecting MFIs to prudential regulation and supervision.

Nevertheless, at present many MFIs do not have adequate standards. The challenge is to find cost-effective ways of improving the standards, in terms of both performance and reporting, of those MFIs that are not currently operating on a sound basis.

Performance and reporting standards of second tier institutions

The role of second tier microfinance institutions was discussed above in the section on arrangements for direct support. In those countries with second tier institutions, these institutions can play a very important role in developing standards for the microfinance sector. Through their lending activities, such institutions have an effective mechanism for enforcing any standards that they develop. It may also be possible for credit rating agencies to develop standards for MFIs and to rate MFIs according to these standards, to make it easier for donor agencies and commercial investors to assess the performance of MFIs and to encourage MFIs to improve their performance.

There is a broad range of experience to draw from in establishing appropriate standards, including the work currently being undertaken by a number of second tier institutions in the region, and work being conducted under the auspices of the Consultative Group to Assist the Poorest (CGAP). Second tier institutions should adopt a number of principles in establishing performance and reporting standards:

- Standards should be based on results achieved rather than the model used. There is a diverse range of institutions involved in microfinance, including financial intermediaries, social intermediaries, and mixed financial/social intermediaries, and appropriate standards should be developed for social intermediation.
- Standards should be raised over time so that MFIs are required to improve their performance progressively. It may also be appropriate to impose differential standards depending on the stage of development of the particular MFI, and to provide for progression from one stage to the next.
- Enforcing standards is just as important as establishing them. Second tier institutions should develop cost-effective methods for off-site and on-site supervision that are appropriate to the operating procedures of MFIs.
- Standards should be developed through a process of wide consultation with MFIs, to ensure that they meet the needs of MFIs and are accepted throughout the sector.

Self-regulation

Another approach to establishing performance and reporting standards for MFIs is through self-regulation. Self-regulation may take a wide variety of forms ranging from a voluntary code of conduct to which MFIs agree to adhere, to a rigorous licensing system administered by an apex body and backed by the force of law.

Establishing standards for self-regulation requires strong apex bodies for MFIs at the national level. Current moves to establish apex bodies for MFIs in a number of countries should be encouraged, while appropriate arrangements should also be put in place in other countries. MFIs should be encouraged to join these apex bodies and become active in their affairs, to ensure that they are well resourced and fully representative of the microfinance sector.

Savings mobilisation and deposit taking

With few exceptions, MFIs are not permitted to accept deposits from the general public unless they establish regulated banks. The Network agrees that non-bank MFIs should generally not be allowed to accept deposits from the public unless appropriate regulations concerning capital adequacy, reserves, liquidity and reporting are in place.

In terms of mobilising savings from members, the position of NGOs engaged in microfinance is somewhat ambiguous in most countries. Generally, regulatory authorities tend not to intervene so long as NGOs mobilise savings from members only. In such cases, however, NGOs do not have a clear legal basis for accepting deposits, and there is always the possibility of sanctions.

Savings facilities provide a valuable service to clients, and can be a key to sustainability. Moreover, requiring borrowers to demonstrate an ability to save before they obtain a loan is also a useful screening device and helps to instil borrower discipline. On the other hand, mobilising savings places a very strong responsibility on an institution to ensure that the savings of poor clients are not at risk. Hence, there is an interrelationship between the standards applying to MFIs and the types of savings facilities offered. Laws governing savings mobilisation by MFIs should be clarified to achieve an appropriate balance between these perspectives.

In many cases, MFIs require loan-linked deposits or compulsory savings deposits as a condition to receiving a loan. Such requirements are an integral part of many if not most microfinance programs, and where clients are net borrowers they impose few prudential risks. They should be seen as a proxy for share capital, or as part of the cost of the loan. The law should be clarified to ensure that MFIs can impose compulsory savings requirements.

Some MFIs also offer voluntary savings facilities to their clients. It is generally not appropriate for MFIs to use voluntary savings in their lending programs unless effective protections are in place. However, the Network considers that subject to the particular country context, MFIs should generally be allowed to mobilise voluntary savings from members, so long as they establish an earmarked account for voluntary savings with a regulated financial institution and other appropriate safeguards are in place.

Regulation of banks

Most institutions engaged in microfinance are specialist MFIs registered as societies, non-profit companies or similar bodies. However, there is also considerable scope for regulated banks to become involved in microfinance. Some specialist MFIs may wish to establish regulated banks, so that they can raise deposits from the general public, although this is not necessarily appropriate for all MFIs. And some traditional banks may wish to become involved in microfinance. However, the extent to which regulated banks become involved in microfinance depends critically on the policy environment.

Licensing and minimum capital requirements

One critical factor affecting the extent to which regulated banks will become involved in microfinance is the scope for the establishment of small banks. Microfinance programs in large banks rarely have a secure position within the bank, although there is a small number of exceptions to this. Smaller banks, by contrast, operate in more localised areas and are more likely to be involved in microfinance.

Of the nine countries in the Network, only two have permissive policy environments for the establishment of small banks. In these two countries, there is considerable microfinance activity by small banks operating at the local level.

In the majority of other countries there is less scope to establish small banks. While some countries may be reluctant to permit their establishment, the Network notes that failures of small banks in some countries have generally resulted from internal mismanagement or flawed government policies. Moreover, performance of banks is not correlated with size. If regulated banks are to play an active role in microfinance it is appropriate that there be some mechanism to enable small banks to be licensed and that there are no other unnecessary restrictions affecting their establishment, subject to the particular country context.

Interest rates

Four of the countries in the Network impose interest rate ceilings on small loans by banks. Such ceilings may limit lending directly to the poor on a commercial basis. Interest rate ceilings on small loans should either be removed or set at levels that are sufficient to enable banks operating efficiently to sustain their microfinance programs.

Prudential regulation and supervision

The Basle Accord recommends that banks should maintain a capital adequacy ratio of at least 8 per cent of risk-weighted assets. However, required capital adequacy ratios should be higher for banks specialising in microfinance than for standard commercial banks, reflecting higher risk and other factors.

Microfinance banks should provision their overdue loans, based on time overdue, more aggressively than conventional banks because of the greater volatility of delinquency. However, provisioning requirements must recognise that microfinance loans are generally not backed by physical collateral. The Network considers that regulators should be flexible in accepting additional indicators of asset quality, such as historical performance of portfolios, statistical sampling of arrears, and adequacy of management information systems in their evaluation of risk.

There are a number of other prudential standards sometimes applied to commercial banks that may not be appropriate for microfinance banks. These include particular reporting requirements, limits on unsecured loans, requirements concerning loan documentation, supervision methods, and branching restrictions. Regulators should review their policies and remove any unnecessary restrictions facing microfinance banks.

Bangkok
7 November 1997

1 Introduction

The policy and regulatory environment for microfinance incorporates a number of elements. These include the policies of governments and donor agencies to support microfinance, the regulatory environment that applies to specialised MFIs, and the extent to which the legal framework enables regulated banks to engage in microfinance.

Until recently, there has been very little research on these key issues. And while three important studies focusing on the regulatory framework have been published recently (see Berenbach & Churchill 1997; Jansson & Wenner 1997; and Rock & Otero 1997), these focus much more on the situation in Latin America than in Asia.

This study considers the policy and regulatory environment from a broad perspective, and with a particular focus on Asia. Individual country studies using a common research framework were undertaken to examine the policy and regulatory environments for microfinance in the nine countries represented in the BWTP Network: Bangladesh, India, Indonesia, Malaysia, Nepal, Pakistan, Philippines, Sri Lanka and Thailand. These studies were conducted in close cooperation with the members of the Network in each country. They also involved interviews with senior officials from a wide variety of institutions including government departments, donor agencies, central banks, microfinance institutions (MFIs), commercial banks, research institutes and other relevant bodies.

These individual country studies, which are included as appendices, each provide a detailed description of the policy and regulatory environment for microfinance in the country concerned and contain a number of recommendations. The main report draws heavily on these nine country studies, highlighting policy measures that have been successful and identifying the key elements of a policy and regulatory environment which would encourage the growth of microfinance on a sustainable basis.

A draft of the study was presented at the Fourth Asia-Pacific Regional Workshop on Banking with the Poor, which was held in Bangkok in 3–7 November 1997 in conjunction with the Asia Regional Conference on *Sustainable* Banking with the Poor. These meetings were organised jointly by the Foundation and the Sustainable Banking with the Poor project of the World Bank. Representatives from the BWTP Network endorsed a statement on the policy and regulatory environment for microfinance in Asia. This was based on the draft study, and is included as a preface to this volume. The study itself has been revised to reflect comments made at the Fourth Regional Workshop, and to incorporate information received since that time.

Following this introduction, chapter 2 offers an overview of microfinance in the region, providing a context for the discussions that follow. Chapter 3 analyses the arrangements by which governments and donor agencies provide support for microfinance, whether through specialist MFIs, the banking system or direct government programs, and identifies current best practice in a number of key areas.

The regulation of non-bank MFIs is considered in chapter 4. The discussion addresses the broad regulatory framework and interest rate restrictions, before moving on to a detailed discussion of experience with alternative approaches to ensuring high performance and reporting standards for MFIs. These include prudential regulation and supervision, the standards of second tier microfinance institutions, and self-regulation. Finally, the chapter discusses the difficult issue of savings mobilisation and deposit taking by MFIs.

Chapter 5 looks at the regulation of banks, insofar as the regulatory framework affects the scope for regulated banks to engage in microfinance. While minimum capital requirements and interest rates are identified as fundamental issues, the chapter also discusses a range of other prudential requirements. Finally, chapter 6 outlines the key conclusions and recommendations of the study.

2 The importance of microfinance

2.1 Background

This chapter provides the context for the detailed discussion of the policy and regulatory environment for microfinance in chapters 3, 4 and 5. Section 2.2 examines the incidence of poverty in the nine countries included in the study, while section 2.3 goes on to consider the role of microfinance in the overall policy framework for poverty reduction. The recent development of a microfinance 'sector', involving specialist microfinance institutions (MFIs) which provide financial services to the poor in an innovative and commercially viable manner, is considered briefly in section 2.4. Section 2.5 discusses the current outreach and self-sufficiency of microfinance programs in the region, while section 2.6 summarises the key points.

2.2 Poverty in Asia

The nine countries included in the study had a total population of some 1,559 million in 1995, around 27.5 per cent of the world's population. They include four of the ten most populous countries in the world, namely India, Indonesia, Pakistan and Bangladesh. Based on national definitions, nearly 500 million people in the nine countries, or 32 per cent of the total population, were living in poverty. More than 425 million of these were in the three large countries in South Asia, namely India (325 million), Bangladesh (57 million) and Pakistan (44 million).

Some basic indicators for the nine countries are provided in table 1. Economic conditions and living standards differ significantly between the countries. While there is overlap in some areas, they can be divided into four broad categories in terms of their economic and social development.

In the first category are Nepal and Bangladesh. They are the two poorest countries in the world outside Africa, with GNP per capita of $200 and $240 respectively in 1995. Indicators of human development are also very low. In both cases life expectancy at birth is below 60, less than 40 per cent of adults are literate, and nearly half the population lives in absolute poverty. These are the least urbanised of the nine countries and have the highest shares of agriculture in GDP. There are also large numbers of landless people in the rural areas relying on self-employment in the informal sector of the economy.

Table 1 Basic indicators, 1995

	South Asia					Southeast Asia			
	Bangladesh	India	Nepal	Pakistan	Sri Lanka	Indonesia	Malaysia	Philippines	Thailand
Population									
Population (millions), 1995	119.8	929.4	21.5	129.9	18.1	193.3	20.1	68.6	58.2
Area ('000km^2)	144	3288	141	796	66	1905	330	300	513
Population density (persons per sq km), 1995	832	283	152	163	274	101	61	229	113
Population, % growth p.a. 1990–1995	1.6%	1.8%	2.5%	2.9%	1.3%	1.6%	2.4%	2.2%	0.9%
Total fertility rate, births per woman, 1995	3.5	3.2	5.3	5.2	2.3	2.7	3.4	3.7	1.8
Labour force (millions), 1995	60	398	10	46	8	89	8	28	34
Urban population (% total), 1995	18%	27%	14%	35%	22%	34%	54%	53%	36%
Economy									
GNP per capita (US$), 1995	$240	$340	$200	$460	$700	$980	$3,890	$1,050	$2,740
GNP per capita at PPP (US$), 1995	$1,380	$1,400	$1,170	$2,230	$3,250	$3,800	$9,020	$2,850	$7,540
GNP per capita, % growth p.a. 1985–1995	2.1%	3.2%	2.4%	1.2%	2.6%	6.0%	5.7%	1.5%	8.4%
Sectoral allocation of GDP (%), 1995									
Agriculture	31%	29%	42%	26%	23%	17%	13%	22%	11%
Industry	18%	29%	22%	24%	25%	42%	43%	32%	40%
Services	52%	41%	36%	50%	52%	41%	44%	46%	49%
Poverty and inequality									
Poverty incidence									
Below national poverty line (%), latest	47.5%	35.0%	42.0%	34.0%	22.4%	11.3%	9.6%	35.7%	13.1%
Below national poverty line (millions), 1995	56.9	325.3	9.0	44.2	4.1	21.8	1.9	24.5	7.6
Gini index, latest (1)	0.283	0.338	0.367	0.312	0.301	0.317	0.484	0.407	0.462
Human development									
Life expectancy at birth (years), 1995	58	62	55	60	72	64	71	66	69
Infant mortality rate (per 1000 live births), 1995	79	68	91	90	16	51	12	39	35
Adult literacy rate (%), 1995	38%	52%	27%	38%	90%	84%	83%	95%	94%
UNDP human development index, 1994	0.368	0.446	0.347	0.445	0.711	0.668	0.832	0.672	0.833
Banking and finance									
M2 / GDP (%), 1995	35.6%	46.0%	33.7%	40.9%	31.8%	46.2%	85.0%	45.4%	73.8%
Bank interest rates–deposits (%), 1995	6.0%	na	na	na	16.1%	na	5.9%	8.4%	11.6%
Bank interest rates–loans (%), 1995	14.0%	16.3%	na	na	14.7%	17.1%	7.6%	14.7%	14.4%
Consumer price inflation (%), 1995	5.2%	12.2%	7.6%	13.0%	7.7%	9.4%	3.4%	8.1%	5.8%
Exchange rate (units per $US), 1996	41.8	36.0	55.1	35.1	55.2	2339.4	2.5	26.2	25.3

(1) Based on distribution of income for Malaysia, and distribution of expenditure for other eight countries.

Sources World Bank 1997a, 1997b; ADB 1997b; UNDP 1997; various national sources

India and Pakistan fall into the second category. They are classified as low-income countries by the World Bank, with GNP per capita of $340 and $460 respectively. They are also classified as having low human development by UNDP. While Pakistan has the higher per capita income, India performs slightly better in terms of human development. Even in India life expectancy is only 62 and nearly half of all adults are illiterate, while in Pakistan these indicators are only marginally better than in Nepal and Bangladesh. In both cases, more than one third of the population lives in absolute poverty.

In the third category are Sri Lanka, Indonesia and the Philippines, with per capita incomes ranging from $700 in Sri Lanka to $1,050 in the Philippines. While all are classified as having medium human development, this is the most diverse of the four groups. Indonesia and the Philippines are middle-income countries. While Sri Lanka is just below the income threshold for middle-income status, it has the best record of the three in terms of human development. In all three countries, indicators such as life expectancy at birth, infant mortality and adult literacy are much better than in the countries in categories one and two, but in Indonesia and the Philippines in particular they fall well short of the levels achieved in the high-income countries. The official incidence of poverty differs considerably between the three countries, at 11 per cent in Indonesia, 22 per cent in Sri Lanka and 36 per cent in the Philippines. Since mid-1997 Indonesia has experienced a severe financial crisis, and the short-term economic outlook is very pessimistic, with poverty expected to increase sharply.

The final category consists of Thailand and Malaysia. While still middle-income countries with per capita incomes of $2,740 and $3,800 respectively, they are clearly much wealthier than any of the other seven countries. The structure of production also differs significantly from the other countries, with less than 15 per cent of GDP derived from agriculture, more than 40 per cent from industry, and much greater reliance on employment in the formal sector of the economy. Both are considered to have high human development by UNDP, although their performance is uneven, with Malaysia's adult literacy rated below those of the Philippines, Sri Lanka and Indonesia, and Thailand's infant mortality higher than that of Sri Lanka. The incidence of poverty is quite low at 10 per cent in Malaysia and 13 per cent in Thailand, although significant pockets of poverty persist, particularly in Thailand. Like Indonesia, Thailand and Malaysia have experienced a severe financial crisis and economic slowdown since mid-1997.

2.3 Poverty reduction and microfinance

With more than 500 million people in the nine countries living in poverty, governments clearly face an enormous challenge to reduce poverty. This is particularly so in the poorest countries and those with the greatest concentrations of poor people.

To achieve rapid and sustainable reductions in poverty it is necessary to have an integrated policy strategy, with the various elements of the strategy reinforcing each other. The World Development Report for 1990 (World Bank 1990) found that poverty can be reduced most effectively through a strategy with two equally important elements.

(1) The first element is to promote the productive use of the poor's most abundant asset, their labour. Broad-based economic growth, through appropriate macroeconomic and microeconomic policies, is critical in this respect. There is also an important role for targeted policies to promote infrastructure development and encourage income-generating activities for the poor.

(2) The second element is to provide basic social services to the poor. The World Bank found that primary health care, family planning, nutrition and primary education are especially important in this regard.

These two elements are mutually reinforcing. Increasing the productivity and incomes of the poor makes it easier for them to access social services such as health care and education. And policies to improve the health and education of the poor enable them to work more productively. The countries that have implemented both parts of the strategy effectively and in a sustained manner have tended to reap the largest gains in terms of poverty reduction. Of the countries in this study, two stand out for their progress in poverty reduction. In Indonesia, in the thirty years to 1996 coinciding with the New Order government of Soeharto, the incidence of poverty declined from close to 70 per cent to just over 11 per cent. In Malaysia, the incidence of poverty has fallen from 42 per cent of households in 1976 to 10 per cent of households in 1995.

In both of these countries, rapid economic growth has increased the demand for labour, creating opportunities for the poor. The two governments have also adopted targeted policies to improve the productivity of the poor, through infrastructure development and income-generating projects. In terms of the second element, both countries have also focused strongly on human development, with a very strong emphasis on improving primary education and nutrition. The mutually reinforcing nature of the two elements described by the World Bank above has contributed to very impressive reductions in poverty. Unfortunately, both countries have recently experienced financial crises, and the short-term economic outlook is not favourable.

Countries that have implemented effective and sustained policies in one of the two areas have been reasonably successful in reducing poverty, but not as successful as those that have implemented both elements effectively. Despite the current crisis, Thailand has been particularly successful at improving employment opportunities for the poor, with more rapid economic growth than even Indonesia and Malaysia. However, there has been less emphasis on targeted programs to improve the productivity of the poor and on providing basic social services. While the incidence of poverty fell from 30 per cent in 1975–74 to 13 per cent in 1992 the benefits of growth have not been spread evenly, with a marked increase in income inequality. Poverty reduction has clearly been slower than in Indonesia and Malaysia.

Sri Lanka, by contrast, has been particularly successful in extending basic social services to the poor. This has contributed to an impressive performance in terms of human development, with indicators such as life expectancy at birth, infant mortality and adult literacy much more favourable than for other countries with similar income levels. On the other hand, Sri Lanka has been less successful in creating opportunities for the poor in employment and income-generating activities. While consistent time series of the incidence of poverty are not available, analysis by the World Bank suggests that Sri Lanka has made good progress in poverty reduction since 1965, with around 22 per cent of the population living below the poverty line in 1990–91. Nevertheless, progress in reducing poverty could have been faster with greater emphasis on measures to improve opportunities for employment and income generation for the poor.

The other five countries included in the study, namely Bangladesh, India, Nepal, Pakistan and the Philippines, have all achieved some reduction in the incidence of poverty. However, the incidence of poverty remains high in these countries, ranging from 34 per cent in Pakistan to 48 per cent in Bangladesh according to the latest estimates. These countries have not been as successful at reducing poverty as the four countries discussed above. While all have implemented a range of policies both to promote employment opportunities and income generating activities for the poor and to extend basic social services, none of these countries has yet been able to achieve rapid and continuous improvements in either of these elements over an extended period of time.

The above discussion demonstrates that rapid and sustainable poverty reduction depends on the interaction of a wide range of policy measures. The availability of microfinance, defined here as the provision of financial services such as savings and credit to poor households, is neither a necessary nor a sufficient condition for rapid poverty reduction. For instance, Malaysia and Thailand have achieved large reductions in poverty with relatively little emphasis on microfinance. And despite the vast outreach of microfinance programs in Bangladesh, progress in reducing poverty has been slow. Clearly, microfinance is only one factor in any strategy for poverty reduction.

Nevertheless, microfinance can play an important role. As noted above, one element of an effective strategy for poverty reduction is to promote the productive use of the poor's labour. This can be done by creating opportunities for wage employment, by raising agricultural productivity among small and marginal farmers, and by increasing opportunities for self-employment. Microfinance is particularly relevant to increasing the productivity of self-employment in the informal sector of the economy. In an environment where economic growth is occurring, microfinance also has the capacity to transmit the benefits of growth more rapidly and more equitably through the informal sector. It is well documented that for many microentrepreneurs, lack of access to financial services is a critical constraint to the establishment or expansion of viable microenterprises (see, for instance, FDC 1992, 1995). Microfinance may also enable small and marginal farmers to purchase the inputs they need to increase their productivity, as well as financing a range of activities adding value to agricultural output and in the rural off-farm economy. Access to savings facilities also plays a key part in enabling the poor to smooth their consumption expenditures, and in financing investments which improve productivity in agriculture and other economic activities.

In most developing countries, opportunities for wage employment in the formal sector of the economy are extremely limited, and the vast majority of poor people rely on self-employment for their livelihood. Better access to financial services, enabling the poor to establish and expand microenterprises and improve their incomes, can be very important in reducing poverty. Even in countries such as Malaysia and Thailand where opportunities for wage employment are greater, many poor households rely on self-employment in microenterprises for their livelihood.

Policies to encourage the development of a viable microfinance sector can also reinforce other poverty reduction policies, and vice versa. Many microfinance programs, including that of the Grameen Bank in Bangladesh, encourage members to develop a socioeconomic agenda covering matters such as health, nutrition and children's education. Even where this emphasis is not explicit, increased empowerment and higher incomes from participation in microfinance programs can reinforce other policies. At the same time, microfinance programs are likely to be more effective in raising members' incomes where rapid growth in the economy and in agricultural output, and better infrastructure, create a demand for the products and services provided by microentrepreneurs. Microfinance programs will also be more effective where inputs such as education and training enable members to use their loans more productively.

2.4 The development of a microfinance sector

How does microfinance overcome the constraints caused by lack of access to financial services? Microfinance can be defined as the provision of financial services, primarily savings and credit, to poor households which do not have access to formal financial institutions. It is widely documented that the formal financial system rarely provides access to poor entrepreneurs in developing economies. Women's World Banking (1995) estimated that in most developing countries, the formal financial system reaches at a maximum the top 25 per cent of the economically active population, leaving the bottom 75 per cent without access to financial services apart from moneylenders. This is because the techniques used by financial institutions do not enable them to lend to the poor in a cost-effective manner (although some countries, notably Indonesia, have a better record in this regard).

Until the 1970s at least, loans for microentrepreneurs were provided primarily through government and donor-funded programs. These programs had relaxed collateral requirements, but otherwise used commercial bank methods. They generally charged subsidised interest rates, based on the view that the poor could not afford to pay market interest rates. They also tended to suffer from politicisation, low repayment rates and high arrears. Reflecting a combination of high cost structures, low interest revenues and low repayments, they required large and ongoing subsidies.

Beginning in the late 1970s, however, there has been an emphasis on establishing financial systems able to reach poor clients on a more sustainable basis, both in Asia and elsewhere. A new set of techniques has been developed and applied by specialist MFIs such as Grameen Bank in Bangladesh, and in the village-level operations of Bank Rakyat Indonesia, to name the two institutions with greatest outreach. While these techniques differ between institutions, Rhyne and Otero (1994) argue that there are three key principles behind them.

The first is knowing the market. The poor are willing to pay for access and convenience. Lending outlets are located near the client, application procedures are simple, and loans are disbursed quickly. Second, successful MFIs use special techniques to slash administrative costs. Simple procedures are used and approvals are decentralised. Borrower groups often handle much of the loan-processing burden. And third, they use special techniques to motivate repayments. MFIs have developed a range of techniques to ensure high repayment rates, including the use of self-selected groups in which members guarantee each other's loans, intensive motivation and supervision of borrowers, incentives for borrowers, progressive lending and compulsory savings requirements.

In recent years MFIs have moved from the margins of the financial system towards the mainstream. It is now more widely accepted that populations traditionally excluded by the formal financial sector can, in fact, be a profitable market niche for innovative banking services. This acceptance is perhaps best demonstrated by the establishment in 1995 of the Consultative Group to Assist the Poorest (CGAP), a multi-donor effort initiated by the World Bank to increase systematically the resources devoted to microfinance. Since then microfinance has continued to gather momentum. The 1997 Microcredit Summit launched a global movement to reach 100 million of the world's poorest families with credit for self-employment and other financial and business services by the year 2005. Much remains to be done, however, to integrate microfinance fully into the mainstream of domestic financial systems, and for orthodox financial institutions, notably commercial banks, to recognise its full potential.

2.5 Current outreach and self-sufficiency of microfinance institutions

Outreach

Despite the rapid growth of MFIs in recent years, their outreach remains very small compared to the potential demand. CGAP (1995) estimated that fewer than 10 million of the few hundred million people who run micro and small enterprises in developing countries have access to financial services. This is as true in the Asian region as it is in other regions, even though many of the largest MFIs in the world are in Asia. The Bank Poor '96 Regional Workshop on Microfinance for the Poor in Asia-Pacific found that:

> Essentially, the task of outreach remains to be done. Of the target poor households in Asia-Pacific, less than 5 per cent have access to financial services. If we exclude Bangladesh — the only country where truly large numbers have been reached — the numbers to whom microfinance services have been extended falls to less than 1 per cent of the target group (Getubig, Remenyi & Quinones 1997, p.10).

In Bangladesh, MFIs have already reached a significant proportion of poor households. Bangladesh boasts a number of the largest MFIs in the world, including Grameen Bank with 2.1 million clients at end-1995, Bangladesh Rural Advancement Committee (BRAC) with 1.5 million clients, and Association for Social Advancement (ASA) with 400,000 clients. Total microfinance clients number at least 6 million, representing not less than one in four rural households in the country.

Microfinance has also achieved significant outreach in Indonesia. It is difficult to estimate the number of poor households with access to microfinance because most institutions are not specifically targeted to the poor. However, financial deregulation has led to a proliferation of financial institutions serving people at all income levels. Bank Rakyat Indonesia serves some 2.6 million borrowers and nearly 18 million savers, including poor clients, through its unit desa system. In addition, there are around 7,300 registered small financial institutions operating at the local level, together with some 2,000 rural banks, plus hundreds of thousands of self-help groups formed as a result of mass campaigns for poverty reduction.

In the other seven countries included in this study, the outreach of microfinance remains limited. While there is a large number of self-help groups in India, the total outreach of genuine microfinance programs is not more than 500,000, a small number in relation to the 65 million poor households in that country. In the Philippines there is a large number of NGOs engaged in microfinance, but most are very small, with only around 30,000 borrowers in total. Outreach of MFIs is also modest in Nepal and Sri Lanka, and negligible in Pakistan. Malaysia and Thailand, where the incidence of poverty is relatively low, are quite well served by MFIs, although the absolute numbers of poor clients are small.

Self-sufficiency

While most successful MFIs were established originally with significant grant funding from donor agencies, there is a strictly limited supply of such funding. Clearly, it will not be possible for the microfinance sector to expand to cover more than a small proportion of the poor in the region on the basis of donor grants. If the number of microfinance clients is to expand significantly, MFIs need access to commercial sources of finance. This in turn requires MFIs to become self-sufficient. Commercial banks will only lend to MFIs if they are satisfied that the MFIs concerned can generate sufficient income to meet their expenses, including the cost of servicing their loans. Similarly, institutional investors will only invest in MFIs if MFIs are able to generate a positive rate of return that is comparable to other investment opportunities.

The Guiding Principles for Selecting and Supporting Intermediaries agreed by donor agencies (Committee of Donor Agencies 1995) define two degrees of self-sufficiency for MFIs and establish indicative 'timetables' for the period over which MFIs should be able to achieve them. CGAP has further clarified these definitions. 'Operational self-sufficiency' requires MFIs to cover all administrative costs and loan losses from operating income. This is calculated by dividing operating income by operating expenses. The Guiding Principles suggest that based on international experience successful MFIs should be able to achieve operational self-sufficiency within three to seven years. 'Financial self-sufficiency' requires microfinance programs to cover all administrative costs, loan losses and financing costs from operating income, after adjusting for inflation and subsidies and treating all funding as if it had a commercial cost. It is suggested that successful intermediaries should achieve financial self-sufficiency within five to ten years.

While the importance of becoming self-sufficient is now widely recognised, few MFIs have yet attained any significant degree of self-sufficiency. Of the 49 MFIs in the Asia-Pacific region that were studied for Bank Poor '96, including virtually all the largest and most successful MFIs in the region, only six were financially self-sufficient.[1] Only two of these, the Association for Social Advancement in Bangladesh (400,000 clients) and SEWA Bank in India (57,000 clients), were reaching substantial numbers of poor clients. The other four MFIs that had achieved financial self-sufficiency all had fewer than 2,000 clients. Another six MFIs, including Grameen Bank, Bank Shinta Daya in Indonesia and the Colombo District Union of the Thrift and Credit Cooperative Societies in Sri Lanka, were more than 80 per cent financially self-sufficient. The remaining 37 MFIs studied were less than 80 per cent financially self-sufficient. Hence, it is clear that most MFIs in the Asia-Pacific region have a long way to go before they become

---

1 It should be noted that the definitions of operational and financial self-sufficiency used in the studies for Bank Poor '96 are slightly different from those recommended in the Guiding Principles and by CGAP.

self-sufficient. These findings are consistent with the experience of CGAP. In its funding guidelines CGAP requires MFIs to be operationally self-sufficient, but of the 116 self-selected institutions which had applied for CGAP funding as of 30 June 1996, only 5 per cent met this criterion (CGAP 1996).

If microfinance is to make an important contribution to poverty reduction in the region, the microfinance sector will need to develop to the stage where it can reach large numbers of poor people on a sustainable basis. This requires increased attention to all aspects of microfinance, including both the internal operations of MFIs and the external policy and regulatory environment in which they operate. As noted in chapter 1, the purpose of this study is to consider how the policy and regulatory environment can best contribute to the development of microfinance.

2.6 Summary

The nine countries included in the study had a total population of some 1,559 million in 1995, around 27.5 per cent of the world's population. While economic conditions and living standards differ significantly between the countries, around 500 million people in the nine countries — or one third of the total population — are living in poverty.

To achieve rapid and sustainable reductions in poverty it is necessary to have an integrated policy strategy. The World Bank has found that poverty can be reduced most effectively through a strategy with two equally important elements. The first element is to promote the productive use of the poor's labour, while the second is to provide basic social services to the poor.

Of the countries in this study, Indonesia and Malaysia stand out for their progress in poverty reduction. These are the only countries that have been able to implement both parts of the strategy consistently and effectively over a sustained period. Thailand and Sri Lanka have also achieved significant reductions in poverty. Thailand has been particularly successful at improving employment opportunities for the poor, but not so effective at providing social services. By contrast, Sri Lanka has been very successful in extending basic social services to the poor but less effective at improving their productivity. The incidence of poverty in these four countries ranges from 10 per cent in Malaysia to 22 per cent in Sri Lanka.

The other five countries included in the study, namely Bangladesh, India, Nepal, Pakistan and the Philippines, have not been so successful in reducing poverty. The incidence of poverty remains high in these countries, ranging from 34 per cent in Pakistan to 48 per cent in Bangladesh.

Microfinance is neither a necessary nor a sufficient condition for rapid poverty reduction. Nevertheless, it can play an important role by increasing the productivity of self-employment in the informal sector of the economy. For such 'microentrepreneurs', lack of access to financial services is often a critical constraint to the establishment or expansion of viable microenterprises. Where opportunities for wage employment in the formal sector of the economy are limited, measures to overcome this constraint can be very important in reducing poverty.

Until the 1970s at least, loans for microentrepreneurs were provided primarily through government and donor-funded programs. Beginning in the late 1970s, however, there has been an emphasis on establishing financial systems able to reach poor clients on a more sustainable basis. In Asia and elsewhere, a new set of techniques has been developed and applied by specialist microfinance institutions (MFIs) such as Grameen Bank in Bangladesh, and in the village level operations of Bank Rakyat Indonesia. It is now generally accepted that populations traditionally excluded by the formal financial sector can, in fact, be a profitable market niche for innovative banking services.

Despite the rapid growth of MFIs in recent years, their outreach remains very small compared to the potential demand. The Bank Poor '96 Regional Workshop on Microfinance for the Poor in Asia-Pacific found that less than 5 per cent of poor households in the Asia-Pacific region have access to financial services. Of the countries in this study, only in Bangladesh and to a lesser extent Indonesia has microfinance reached a significant proportion of poor households.

It is now widely recognised that if the number of microfinance clients is to expand significantly, MFIs need to become self-sufficient. However, few MFIs have yet attained any significant degree of self-sufficiency. Of the 49 MFIs in the Asia-Pacific region that were studied for Bank Poor '96, including virtually all the largest and most successful MFIs in the region, only six were financially self-sufficient and only two of these were reaching substantial numbers of poor clients.

While microfinance has the potential to make an important contribution to poverty reduction in the region, this requires the development of a microfinance sector that is able to reach large numbers of poor people on a sustainable basis. This, in turn, requires increased attention to all aspects of microfinance, including both the internal operations of MFIs and the external policy and regulatory environment in which they operate. The purpose of this study is to consider how the policy and regulatory environment can best contribute to the development of microfinance.

3 Arrangements for direct support

3.1 Background

As noted in chapter 2, it is now generally accepted that microfinance institutions (MFIs) need to become self-sufficient if they are to expand their outreach to cover a significant proportion of poor people in Asia. Public resources, from governments and donor agencies, are strictly limited and MFIs cannot rely on ever increasing amounts of public resources to expand their outreach. Increasing self-sufficiency enables MFIs to reach more poor people without a commensurate increase in the amount of public resources devoted to microfinance. Indeed, where MFIs are operating at full financial self-sufficiency, direct support by governments and donor agencies is no longer necessary. Fully self-sufficient programs are able to meet all administrative costs, loan losses and financing costs from operating income, and do not need any grants or concessional loans from government or donor agencies. In the long term, the ideal situation would be for governments and donor agencies to withdraw all direct support from microfinance, and redirect such expenditures to other poverty reduction programs that are not able to operate on a commercial basis.

Nevertheless, such a situation is a long way off. In all countries in this study except for Pakistan, governments and/or donor agencies have spent large sums of money to support the development of microfinance. This support has been critical in enabling MFIs to become established and to increase their outreach. It is no accident that in Pakistan, where there has been little direct support for microfinance, the outreach of MFIs is far less than in any other country in the study. And even in Pakistan, those MFIs that do exist have relied heavily on the support of various donor agencies. The experience of the countries in the study suggests that active support from government and/or donor agencies, including direct financial support, is a necessary catalyst to the establishment of a viable microfinance sector.

This is largely because achieving self-sufficiency takes a considerable period of time. The Guiding Principles for Selecting and Supporting Intermediaries (Committee of Donor Agencies 1995) establish indicative 'timetables' for the period over which MFIs should be able to achieve self-sufficiency. Based on some assumptions about the rate of expansion of outreach, they suggest that successful MFIs should be able to achieve operational self-sufficiency within three to seven years, and financial self-sufficiency within five to ten years. To set up their programs in the first place, and for a number of years thereafter, they need to be subsidised. Initially, they will require external funding for both operating expenses and loanable funds. Once they reach operational self-sufficiency, they will be able to meet operating expenses from their income, but loanable funds will still need to be subsidised until they attain full financial self-sufficiency. It should also be noted that, in practice, most MFIs have not been able to attain self-sufficiency in accordance with the timetables proposed in the Guiding Principles.

To reach self-sufficiency, it is generally necessary for an MFI to realise significant economies of scale. A larger institution is generally better able than a small one to develop streamlined and cost-effective systems in areas such as administration and staff training, and to achieve high ratios of clients per employee. To achieve the scale necessary for self-sufficiency within a reasonable time frame, it is necessary to go through an expansion phase relatively early in the life of the institution. This requires a considerable input of resources for capacity building and institutional development. In addition to meeting ordinary operational expenses, governments and/or donor agencies will need to meet the costs of scaling up operations if large, viable MFIs are to emerge.

For these reasons, direct financial support from governments and donor agencies is critical to the development of a microfinance sector. Governments and donor agencies may also support microfinance in other ways, such as providing technical assistance, requiring banks and other regulated financial institutions to engage in microfinance, or through pilot programs designed to demonstrate the viability of microfinance and thereby encourage the private and non-government sectors to become involved in this sector.

Direct support for microfinance can also be channelled through different types of institutions. This chapter looks at the advantages and disadvantages of providing support through a number of different types of institutions, and how support through each may be improved. Section 3.2 discusses support for individual MFIs, while section 3.3 considers the tendency for support to be channelled increasingly through second tier microfinance institutions. Section 3.4 looks at support to microfinance through the banking system. Such support may be provided in different ways, such as requiring banks to allocate some of their portfolio to microfinance, channelling funds through the banking system to final borrowers, or supporting linkages between banks and MFIs. Section 3.5 looks at programs operated directly by government agencies, while section 3.6 summarises the key findings.

3.2 Support for individual microfinance institutions

Country experiences

As noted above, MFIs in all countries have received considerable support from the government and/or donor agencies. In the past, most of this has been in the form of financial assistance from the government or donor agency direct to an individual MFI.

In Bangladesh, the country with by far the greatest outreach of microfinance, MFIs have received large amounts of support. The Grameen Bank itself has received considerable support from the government, Bangladesh Bank and donor agencies. Following the success of the initial experimental project by the University of Chittagong, the Grameen Bank project was established in 1979 with support from Bangladesh Bank and later from nationalised commercial banks. By end-1995, Grameen Bank had received donor grants amounting to $84 million for its revolving loan fund. It has also continued to receive support from the government and government agencies. For instance, Bangladesh Bank provided a line of credit of $145 million in 1993–94 at an interest rate of 6 per cent, although less than half of this was drawn down. Grameen Bank has also issued bonds guaranteed by the government, and the nationalised commercial banks purchased around $360 million of such bonds in early 1995 with the encouragement of the government.

Many other MFIs in Bangladesh have also relied on donor funds, especially during the establishment phase, with around 250 MFIs currently receiving foreign donations for both operational costs and loan capital. Large inflows of subsidised donor capital have been instrumental in the proliferation and expansion of MFIs. Nevertheless, since the late 1980s and early 1990s, donor funds have become harder to come by.

This important role for government and donor agencies is mirrored in most other countries. Few if any specialist MFIs with significant outreach to poor clients have been established without the support of such funding agencies. In Indonesia, where the autonomous role of non-governmental organisations (NGOs) is less firmly established, most MFIs have received assistance in the context of particular government-initiated programs rather than support for independent operations. In the Philippines, the major MFIs have received support from a large number of government programs which operate through the non-government sector. Moreover, numerous official and private donor agencies have seen microfinance as an effective mechanism for poverty reduction. In India, the myriad of MFIs and NGOs involved in promoting self-help groups (SHGs) rely heavily on funding from various donor agencies to meet their administrative expenses.

The situation is similar in Sri Lanka and Nepal, where MFIs have been supported by a wide range of external donors as well as some government programs. In Malaysia, the government has provided extensive support to the dominant MFI, Amanah Ikhtiar Malaysia (AIM), while the smaller institutions have relied on support mainly from domestic private sources. Even in Pakistan where very few MFIs exist, all significant initiatives have received support from official and/or private donor agencies from abroad.

This support for individual MFIs has been critical in enabling them to establish in the first place, and subsequently to expand their outreach and increase their self-sufficiency. Without this support, the microfinance sector would not have developed to anything like its current size. Indeed, it is unlikely that there would be a microfinance sector at all, in the sense of specialist MFIs providing financial services to the poor in an innovative and commercially viable manner.

Nevertheless, it is probably fair to say that the development of microfinance and the success of leading MFIs owes more to the vision of their founders and management, than to the particular criteria used by government and donor agencies for supporting MFIs. Support has been largely ad hoc in nature, and has generally not been explicitly designed to maximise the twin objectives of outreach and sustainability in the most cost-effective manner.

The Guiding Principles

The Guiding Principles for Selecting and Supporting Intermediaries agreed by major donor agencies in October 1995 provide a number of suggestions as to how support by donors and government can best be directed to maximising outreach and sustainability. Most importantly, governments and donor agencies should only support institutions which demonstrate a capacity to reach poor clients on a sustainable basis. The Guiding Principles suggest that such MFIs should have three clusters of characteristics, either in their current operations or through credible plans underpinned by concrete measures.

First, they should be strong institutions. They should have institutional cultures and structures that can support sustained service delivery to a significant and growing number of low-income clients. This includes sound governance, freedom from political interference, and strong business plans for expansion and sustainability. They should also have accurate management information systems that are actively used to make decisions, systems that manage small transactions efficiently, and meaningful, transparent financial reporting that conforms to international standards.

The second cluster relates to quality of services and outreach. MFIs seeking support should focus on the poor and have lending terms and conditions that meet the needs of their clients, such as quick, simple and convenient access to small loans. Where possible they should offer savings services. They should also demonstrate significant progress in expanding outreach.

Third, institutions should have sound financial performance. They should charge interest rates that are sufficient to cover the full costs of lending after a reasonable start-up period. They should maintain low arrears. They should have clear plans for steadily reducing dependence on subsidies and for attaining operational and financial self-sufficiency within a reasonable time period. And they should have plans for building a solid and growing funding base through mobilisation of commercial funds from depositors and/or the financial system.

The Guiding Principles also consider the types of support that donor agencies should provide. They argue that grants should only be given to cover operating losses during a clear, time-limited, start-up or expansion phase. On the other hand, support for institutional development is appropriate at all stages of an institution's life, but should become more selective and specialised as institutions evolve. Support through soft loans for on-lending is appropriate for MFIs that meet performance standards. However, it is also important that MFIs seek loan capital from commercial sources.

The Guiding Principles also note that grants for equity can be of strategic importance in enabling MFIs to build a capital base. A sound equity position is important to generate investment income, build the loan portfolio, and leverage funds from commercial banks and capital markets. As such, they can be a catalyst and complement to domestic mobilisation of funds. Grants for equity can also help MFIs seeking to become formal financial institutions to meet minimum capital requirements.

In brief, if governments and donor agencies wish to ensure that their support for microfinance has maximum impact, they need to look very carefully at the institutions they support and ensure that such institutions meet a number of key criteria. While the major donor agencies have endorsed these principles, it is fair to say that they are not always followed in practice. It would be appropriate for all governments and donor agencies to ensure that their support for MFIs is consistent with these principles.

3.3 The role of second tier microfinance institutions

Country experiences

Bangladesh

Most countries included in the study have some form of 'second tier' microfinance institution which channels funds from the government and/or donor agencies to individual MFIs. The largest and most successful second tier institution is the Palli Karma Sahayak Foundation (PKSF) in Bangladesh. PKSF was established as a private non-profit organisation in 1990, and has received a total of $17.9 million from the government of Bangladesh. It is governed by a general body of fifteen people, the majority of whom are from outside government. By December 1996 PKSF had disbursed loans of $31.6 million to 135 MFIs with a demonstrated capacity or potential capacity in microfinance, for on-lending to final borrowers. The repayment rate by MFIs on loans from PKSF was above 98 per cent. A total of 546,000 final borrowers had obtained loans through these facilities.

By all accounts, PKSF has operated very successfully. A recent World Bank review (1996) found that its operating policies and procedures were quite satisfactory, with sound and conservative credit approval policies, intensive credit supervision, and comprehensive external audit. The World Bank poverty alleviation microfinance project provides a line of credit of $109 million to PKSF for on-lending to MFIs, and a further $6 million for technical assistance for capacity and institution building for MFIs, PKSF and the Bangladesh Bank. It should be noted that PKSF only lends to MFIs for on-lending to final borrowers. It does not provide funds, whether in the form of grants or soft loans, for scaling-up operations, institutional development or increasing equity. It does, however, provide training and advisory services, and conducts research.

India

In India, there are no fewer than three second tier microfinance institutions which channel funds to specialist MFIs at concessional interest rates. The largest of these is Rashtriya Mahila Kosh (RMK), established by the government in 1993 with a corpus fund of $8.6 million. By March 1997 it had disbursed around $5.7 million to NGOs for on-lending. The Small Industries Development Bank of India (SIDBI) has also operated a microcredit scheme since 1994, and by March 1997 had provided loans of $2.8 million to 79 NGOs. Finally, the National Bank for Agriculture and Rural Development (NABARD) provides a small amount of revolving fund assistance to NGOs for on-lending to self-help groups (SHGs).

A major weakness in the programs of RMK and SIDBI is that their interest rate policies make it very difficult if not impossible for their partner MFIs to be self-sufficient. The interest rate charged by RMK to its partners is 8 per cent, and they are required to lend to SHGs at 12 per cent, a margin of only 4 percentage points. While MFIs can obtain some interest rate relief from RMK, this only enables them to increase the margin to 6.5 percentage points. SIDBI lends to MFIs at 9 per cent, and the MFIs are required to on-lend to SHGs at a rate not higher than 15 per cent, a mark-up of 6 percentage points. These margins are not enough to enable MFIs to cover their costs, and MFIs participating in the programs are only able to operate through grants from donor agencies and other sources, which meet a large proportion of their costs. This greatly inhibits their ability to expand, and reduces the scope for new MFIs to be established. On the other hand, one very positive feature of all three Indian programs is the availability of capacity building funds to enable MFIs to strengthen their capabilities and scale up their operations.

Sri Lanka

There is also a second tier microfinance institution in Sri Lanka. The National Development Trust Fund (NDTF), originally known as the Janasaviya Trust Fund (JTF), was established in 1991. It is governed by a 20-member board of trustees, selected by the government and comprising around half public sector and half private sector representatives. Its main function is to manage a credit fund for disbursing credit to partner organisations, but it also manages a human resources development fund for providing skills training to beneficiaries, a rural works fund, and a nutrition fund. A credit fund of $35 million was established with support from the World Bank, the government of the Federal Republic of Germany and the government of Sri Lanka. By March 1997, it had provided funds totalling $21.5 million to 157 partner organisations, including commercial banks, regional rural development banks, thrift and credit cooperative societies and NGOs. NDTF also provides assistance to partner organisations for institutional development.

NDTF has achieved a solid repayment rate of 90 to 95 per cent on its loans to partner organisations. However, it has experienced a number of difficulties, to the extent that the mid-term project review by the World Bank in May 1995 classified the project as a 'problem' project. Difficulties included inadequate processes for selecting partner organisations, inadequate monitoring and supervision of partner organisations, and concerns about the targeting of the program. These failures appear to reflect a number of factors. Some commentators stated that NDTF was under pressure to disburse funds too quickly, and that there were not enough sound MFIs available to use as partner organisations. It would also appear that NDTF did not have sufficient staff with the technical skills to implement the program properly. Finally, some commentators pointed to politicisation of the organisation. More recently, some measures have been implemented to try to overcome these problems, and there appears to have been a marked improvement in its performance.

Philippines

In the Philippines, the People's Credit and Finance Corporation (PCFC) was established in 1995 as a government finance company for lending to the poor. It is incorporated under the Corporations Act and regulated by the Securities and Exchange Commission. PCFC defines MFIs broadly, lending to NGOs, rural banks, cooperatives and other intermediaries as 'conduits' for on-lending to the poor. It aims to ensure that such intermediaries are replicable, self-sustaining and operationally viable. The National Credit Council envisages that the corporation should gradually replace many of the other lending programs operated by line agencies of government.

By December 1996 PCFC had lent a total of $10.8 million to 76 conduits, benefiting some 32,000 final borrowers. PCFC is also the executing agency for a $26.3 million program funded by a loan from the Asian Development Bank (ADB) and the International Fund for Agricultural Development (IFAD). These funds are to be provided exclusively for PCFC to support MFIs replicating the Grameen Bank approach, even though there is a wide variety of models being used in the Philippines. In mid-1997, PCFC was funding 58 conduit institutions from its other reserves, of which only 17 were Grameen replicators.

PCFC also loans funds to conduits for capacity building. These are soft loans and although they are limited to 20 per cent of total outstandings, they are a source of concern given the need for PCFC to show a profit in the lead-up to privatisation (the ADB is requiring PCFC to complete a privatisation plan by mid-1998, with a view to completing the process by end-1999). After privatisation, the government may need to accept greater responsibility for capacity-building requirements of MFIs.

Thailand

In Thailand there are two institutions, the Government Savings Bank (GSB) and the Urban Community Development Office (UCDO), which lend to cooperatives and community organisations involved in microfinance. Unlike most of the NGOs and partner organisations which borrow from second tier institutions in other countries, the cooperatives and community organisations which borrow from GSB and UCDO are owned by their members and tend to be small. Most of them are not registered and operate on an informal basis. By February 1997 GSB had provided loans to some 1,360 organisations with a total membership of 188,000. UCDO had approved loans of $4.9 million to 103 organisations. As well as providing loans, both GSB and UCDO provide the organisations with technical support. The government is currently planning to establish the Community Organisation Development Institute (CODI) which will take over the overall policy responsibility for the two programs. But it is expected that, at least initially, GSB and UCDO will continue to administer the schemes.

Other countries

Nepal also has a second tier institution for channelling funds to NGOs engaged in microfinance, but it is much smaller than comparable institutions in other countries. The government established the Rural Self-Reliance Fund (RSRF) in 1991 with a one-off contribution of $400,000. By January 1997, RSRF had disbursed around $300,000 to some 54 NGOs. Eligible NGOs are those that are registered with the government and permitted by the central bank to engage in limited banking.

There is currently no second tier microfinance institution in Pakistan, but the government is proposing to establish the Poverty Alleviation Fund, with support from the World Bank, to perform this role. In Malaysia, the Credit Guarantee Corporation (CGC) has performed the role of a second tier microfinance institution to a minor extent as an adjunct to its primary responsibilities. The small number of MFIs and more limited demand for microfinance in that country reduce the need for a specialist second tier institution.

Interestingly, there is no institution in Indonesia that performs the role of a second tier microfinance institution, despite the prominence of microfinance. This reflects greater emphasis in that country on a financial systems development approach to microfinance, with microfinance flowing as a result of the development of effective formal financial institutions. NGOs play a relatively minor role in the Indonesian situation, although government-supported community groups are important players.

Some lessons

Importance of second tier institutions

Where they operate well, second tier microfinance institutions are a very effective means for governments and donor agencies to channel support to MFIs. Such institutions have a number of advantages over the traditional approach of providing support to individual MFIs on a largely ad hoc basis. As noted above, if governments and donor agencies are to maximise the effectiveness of their support for microfinance, they need to look very carefully at the MFIs they support, and ensure that such institutions meet a number of key criteria. This requires a detailed appraisal of the institution, and regular monitoring against the various criteria. Clearly, it is much more efficient for one institution to conduct this analysis than for different government and donor agencies to do their own appraisals and evaluations. Moreover, if all the support for a particular MFI can be channelled through one agency, it is much easier to ensure that it is complementary and directed to the same objectives. This can avoid the situation where different government and donor agencies have different and possibly inconsistent objectives, as is often the case at present.

An effective second tier institution can also ensure that all MFIs operate on a level playing field, with support available to all MFIs meeting predetermined standards on the same terms and conditions. Moreover, second tier institutions can ensure that the MFIs that borrow from them face common performance and reporting standards, rather than different standards imposed by different donor agencies, or no standards at all as is often the case at present. By setting appropriate standards, second tier institutions can contribute significantly to a more efficient and professional microfinance sector. These issues are discussed in more detail in chapter 4.

Second tier institutions also offer advantages for MFIs. They are a one-stop funding source, and can avoid the delays that often arise when relying on other funding sources. They can also facilitate training to MFIs, and enable exchange of best practice between them.

For all of these reasons, it would be desirable for governments and donor agencies to channel their support for microfinance, as far as possible, through efficient and well-managed second tier microfinance institutions. In countries with more than one second tier institution, it is important to ensure that the different institutions adopt consistent standards and policies.

At the same time, there is evidence both from Asia and from other regions that second tier institutions do not always operate on a sound basis. For instance, Fruman and Goldberg (1997) comment that second tier institutions only work well when there are high standards, clear objectives and managerial authority. Where these conditions are not met, they are fraught with administrative, political and technical difficulties. They also point out that second tier institutions are most effective when there is already a group of strong retail MFIs, such as in Bangladesh. In countries that do not have a well-developed microfinance sector, it may be very difficult to establish an effective second tier institution.

Performance and reporting standards

If second tier institutions are to play an effective role, it is clear that there are a number of critical issues that need to be addressed. First and most important, it is important that second tier institutions establish and enforce appropriate performance and reporting standards for the MFIs that they fund. In some countries second tier institutions have not been sufficiently rigorous in establishing and enforcing such standards. Insufficient attention to the performance of partner MFIs represents a missed opportunity to improve the outreach and sustainability of the microfinance sector. In the extreme it can also reduce the ability of the partner organisations to repay their loans and undermine the viability of the second tier institution itself. However, it should be noted that even the institutions discussed above which are not performing as well have maintained repayment rates of at least 90 per cent on loans to their partner organisations, while the best institutions have maintained repayment rates of close to 100 per cent.

The standards to be enforced should be based primarily on outreach and financial criteria. Second tier institutions should not restrict support to any particular model or models of microfinance, as this may inhibit the development of new approaches to microfinance capable of satisfying appropriate financial norms. There is scope for a diversity of models and institutional forms, including financial intermediaries, social intermediaries and mixed financial/social intermediaries.

Pressure to expand

Second, pressure to expand too rapidly may lead to problems. While in Bangladesh there is a large number of well-managed MFIs able to meet fairly rigorous performance and reporting standards, this is not the case in most other countries. Pressure to meet unrealistic disbursement targets may cause institutions to lower their standards and lend to some ineffective MFIs, as in the case of NDTF in Sri Lanka. In most countries, it will take time for large numbers of MFIs to reach the standards required by a prudent second tier institution. This is particularly relevant in countries such as Pakistan, where there are currently very few MFIs operating on a sound basis.

Restrictive interest rate policies

Third, second tier institutions should avoid restrictive interest rate policies. In India, the major second tier institutions impose ceilings on the interest rates that their partner MFIs can charge borrowers, at levels which make it difficult if not impossible for the MFIs to achieve self-sufficiency. This means that they have to rely on donor grants to fund their operations, and severely restricts their ability to expand their outreach. In most cases, there would not appear to be any need for second tier institutions to impose interest rate ceilings on their partners. If they do impose ceilings, they should ensure that the margins permitted are sufficient to enable MFIs to meet all of the costs of their operations.

Support for capacity building

Fourth, some second tier institutions, most notably PKSF in Bangladesh, only lend to MFIs for on-lending to final borrowers. PKSF does not provide funds, whether in the form of grants or soft loans, for scaling-up operations, institutional development or increasing equity. In many countries, funds for these activities are at least as important in enabling MFIs to increase their outreach and sustainability as funds for on-lending. It would therefore be appropriate for second tier institutions to fund scaling-up, institutional development and equity as well as lending. Appropriate criteria would need to be established for accessing support for each of these activities.

It should be noted that while PCFC in the Philippines makes soft loans to MFIs to finance capacity building, the need to become more profitable in preparation for privatisation imposes a strain on its ability to undertake capacity building. Where a second tier institution is privatised, government should accept some responsibility to finance capacity building of MFIs.

Importance of independence

Fifth, it is critical that second tier institutions operate as independent entities and are not politicised. Some commentators suggested that the performance of NDTF in Sri Lanka had been affected by politicisation, and this also appears to have been a factor affecting institutions in some other countries. By contrast, one of the strengths of PKSF in Bangladesh is that it appears to have been able to operate independently with little or no political interference. The extent to which institutions are able to operate independently partly reflects the overall political culture of the country, and in some cases it may be extremely difficult to avoid political interference completely. Nevertheless, possible techniques for minimising politicisation include spelling out the objectives of the institution as simply and clearly as possible, making the board of directors directly responsible for achieving these objectives, limiting the number of public sector representatives on the board, appointing board members for fixed terms, and enabling various private and non-government bodies to appoint representatives to the board directly.

3.4 Support through the banking system

In her study of the role of commercial banks in microfinance, Goodwin-Groen (forthcoming) notes that banks can engage in microfinance in a wide variety of ways. She presents a taxonomy of twelve different ways, nine of which involve a government mandate or government support. While this section considers government support through the banking system in a much more simplified framework, it is important to recognise that there is considerable overlap and blurring between the categories discussed below.

First, this section looks at directed credit schemes where banks lend to fulfil a specific government mandate. While such schemes are considered together in this section, they may take a variety of different forms. In some cases banks may be required to lend at subsidised rates, while in other cases they may lend at commercial rates. Moreover, they may lend directly to individual borrowers, or they may make use of non-governmental organisations (NGOs) or self-help groups (SHGs) as financial or social intermediaries.

Second, it considers government programs where subsidised government money is channelled through the banking system. Again, banks can lend to individual borrowers under such programs, or they can involve NGOs and SHGs in the program. Finally, it goes on to look at government programs to encourage linkages between banks and specialised MFIs. While such programs may be promoted by government, their objective is to facilitate such linkages on a purely commercial basis, without involvement from government.

Directed credit schemes

Seven of the nine countries included in the study impose directed credit requirements, whereby banks are required to lend a certain proportion of their loan portfolio to particular sectors. Only Bangladesh and Sri Lanka have abolished all such sectoral lending requirements.

In Thailand and the Philippines, the requirements relate to broad sectoral allocations only. Commercial banks in Thailand are required to lend 20 per cent of their total deposits from the previous year to the rural sector. In the Philippines, banking institutions are required to allocate at least 25 per cent of loanable funds to certain specified sectors, including agriculture. In these countries there is no requirement on banks to lend to the poor. Similarly in Malaysia, Bank Negara has three lending guidelines requiring banks to lend to priority sectors of the economy, but none of these directly targets poor borrowers.

In Indonesia since 1990 the government has instructed commercial banks to allocate 20 per cent of their advances to 'small' business. Small-scale business credits (KUK) consist of investment and working capital loans extended to small-scale entrepreneurs, with a maximum overall credit ceiling of Rp350 million ($150,000). While microcredit lending is included in this category, the relatively high ceiling on assets below which the entrepreneur is classified as 'small' and the generous ceiling on individual loans make it clear that this government requirement is concerned only incidentally with stimulating support for microfinance and has very little direct relevance for poverty alleviation. Its primary purpose is to satisfy pressures from indigenous Indonesian entrepreneurs who feel disadvantaged relative to ethnic Chinese business interests which are over-represented in medium- to large-scale enterprise. It is relevant to our concerns to note that commercial banks which have difficulty in reaching the 20 per cent target are entitled to count for that purpose credit extended to the small rural banks (BPRs) which deal primarily with small business and microenterprise. These banks are discussed in chapter 5.

The remaining countries make more attempt to target poor borrowers through directed credit. India has perhaps the most elaborate requirements. All commercial banks and regional rural banks are required to lend 40 per cent of net bank credit to priority sectors. In broad terms, at least 18 per cent of lending must be to agriculture. A further 10 per cent must be to weaker sections, such as small and marginal farmers, rural artisans and agricultural labourers. The remaining 12 per cent is unmarked, and can be for either of the above categories or for small-scale industry. Of the lending to small-scale industry, 40 per cent must be for tiny industry. Most lending to priority sectors is eligible for refinancing from the National Bank for Agriculture and Rural Development (NABARD). The repayment rate on priority sector lending is generally low, in the range of 60 to 65 per cent.

In Pakistan, the State Bank administers a scheme requiring some banks to lend a certain proportion of their loans to agriculture, and within that to small farmers. The scheme applies to the three longstanding state-owned commercial banks, the two privatised commercial banks, the Agricultural Development Bank and the cooperative banks. There is a complex procedure for determining the allocations for individual banks, but in the case of commercial banks it is understood that the requirements mean that around 2.5 per cent of the value of loans outstanding must be allocated to small farmers. However, it is unlikely that many poor farmers benefit from this allocation. It is understood that around 70 per cent of farmers fall within the definition of small farmers and, even so, some large farmers have managed to find ways of obtaining loans. Repayment rates have increased in recent years, but are still only in the 70 to 75 per cent range.

In Nepal, commercial banks are required to set aside 12 per cent of their loan portfolio for priority sector lending under the Intensive Banking Program (IBP). Within this, 3 per cent of their loan portfolio must be devoted to the 'hard core poor'. However, there is no definition for the 'hard core poor', and loans up to Rs15,000 ($270) to individual borrowers are regarded as meeting this requirement. The recovery rate under the IBP was estimated at 46 per cent in 1995–96, reflecting weak supervision, untrained bank personnel and lack of incentives. There are also suggestions that most of the resources have gone to the non-poor.

Other things being equal, directed credit schemes which target the poor cause banks to lend more to poor borrowers than they otherwise would. Nevertheless, such schemes tend to be an inefficient means of reaching the poor. Many of the considerations discussed below relating to the implementation of government microfinance programs through commercial banks also apply here, with most participating banks not having the commitment to make the far-reaching changes that are necessary to operate successful microfinance programs. As such, their priority sector lending to the poor tends to be poorly targeted and to suffer from low repayment rates. While such schemes do not necessarily impose a cost to the budget (although where refinancing is involved they may), they reduce the efficiency of the financial system, and therefore impose resource costs on the economy as a whole. Again, experience with such schemes suggests that there are much more efficient ways of encouraging microfinance than through directed credit requirements, and that a more effective way for governments to encourage regulated banks to become involved in microfinance is to ensure an appropriate regulatory and prudential framework.

Programs channelled through the banking system

India

In some countries, the government operates specific microfinance programs in which funds are channelled through the banks. By far the largest of these is the Integrated Rural Development Programme (IRDP) in India. This program involves the provision of credit to the poor by banks, with a cash subsidy provided to borrowers by the government. Beneficiaries are selected by local village assemblies on the basis of a survey by local officials of households below the poverty line, and are then screened by the banks. It is designed to assist the poorest of the poor, with reservations for scheduled castes and tribes (50 per cent), women (40 per cent) and the physically handicapped (3 per cent).

There is no specific interest rate set under the program, but as with all small loans by commercial banks, there is a ceiling of 12 per cent. The maximum loan size under the IRDP is Rs25,000 ($690), with the average loan size around Rs15,000 ($420). Lending by banks under the IRDP is eligible for refinancing from NABARD. As at August 1996, over 49 million loans had been advanced under the program since it began in 1978.

Numerous evaluation studies have shown that the IRDP has not met its objectives. For instance, the Interim Report of the Expert Committee on the IRDP, constituted by the Reserve Bank of India (1995), found the following shortcomings:

(1) There was inappropriate identification of borrowers, with the subsidies often being captured by better-off households.

(2) The provision of the subsidy at the beginning of the loan had caused leakages and malpractices, such as encouraging beneficiaries to dispose of the assets purchased with the loan and simply pocket the subsidy.

(3) Repayment rates were very low, with the cumulative repayment rate having declined to 30.9 per cent by end-June 1993.

Recently, some changes have been made to the operation of the scheme, in response to this report. It remains to be seen to what extent these changes will lead to an improvement in the performance of the program.

Indonesia

Indonesia has a number of programs in which credit is channelled through the banking system, with varying degrees of effectiveness and varying degrees of relevance to poverty alleviation. Possibly the most successful, the P4K project (income-generating project for marginal farmers and landless) is conducted by the Ministry of Agriculture and has a mass character. It has employed Bank Rakyat Indonesia's field staff, community facilitators and 'small farmer groups' to develop a savings and credit scheme which the International Fund for Agricultural Development (IFAD) is said to regard as the best it has supported in Asia. Bank Rakyat Indonesia covers its costs, and final borrowers (who number some 480,000) pay market-related interest rates.

The central bank, Bank Indonesia, has a targeted microcredit project which is based on a poverty line, with one-third of borrowers 'poor' and the remainder 'nearly poor'. Financial development at the grassroots level is at least as important an objective as poverty alleviation for this project. The rural banks (BPRs), other small financial institutions and NGOs are involved in the disbursement process and interest rates are set to cover costs. Bank Indonesia also channels 'liquidity credits' to cooperatives, with funds from commercial banks, in the ratio of 3 to 1. The central bank credits are subsidised and provide generous margins to support the cooperatives, with interest rates to final borrowers (few of whom are below the poverty line) below market rates. Another Bank Indonesia initiative is the PHBK (program linking banks with self-help groups), discussed below in the section on linkages between banks and specialist MFIs.

Malaysia

A much smaller scheme operates in Malaysia and Sri Lanka. In Malaysia, commercial banks serve as a conduit for a number of loan schemes operated by CGC. The main scheme is the loan fund for hawkers and petty traders. The scheme is funded through a one-off soft loan from the government to CGC of RM120 million ($48 million). This money is on-lent to commercial banks and finance companies free of interest, and banks lend a maximum of RM10,000 ($4,000) to final borrowers at an interest rate of 4 per cent. While the scheme has achieved high repayment rates, it was reported that it does not generally reach poor borrowers.

Sri Lanka

In Sri Lanka, the government has recently introduced the Samurdhi Development Credit Scheme, targeted at welfare beneficiaries. The scheme is implemented by the Ministry of Youth Affairs, Sports and Rural Development in collaboration with two state commercial banks. The government has provided Rs500 million ($9.1 million) to the two participating banks for 1997. Borrowers are selected by village task forces, and receive loans of between Rs2,500 ($45) and Rs10,000 ($180) at an interest rate of 10 per cent. Because of the newness of the scheme, no data on its performance are available at this stage.

Thailand

In Thailand, one of the largest microfinance programs is the credit program for rural development, administered by the Government Savings Bank (GSB) and referred to in section 3.3. The program provides loans to savings and credit organisations in rural areas at an interest rate of 7 per cent. To date 1,360 organisations with a total membership of 188,000 have obtained loans, and repayment rates are reported to be high. The program appears to have been more successful than most other microfinance programs channelled through the banking system. This is very likely because GSB operates through linkages with savings and credit organisations, and does not lend to final borrowers in its own right.

Nepal

Nepal also has programs channelled through the banking system. The Production Credit for Rural Women (PCRW) scheme was introduced with assistance from IFAD, and channels funds through three public sector banks direct to self-help groups. It has been reasonably successful with a cumulative repayment rate of around 82 per cent, but delivery costs are quite high. The Micro Credit Project for Women (MCPW) is supported by the ADB. It is channelled through two state commercial banks, and involves NGOs as financial intermediaries. Repayment is reported to be close to 100 per cent, very likely reflecting the use of NGOs.

Pakistan

In Pakistan the First Women Bank, a state commercial bank, administers a small fund of Rs48 million ($1.4 million) provided by the Department of Women's Development. From this fund, the bank provides small loans at a mark-up of 12 per cent to poor women. Loans are generally provided to individual borrowers, although in some cases borrowers organise themselves into groups and provide group guarantees. However, 22 NGOs are associated with the program as social intermediaries, in identifying and training borrowers. The bank has also lent to five NGOs as financial intermediaries for on-lending to final borrowers. To date, the program has provided loans to around 5,040 women and achieved a cumulative repayment rate of around 97 per cent. This successful performance may reflect the fact that First Women Bank is a relatively small bank with a particular focus on women, and the use of NGOs as financial and social intermediaries.

Conclusions

Based on experience in Asia and elsewhere, it is fair to say that the implementation of government microfinance programs through commercial banks has generally not been successful, at least where commercial banks have lent directly to final borrowers without using NGOs as financial or social intermediaries. While it is clear that banks can establish successful microfinance programs, it is equally clear that this takes a great deal of effort and commitment. In the past at least, most banks have not had the commitment to make the thoroughgoing changes in organisational design and financial technologies that are necessary to operate successful microfinance programs.

Moreover, participation in government microfinance programs is unlikely to induce them to make these changes. Such schemes are generally implemented through very large, often state-owned commercial banks, and account for only a small proportion of their total loans outstanding. They are therefore seen as marginal to their overall operations. Often the loanable funds come from a specific government allocation or are guaranteed by the government, reducing the incentive for intensive follow-up to ensure high repayment rates. There is little incentive for the banks to ensure that such programs reach genuinely poor borrowers. And interest rates are generally kept too low for commercial banks to operate such schemes on a sustainable basis, even if they had the commitment to do so. Hence, it is not surprising that such schemes tend to be poorly targeted and to suffer from low repayment rates.

Such schemes may also 'crowd out' other microfinance programs, not only by absorbing scarce public funds, but also by making it more difficult for other programs to charge market interest rates and by eroding repayment discipline. Where public funds are available for microfinance, it would appear much more appropriate to channel them through second tier microfinance institutions and specialist MFIs, rather than through the banking system. There is also no reason why small banks with a commitment to microfinance and which meet the required performance and reporting standards cannot borrow from second tier institutions. In the Philippines a number of rural banks have borrowed from PCFC, and in Sri Lanka NDTF has lent to a number of regional rural development banks.

An apparent exception to this analysis is in Indonesia, where some microfinance programs channelled through banks, in particular Bank Rakyat Indonesia and the BPRs, appear to have been successful. This is because these banks have a genuine commitment to outreach, and the success of their efforts in this regard brings them into the market for microfinance. Their appropriate organisation, products and procedures contribute to their success at the bottom end of the market. Moreover, their role as a conduit for various government programs is only one aspect (and in many cases a relatively minor one) of their overall involvement in the microfinance sector. Hence, in Indonesia, Bank Rakyat Indonesia and the network of BPRs may be suitable vehicles for the implementation of microfinance programs.

In general, however, the most effective way for governments to encourage regulated banks to become involved in microfinance is to ensure an appropriate regulatory and prudential framework. With an appropriate framework, those banks which wish to become involved in microfinance will be able to do so on a commercial basis, while those that do not will be able to concentrate on other activities. These issues are discussed in more detail in chapter 5.

Linkages between banks and specialised microfinance institutions

One important way in which commercial banks can become involved in microfinance is through linkages with NGOs and SHGs. This approach combines the strength of commercial banks in financial management with the ability of NGOs to reach the poor. In many cases, community-based NGOs may have an advantage over commercial banks in reaching the poor, reflecting factors such as proximity, trust, commitment, flexibility and responsiveness. Linkages between banks and NGOs and SHGs may take a variety of forms. For instance, NGOs may act as financial intermediaries, with banks extending loans to NGOs and the NGOs on-lending to final borrowers. Alternatively, NGOs may act as social intermediaries, selecting and motivating groups of borrowers on behalf of banks, but with the loan contract being between the bank and the final borrower. Commercial banks may also lend to institutions involved in microfinance that are not NGOs, such as second tier microfinance institutions, rural banks, cooperatives and others.

The Foundation for Development Cooperation (1992 and 1995) has demonstrated that such linkages have considerable potential to provide financial services to the poor on a sustainable basis. Nevertheless, it must be said that progress in establishing such linkages has been slow, and there are relatively few examples of linkages except where they have been promoted by specific government programs as discussed below. In Bangladesh and Nepal, some state commercial banks have established linkages with MFIs on a commercial basis and outside the framework of specific government programs, but to date no private commercial banks have done so in those countries. In Sri Lanka a private commercial bank, Hatton National Bank, has established a very successful microfinance program which includes using NGOs as social intermediaries (this program is discussed in detail in Gallardo, Randhawa and Sacay, 1997). Such examples, however, are still comparatively rare.

In most countries included in the study there are no specific regulatory impediments to linkages. In some countries, the use of NGOs as social intermediaries may be constrained by interest rate ceilings which prevent banks from lending on a commercial basis to microentrepreneurs. These issues are discussed in chapter 5. Some other general regulations affecting banks or NGOs may also reduce the scope for linkages. Nevertheless, the major obstacles to linkages relate to matters other than the regulatory environment.

The only exception to this is Pakistan, where banking regulations make it extremely difficult for commercial banks to establish linkages. First, banks are only permitted to make unsecured loans up to Rs100,000 ($2,850). This rule greatly restricts the scope for banks to lend to NGOs, village organisations or SHGs for on-lending to poor borrowers, as such organisations generally have little to offer by way of security. Second, other than individuals, banks are only allowed to lend to structured bodies which meet certain conditions. For instance, structured bodies are required to maintain audited accounts, and are subject to regulations concerning debt-equity ratios and other matters. This makes it very difficult for banks to lend to relatively informal group structures such as village organisations and SHGs. The Aga Khan Rural Support Program is currently holding discussions with the State Bank to amend these rules or to exempt loans to NGOs and village organisations from these requirements. Nevertheless, as they stand, these restrictions are clearly a major barrier to banks establishing linkages with NGOs and SHGs. In other countries there are no major policy barriers to linkages.

However, other than in India and Indonesia, there is little positive support for linkages from policymakers.

India

In India NABARD, which was established by the Reserve Bank in 1982 as the apex body for rural credit, has an active program for linking banks with SHGs, and has issued detailed guidelines to banks about how to facilitate such linkages. The main features of the program are as follows:

(1) The banks extend loans to SHGs either directly or through NGOs. In around 94 per cent of cases, the SHGs have been initiated and promoted by NGOs. In around two-thirds of these cases the NGOs have acted as social intermediaries, and the loan contract has been between the bank and SHG. This is NABARD's preferred model, and is the one adopted by major NGOs such as the Mysore Resettlement and Development Agency (MYRADA). In around one-third of cases, the NGOs have acted as financial intermediaries, and have borrowed from banks and on-lent to the SHGs. NABARD, however, has sought to discourage this model.

(2) The banks lend at an interest rate of 10.5 per cent if lending through an NGO, or 12 per cent if lending directly to an SHG. Where the bank lends to an NGO, the NGO on-lends to SHGs at 12 per cent. The banks receive refinancing from NABARD at 6.5 per cent.

(3) Loans from banks to NGOs and SHGs are generally for three years, but loans from SHGs to members are flexible, with terms determined by the members. SHGs normally charge interest rates of between 24 and 36 per cent.

As of March 1997, a total of 8,546 SHGs, with a total membership of more than 150,000, had been linked to banks. Banks had lent Rs111 million ($3.1 million) to these groups, and had received refinancing from NABARD of Rs103 million ($2.9 million). Twenty-six (26) state commercial banks, two private commercial banks, 67 regional rural banks, seven cooperative banks and 166 NGOs had been involved in the program. As well as providing refinancing, NABARD has also supported linkages between banks and SHGs in a variety of other ways. For instance, it has funded exposure and training to commercial bank staff to enable them to understand the program and the advantages that it offers to banks. Training is normally provided by NGOs and training institutes. By September 1996, around 2,200 bank officers had received training and exposure.

While the NABARD program is a positive initiative, it should be noted that it is not sustainable in its current form. In particular, the mark-ups do not provide anywhere near a sufficient margin for NGOs to recover the costs of forming and motivating SHGs. Where NGOs act as social intermediaries, the mark-up between bank and SHG is only 5.5 percentage points. In practice, banks retain this margin and do not reimburse the NGOs for their costs, which in any case are likely to be above 5.5 percentage points. Where NGOs act as financial intermediaries, the mark-up is only 1.5 percentage points. Hence, NGOs are only able to participate in the program if they can obtain donor funds to subsidise these activities. This is likely to mitigate against expansion of the program.

Indonesia

In Indonesia, the PHBK (project linking banks with SHGs) has been implemented with German technical assistance. It originally concentrated on nurturing linkages between branches of various state commercial banks (although private commercial banks are now involved to some degree) with NGOs and state-sponsored agencies which are active in organising the poor into SHGs for savings and credit management. The growing involvement of rural banks in the PHBK scheme has permitted an acceleration in recent times in the numbers of clients and volume of credit disbursed via linkages, at a rate of 10 per cent per month. Some 400 banks, 183 'self-help promoting institutions' (including NGOs) and 6,800 groups were involved in September 1996. Interest rates are market based and transaction costs are covered by interest margins. The project is a painstaking attempt to build a sustainable system for credit and savings mobilisation, with limited outreach as yet.

The freedom of banks, NGOs and SHGs to set interest rates at sustainable levels in Indonesia's deregulated financial environment, and the absence of central bank refinancing, are other factors which distinguish the Indonesian situation from that in India. The preferred model of linkage is one in which the role of the NGO or other intermediating agency is social; financial transactions occur directly between the bank branch and the SHG. Some rural banks are moving directly to organise their own groups, cutting out the role of the 'social intermediary' in some cases.

Comment

Other countries have not adopted comparable programs. In Bangladesh, the central bank conducted a seminar on linkages in 1994, and it has issued a number of circulars to commercial banks encouraging them to establish linkages with NGOs for lending to the poor. Nevertheless, the commercial banks commented that it is necessary for the central bank to take a more proactive role. In Nepal, the proposed Financial Intermediation Act will be an important step in establishing the financial intermediary role of NGOs and MFIs. In these and in other countries, it would be appropriate for the central bank to take a more active role in encouraging linkages by documenting and publicising successful examples, issuing clear guidelines that the banks could follow, providing training to banks, encouraging ratings systems for MFIs, and more generally promoting change in the culture of banking. This would be conducive to an environment in which such linkages would occur on a commercial basis, outside the framework of government programs. The guidelines issued by NABARD in India may be a useful starting point, although they would need to be adapted to ensure that programs are sustainable and to suit the institutional framework in other countries.

3.5 Programs operated directly by government agencies

The other main category of microfinance programs is those operated directly by government agencies. This is a diverse category, with few commonalities among schemes. While most countries have such programs, most are small and not well documented. Nevertheless, the information that is available suggests that most microfinance programs operated by government agencies suffer from high costs and low repayment rates, and in many cases do not reach poor borrowers.

Bangladesh

There have been a number of microfinance programs administered by government agencies in Bangladesh. One of the largest and most successful of these is the RD-12 program of the Bangladesh Rural Development Board (BRDB), with some 328,000 borrowers as at December 1995. BRDB is a semi-autonomous government agency with its own board of directors. In addition, the RD-12 project has a central coordinating committee, including representatives from the Canadian International Development Agency (CIDA), which meets once every six months to decide on overall policy matters relating to the project. The project borrows heavily from the experience of NGOs involved in microfinance, including the Grameen Bank and Bangladesh Rural Advancement Committee (BRAC), with the lending methodology based on the Grameen Bank model.

The project has performed very well compared to most other government microfinance programs both in Bangladesh and in other countries, with a recovery rate of 91 per cent in 1993. Its success demonstrates that by using best practice techniques and ensuring relatively independent management free from political interference, it is possible for government agencies to establish effective microfinance programs. Nevertheless, the repayment rates achieved by RD-12 are still below those achieved by leading MFIs in Bangladesh. RD-12 has also not been under as much pressure as the NGO programs to minimise costs and become sustainable. Moreover, it is understood that most other government programs have not been nearly as successful as RD-12.

Indonesia

In Indonesia, there are two major new microfinance programs of a mass character operated by government agencies. These represent something of a reversal in the trend towards sustainability in government programs in that country. The IDT (Inpres Desa Tertinggal or Presidential Instruction relating to backward villages) is a presidential initiative programmed in Indonesia's sixth Five Year Plan (1993–1998). Prompted by perceptions of growing relative poverty and regional income inequality and coordinated by the National Development Planning Board, it calls on interdepartmental resources to channel funds to more than 20,000 'backward' villages, primarily through grants to provide seed capital for the economic activities of the poor who are organised in self-help groups. The groups themselves decide the terms on which funds will be on-lent to members. Other resources are provided to facilitate the preparation of these groups, and to improve infrastructure in the chosen villages. It is hoped that after some period of funding, the groups will 'graduate' to more commercial sources of funding (such as the PHBK program of Bank Indonesia). It is not clear that sustainability is a primary goal, in that groups hold what is essentially a revolving fund and substantial leakage may be occurring. Coverage of the program was some 107,000 groups and 2.9 million people at end-1996. By mid-1997 some 3 million households were said to have received seed capital averaging $81 per household.

The Prosperous Family program was initiated in March 1996 and over a twelve-month period channelled funds to the mothers of some 9.8 million families. This was possible because it employed the infrastructure of Indonesia's national family planning agency, which is far-reaching and effective, and the existing structure of groups organised for family planning and maternal and child health. The program is another Presidential initiative, and a direct reaction to political concerns about inequality. Women beneficiaries are stratified by economic status and perceived 'readiness' to handle credit effectively. The poorest start with savings, and initial small grants are designed to provide an incentive for individual saving. After some savings have been accumulated, women progress to receiving very small loans, at a highly concessional interest rate of 6 per cent. Much criticism is directed at the small size of these loans and at the capacities of family planning and health field staff to generate economic activity among the poor. The scheme is still too new, and the numbers too large, for any careful evaluation. It remains to be seen (for both IDT and Prosperous Family) whether concerns for institutional development and sustainability will prevail over the attraction of short-term political gains from widespread disbursement of cash.

Philippines

In the Philippines, a recent audit of microfinance programs by the National Credit Council (NCC) uncovered at least 111 government credit programs. Many of these involve government agencies lending directly to final borrowers. These government credit programs have been criticised for being inefficient, highly politicised, uncoordinated and unsustainable. For instance, Llanto, Garcia and Callanta (1996, p.14) comment that:

> . . . Philippine experience has shown the huge inefficiency and high costs of using government non-financial institutions to implement credit programs. Recent research has shown the unsustainability of government supply-led credit programs, the great capacity for leakage of the benefits of government credit programs to the non-poor, the duplication and overlapping of a number of credit programs leading to gross inefficiencies, the distortion of the financial market and weakening of private sector incentive to innovate.

The Department of Finance and the NCC are currently working to rationalise these programs. The NCC guidelines provide that government line agencies should focus on technical assistance and capacity building, and should channel all their lending activities through banks and MFIs. Political and bureaucratic resistance leaves the ultimate outcome in doubt.

Thailand

Another large government microfinance program is the poverty alleviation project operated by the Community Development Department in Thailand. The program operates only in villages that are identified as poor, and individual borrowers are also means tested. A revolving fund is established in each village, and borrowers are identified by local government authorities using basic minimum needs data collected by the village. Loans to individual borrowers are interest free, with administrative costs met through the budget. By 1995, around B2.8 billion ($110 million) had been advanced to village welfare committees in around 10,000 villages, and nearly B1 billion ($40 million) had been on-lent to final borrowers. The program is clearly not sustainable, and analysis by the World Bank suggests that repayment rates are very low.

Comment

Based on these experiences, it appears that government microfinance programs that lend directly to final borrowers are rarely cost-effective. Moreover, they may 'crowd out' more effective microfinance programs. In general, it would be appropriate to abolish such programs and channel the funds through well-managed MFIs instead. Direct government programs should only be retained where it can be shown through a rigorous evaluation that, taking all direct and indirect subsidies into account, they are as cost-effective as leading MFIs.

In a number of countries, governments have forgiven certain categories of small loans under their own programs or by state commercial banks. Two particular examples are the 1991 decision by the government of Bangladesh to forgive all agricultural loans up to Tk5,000 ($120), and the periodic debt waivers by successive governments in Sri Lanka, most recently in 1995. However, debt forgiveness is not confined to these two countries. These episodes have created major problems for MFIs. Clearly, failure to ensure high repayment rates in other parts of the financial system reduces overall borrower discipline and makes it much harder for MFIs to maintain high repayment rates. Governments should avoid debt forgiveness for small loans in the future.

3.6 Summary and recommendations

Active support from government and/or donor agencies, including direct financial support, is a necessary catalyst to the establishment of a viable microfinance sector. While microfinance institutions (MFIs) should strive for self-sufficiency, attaining it takes a considerable period of time. To set up their programs and for a number of years thereafter, MFIs need to be subsidised. Expanding to achieve economies of scale also requires a considerable input of resources for capacity building and institutional development.

Support for individual microfinance institutions

MFIs in all countries have received considerable support from the government and/or donor agencies. In the past, most of this has been in the form of financial assistance direct to an individual MFI. This support has been critical in enabling them to establish, and to increase their outreach and self-sufficiency. Without this support, it is unlikely that there would be a microfinance sector at all, in the sense of specialist MFIs providing financial services to the poor in an innovative and commercially viable manner.

Nevertheless, the development of microfinance and the success of leading MFIs owes more to the vision of their founders and management than to the criteria used by government and donor agencies for supporting them. Support has been largely ad hoc in nature, and has generally not been explicitly designed to maximise the twin objectives of outreach and sustainability in the most cost-effective manner.

Direct support for MFIs towards outreach and sustainability

The Guiding Principles for Selecting and Supporting Intermediaries, agreed by major donor agencies in October 1995, provide a number of suggestions as to how support by donors and government can best be directed to maximising outreach and sustainability. Most importantly, governments and donor agencies should only support institutions which demonstrate a capacity to reach poor clients on a sustainable basis. Support should be directed to institutions with demonstrated performance or credible plans in terms of institutional strengths, quality of services and outreach, and financial performance. The Guiding Principles also consider the types of support that donor agencies should provide.

While the major donor agencies have endorsed these principles, they are not always followed in practice. All governments and donor agencies should ensure that their support for MFIs is consistent with the Guiding Principles.

The role of second tier microfinance institutions

Most countries included in the study have some form of 'second tier' microfinance institution which channels funds from the government and/or donor agencies to individual MFIs. The largest and most successful second tier institution is the Palli Karma Sahayak Foundation (PKSF) in Bangladesh. Second tier institutions are also an important part of the microfinance sector in India, Sri Lanka, the Philippines and Thailand.

Where they operate well, second tier microfinance institutions are a very effective means for supporting MFIs. It is much more efficient for one institution to analyse and monitor the performance of individual MFIs than for different government and donor agencies to do their own appraisals and evaluations. Moreover, if all the support for a particular MFI can be channelled through one agency, it is much easier to ensure that it is complementary and directed to the same objectives.

Channel support for microfinance through well-managed second tier institutions

For these reasons, governments and donor agencies as much as possible should channel their support for microfinance through efficient and well-managed second tier microfinance institutions. In countries with more than one second tier institution, governments should ensure that the different institutions adopt consistent standards and policies.

Ensure sound operations of second tier institutions

At the same time, there is evidence both from Asia and from other regions that second tier institutions do not always operate on a sound basis, and may be subject to significant administrative, political and technical difficulties. If second tier institutions are to play an effective role, it is clear that there are a number of critical issues that need to be addressed.

First and most important, second tier institutions should establish and enforce appropriate performance and reporting standards for the MFIs that they fund. They should support MFIs based on the standards they achieve, rather than the model they follow. Second, pressure to meet unrealistic disbursement targets may cause institutions to lower their standards and be counter-productive.

Third, second tier institutions should avoid restrictive interest rate policies. In India, for instance, the major second tier institutions impose ceilings on the interest rates that their partner MFIs can charge borrowers, at levels which make it difficult if not impossible for the MFIs to achieve self-sufficiency.

Fourth, some second tier institutions only lend to MFIs for on-lending to final borrowers. They should develop appropriate criteria for funding scaling-up, institutional development and equity, as well as providing loanable funds. Where privatisation is envisaged, other arrangements for such support must be assured.

Fifth, it is critical that second tier institutions operate as independent entities and are not politicised. Some commentators suggested that the performance of the National Development Trust Fund (NDTF) in Sri Lanka had been affected by politicisation, and this also appears to have been a factor affecting institutions in some other countries.

Support through the banking system

Seven of the nine countries included in the study impose directed credit requirements, whereby banks are required to lend a certain proportion of their loan portfolio to particular sectors. Other things being equal, directed credit schemes which target the poor will cause banks to lend more to poor borrowers than would otherwise be the case. However, they are an inefficient means of reaching the poor, and impose economic costs.

Channel public funds through second tier institutions and specialist MFIs rather than banks

In some countries, the government operates specific microfinance programs in which funds are channelled through the banks. The largest of these programs is IRDP in India. Such programs have generally not been successful, and may 'crowd out' more effective programs. Where public funds are available to support microfinance, it is more appropriate to channel them through second tier microfinance institutions and specialist MFIs, rather than through the banking system. The most effective way for governments to encourage regulated banks to become involved in microfinance is to ensure an appropriate regulatory and prudential framework, rather than through direct financial support. On the other hand there is also no reason why small banks with a commitment to microfinance should not borrow from second tier institutions.

An apparent exception to this analysis is in Indonesia, where some microfinance programs channelled through banks, in particular, Bank Rakyat Indonesia and the rural banks (BPRs), appear to have been successful. This is because these banks have a genuine commitment to outreach, as well as appropriate organisation, products and procedures. Hence, in Indonesia, banks already involved in microfinance may be suitable vehicles for the implementation of government microfinance programs.

Encourage commercial bank involvement via linkages

One important way in which commercial banks can become involved in microfinance is through linkages with non-governmental organisations (NGOs) and self-help groups (SHGs). The only country included in the study with specific regulatory impediments to such linkages is Pakistan. However, other than in India and Indonesia, there is little positive support for linkages from policymakers, and even in India the program is not sustainable because the mark-ups that banks and NGOs can charge do not provide anywhere near a sufficient margin for NGOs to recover the costs of forming and motivating SHGs. Central banks should take a more active role in encouraging linkages by documenting and publicising successful examples, issuing clear guidelines that the banks could follow, and other measures. This would be conducive to an environment in which such linkages would occur on a commercial basis, outside the framework of government programs.

Programs operated directly by government agencies

The other main category of microfinance programs is those operated directly by government agencies. The largest and possibly the most successful such program is the RD-12 program of the Bangladesh Rural Development Board (BRDB). Its success demonstrates that by using best practice techniques and ensuring relatively independent management free from political interference, it is possible for government agencies to establish effective microfinance programs. Nevertheless, its performance is still not as good as that of leading MFIs in Bangladesh.

In the Philippines, a recent audit of microfinance programs by the National Credit Council (NCC) uncovered at least 111 government credit programs, many involving government agencies lending directly to final borrowers. These government credit programs have been criticised for being inefficient, highly politicised, uncoordinated and unsustainable. Fragmentary evidence suggests that these criticisms could also be levelled at most direct government microfinance programs in other countries.

In Indonesia, while there is not the proliferation of line agency programs observed in the Philippines, there are several such programs. Two have achieved mass outreach in a short period, with the Inpres Desa Tertinggal (IDT) reaching more than 3 million households in less than four years, and the Prosperous Family program reaching almost 10 million households in a single year. Considerations of institutional development and sustainability may have been casualties in the face of the government's need to be seen to be responding to popular concern about regional and interpersonal income inequalities.

Abolish direct government microfinance programs

In general, governments should abolish direct microfinance programs and channel the funds through well-managed second tier microfinance institutions or MFIs instead. Direct government programs should only be retained where it can be shown through a rigorous evaluation that they are as cost-effective as leading MFIs, taking all direct and indirect subsidies into account.

Avoid debt forgiveness for small loans

In a number of countries, governments have forgiven certain categories of small loans under their own programs or by state commercial banks. These episodes have created major problems for MFIs. Governments should avoid debt forgiveness for small loans in the future.

4 Regulation of non-bank microfinance institutions

4.1 Background

The regulatory environment for microfinance institutions (MFIs) is very important if the microfinance sector is to achieve significant outreach on a sustainable basis. On the one hand, if MFIs are to flourish they should be able to operate relatively freely without unnecessary restrictions, and charge interest rates and fees that are sufficient to cover their costs. On the other hand, it is appropriate to have some kind of framework to encourage MFIs to meet certain minimum performance and reporting standards and to improve their performance over time. Berenbach and Churchill (1997, p.1) discuss the task at hand in the following terms:

> As unregulated financial entities, the better microfinance institutions have had considerable freedom to adapt operating methods to serve their target markets effectively. This has led to the development of a small but growing number of robust, specialised financial institutions, innovative delivery methods, and an extension of the financial services market. When regulation is warranted, it requires coherent prudential guidelines that will allow the growth of the microfinance sector while protecting the interests of small savers and supporting the integrity of the financial sector as a whole.

This chapter considers the regulation of non-bank MFIs. Section 4.2 considers the broad regulatory framework, while regulations concerning interest rates are discussed in section 4.3. The subsequent three sections discuss alternative ways to ensure high standards within the microfinance sector, starting with an analysis of the scope for prudential regulation and supervision in section 4.4. This is followed by a discussion of the performance and reporting standards of second tier microfinance institutions in section 4.5, while section 4.6 covers matters to do with self-regulation. Section 4.7 discusses the difficult issue of savings mobilisation and deposit taking by MFIs, while section 4.8 summarises the chapter and provides recommendations.

4.2 The broad regulatory framework

Specific regulatory provisions for microfinance

In general, there is no separate regulatory framework for MFIs, and they are subject to the same regulatory framework as other NGOs or cooperatives. The one exception to this is the Grameen Bank in Bangladesh. The Grameen Bank is regulated under its own ordinance, the Grameen Bank Ordinance 1983. The ordinance specifically provides that laws relating to banking shall not apply to the Grameen Bank. According to the ordinance, the function of the bank will be to provide credit, with or without collateral security, to landless persons for all kinds of economic activities including housing. The ordinance further specifies a range of activities that the bank may undertake, including accepting money on deposit. The bank is not permitted to transact any kind of business other than those authorised. For instance, it is not permitted to engage in foreign exchange transactions. This legislation was specifically enacted to cover the Grameen Bank, and is tailored to its particular needs and circumstances.

It should be noted, however, that the ordinance applies only to the Grameen Bank. It does not cover other MFIs operating in Bangladesh. These are governed by the general provisions relating to NGOs in that country.

Non-government organisations

In most countries, MFIs are permitted to provide loans to poor clients so long as they are registered under one or other of the provisions applying to NGOs in general.

In India, Bangladesh and Pakistan, the provisions for NGOs to obtain registration are very similar, reflecting their common colonial heritage. In all of these countries, two options for registration are as a society under the Societies Registration Act of 1860, or as a trust under the Trusts Act of 1882, both dating from the colonial era. These Acts have been amended in each of the three countries, and in India they are administered by the state governments. Hence, requirements differ slightly between the different countries and in the case of India, between different states. Nevertheless, to be registered under these Acts, NGOs must generally have a memorandum of association and rules and regulations, or some similar document, covering such matters as the name of the organisation, objectives, membership, management committee and organisational structure. NGOs are also generally required to provide an annual report and financial statements to the regulatory agency. In most cases, these requirements for registration are relatively straightforward to fulfil. There are also some other options for registration, with broadly similar requirements. For instance, in Bangladesh some MFIs are registered as non-profit companies or charitable trusts, while in Pakistan some are registered as non-profit companies or voluntary social welfare agencies.

The framework for registration is also quite similar in Nepal and Sri Lanka. In Nepal, most MFIs are registered as societies under the Societies Registration Act of 1978, and are subject to similar requirements to NGOs registered as societies in the other South Asian countries. In Sri Lanka, there are three avenues for NGOs to obtain registration. Some large NGOs have been incorporated under their own Acts of Parliament. This is probably the most complicated method. The other options are to be registered as a non-profit company or as a society. Even though these various provisions for registration are not particularly onerous, there is no requirement for NGOs to be registered at all. It is quite possible for an NGO in Sri Lanka to operate a microfinance program without being registered under any Act of Parliament and without being accountable to any regulatory agency, although unregistered NGOs may have difficulty in attracting external funds.

In the Philippines, MFIs are classed along with other NGOs as 'non-stock, non-profit' organisations, and are registered with the Securities and Exchange Commission. While the system is different, the requirements for registration are quite similar to those applying in the countries discussed above. They must have a board of directors, and must file articles of incorporation and by-laws. They are also required to provide audited annual financial statements to the commission. In Indonesia, NGOs register as foundations, a legal entity which is simple to establish and extremely elastic in regard to the uses to which it can be put. NGOs intending to engage in lending do not require permission or specific registration in regard to credit activities.

In Malaysia and Thailand, it is more difficult for an MFI to meet the legal requirements to establish a microfinance program. In Malaysia there are three main options for NGOs in terms of registration: as a trust, as a non-profit company, or as a society. The requirements for registration are generally quite straightforward However, registration under these provisions does not permit an NGO to engage in microfinance. Under Malaysian law, only specified institutions such as banks, cooperative societies and licensed moneylenders are permitted to lend money in consideration of a larger sum being repaid. If NGOs are to operate as MFIs and make loans, they need to obtain a specific exemption from the provisions of the Moneylenders Act of 1951. Such exemption must be obtained on a one-off basis from the Minister of Housing and Local Government, and is generally granted for a period of three to four years. There are no clear criteria for obtaining an exemption, and some commentators stated that it may be difficult for smaller NGOs without connections to obtain an exemption.

In Thailand, NGOs are generally registered as associations or foundations. Associations and foundations are not permitted to undertake business activities, and it is not clear if these organisations are strictly entitled to provide microfinance services. A number of multi-purpose NGOs which operate microfinance programs are registered under these provisions, and the authorities have tended not to intervene. However, these organisational forms would not appear to be appropriate for specialist MFIs which provide financial services only. One such specialist MFI found that the simplest way to obtain a legal identity was to register as a company under the Civil and Commercial Code. However, to register as a company, it is necessary to meet a minimum capital requirement of B500,000 ($19,760), and this may be prohibitive for a small NGO wishing to engage in microfinance.

Cooperative societies

All countries included in the study have long-established cooperative movements, including credit cooperatives. The legislation governing the establishment of cooperatives is quite similar in most countries. In general, a minimum of around ten members is necessary to establish a cooperative. Cooperatives are required to be non-discriminatory in membership and must have a democratic structure, with all members having equal voting rights. They are also generally required to have by-laws according to a standard format, covering matters such as name and objects, membership rules, power and functions of the general body, frequency of meetings, and the size and composition of the board of directors.

In most countries in South Asia and also in Indonesia, credit cooperatives have been largely unsuccessful in extending financial services to poor households. Generally, the cooperative movement includes people of all income levels within a particular village or community, and does not target the poor. Moreover, management of the cooperative movement has been inadequate in most countries.

In some countries such as India and Pakistan, a large proportion of cooperatives is reported to be non-functional, due to financial mismanagement and inability to recover dues. Even where they are functional, management is often dominated by rural elites, with funds allocated on the basis of patronage rather than needs. Frequently they rely heavily on government funds and are largely owned and controlled by governments. In India and Pakistan, for instance, state and provincial cooperative departments have the right to be represented on the board of directors, and can exert considerable influence on the management of cooperatives. For instance, permission may be needed to hold elections, invest funds, change their area of operations, use funds from their reserves, and similar matters. In Indonesia also, the officially sponsored cooperatives have been described as smothered by government bureaucracy. These controls make it very difficult for cooperatives to function efficiently or effectively. Nevertheless, in India in particular there is a small number of highly successful cooperative banks and societies which are devoted specifically to providing financial services to the poor, such as SEWA Bank and Working Women's Forum.

In India, the state of Andhra Pradesh has recently passed the Mutually Aided Cooperative Societies Act of 1995, designed to remove cooperatives from many of the administrative controls of the state and make them more self-reliant and autonomous. It is understood that the states have given in-principle agreement to the government of India to pass a similar law at the national level, which would apply throughout India. This would provide the opportunity to streamline the regulatory requirements facing cooperatives and remove unnecessary requirements.

In contrast to the other countries in South Asia, the credit cooperative movement in Sri Lanka has been highly successful and does not rely on the government for funding. Nevertheless, the regulatory framework is quite similar to that applying in other countries in South Asia, and the Federation of Thrift and Credit Cooperative

Societies commented that it found the regulatory framework restrictive in a number of ways. The law gives considerable discretion to the Minister and to the Registrar of Cooperative Societies, and requires their approval for numerous activities undertaken by the societies. For instance, various staffing decisions, relatively small capital purchases, and even large loans to borrowers require approval from the registrar. These requirements are cumbersome and inefficient.

In the Southeast Asian countries other than Indonesia, the regulatory environment for cooperatives appears to be less intrusive. In Thailand and to a lesser extent the Philippines, the cooperative movement is an important player in the microfinance sector. Credit cooperatives in these countries did not report that the regulatory environment was an impediment to their efficient operation.

Self-help groups and small community organisations

In all countries there is a wide variety of small, informal savings and loans groups, such as rotating savings and credit associations (ROSCAs) which operate informally and are not registered. In at least three countries, these or similar groups have been institutionalised to some extent by involving them in formal microfinance programs. In India self-help groups (SHGs) are an integral part of the National Bank for Agriculture and Rural Development (NABARD) program for linking banks and SHGs. Nevertheless, they are generally not registered. Under Indian law, SHGs are only required to be registered (as a society, trust or cooperative) if they have more than 20 members. For this reason, many SHGs restrict their membership to 20 persons or less. It is also understood that some larger SHGs operate informally and are not registered.

Indonesia has hundreds and thousands of groups engaged in savings and credit. Some of these are indigenous, based on traditional custom, while others are the result of action by government agencies, community groups and NGOs to form groups in connection with various government-initiated microfinance schemes. These include Bank Indonesia's microcredit project and program linking banks with self-help groups (PHBK), the income-generating project for marginal farmers and landless (P4K) of the Ministry of Agriculture, and the newer mass programs (Inpres Desa Tertinggal (IDT) and Prosperous Family program). There is no provision for registration of SHGs, nor are they regulated except in the context of the particular government program from which they arise.

Similarly in Thailand, some of the community organisations involved in the microfinance programs of the Government Savings Bank (GSB) and Urban Community Development Office (UCDO) are registered as cooperatives. However, most are unregistered and operate informally. For instance, figures from UCDO show that of the 385 members with savings activities, only 66 are legally registered as cooperatives while the other 319 are not registered and operate informally.

Regulatory controls

In some countries, MFIs face additional regulatory controls that are not of a prudential nature. For instance, in Bangladesh all NGOs which receive foreign donations are required to be registered with the NGO Affairs Bureau. They are required to seek approval each time before they can receive a foreign donation, including providing detailed budgets of how the funds are to be used. The NGO Affairs Bureau considers these applications and also circulates them to relevant ministries. Through this process, the NGO Affairs Bureau and other ministries have wide powers to regulate the activities of MFIs. Most MFIs felt that the bureau operates in a relatively flexible manner, and seeks to solve problems through discussion and negotiation rather than through arbitrary rulings. Nevertheless, it was felt that there is not always a level playing field between MFIs. For instance, some MFIs have been required to liaise with other MFIs and NGO bodies as to the coverage of their operations, or have been asked not to provide services in some areas, thereby limiting competition between MFIs.

In India, all NGOs receiving grants from foreign sources are subject to registration and reporting requirements with the Ministry of Home Affairs. In general, this procedure is not onerous. However, if not all of the grant is spent, approval from the Ministry of Finance is necessary to return the unspent portion to the donor, and this can take some time. In the case of loans from foreign sources there are further complications. Approval from the Ministry of Finance is needed before any loan can be received from foreign sources, and such approval can be difficult to obtain. Moreover, it is necessary to obtain approval from the Reserve Bank every time a repayment is made. This requires a detailed utilisation report, and NGOs commented that this report is quite onerous to complete. While the requirement for approval can be waived by the Reserve Bank, it is still necessary to complete the utilisation report. These restrictions reflect a desire on the part of the authorities to conserve foreign exchange, but are cumbersome and can place a significant administrative burden on MFIs.

Comment

In some countries, most notably Bangladesh and the Philippines, there has been some discussion as to whether there should be a separate registration process for MFIs. This may offer some advantages, in terms of establishing a regulatory framework that specifically caters for the needs of MFIs and ensuring that all MFIs in the country face the same requirements. Nevertheless, it would appear that in most cases the present processes for registration work reasonably well. In most countries, it is relatively easy for MFIs to obtain registration under the general provisions applying to NGOs and cooperatives. The only exceptions to this appear to be Malaysia and Thailand. In these countries, governments should establish simple registration procedures for NGOs wishing to engage in microfinance.

In all countries, it is quite easy for NGOs to obtain registration. The broad requirements, such as having a memorandum of association or some similar document and preparing an annual report and financial statements, are quite simple and should pose no problem to any well-managed MFI. However, even though these requirements are not particularly onerous, in many countries they are not enforced rigorously. In some countries, this relatively lax regime may have enabled some unscrupulous operators to set up and take advantage of clients. In Bangladesh, for instance, it was reported that there have been a number of examples of fraud by MFIs. Some MFIs have set up and obtained compulsory savings from members by promising to give them loans. However, the loans have not been forthcoming and their principals have absconded with members' savings. Similarly in Sri Lanka, it would appear that the unstructured regime has led to some problems, with some NGOs reportedly engaging in activities of a controversial nature.

While these cases have not been all that widespread, a number of poor clients have lost their money. Moreover, such fraud has the potential to undermine the confidence of borrowers in the vast majority of MFIs that are operating legitimately. To prevent such abuses, it would be appropriate to tighten up the regulatory framework. NGOs engaged in microfinance should be required to be registered, and regulatory agencies should undertake simple monitoring of their activities to reduce the scope for fraud. This may involve character checks on directors, and more rigorous enforcement of the requirements for the provision of annual reports and audited financial statements.

On the other hand, in some cases MFIs are subject to unnecessary and burdensome rules and regulations, and the rules are not transparent. This is most apparent in the case of cooperative societies, especially in South Asia. Governments should review the regulatory requirements facing cooperatives, with a view to making them more independent of government, limiting the discretionary power available to regulatory agencies, and removing unnecessary requirements.

Similar problems exist in the case of NGOs, albeit to a lesser degree in most cases. In Sri Lanka, Indonesia and Pakistan, for instance, the environment for NGOs has at times been highly politicised, with NGOs subject to considerable uncertainty. As noted above, the discretion granted to the NGO Affairs Bureau and other ministries in Bangladesh through the foreign donations approval process also leads to some uncertainty. In all cases, unnecessary restrictions should be removed, and the discretionary powers vested in regulatory agencies should be limited as much as possible. All regulatory requirements should be set out as clearly and transparently as possible, and any MFI that meets them should be free to operate without restriction.

4.3 Interest rates

Only two countries impose general ceilings on the interest rates that MFIs can charge borrowers. In Nepal, NGOs are subject to an interest rate ceiling of 15 per cent. In addition, they are permitted to impose a 3 per cent service charge, yielding a maximum effective rate of interest of 18 per cent. This restriction applies only to NGOs, with banks and cooperatives free to determine their own interest rates. In Thailand, there is a general ceiling of 15 per cent on interest rates. This ceiling applies to all bodies and transactions unless they are specifically excluded. Thrift and credit cooperatives are excluded from the ceiling, but are subject to a separate interest rate ceiling of 19 per cent. Other MFIs, such as agricultural cooperatives, informal organisations, private and NGO microfinance programs and private transactions, are subject to the 15 per cent ceiling. It is understood that registered cooperatives generally stay within the relevant ceilings, but that unregistered community organisations generally charge higher interest rates.

In both of these countries, the ceilings are generally too low for MFIs to cover their costs. In Thailand this is implicitly recognised by regulatory agencies, in that they do not enforce the ceilings, even in the case of MFIs that receive funding under government microfinance programs.

In other countries, there is no general ceiling applying to MFIs. However, this does not always mean that MFIs are free to determine their own interest rates. For instance, in India, MFIs are subject to interest rate ceilings if they borrow from second tier institutions such as Rashtriya Mahila Kosh (RMK) or the Small Industries Development Bank of India (SIDBI), or if they participate in the National Bank for Agriculture and Rural Development (NABARD) program for linking banks and self-help groups. As noted in chapter 3, these ceilings make it extremely difficult if not impossible for them to achieve self-sufficiency. Moreover, while there are no legal restrictions on the interest rates cooperatives can charge, in some cases state governments control the interest rates that cooperatives can charge through their ownership of shares in them. This may make it difficult for cooperatives to cover their costs and operate on a commercial basis.

In Pakistan, there are no regulations concerning the mark-ups that NGOs involved in microfinance can charge borrowers. However, mark-ups charged by cooperatives are regulated, with a ceiling of 14 per cent on loans from the primary societies to final borrowers. There is also considerable social and political pressure on financial institutions in general, including MFIs, to keep mark-ups low, and it would appear that this 'moral suasion' has a significant effect on MFIs.

In Bangladesh, MFIs generally have much more freedom to charge market interest rates at a level sufficient to cover their costs. However, some MFIs reported that the NGO Affairs Bureau and other ministries have sought to influence their interest rates when approving foreign donations. It is understood that some MFIs have agreed to reduce their interest rates. Recently, the NGO Affairs Bureau has held informal discussions with some of the larger MFIs about the possibility of an overall interest rate ceiling to apply to all MFIs, but no decision has been taken.

More generally, other aspects of the policy environment can affect the ability of MFIs to charge full-cost interest rates. For instance, in the Philippines the proliferation of government-sponsored credit schemes introduces substantial subsidy elements into microfinance and leads to market distortions, making it harder for NGO programs to cover their costs. This is also true in other countries, including Indonesia, Sri Lanka and Malaysia. In Indonesia, for instance, while MFIs are free to set their own interest rates, mass programs providing credit to the poor on a grant basis (the Inpres Desa Tertinggal (IDT) program), or at heavily subsidised rates (the Prosperous Family program) have introduced distortions into the microfinance market.

All of these measures impede the development of microfinance on a sustainable basis. Countries that impose interest rate ceilings should either remove them or set them at levels that are consistent with the sustainability of efficient, well-managed MFIs. Other countries should examine policies designed to support microfinance, to ensure that such policies do not reduce the interest rate margins available to MFIs and make it difficult for them to operate sustainably. It would also be desirable if all governments could positively encourage MFIs to charge interest rates sufficient to cover all of their long-term costs, including operating and financing costs and the cost of their capital, after adjusting for inflation and subsidies.

4.4 Prudential regulation and supervision

In most areas covered by this study, the policy and regulatory environment differs substantially from country to country. However, in one area there is almost complete uniformity. Microfinance institutions (MFIs) which do not accept deposits from the general public are not subject to prudential regulation or supervision by a government agency in any country included in the study. MFIs are not subject to any minimum capital requirements beyond the nominal requirements that may be necessary to register as a society or similar body. Nor are there any prudential regulations covering matters such as capital adequacy, liquidity, reserves or loan loss provisioning in any country.

There are also no compulsory reporting requirements designed specifically with the needs of MFIs in mind. As noted above, in most countries MFIs are required to be registered as societies or some similar organisational form, and are required to produce annual financial statements. In some cases, these financial statements are required to be audited. Some regulatory agencies also require additional data about certain aspects of the operations of MFIs, such as the NGO Affairs Bureau in Bangladesh which requires detailed acquittals of foreign donations. However, these financial reports are not designed to be used for prudential supervision, and are not suitable for this purpose. Most importantly, the data are collected on an annual basis only, and therefore cannot be used for regular and timely supervision. Moreover, much of the information that a supervisory agency would generally require from financial institutions, such as detailed portfolio information, is not collected. Regulatory agencies do not collect the type of information that is needed to monitor the sustainability or risk of the operations of MFIs, and do not in fact attempt any such monitoring.

Is this absence of a framework for prudential regulation and supervision a weakness that countries should seek to rectify? The general consensus among academics and practitioners in the international microfinance community is that it is not. It is generally agreed that where MFIs do not accept deposits from the public, it is unnecessary and may even be counter-productive to subject them to formal prudential regulation and supervision by a government agency. For instance, CGAP (1996, p.1) argues that:

> In most countries 85 per cent of MFIs are not financial intermediaries — i.e. they are lenders only, and do not take deposits from the public. There is probably no strong reason for public prudential oversight of such MFIs, since protection of depositors is usually viewed as the principal rationale for such oversight.

Berenbach and Churchill (1997, p.27) make the case even more strongly. They argue that:

> Regulators are primarily responsible for two things: (1) to preserve the integrity of the financial system and (2) to protect small depositors. Almost all the experts who advised this research felt strongly that as long as MFIs do not mobilise savings from the general public, they should not be regulated.

In most countries, there would also be significant practical difficulties in subjecting MFIs to prudential regulation and supervision. One issue would be to find a suitable regulatory agency to regulate them. Most central banks in the region do not have a unit responsible for microfinance, and do not have a sound knowledge and understanding of the requirements of MFIs. A number of commentators from more than one country have argued that in the absence of significant changes in the methods of regulation and supervision, placing MFIs under the supervision of the central bank would be likely to stifle them. It is also not obvious that there are any other government agencies that would be better placed to regulate and supervise MFIs.

Moreover, in most countries the cost of subjecting MFIs to full prudential regulation and supervision would be prohibitive. In Bangladesh, for instance, there are around 1,000 NGOs involved in microfinance. And while MFIs in other countries do not have nearly the same outreach as in Bangladesh, the number of MFIs is not necessarily less. In India there are perhaps as many NGOs engaged in microfinance as in Bangladesh, plus some 90,000 primary agricultural credit societies and thousands of self-help groups. In the Philippines, there are some 500 MFIs reaching a combined total of only 30,000 borrowers. In Thailand there are more than 1,500 community organisations engaged in microfinance. Clearly, it would not be possible to subject all of these bodies to prudential regulation and supervision. In summary, full prudential regulation and supervision by a regulatory agency of MFIs which do not accept deposits from the public would appear neither desirable nor practicable.

Are some standards necessary?

While full prudential regulation and supervision may not be an option, it is nevertheless important to establish some mechanisms for ensuring that MFIs maintain high standards in their operations. It is clear that at present most MFIs are not operating on a sound basis. For instance, in an analysis of MFIs in Bangladesh, the World Bank (1996) noted that the accounting, management information systems and external audit policies and standards followed by the large MFIs are good and comprehensive. However, for the most part, the standards adopted by the small and medium MFIs need to be substantially upgraded. Inadequate standards are likely to threaten the long-term viability of such MFIs, potentially leading to reduced confidence in the sector as a whole. For this reason, most commentators in our Bangladesh country study considered that some standards for MFIs are necessary.

This is even more true in other countries, with many MFIs appearing to have inadequate and unsound practices and procedures. In the case of the Philippines, for instance, Llanto et al. (1996) found that a number of major MFIs have inadequate financial reporting and monitoring, making it difficult to determine past due loans and the extent of arrears. They also found that the absence of adequate and sound performance standards and a standardised accounting and reporting system makes it difficult to evaluate the relative performance of MFIs. They concluded (p.21) that:

> In sum, internal financial policies and practices need a lot of improvement, particularly in the installation of sound financial reporting and monitoring systems, portfolio management, assessment and management of risks, product packaging and pricing, management of loan arrears and strategic business planning. Related to these will be the need to upgrade and institutionalise performance standards, particularly in loan repayment, appreciation of loan default and ageing of delinquent accounts, and the installation of appropriate accounting and internal audit systems.

These findings are consistent with the survey of MFIs conducted by Sustainable Banking with the Poor (1996). Only a few of the questions in the survey relied on accurate accounting. The authors commented (p.4) that:

> While these basic figures should be relatively standard throughout the world, it was disappointing to see numerous institutions (mainly NGOs) that reported implausible figures. . . If some managers of microfinance institutions are unable to answer questions about their own costs and arrears without the help of outside experts, how can they be expected to run sustainable financial institutions? Clearly, a greater emphasis on financial monitoring and reporting using standardised accounting is needed.

The challenge is therefore to find cost-effective ways of improving the standards, in terms of both performance and reporting, of the large numbers of MFIs that are not currently operating on a sound basis. While it may not be possible to reach all MFIs, it is desirable to establish mechanisms to ensure that at least the major MFIs are able to reach and maintain high standards. Some possible approaches are discussed in sections 4.5 and 4.6 below.

4.5 Performance and reporting standards of second tier institutions

In many countries, one very promising avenue for ensuring that microfinance institutions (MFIs) operate on a sound basis is through the lending policies of second tier microfinance institutions. Such institutions are not regulatory agencies, and cannot impose any legal obligation on MFIs to meet their standards. However, they can require MFIs that borrow from them to meet certain performance and reporting standards. In countries where there is one dominant second tier institution and this institution is a significant source of funds for MFIs, there is a powerful incentive for MFIs to meet these standards.

Bangladesh

The second tier institution that is making most progress in establishing performance and reporting standards is Palli Karma Sahayak Foundation (PKSF) in Bangladesh. It encourages MFIs to recover at least their recurring administrative and funding costs from interest income. It imposes a minimum lending rate of 16 per cent to ensure that MFIs do not lend below commercial bank rates, and to promote cost recovery from operations. It also encourages MFIs with outside sources of income to set aside a portion of interest income as reserves. Finally, it requires all MFIs to have a savings program for members, and generally requires that these savings be kept in a bank. Only those MFIs with a good track record and high standards of financial accounting are allowed to use savings in credit programs. PKSF also imposes a number of requirements in terms of the type of loan program that MFIs must offer to be eligible for funding.

In terms of reporting, PKSF requires monthly reports from all MFIs borrowing from it, covering information on the number of loans, disbursements, loans outstanding, recovery of principal and interest, and repayment rates. It monitors repayment rates (measured as repayments collected as a percentage of repayments due), and seeks to ensure that repayment rates remain above 98 per cent. MFIs borrowing from PKSF commented that PKSF is active in following up on these reports. It visits all borrowing MFIs at least four times a year for on-site inspections, and MFIs reported that these inspections are very rigorous. It audits each borrower MFI once a year, and in addition PKSF's external auditor audits one third of these MFIs each year.

While PKSF is rigorous in supervising the MFIs that it funds, some of the performance standards that it uses to measure their performance are quite general. The World Bank poverty alleviation microfinance project provides for refinement of these standards, and it is envisaged that MFIs will only be eligible for support if they meet these criteria. In particular, PKSF is to receive technical assistance to establish standards in a number of important areas, namely:

(1) Standards for loan classification and provisioning. Draft standards were released in early 1997. Broadly, the draft standards provide for a provision of 50 per cent of the outstanding balance for doubtful loans (all loans past expiry which have not been paid off), and 100 per cent of the outstanding balance for bad loans (all loans one year or more past expiry which have not been paid off).

(2) Standards for savings facilities. Draft standards were expected to be released in 1997.

(3) Uniform accounting policies in respect of reporting repayment rates, arrears, rescheduling, portfolio quality, etc. and audit standards.

(4) Standards for measuring MFIs' progress in terms of sustainability.

(5) In the case of multi-purpose NGOs, guidelines for measuring and separating the costs of delivering financial and non-financial services.

PKSF is clearly a leader in developing performance and reporting standards for MFIs, and in developing techniques for monitoring and supervision. It is likely that many of the standards currently being developed will be useful in other countries as well.

The Philippines

In the Philippines, the People's Credit and Finance Corporation (PCFC) also imposes certain conditions on MFIs before they can obtain loans from it. Most importantly, they must have a three-year track record in lending, their working capital must be at least Ps250,000 ($9,500), lending operations must be segregated from other activities with appropriate full-time staff, past due loans must be not more than 20 per cent, they must not have any loans in arrears to PCFC or other agencies, and 'established systems of proven effectiveness' must be in place.

Interestingly, PCFC has set different minimum performance standards for MFIs depending on their stage of operations, with different standards for start-up, intermediate and advanced institutions. It feels the need to recognise that institutions progress as their capacities improve, and to provide for this progression in the standards. In this way, PCFC sees its role as an explicitly dynamic one, of not only enforcing standards but of facilitating the progression of institutions over time:

(1) In terms of outreach, the guideline is for 500 borrowers for start-up institutions, 1,500 for intermediate institutions and 5,000 for advanced institutions.

(2) PCFC has set minimum performance standards for viability (cost recovery) of 50 per cent for start-up institutions, 75 per cent for intermediate institutions and 100 per cent for advanced institutions.

(3) The minimum collection rate also varies depending on the stage of development of the institution, ranging from 90 per cent for start-up institutions, to 95 per cent for intermediate institutions to above 98 per cent for advanced ones.

PCFC has also set guidelines relating to such qualitative issues as governance, information systems and staffing, to benchmark the standards thought necessary at each stage of an institution's development.

Sri Lanka

If the performance of the microfinance sector is to improve over time, it is important to ensure that the standards that are developed are actually enforced. In Sri Lanka, the National Development Trust Fund (NDTF) has laid down quite detailed operational procedures for partner organisations which borrow from it. According to the guidelines, an organisation must have legal status and must have at least two years experience in lending to the poor, with a recovery rate of at least 90 per cent over the last year. In addition, it must meet a number of other criteria relating to financial viability, savings mobilisation, and management and accounting. In the past, however, these conditions were not enforced. Many partner organisations with little or no previous experience in microfinance were given loans. An external audit of partner organisations completed in August 1996 found that a significant number had not maintained proper accounting records and did not follow generally accepted accounting principles.

Since 1995 the requirements in terms of experience and repayment rates have been enforced more rigorously. NDTF has also introduced a number of more specific prudential requirements. In particular, partner organisations are required to:

(1) Maintain a group contingency fund, established by deducting 5 per cent of the principal of all loans, and subject to certain conditions.

(2) Establish a loan loss reserve as a provision against defaults. A minimum of 20 per cent of interest earned on sub-loans must be retained in the reserve, which must be invested in an interest-earning bank account.

(3) Maintain a minimum of 35 per cent of members' savings in reserve at all times.

In terms of financial reporting, NDTF requires partner organisations to have their accounts audited by a qualified auditor. Partner organisations are also required to provide a quarterly report to NDTF, but this is very brief and does not provide the information needed for prudential monitoring of their activities.

India

In India, there are at least three official second tier institutions which on-lend to specialist MFIs. However, none of them imposes rigorous performance and reporting standards. The second tier institution with the largest lending program is

Rashtriya Mahila Kosh (RMK). For a partner organisation to borrow from RMK, it should have at least three years experience in thrift and credit administration, a 90 per cent recovery performance during the last three years (in practice, RMK generally accepts a recovery rate in the range of 80 to 90 per cent), satisfactory funds management and financial performance, and a good track record of work in the socioeconomic field. These requirements are all quite general in nature. There are also a number of requirements relating to loans by the partner organisations to individual borrowers. Further, partner organisations are supposed to maintain 10 per cent of the loan provided by RMK as reserves, but this is not strictly enforced.

Reporting standards are also not sufficient to enable proper prudential monitoring. Partner organisations are required to submit monthly and quarterly reports to RMK, but these deal with the utilisation of the loan from RMK and do not cover data necessary for monitoring their overall financial performance. They are also required to submit annual financial statements audited by a registered chartered accountant. The performance and reporting standards imposed by two other significant second tier institutions, the Small Industries Development Bank of India (SIDBI) and the National Bank for Agriculture and Rural Development (NABARD) are even less specific that those imposed by RMK and do not provide a basis for monitoring the financial performance of the NGO.

Thailand

Where community organisations in Thailand obtain funds from the Government Savings Bank (GSB) or Urban Community Development Office (UCDO), they are subject to various requirements. To become a member of the GSB program, a community organisation is required to have operated a savings program for at least six months and to provide a financial statement and details of the group's operating performance during that period. Moreover, every month, organisations are requested to provide a trial balance and some basic portfolio data to the bank. The requirements for members of the UCDO program are broadly similar, with some slight differences. For instance, in addition to operating a savings program for six months, UCDO encourages organisations to operate a loans program from their own funds for three months before they obtain a loan.

Both programs also impose limits on the amount that they will lend to a community organisation. GSB tailors the amount of the loan to the particular circumstances of the group, but with a maximum of five times the group's own funds. Under the UCDO program the maximum loan amount is set at ten times the value of the group's own savings, reflecting the fact that loans are also given for housing. However, it is preferred that groups build up gradually to this amount. These limits are of a quasi-prudential nature in that, to some extent, they restrict the degree to which organisations can leverage members' savings to obtain external resources. However, the limits apply only to loans from GSB and UCDO, and do not prevent organisations from obtaining loans from other sources.

UCDO intends to strengthen its guidelines progressively in the future. For instance, it has been giving some thought to developing standards for loan loss provisioning. It should also be noted that UCDO places a great deal of emphasis on developing its standards through a process of consultation with community organisations.

International networks and agencies

In developing standards for MFIs it is also important to look at work being done on performance standards by international networks and agencies. A number of organisations, including the SEEP Network, ACCION International and the International Financial Advisory Group, have sought to define key performance standards for MFIs.

In 1992, ACCION International designed an instrument for assessing MFIs which took the CAMEL analysis as its conceptual framework. While it uses the same five areas of financial and managerial performance as the conventional CAMEL instrument, the indicators are designed specifically with the microfinance sector in mind.

The ACCION CAMEL is discussed in detail in Saltzman, Rock and Salinger (1998). It was designed to be independent of any methodological biases, and can be applied to any type of institution servicing the microenterprise sector. Its objective is to lead MFIs towards accessing financial markets, so only those aspects that 'the market' deems relevant and important are included in the CAMEL rating. Hence, the rating does not consider issues such as poverty targeting or social impact. It is also designed to relate specifically to Latin American MFIs operating in urban environments, who make up the majority of ACCION affiliates. The five areas examined are as follows:

(1) *Capital adequacy*. This covers the capital position of the MFI, including its capacity to support growth in the loan portfolio, and its ability to raise additional equity in the case of losses.

(2) *Asset quality*. This area covers the overall quality of the loan portfolio, including the level of portfolio at risk and write-offs, and the appropriateness of the portfolio classification system, collection procedures and write-off policies. The quality of other assets is also examined.

(3) *Management*. The focus here is on human resource policy, general management, management information systems, internal control and auditing, and strategic planning and budgeting.

(4) *Earnings*. This area examines the key components of revenues and expenses, including operational efficiency, interest rate policy, and return on equity and assets.

(5) *Liquidity*. Finally, this component looks at the institution's ability to project funding needs in general, and credit demand in particular.

The instrument analyses and rates 21 key indicators relating to these five areas. There are eight quantitative indicators contributing 48 per cent of the final rating, and 13 qualitative indicators contributing 52 per cent of the final rating. MFIs are given overall alphabetical ratings based on their scores on these indicators:

(1) An 'A' classification indicates an MFI with strong financial performance in all of the key areas analysed.

(2) A 'B' rating generally indicates that the MFI is undergoing a difficult period which is adversely affecting its normally strong financial condition.

(3) An MFI receiving a 'C' classification is experiencing fundamental problems administering its credit program, with basic weaknesses in various key indicators.

(4) A 'D' rating implies that the MFI should not be operating a credit program.

(5) A classification of 'NC' (not rated) is given where it is impossible to assess the MFI due to a lack of basic operational information or because the MFI has not embraced the most minimal characteristics of an acceptable credit program.

Out of 11 MFIs evaluated to date, one received an 'A' rating in its most recent evaluation, while the other ten all received 'B' ratings in their most recent evaluations.

While the CAMEL review is comprehensive, it is also intensive. A first-time review requires a team of three to four people for ten working days to gather, adjust and analyse the financial and management information necessary to conduct the analysis. Even where a review has previously been completed, the team consists of three people working eight days on site. Clearly, it would be very difficult for second tier institutions to devote this much time to each of their partner MFIs on a regular basis. Nevertheless, the instrument provides a number of very useful insights into developing performance and reporting standards.

Most recently, the Consultative Group to Assist the Poorest (CGAP) has become a focal point for developing industry standards in microfinance. CGAP is currently developing a number of tools which are designed, among other things, to foster the development of industry standards in reporting and performance measures, and to bring greater transparency to the industry. These build on existing systems used by leading MFIs and networks, and are tailored to meet the needs of MFI managers.

The first of these is the format for appraisal of MFIs, which has already been released. The format is divided into four main sections:

(1) *Institutional factors*. This section examines issues such as governance, leadership, human resource management, organisational structure, management information systems, and internal audit and control.

(2) *Services, clientele and market of the MFI*. This section looks at the type and quality of services provided, breadth and depth of outreach, targeting of poor clients, and similar issues.

(3) *Strategic objectives*. This section considers issues related to the MFI's mission statement and objectives, business plan and financial projections. The objective is to assess the extent to which these factors will facilitate increased outreach on a financially sustainable basis.

(4) *Financial performance*. This section presents the MFI's financial statements in standard format adjusted for inflation and subsidies. It then goes on to calculate a number of ratios designed to assess profitability, efficiency and portfolio quality, and looks at other issues concerning financial management and performance.

The format does not actually establish specific performance standards that MFIs should meet in each of these areas. Nevertheless, many of the items could be turned quite easily into specific, measurable criteria that could be used by second tier institutions in monitoring and supervising MFIs that borrow from them. The minimum standards required could differ between countries depending on the size and quality of MFIs in the particular country, and by institution depending on the stage of development of the particular institution.

CGAP is currently finalising a number of other tools for practitioners: in particular, guidelines for business planning and financial modelling for MFIs; a handbook to assist with the external audit of MFIs; and a handbook for management information systems for MFIs. These tools should also be very useful to second tier institutions in developing appropriate standards for MFIs and appropriate methodologies for supervising them.

Comment

This section has surveyed the work being done by second tier microfinance institutions in a number of countries, in developing performance and reporting standards for the MFIs that they fund. While these experiences are diverse, it is possible to offer a number of general comments.

First, in those countries which have active second tier microfinance institutions, these institutions can play a very important role in developing standards for the microfinance sector. This role fits in well with their other activities. Quite apart from issues to do with overall sectoral standards, such institutions need to develop methodologies for assessing MFIs in order to protect their own loan portfolios. Hence, much of the work associated with developing performance and reporting standards needs to be done in any case. Moreover, such institutions have an effective mechanism for enforcing any standards that they develop, as any MFIs which borrow from them, or intend to borrow from them in the future, will need to meet the required standards. Over time, there is considerable potential for such standards to become accepted as sectoral norms, at least by the more significant MFIs, even if they themselves do not borrow from the second tier institution. It may also be possible for credit rating agencies to develop standards for MFIs and to rate MFIs according to these standards, to make it easier for donor agencies and commercial investors to assess the performance of MFIs and to encourage MFIs to improve their performance.

Second, standards should be based on results achieved rather than the model used. There is a diverse range of institutions involved in microfinance, including financial intermediaries, social intermediaries and mixed financial/social intermediaries. Standards for social intermediation should also be developed.

Third, standards should have a proactive role in facilitating improvement in the performance of the microfinance sector over time. While all second tier institutions need to ensure that the quality of their loan portfolio is maintained, countries with relatively undeveloped microfinance sectors, such as Pakistan, may not be able to impose standards as rigorous as those imposed in countries such as Bangladesh. However, standards should be raised over time so that MFIs are gradually forced to improve their performance. It may also be appropriate to impose differential standards depending on the stage of development of the particular MFI, and to provide for progression from one stage to the next. Second tier institutions also have an important developmental role in assisting MFIs to improve their performance so that they can meet the standards.

Fourth, enforcing standards is just as important as establishing them. This involves developing cost-effective methods for off-site and on-site supervision that are suitable to the operating procedures of MFIs. The approaches used by PKSF in Bangladesh, and the work being done by CGAP on external audit, may be particularly instructive here.

Fifth, in countries such as India and Thailand with more than one second tier institution, it is important that they establish common, or at least consistent, standards. Sixth, standards should be developed through a process of wide consultation with MFIs, to ensure that they meet the needs of MFIs and are accepted throughout the sector.

4.6 Self-regulation

Another approach to establishing performance and reporting standards for microfinance institutions (MFIs) is through self-regulation. Self-regulation may take a wide variety of forms, ranging from a voluntary code of conduct to which MFIs agree to adhere, to a rigorous licensing system administered by an apex body and backed by the force of law. In between, there is a wide variety of possibilities with varying degrees of monitoring and compulsion.

The feasibility of various forms of self-regulation depends on a range of factors, including the extent to which there is an apex body that can represent MFIs as a whole, the quantum of resources available for monitoring and supervision, and the availability of incentives and/or sanctions to enforce compliance. Self-regulation can be an alternative to, or can supplement, prudential regulation and supervision by a government agency or the performance and reporting standards of a second tier institution.

Philippines

The country that is making the greatest progress in developing standards for self-regulation is the Philippines. A major new initiative, the Developing Standards for Microfinance Project (DSMP) was set up in 1996 with funding from USAID. A coalition known as the Philippine Coalition for Microfinance Standards has been formed under the project to develop and promote standards for MFIs. The coalition has 55 member institutions, including leading MFIs, the central bank, the People's Credit and Finance Corporation (PCFC), government and donor agencies, and others.

The coalition has begun to build the database for benchmarking and standard setting, and has commenced documenting best practice among MFIs in the Philippines. The objective is to arrive at benchmarks or standards for good practice for a national microfinance summit in 1998. In establishing the benchmarks, the following indicators are to be observed:

(1) Organisational and operational factors (organisation structure, culture and capacity, management information systems, operational efficiency, etc.)

(2) Outreach and services (scale and depth of outreach, range and quality of services, etc.)

(3) Financial sustainability (self-sufficiency, portfolio quality, etc.).

Developing performance standards in these areas is the first step in the process. Further steps include assisting MFIs to adopt the standards, and moving beyond that to ensure widespread implementation of them by MFIs. The DSMP is also working towards the development of a 'capacity measurement system' to identify the strengths and weaknesses of individual MFIs. This implies a rating system for MFIs based on the indicators which have been developed. A rating system would be useful to domestic financial institutions which need information to assess the bankability of MFIs, and to government and donor agencies in identifying areas for intervention and support.

As noted above, a key issue in any system of self-regulation is compliance. While there are currently two major networks of MFIs in the Philippines, both have limited membership. The Association of Philippine Partners in Enterprise Development (APPEND) has nine member institutions, while PHILNET, a group of Grameen replicators, has seven members. It is not clear how the new coalition will seek to ensure that individual MFIs comply with the standards. One option may be to create a new apex body covering all major MFIs. Another option may be to back the standards with some form of incentives or sanctions, such as through the legal system or through the policies of a second tier institution. The coalition itself suggests that '. . . this may involve establishing a system of accrediting NGOs which have adopted the standards, a system of reporting and validation, and a system of rewards or penalties for compliance or non-compliance' (Microfinance Coalition for Standards 1997).

Other countries

No other country included in the study has progressed as far as the Philippines in establishing standards for self-regulation. The apex body for MFIs in Bangladesh is the Credit and Development Forum (CDF), which was established in 1992. CDF currently has 662 members. It includes most major MFIs, but not the Grameen Bank, which is not an NGO. CDF is making significant progress in a number of important areas. Nevertheless, there is a lack of consensus on policy and other issues among the major MFIs operating in Bangladesh, and this limits the ability of CDF to fulfil all of the functions of an apex body for the microfinance sector. While it could play a very useful role in developing a voluntary code of conduct or similar mechanism for self-regulation, it would not appear at this stage to have the resources or the authority to enforce a more rigorous model of self-regulation based on compulsion.

In other countries, apex bodies for MFIs are only just starting to be established. In India, a proposed apex body, the All India Association of Micro Enterprises Development (AIAMED) Network was registered in February 1997. It is conducting a series of seven regional coordination consultations in different regions, and some 400 MFIs have expressed an interest in attending these consultations, including the most prominent MFIs.

In Sri Lanka, there is a very effective apex body for the credit cooperative movement, in the form of the Federation of Thrift and Credit Cooperative Societies (FTCCS). Below the federation are 33 district unions, which in turn are responsible for some 8,340 primary societies. The federation coordinates guidelines and procedures for the operation of primary societies. For instance, it has introduced standard loan documentation and other forms for all primary societies. In turn, the district unions supervise the day-to-day activities of the primary societies. The primary societies are required to provide monthly financial statements, covering portfolio data, income and expenses, and balance sheet data, to the district union. Officers from the district union monitor this information and conduct visits to the primary societies. Hence, there is a well-developed structure for coordination and self-regulation, with the federation and district unions providing a range of services to the primary societies.

However, there is no apex body for MFIs as a whole. An informal forum for NGOs was established in early 1995 under the auspices of UNDP, and meets once every two months. There are around 55 members, with about 35 attending meetings regularly, but only around ten to twelve of the participants are local NGOs.

In Indonesia, an organisation of NGOs associated with the Bank Indonesia linkage program exists, but is currently inactive. There are also plans to establish an apex body for NGOs engaged in microfinance in Pakistan. A planning committee has been established consisting of major NGOs involved in microfinance, and the committee intends to organise a workshop, with funding from the Asia Foundation, to look at relevant issues. In the other countries included in the study, namely Malaysia, Nepal and Thailand, there do not appear to be any concrete moves to establish apex bodies for MFIs.

Comment

Self-regulation is a very attractive way of establishing appropriate standards for MFIs. Establishing standards through self-regulation can avoid the tendency for regulatory agencies to impose burdensome regulations that do not take account of the specific needs of MFIs. Self-regulation also ensures ownership of the standards by the MFIs themselves, and there is likely to be much greater acceptance of standards established through self-regulation than of standards imposed from above.

While there are many forms of self-regulation, more rigorous models require some mechanism for achieving compliance, through regular monitoring and a system of incentives or sanctions. This is likely to require a very effective and representative apex body for the MFI sector. Bangladesh and the Philippines have better developed networks of MFIs than the other countries in this study. Nevertheless, it is doubtful even in these cases that the apex bodies have the necessary resources or authority to monitor individual MFIs regularly and ensure that they meet the agreed standards. Hence, systems of self-regulation may need to be reinforced with some legal or quasi-legal system of incentives or compulsion. It is instructive that the Philippine Coalition for Microfinance Standards appears to be thinking along these lines.

Recent moves to establish apex bodies for MFIs in a number of countries should be encouraged, while appropriate arrangements should be put in place in other countries. Apex bodies have the potential to undertake a range of important activities, including information exchange, training, research, and policy dialogue with governments and donor agencies. Over time, they may also become focal points for the establishment of standards for self-regulation. MFIs should be encouraged to join these apex bodies and become active in their affairs, to ensure that they are well resourced and fully representative of the microfinance sector.

4.7 Savings mobilisation and deposit taking

Accepting deposits from the general public

So far, this chapter has not discussed the question of savings mobilisation and deposit taking by microfinance institutions (MFIs). In almost all cases, it is clear that MFIs cannot accept deposits from the general public unless they establish regulated banks.

There are several cases in the countries included in the study where MFIs are permitted to accept deposits from the public. First, in Bangladesh the Grameen Bank Ordinance provides scope for the Grameen Bank to accept deposits from the general public as well as from its members (while the Grameen Bank is classified as a specialised development bank, it is not really a regulated bank in that it is not subject to prudential regulation and supervision by the central bank). To date, however, the Grameen Bank has not actually raised deposits from the general public.

Second, in Sri Lanka and Bangladesh the law specifically permits cooperative societies to receive deposits from persons who are not members. In Sri Lanka, many thrift and credit cooperative societies (TCCSs) are now actively seeking deposits from non-members by offering competitive interest rates, and deposits by non-members account for around 15 per cent of total deposits. Given the lack of prudential requirements, it is perhaps surprising that societies should be permitted to receive deposits from non-members. Indeed, the federation itself commented that the lack of prudential requirements reduces the credibility of societies as deposit-taking institutions, making it difficult for them to attract deposits on a large scale.

Third, in Nepal the central bank has permitted two large NGOs, namely Nirdhan and the Center for Self-Help Development (CSD), to accept savings deposits from non-members pursuant to the 'limited banking' arrangements instituted in 1994. Under these arrangements, the two NGOs are permitted to accept savings deposits, but are not allowed to engage in other banking activities such as foreign exchange and bills transactions. These NGOs are subject to a number of prudential requirements, including a liquidity requirement of 10 per cent and loan loss provisioning requirements similar to those applying to banks.

Finally, in Indonesia there is a range of small non-bank financial institutions, many of them supervised by provincial governments, which are empowered to accept deposits. These provide microfinance services.

In general, MFIs should not be permitted to accept deposits from the public unless appropriate regulations concerning capital adequacy, reserves, liquidity and reporting are in place. Accepting deposits from the public places a very heavy responsibility on any institution. As Berenbach and Churchill (1997, pp.58–59) argue:

> . . . very few NGOs have the right management, financial discipline, information systems and profitability to be safe deposit takers. In addition, no institution should be allowed to take savings if its ownership and governance structure is not appropriate for that function. If an institution is capitalised with donor money and retained earnings, and therefore does not have owners in the traditional sense, then it is hard to justify the authorisation of deposit-taking services.[1]

Mobilising savings from members

In all countries, it is clear that cooperatives are permitted to mobilise savings from their members for on-lending. However, in most cases the position of NGOs engaged in microfinance is somewhat ambiguous. Generally, regulatory authorities tend not to intervene so long as they mobilise savings from members only. In such cases, however, NGOs do not have a clear legal basis for accepting deposits, and there is always the possibility of sanctions.

This is best illustrated by the case of Sri Lanka. According to the law, NGOs in Sri Lanka are not allowed to provide any savings facilities. This applies to all deposits, whether from members or non-members, and includes compulsory savings that may be a pre-condition for obtaining a microfinance loan. Any such savings must be invested in a bank account, and cannot be used for re-lending by the NGO. In practice, the prohibition on mobilising savings has generally not been applied strictly. Indeed, major government programs such as the National Development Trust Fund (NDTF) and the Small Farmers and Landless Credit (SFLC) project have required NGOs borrowing from them to establish savings programs, and have encouraged them to use these savings in their credit programs. On the other hand, in 1992 the largest NGO, Sarvodaya, was prosecuted for mobilising savings and required to return all savings to members. It now mobilises savings only through independent primary societies, and these are not remitted to Sarvodaya itself. Clearly, the current situation leads to a great deal of uncertainty.

In the Philippines too, the legal situation with regard to mobilising savings from members is unclear. Under the Banking Act, NGOs are not permitted to accept savings and deposits in any form. Many NGOs are reported to have informal deposit-taking relationships with members, using devices such as accepting funds for 'capital build-up'. Llanto et al. (1996) comment that this is skating on thin ice because of potential legal sanctions against this illegal activity. The legal situation is also somewhat ambiguous in a number of other countries, including Bangladesh, India, Indonesia and Malaysia. In Indonesia, inability to access capital resources

---

1 It should be noted that some countries in other regions are creating special categories of MFIs that are permitted to accept deposits from the public under certain circumstances (see Berenbach & Churchill, 1997). These include entities for the development of small and micro enterprises in Peru, and private financial funds in Bolivia. These are regulated financial institutions, but are not banks and are only authorised to provide a limited range of financial services.

through savings mobilisation is a factor in the movement by some NGOs to create rural banks (BPRs).

One country that has clarified this situation is Nepal, where the central bank has issued two types of 'limited banking' authorisations. In the first category two large NGOs have been authorised to accept savings deposits from both members and non-members, as discussed above. There is also a second category, whereby NGOs are permitted to mobilise savings from members. To date, 380 NGOs have been authorised under this category.

Comment

The question of savings mobilisation by MFIs is a difficult one for regulators. On the one hand, savings facilities provide a valuable service to clients, and can be important in reducing poverty. Requiring borrowers to demonstrate an ability to save before they obtain a loan is also a useful screening device and helps to instil borrower discipline. Just about all successful microfinance programs operate on the principle of 'savings first, credit later'. On the other hand, mobilising savings places a very strong responsibility on an institution to ensure that the savings of poor clients are not at risk. Hence there is an inter-relationship between the standards applying to MFIs and the types of savings facilities offered.

In many cases, MFIs require loan-linked deposits or compulsory savings as a pre-condition to receiving a loan. CGAP (1996) argues that such savings should probably be thought of as part of the cost of the loan, rather than as true financial intermediation requiring public intervention to protect depositors. At any point in time, the vast majority of clients with compulsory savings deposits will also have loans, and will be net borrowers. As such, their savings are not at risk if the institution encounters financial difficulties. Such compulsory savings requirements are an integral part of many if not most microfinance programs. The law should be clarified to make it clear that MFIs are permitted to impose compulsory savings requirements. It would also seem appropriate to permit MFIs to use compulsory savings in their lending programs.

Some MFIs also offer voluntary savings facilities to their clients. Voluntary savings are a very important service, especially in areas where clients do not have access to any other formal savings facilities. In general, it would be appropriate to permit MFIs to accept voluntary savings from their members. Nevertheless, as noted above, accepting voluntary savings imposes a heavy responsibility on MFIs in terms of financial management. For these reasons, it would generally not seem appropriate to permit MFIs to use voluntary savings in their lending programs unless effective protections are in place. One option is to require MFIs to establish an earmarked account for voluntary savings with a regulated financial institution, with the MFI maintaining shadow accounts for each individual client. It should be noted that in Bangladesh, the Palli Karma Sahayak Foundation (PKSF) generally requires MFIs that borrow from it to keep members' savings in a bank account, and only those MFIs with a good track record and high standards of financial accounting are permitted to use savings in credit programs.

As noted above, in all countries member-owned institutions following the cooperative structure are permitted to mobilise savings from members. Chaves and Gonzalez-Vega (1994, p.73) note that:

> Regulators have tended to allow member-owned organisations to govern themselves to a greater degree than investor-owned banks, on the presumption that members will look after their own best interests. Although this is true to some degree, there are sufficient problems — as testified by the history of the credit union movement — to warrant outside regulation and supervision.

This suggests that it is also important to have a sound legal framework regulating the activities of the cooperative movement, and an effective apex body which is able to supervise the activities of individual credit cooperatives. As noted above, in most countries these conditions are not met.

In the case of community groups, CGAP argues that public supervision is both unnecessary and impractical for 'community groups which accept voluntary savings from a few dozen members, who know each other and who control the group's lending decisions'. In a sense it is debatable that supervision is unnecessary, in that such community organisations can and do experience financial difficulties. On the other hand, in most cases it is clearly not practical to monitor their activities or to restrict the uses to which they put members' savings.

4.8 Summary and recommendations

The broad regulatory framework

Establish simple, appropriate registration procedures for MFIs

In most countries, microfinance institutions (MFIs) are able to obtain registration under the general provisions applying to non-governmental organisations (NGOs) and cooperatives. The broad requirements, such as having a memorandum of association or some similar document and preparing an annual report and financial statements, are quite simple and should pose no problem to any well-managed MFI. The only exceptions to this appear to be Malaysia and Thailand, where the usual registration procedures for NGOs may not permit an institution to engage in microfinance. In these countries, governments should establish simple registration procedures suitable for MFIs.

Require registration for MFIs and ensure simple monitoring

Even though the requirements for registration are generally not onerous, in many countries they are not enforced rigorously. In some countries, this relatively lax regime may have enabled some unscrupulous operators to set up and take advantage of clients. NGOs engaged in microfinance should be required to be registered, and regulatory agencies should undertake simple monitoring of their activities to reduce the scope for fraud.

Remove unnecessary regulation of NGOs and cooperatives

On the other hand, in some cases MFIs are subject to unnecessary and burdensome rules and regulations, and the rules are not transparent. This is most apparent in the case of cooperative societies, especially in South Asia. Governments should review the regulatory requirements facing cooperatives, with a view to making them more independent of government, limiting the discretionary power available to regulatory agencies, and removing unnecessary requirements. Similar problems exist for NGOs in some countries, albeit to a lesser degree. In all cases, unnecessary restrictions should be removed, and the discretionary powers vested in regulatory agencies should be limited as much as possible.

Interest rates

Only two countries, Nepal and Thailand, impose general ceilings on the interest rates that MFIs can charge borrowers. In both of these countries, the ceilings are generally too low for MFIs to cover their costs. In fact, in Thailand this is implicitly recognised by regulatory agencies, in that they do not enforce the ceilings.

In other countries, there is no general ceiling applying to MFIs. However, this does not always mean that MFIs are free to determine their own interest rates. In a number of countries, there are ceilings on interest rates under government microfinance programs or as a result of various other actions by government.

Remove interest rate ceilings and other restrictive practices

All of these measures impede the development of microfinance on a sustainable basis. Countries that impose interest rate ceilings should either remove them or set them at levels that are consistent with the sustainability of efficient, well-managed MFIs. Other countries should examine policies designed to support microfinance, to ensure that such policies do not reduce the interest rate margins available to MFIs and make it difficult for them to operate sustainably.

Prudential regulation and supervision

In most areas covered by this study, the policy and regulatory environment differs substantially from country to country. However, in one area there is almost complete uniformity. MFIs which do not accept deposits from the general public are not subject to prudential regulation or supervision by a government agency in any country included in the study. There are also no compulsory reporting requirements designed specifically with the needs of MFIs in mind.

Do not introduce prudential regulation for MFIs

This lack of prudential regulation is appropriate. It is generally agreed that where MFIs do not accept deposits from the public, it is unnecessary to subject them to formal prudential regulation and supervision by a government agency. In most countries, there would also be significant practical difficulties in subjecting MFIs to prudential regulation and supervision.

Find ways to improve MFI performance and reporting standards

Nevertheless, it is clear that at present most MFIs do not have adequate standards. The challenge is to find cost-effective ways of improving the standards, in terms of both performance and reporting, of the large numbers of MFIs that are not currently operating on a sound basis.

Performance and reporting standards of second tier institutions

In those countries with second tier microfinance institutions, these institutions can play a very important role in developing standards for the microfinance sector. This role fits in well with their other activities. Moreover, such institutions have an effective mechanism for enforcing any standards that they develop, as any MFIs which borrow from them, or intend to borrow from them in the future, will need to meet the required standards. There is a broad range of experience to draw from in establishing appropriate standards, including the work currently being undertaken by Palli Karma Sahayak Foundation (PKSF) in Bangladesh and other second tier institutions in the region, and work being conducted under the auspices of ACCION International and CGAP.

Establish and enforce appropriate standards for MFIs to improve their performance over time

Standards should be based on results achieved, rather than the model used. They should have a proactive role in facilitating improvement in the performance of the microfinance sector over time. Countries with relatively undeveloped microfinance sectors may not be able to impose standards as rigorous as those imposed in countries such as Bangladesh. However, standards should be raised over time so that MFIs are gradually forced to improve their performance. It may also be appropriate to impose differential standards depending on the stage of development of the particular MFI, and to provide for progression from one stage to the next.

Enforcing standards is just as important as establishing them. This involves developing cost-effective methods for off-site and on-site supervision that are suitable to the operating procedures of MFIs. Standards should be developed through a process of wide consultation with MFIs, to ensure that they meet the needs of MFIs and are accepted throughout the sector.

Self-regulation

Another approach to establishing performance and reporting standards for MFIs is through self-regulation. Self-regulation may take a wide variety of forms, ranging from a voluntary code of conduct to which MFIs agree to adhere, to a rigorous licensing system administered by an apex body and backed by the force of law. The feasibility of various forms of self-regulation depends on a range of factors, including the extent to which there is a apex body that can represent MFIs as a whole, the quantum of resources available for monitoring and supervision, and the availability of incentives and/or sanctions to enforce compliance.

Reinforce self-regulation by MFIs through incentives

The Philippine Coalition for Microfinance Standards is the most important initiative for self-regulation in the region. Bangladesh and the Philippines have better developed networks of MFIs than the other countries in the study, but even here it is doubtful that the apex bodies have the necessary resources or authority to monitor individual MFIs regularly and ensure that they meet the agreed standards. Hence, systems of self-regulation may need to be reinforced with some legal or quasi-legal system of incentives or compulsion.

Encourage establishment of apex MFI bodies

Recent moves to establish apex bodies for MFIs in a number of countries should be encouraged, while appropriate arrangements should be put in place in other countries. MFIs should be encouraged to join these apex bodies and become active in their affairs, to ensure that they are well resourced and fully representative of the microfinance sector.

Savings mobilisation and deposit taking

In general, MFIs are not permitted to accept deposits from the general public unless they establish regulated banks, although there are several exceptions to this in the countries included in the study. Prohibiting non-bank MFIs from accepting deposits from the public is generally appropriate, as accepting deposits from the public places a very heavy responsibility on any institution.

In terms of mobilising savings from members, the position of NGOs engaged in microfinance is somewhat ambiguous in most countries. Generally, regulatory authorities tend not to intervene so long as they mobilise savings from members only. In such cases, however, NGOs do not have a clear legal basis for accepting deposits, and there is always the possibility of sanctions. One country that has clarified this situation is Nepal. The central bank has established 'limited banking' arrangements for authorising NGOs to accept deposits, and 380 NGOs have been authorised to mobilise savings from members under these arrangements.

While the question of savings mobilisation by MFIs is a difficult one for regulators, savings facilities provide a valuable service to clients, and can be important in reducing poverty. Moreover, requiring borrowers to demonstrate an ability to save before they obtain a loan is also a useful screening device and helps to instil borrower discipline.

Clarify right of MFIs to require loan-linked deposits or compulsory savings

In many cases, MFIs require loan-linked deposits or compulsory savings deposits as a condition to receiving a loan. Such compulsory savings requirements are an integral part of many if not most microfinance programs, and impose few prudential risks. The law should be clarified to make it clear that MFIs are permitted to impose compulsory savings requirements. It would also seem appropriate to permit MFIs to use compulsory savings in their lending programs.

Allow MFIs to mobilise voluntary savings with safeguards

Some MFIs also offer voluntary savings facilities to their clients. It would generally not seem appropriate to permit MFIs to use voluntary savings in their lending programs unless effective protections are in place. One option is to permit MFIs to mobilise voluntary savings from members if they establish an earmarked account for voluntary savings with a regulated financial institution.

In all countries, cooperatives are permitted to mobilise savings from their members for on-lending. To protect these savings, it is important to have a sound legal framework regulating the activities of the cooperative movement, and an effective apex body which is able to supervise the activities of individual credit cooperatives. In most countries these conditions are currently not met.

5 Regulation of banks

5.1 Background

While most institutions engaged in microfinance are specialist microfinance institutions (MFIs) registered as societies, non-profit companies or similar bodies, there is also considerable scope for regulated banks to become involved in microfinance.[1]

In the past, most banks have tended to steer clear of microfinance, because they have regarded it as too risky and expensive, and it is clear that traditional banking methods and procedures are inappropriate for microfinance. As noted by Baydas, Graham and Valenzuela (1997), banks need to resolve a number of critical issues relating to commitment, organisational design, financial technology, human resources and cost-effectiveness if they are to enter the microfinance market successfully. Nevertheless, Baydas et al. note that if banks can learn from specialist MFIs and adjust their methods, they actually have a number of advantages over specialist MFIs that may put them in a very good position to establish microfinance programs:

- As regulated institutions, they are subject to a variety of standards which help to ensure prudent management.
- Many have physical infrastructure, including a large network of branches, from which they can reach out to large numbers of microfinance clients.
- They have their own sources of funds, such as deposits and equity capital, and hence do not have to rely on scarce and volatile donor resources.
- Their ownership structures encourage sound governance and profitability.[2]

The relationship between microfinance and the regulated banking system flows in both directions. In most countries, only regulated banks are permitted to raise deposits from the general public. Given the strong fiduciary relationship between deposit taking institutions and their clients, this is appropriate. Some specialist MFIs may wish to establish regulated banks, so that they can raise deposits from the general public and, more generally, increase their credibility with investors and

---

1 This discussion focuses on banks which are regulated by the central bank. In some countries there are other institutions referred to as 'banks', which are not regulated by the central bank and are generally subject to little prudential regulation and supervision. These include the cooperative banks in Pakistan and the cooperative rural banks in Sri Lanka.

2 The role of commercial banks in microfinance is discussed in detail in a recent study conducted by Goodwin-Groen (forthcoming).

depositors. Offering full deposit services enables them to offer a broader range of financial services to the poor, with some studies suggesting that savings facilities are just as important to the poor as credit. Moreover, a bigger deposit base gives MFIs access to an additional source of funds, enabling them to expand their operations. A number of specialist MFIs in countries included in this study, including the Bangladesh Rural Advancement Committee in Bangladesh, the Aga Khan Rural Support Programme in Pakistan, TSPI Development Corporation in the Philippines, and the Federation of Thrift and Credit Cooperative Societies in Sri Lanka, are currently seeking to establish banks. On the other hand, it is not necessary or desirable for all specialist MFIs to establish regulated banks. Establishing a regulated bank raises a number of complex issues, and may lead to a change of focus away from the original objectives of the institution. It may not be an appropriate path for all MFIs to follow.

From the other side, some traditional banks may wish to become involved in microfinance. As noted above, banks have a number of advantages that make them well placed to move into the microfinance sector. Where they adopt appropriate operational procedures, microfinance can be a profitable activity. The involvement of regulated banks in microfinance is most common in Indonesia, where there is a large number of banks providing financial services in the rural areas, including to poor clients. While Bank Rakyat Indonesia is the largest and most famous of these, there are also many small banks operating in more localised areas. To a lesser extent, regulated banks are also becoming involved in microfinance in the Philippines, and in a number of the other countries included in this study. Banks may be involved in microfinance either through direct lending to the poor, or through linkages with specialist MFIs.

The extent to which regulated banks become involved in microfinance depends critically on the policy environment. As noted in chapter 3, in some countries the government operates specific microfinance programs in which funds are channelled through the banks to borrowers who meet certain criteria. Most countries also continue to impose various directed credit requirements, whereby banks are required to lend a certain proportion of their loan portfolio to particular sectors, which may include the poor. Hence, regulated banks may become involved in microfinance as a result of specific government requirements.

Banks may also become involved in microfinance as a matter of choice, because they see it as a profitable activity. This depends importantly on the regulatory and prudential framework. In many ways, the regulatory and prudential framework is more critical for regulated banks than it is for specialist MFIs. As noted by Baydas et al:

> Non-bank microlending NGOs can operate in a repressed financial market environment since they are not subject to the regulatory interest rate ceilings, high reserve requirements and selective (i.e. targeted) credit policies characteristic of these markets. Commercial banks, however, cannot escape these regulations that, in the end, reduce their profit margins. Rarely have commercial banks considered

microfinance initiatives while operating under a regime of financial repression (pp.8–9).

This chapter considers a number of matters relating to the regulatory framework that are particularly relevant to the scope for banks to engage in microfinance. Section 5.2 looks at issues of licensing and minimum capital requirements, while section 5.3 deals with regulations relating to interest rates. A range of issues relating to prudential regulation and supervision are considered in section 5.4, while section 5.5 summarises the chapter and provides recommendations.

5.2 Licensing and minimum capital requirements

One critical factor affecting the extent to which regulated banks will become involved in microfinance is the scope for the establishment of small banks. Baydas et al. found that microfinance programs rarely have a secure position in large banks. Microfinance programs generally do not rank highly among the operational divisions within the bank, and the future of programs depends strongly on the support of a few important shareholders or bank officers. While some large banks such as Bank Rakyat Indonesia have been able to extend the range of their commercial banking functions successfully and profitably into the domain of microfinance, this is the exception rather than the rule.

Smaller banks, by contrast, operate in more localised areas and are more likely to serve niche markets. Baydas et al. found that where smaller banks are involved in microfinance, they tend to have a larger percentage of their portfolio in microfinance and there is a stronger institutional commitment to it, as compared to larger banks. It is also easier to establish an institutional culture geared towards servicing a lower income clientele with specialised products.

The scope for establishing small banks is also of critical importance to specialist MFIs wishing to establish regulated banks. Clearly, such institutions are unlikely to be able to muster the capital to establish a commercial bank of national significance offering the full range of financial services. Unless there is provision to establish smaller banks, they will not be able to become regulated financial institutions and offer full deposit services. For these reasons, if regulated banks are to play an active role in microfinance, it is essential that there be some mechanism to enable small banks to be licensed. In large part, this means that minimum capital requirements for the establishment of a new bank should be realistic for a small bank operating at a local level. It also means that there should not be other restrictions preventing the establishment of small banks. Jansson and Wenner (1997) note that a further issue is whether NGOs establishing banks should be permitted to use the net present value of loan portfolios as capital.

Does relaxing minimum capital requirements increase prudential risks? Chaves and Gonzalez-Vega (1994, p.64) distinguish clearly between capital adequacy ratios and minimum capital requirements:

> Capital adequacy regulations in the form of some minimum solvency ratio create good incentives. This makes for sound regulation. But capital adequacy requirements as an absolute minimum amount of equity to enter the industry are, conceptually, anticompetitive. The only justification for this latter type of regulation is a pragmatic one that has to do with the difficulty of supervising large numbers of intermediaries with small scale operations.

Following this line of argument, the major cost of permitting the establishment of small banks will be the additional cost to the central bank of regulating and supervising them. While this cost may be not insignificant, it would appear a relatively small price to pay if the result is to increase significantly the outreach of financial services in the rural areas, including to poor clients.

CGAP (1996) and Berenbach and Churchill (1997) are less emphatic. They note that the more capital a financial institution has, the better able it is to sustain losses. Moreover, the more money owners of financial institutions have at stake, the greater the incentive to avoid high-risk decisions. They point to particular risks in the case of NGOs-turned-banks, where much of the capital may come from investors who are not primarily motivated by commercial concerns, and so have less incentive than other investors to avoid risky behaviour. Nevertheless, central banks may minimise these risks by looking at the source of capital and proposed ownership structure, limiting any one shareholder to a fixed percentage of the share capital, and scrutinising the management of the proposed bank.

Of the nine countries included in this study, only two have a permissive policy environment for the establishment of small banks.[3] For Indonesia, the category of rural banks (known by their Indonesian acronym BPR), was mentioned in chapter 3. Under the Banking Act of 1992, the government of Indonesia determined that there should be only two categories of banks in Indonesia, commercial banks and rural banks. The former provide general banking services with access to the payments system, while the latter may accept deposits only in the form of time deposits, savings or other similar forms. Rural banks, which may be structured in such forms as regional government enterprises, cooperatives or limited liability companies are entitled to extend credits and may also place funds in central bank money market instruments or with other banks.

Both categories of banks are subject to the supervision of Bank Indonesia, the central bank. In principle, both are subject to broadly the same prudential and regulatory regime, with regard to such requirements as capital adequacy ratio, legal lending limit (related party transactions), loan to deposit ratio, debt provisioning and bank ratings according to CAMEL factors. Rural banks are quite restricted in regard to the geographic area of their operations, with their expansion being

3 A number of countries in other regions have enacted provisions for the establishment of small banks and/or special categories of MFIs which can accept deposits from the general public. Berenbach and Churchill (1997) discuss the situation in Peru, Bolivia and West Africa. Jansson and Wenner (1997) note that Nicaragua and El Salvador are considering similar reforms.

confined to adjacent municipalities or subdistricts. Despite their name, 'rural' banks may also be established in urban areas. However, rural banks are somewhat more lightly regulated than commercial banks in terms of the requirements for qualifications of directors (although at least 50 per cent of nominees for a rural bank board must have not less than one year's experience in banking operations).

The principal difference relates to the minimum capital requirements for the two types of bank. Unlike commercial banks, a rural bank may be established with as little as Rp50 million ($21,300) in capital. Such banks are frequently very modest operations and their client bases can extend well down the income distribution to include low-income people and microentrepreneurs. They are playing an increasingly important role in the program established by Bank Indonesia to create linkages between banks and NGOs for the provision of credit to the poor. Some are moving quite proactively to create self-help groups among poor clients to minimise the transaction costs of dealing with this class of very small customer. In an environment where NGOs appear not to flourish, they are beginning to play a significant role in microfinance. It should be noted, however, that the recent financial crisis has led to the closure of a number of rural banks and may also lead to a tightening of the requirements for the establishment of rural banks.

There is also considerable scope to establish small banks in the Philippines. While the minimum capital requirement for a commercial bank is Ps2 billion ($76.3 million), it is possible to establish thrift banks and rural banks with much lower capital. The requirement for a thrift bank is Ps250 million ($9.5 million) if the head office is in Metro Manila, and Ps40 million ($1.5 million) if the head office is outside Metro Manila. In the case of rural banks, the minimum capital requirement varies from Ps20 million ($0.8 million) down to Ps2 million ($80,000), depending on the location of the head office. While thrift banks and rural banks are more restricted in their operations than commercial banks, particularly with respect to their areas of operation, they are permitted to provide the full range of deposit services. This policy environment has facilitated the establishment of a large number of small banks, with some 108 thrift banks and 805 rural banks (the latter including some 47 cooperative rural banks) under the supervision of the central bank. The cooperative rural banks have been singled out for praise by the World Bank for their capacity to provide microfinance services profitably.

In the other seven countries, there is much less scope to establish small banks. In all cases, the minimum capital requirement to establish a commercial bank is high, ranging from $4.8 million in Bangladesh to $29.6 million in Thailand. This would generally be too high for someone wishing to establish a small localised bank. Moreover, even meeting the minimum capital and other requirements for the establishment of a commercial bank does not mean that it is possible to obtain a licence. To establish a commercial bank in Pakistan, it is necessary to open a branch in each of the four provinces and in the disputed territory of Kashmir. In Bangladesh, Malaysia and Thailand, the central bank is actively trying to restrict the number of commercial banks, and it is unlikely that any new bank would be licensed even if it met all the criteria.

In these four countries (that is, Bangladesh, Malaysia, Pakistan and Thailand), the retail banking system is essentially limited to commercial banks and state development banks, with no network of small regulated banks. No regulated banks other than commercial banks are permitted to offer full deposit services. Hence, there is effectively very little scope to establish a small bank offering full deposit and loan services. While there may be some scope to be licensed as some other type of bank (for example, as an investment bank in Pakistan, the route currently being used by the Aga Khan Rural Support Program to establish a bank), this is clearly a very imperfect solution that permits only a limited range of deposit services.

In Nepal, the banking system has traditionally consisted of commercial banks and state development banks. However, since 1994, five regional rural development banks have been established to lend to 'deprived' sections of society using the Grameen Bank model. These banks are owned as to 75 per cent by the government and central bank, with the balance being subscribed by other banks and financial institutions. While their initial performance has been promising, it was reported that they are increasingly being plagued by political pressure and interference with their operations. Following passage of the Development Bank Act 1996, it is also possible for private interests to establish development banks mandated to focus on low-income families. The minimum capital requirement is Rs10 million ($180,000), and it is understood that a private development bank is to be licensed shortly.

In India and Sri Lanka, there has long been a network of small banks, with the regulated banking system including commercial banks, state development banks, regional rural development banks and, in the case of India, cooperative banks.[4] Regional rural development banks and cooperative banks operate at the regional level, and to some limited extent are involved in microfinance. However, they are essentially owned and/or controlled by the government, and in most cases their performance has been poor. There is no scope for private shareholders to establish new regional rural development banks. In India, there may be some limited scope to establish new urban cooperative banks. This is the route taken by one prominent MFI, SEWA Bank, but it is not clear if it would be open to other institutions.

In both India and Sri Lanka, there have been some recent initiatives to encourage the establishment of smaller banks. In India, the Reserve Bank has created special provisions for the establishment of local area banks with a minimum capital requirement of Rs50 million ($1.4 million). They are permitted to offer the full range of banking services, but their operations are limited to three geographically contiguous districts. Similarly, in Sri Lanka, the government has recently made it

---

4 Some other countries, including Sri Lanka, also have cooperative banks, but these are more in the nature of credit cooperatives. Only in India are they regulated by the central bank.

easier for specialised banks to be licensed, with a minimum capital requirement of Rs100 million ($1.8 million). While these provisions make it easier to establish smaller banks, the minimum capital requirements are still quite high.

5.3 Interest rates

One critical constraint which may prevent regulated banks from lending directly to the poor relates to interest rates. Microfinance is an inherently costly activity. Effective microfinance programs require intensive inputs in motivating and training borrowers and in follow-up, with regular monitoring and frequent loan repayments. Programs must go to where the borrowers are, rather than being located in regional centres. All of these factors add to costs. And loan amounts are small, implying low interest income per loan. To be sustainable, microfinance programs must therefore charge higher rates of interest than those charged on other loans. This is true regardless of whether programs are undertaken by specialised MFIs or regulated banks. The Grameen Bank, the largest and one of the most efficient microfinance programs in the world, charges an effective interest rate of 20 per cent per annum, and most smaller programs need to charge considerably more than this to be sustainable. Even if regulated banks adopt the techniques of specialist MFIs, they need to charge higher interest rates on their microfinance loans than on their other loans if their microfinance programs are to be sustainable.

Four of the countries included in the study impose interest rate ceilings on small loans by banks. In Bangladesh, interest rate ceilings apply to bank loans for small-scale cottage industries (12 per cent) and agriculture (14 per cent). In India, commercial bank loans below Rs25,000 ($690) are subject to a ceiling of 12 per cent, while loans between Rs25,000 ($690) and Rs200,000 ($5,560) are subject to a ceiling of 13.5 per cent (these ceilings only apply to loans by commercial banks, and do not apply to loans by regional rural banks or cooperative banks). In Malaysia, bank loans are subject to a general ceiling equal to the base lending rate plus 4 percentage points, with lower ceilings for some specific categories of loans. In Nepal, the maximum mark-up between deposit rates and loan rates is 6 percentage points. All of these requirements effectively preclude regulated banks from lending direct to poor borrowers on a sustainable basis. It is not surprising that in all of these countries, regulated banks tend only to lend to poor borrowers where they are required to by law or where they can access special government funds. This is also the case in Pakistan, where there is no formal interest rate ceiling but where banks generally charge small borrowers at the minimum rate of 14 per cent because of perceived social pressures.

The remaining four countries, Indonesia, Philippines, Sri Lanka and Thailand, have no interest rate ceilings, with banks free to determine their own interest rates in line with costs and market conditions. In two of these countries, most especially Indonesia and to a lesser extent the Philippines, regulated banks are involved in microfinance to a significant extent. Clearly, deregulated interest rates are an important factor in encouraging them to become involved in the microfinance sector. It is understood that rural banks in Indonesia charge interest rates up to 3 to 4 per cent per month, while Goodwin-Groen (forthcoming) notes that in the Philippines, rural banks charge interest rates of around 34 per cent annually.

5.4 Prudential regulation and supervision

Reserve and liquidity requirements

Another factor which may discourage banks from becoming involved in microfinance is high reserve requirements. In many developing countries, regulatory authorities have used reserve requirements to limit monetary expansion in the banking system and thereby control inflation. The higher the reserve requirement, the less the deposit base available for on-lending and the less likely are banks to engage in microfinance.

In the past, a number of countries in Asia have maintained high reserve requirements. However, these have been reduced significantly in recent years as they have deregulated their banking systems. Of the countries included in the study, Malaysia has the highest reserve requirement, with banks required to hold cash reserves with the central bank equal to 13.5 per cent of deposit liabilities. In the Philippines, the reserve requirement for commercial banks is 13 per cent, but requirements are lower for thrift banks and rural banks, with savings and time deposits treated more leniently than demand deposits. Similarly in India, the reserve requirement is currently 10 per cent for commercial banks, but only 3 per cent for other banks. All other countries have reserve requirements of less than 10 per cent. Hence, for the countries in the study, reserve requirements appear to be set primarily on prudential rather than macroeconomic grounds, and do not appear to be a constraint to the development of microfinance.

Chaves and Gonzalez-Vega (1994) and CGAP (1996) comment that small banks are likely to be exposed to high levels of liquidity risk, particularly seasonal liquidity risk. They suggest that it may sometimes be prudent to set relatively high liquidity standards. Similarly, Christen (1997) notes that liquidity management is an extremely important area, and one in which MFIs tend to be weak. On the other hand, he points out that what may be an appropriate liquidity ratio depends very much on the particular circumstances facing the institution concerned, such as seasonal factors and plans for expansion. He argues that this makes liquidity management less susceptible to regulation and supervision than some other areas. For the countries included in the study, statutory liquidity requirements (over and above reserve requirements) range from zero in Thailand to 25 per cent in India and Pakistan.

Capital adequacy ratios

In terms of capital adequacy ratios, the Basle Accord recommends that banks should maintain capital at least equal to 8 per cent of risk-weighted assets, equivalent to a gearing multiple of slightly over 12:1. Most of the countries in this study have adopted this standard. Thailand and the Philippines have adopted slightly higher standards of 8.5 and 10 per cent of risk-weighted assets respectively, whereas in Pakistan banks must maintain capital equal to at least 7.5 per cent of time and deposit liabilities, a slightly lower standard than that recommended by the Basle Accord.

Most commentators suggest that the capital adequacy ratio should be higher for small and microfinance banks than for commercial banks. There are a number of reasons for this. First, as noted above, in the case of banks established out of the NGO movement, much of the capital may come from investors who are not primarily motivated by commercial concerns.[5] Such investors may have priorities other than rigorously safeguarding their capital. Second, such banks will generally be restricted to certain geographic areas or client groups, leading to less diversified portfolios than other banks. Third, because such banks operate with relatively high costs and high interest rates on loans, a given percentage of non-performing loans will decapitalise them faster than commercial banks. Fourth, banking regulators have little experience with small banks. Some have suggested capital adequacy ratios of 20 per cent or higher, at least initially, while others have suggested more modest figures such as 12 per cent.

Loan classification and provisioning

Loan classification and provisioning is another problematic area for banks specialising in microfinance. While microfinance portfolios often show lower delinquency than commercial bank portfolios, delinquency tends to be more volatile. For this reason, CGAP (1996) suggests that microfinance banks should provision their overdue loans (based on time overdue) more aggressively than conventional banks. On the other hand, some regulations for loan provisioning require high provisions for unsecured loans, even where such loans are not overdue. Clearly, such regulations are inappropriate for microfinance banks. CGAP suggests that regulators should be flexible in considering alternative indicators of asset quality, such as historical performance of portfolios, statistical sampling of arrears, and the adequacy of management information systems and policies for dealing with arrears.

What provisioning requirements are appropriate for microfinance banks? One approach would be for regulators to use the same provisions that CGAP (1997a) has proposed for MFIs, as follows.

5 The Basle Accord requires banks to have at least half of their capital in the form of paid-in shares, to ensure that owners see themselves as having a stake in the institution's future.

Time in arrears	Loan loss provision
1 to 30 days	10% of unpaid balance
31 to 90 days	25% of unpaid balance
91 to 180 days	50% of unpaid balance
more than 180 days	100% of unpaid balance

These are stricter, in terms of the provision required for loans with a given length of time in arrears, than those applying to commercial banks under the Basle Accord, but are not quite as strict as those used in the ACCION CAMEL instrument for MFIs. The provisioning requirements in the Basle Accord have been adopted by most of the countries in this study. Some countries, including the Philippines and Thailand, require higher provisions for unsecured loans than for secured loans that are the same length of time in arrears.

Reporting requirements

Berenbach and Churchill (1997) argue that reporting formats used for large commercial banks may not be appropriate for small microfinance banks. They comment that reporting formats were originally conceived for banks with fewer, larger transactions, while microfinance banks are more concerned with aggregate indicators. Since their portfolios consist of thousands of small loans, it is not necessary nor realistic to monitor the performance of each individual loan, and portfolio reporting formats should be appropriate to the volume, loan size and term of microfinance loans.

For those countries in the study that have small regulated banks (India, Indonesia and the Philippines), reporting requirements are broadly similar for all categories of banks. Nevertheless, small banks did not comment that these requirements were overly difficult for them to fulfil. For instance, one urban cooperative bank in India that is heavily involved in microfinance commented that it found the reporting requirements rigorous but realistic. It may also be the case that, in practice, small banks are not supervised as rigorously as larger ones. In Indonesia, for instance, the current financial crisis has given rise to suggestions that some rural banks have not been adequately supervised.

Other prudential requirements

Berenbach and Churchill (1997) noted a number of other problems that may apply when standard banking regulation and supervision is applied to small banks or banks with substantial microfinance portfolios.

In many countries, bank regulations limit the percentage of the portfolio that may be extended as unsecured loans. Clearly, regulations of this nature will limit the share of a bank's portfolio that can be devoted to microfinance. Nevertheless, such regulations do not appear to be a constraint in the countries included in this study. The only country to impose restrictions on unsecured lending by banks is Pakistan, which only permits banks to make unsecured loans up to Rs100,000 ($2,850) in the case of loans of less than three years for trade, commerce or business, and Rs25,000 ($710) for other loans. These ceilings are high enough to enable the banks to engage in direct lending to the poor without security, should they wish to do so.

Sometimes regulations concerning loan documentation are not appropriate for microloans. It is not clear if this is a constraint in the countries included in this study. None of the central banks reported any regulations of this nature, leaving the question of loan documentation to the discretion of individual banks.

Supervision methods used by bank regulators may not be appropriate for microfinance portfolios. Berenbach and Churchill noted that bank examiners usually review 30 per cent of a bank's loans. Clearly, this is not feasible in the case of microloans, and such procedures would need to be adjusted. Christen (1997) also suggests that supervisors need to adopt a different mindset when dealing with microfinance banks. The instinctive reaction of regulators to increased loan delinquency and management weakness may be to suggest greater administrative controls, essentially meaning greater hierarchy and bureaucracy, but this is likely to be inappropriate in the case of microfinance banks.

In some countries banking regulators must approve the opening of new branches, or branches may have limited flexibility regarding services and opening hours. Berenbach and Churchill comment that in some cases regulators have queried the location of branches in poor, remote communities that are perceived as unsafe, but these are precisely the areas where banks providing microfinance services should set up branches. Another issue is that banks with large microfinance portfolios will inevitably have higher ratios of operational costs to average portfolio than other banks. When conducting the standard CAMEL rating, regulators should therefore compare microfinance banks with other banks with similar loan portfolios.

5.5 Summary and recommendations

Most institutions engaged in microfinance are specialist microfinance institutions (MFIs) registered as societies, non-profit companies or similar bodies. However, there is also considerable scope for regulated banks to become involved in microfinance. Some specialist MFIs may wish to establish regulated banks, so that they can raise deposits from the general public, and more generally increase their credibility with investors and depositors. And some traditional banks may wish to become involved in microfinance. However, the extent to which regulated banks become involved in microfinance depends critically on the policy environment.

Licensing and minimum capital requirements

One critical factor affecting the extent to which regulated banks will become involved in microfinance is the scope for the establishment of small banks. Microfinance programs in large banks rarely have a secure position within the bank, although the *unit desa* system of Bank Rakyat Indonesia is a major exception to this. The particular combination of supportive policy and regulatory environment and political leadership which underlies the success of Bank Rakyat Indonesia deserves close study throughout the region.

Smaller banks, by contrast, operate in more localised areas and are more likely to be involved in microfinance. Of the nine countries included in this study, only Indonesia and the Philippines have a permissive policy environment for the establishment of small banks. In these two countries, there is considerable microfinance activity by small banks operating at the local level. In the other seven countries, there is much less scope to establish small banks. In Bangladesh, Malaysia, Pakistan and Thailand there is no network of small regulated banks. In India and Sri Lanka there is a network of regional rural development banks which are involved in microfinance to some extent, but they are essentially controlled by the government and in most cases their performance has been poor. In Nepal the government has recently established regional rural development banks with a specific microfinance mandate, but they are subject to increasing political pressure.

Establish a practical framework for licensing small banks

If regulated banks are to play an active role in microfinance, it is important that there be some mechanism to enable small banks to be licensed. Governments should ensure that the minimum capital requirements for establishing a bank are realistic for small banks operating at the local level, and that there are no other restrictions affecting the establishment of small banks.

Interest rates

Remove interest rate ceilings

Four of the countries included in the study impose interest rate ceilings on small loans by banks. Such ceilings may prevent banks from lending directly to the poor. Microfinance is an inherently costly activity, and if it is to be sustainable, interest rates on microloans must be higher than on other loans. Interest rate ceilings on small loans should be removed, or at the very least set at levels that are sufficient to enable banks to operate microfinance programs sustainably.

Prudential regulation and supervision

High reserve requirements may also discourage banks from becoming involved in microfinance. For the countries in the study, however, reserve requirements appear to be set primarily on prudential rather than macroeconomic grounds, and do not appear to constitute a barrier to microfinance. While microfinance may give rise to liquidity risk, it is not clear that small banks should face higher statutory liquidity requirements than large banks.

Establish appropriate capital adequacy ratios for microfinance banks

The Basle Accord recommends that banks should maintain a capital adequacy ratio of at least 8 per cent of risk-weighted assets. However, required capital adequacy ratios should be higher for small microfinance banks than for standard commercial banks, reflecting higher risk and other factors. Some commentators have suggested capital adequacy ratios of 20 per cent or higher, at least initially, while others have suggested more modest figures such as 12 per cent.

Establish appropriate provisioning requirements for microfinance banks

Microfinance banks should provision their overdue loans, based on time overdue, more aggressively than conventional banks because of the greater volatility of delinquency. On the other hand, provisioning requirements must take account of the fact that microfinance loans are generally unsecured. Regulators should be flexible in accepting additional indicators of asset quality, such as historical performance of portfolios, statistical sampling of arrears, and adequacy of management information systems in their evaluation of risk.

Review other policies affecting microfinance banks

There are a number of other prudential standards sometimes applied to commercial banks that may not be appropriate for microfinance banks. These include reporting requirements, limits on unsecured loans, requirements concerning loan documentation, supervision methods, and branching restrictions. While the study did not identify any specific impediments in these areas, regulators should review their policies and remove any unnecessary restrictions facing microfinance banks.

6 Conclusion

Lack of access to financial services is often a critical constraint to the establishment or expansion of viable microenterprises. It is now generally accepted that populations traditionally excluded from the formal financial sector can, in fact, be a profitable market niche for innovative banking services, and that microfinance can be very important in reducing poverty.

Despite the rapid growth of microfinance institutions (MFIs) in recent years their outreach remains very small compared to the potential demand. Moreover, few MFIs have yet attained any significant degree of self-sufficiency. While microfinance has the potential to make an important contribution to poverty reduction in the region, this requires the development of a microfinance sector that is able to reach large numbers of poor people on a sustainable basis.

This, in turn, requires increased attention to all aspects of microfinance, including the policy and regulatory environment. While the nine countries included in the study differ in terms of their level of economic development, social conditions and institutional structure, the study suggests that an effective policy and regulatory environment for microfinance is likely to include a number of common elements.

Arrangements for direct support

Active support from government and/or donor agencies, including direct financial support, is a necessary catalyst to the establishment of a viable microfinance sector.

MFIs in all countries have received considerable support from their governments and/or donor agencies. In the past, most of this has been in the form of financial assistance direct to an individual MFI. This support has been largely ad hoc in nature. The Guiding Principles for Selecting and Supporting Intermediaries, agreed by major donor agencies in October 1995, provide a number of suggestions as to how support by donors and government can best be directed to maximising outreach and sustainability. All governments and donor agencies should ensure that their support for MFIs is consistent with the Guiding Principles.

Most countries included in the study have some form of second tier microfinance institution which channels funds from the government and/or donor agencies to individual MFIs. The most successful of these is the Palli Karma Sahayak Foundation (PKSF) in Bangladesh. Where they operate well, second tier microfinance institutions are a very effective means for supporting MFIs. Governments and donor agencies should channel their support for microfinance, as much as possible, through efficient and well-managed second tier institutions.

At the same time, there is evidence both from Asia and from other regions that second tier institutions do not always operate on a sound basis, and may be subject to significant administrative, political and technical difficulties. If second tier institutions are to play an effective role, it is clear that there are a number of critical issues that need to be addressed.

Most importantly, they should establish and enforce appropriate performance and reporting standards for the MFIs that they fund. They should also operate as independent entities, support MFIs based on the standards they achieve rather than the model they follow, avoid restrictive interest rate policies, and develop appropriate criteria for funding scaling-up, institutional development and equity.

Seven of the nine countries included in the study still impose directed credit requirements, whereby banks are required to lend a certain proportion of their loan portfolio to particular sectors. These are an inefficient means of reaching the poor, and impose economic costs.

In some countries, the government operates specific microfinance programs in which funds are channelled through the banks. Such programs have generally not been successful and may 'crowd out' more effective programs. Where public funds are available to support microfinance, it is more appropriate to channel them through second tier microfinance institutions and specialist MFIs, rather than through the banking system. An apparent exception to this analysis is in Indonesia, where some microfinance programs channelled through banks with a genuine commitment to outreach, in particular, Bank Rakyat Indonesia and the rural banks (BPRs), appear to have been successful.

One important way in which commercial banks can become involved in microfinance is through linkages with NGOs and self-help groups. Other than in India and Indonesia, there is little positive support for linkages from policymakers. Central banks should take a more active role in encouraging linkages, by documenting and publicising successful examples, issuing clear guidelines that the banks can follow, and other measures.

The other main category of microfinance programs is those operated directly by government agencies. In general, governments should abolish direct microfinance programs and channel the funds through well-managed second tier microfinance institutions or MFIs instead.

Regulation of non-bank microfinance institutions

In most countries, MFIs are able to obtain registration under the general provisions applying to NGOs and cooperatives. The broad requirements are generally quite simple. The only exceptions to this appear to be Malaysia and Thailand, where the usual registration procedures for NGOs may not permit an institution to engage in microfinance. In these countries, governments should establish simple registration procedures suitable for MFIs.

NGOs engaged in microfinance should be required to be registered. On the other hand, in some cases MFIs are subject to unnecessary and burdensome rules and regulations, and the rules are not transparent. Unnecessary restrictions should be removed, and the discretionary powers vested in regulatory agencies should be limited as much as possible.

Only two countries, Nepal and Thailand, impose general ceilings on the interest rates that MFIs can charge borrowers. In a number of other countries, however, there are ceilings on interest rates under government microfinance programs or as a result of various other actions by government. Countries that impose interest rate ceilings should either remove them or set them at levels that are consistent with the sustainability of efficient, well-managed MFIs. Other countries should avoid policies that reduce the interest rate margins available to MFIs.

MFIs which do not accept deposits from the general public are not subject to prudential regulation or supervision by a government agency in any country included in the study. There are also no compulsory reporting requirements designed specifically with the needs of MFIs in mind. This situation is appropriate. It is generally agreed that where MFIs do not accept deposits from the public, it is unnecessary to subject them to full prudential regulation and supervision.

Nevertheless, it is clear that at present, most MFIs do not have adequate standards. The challenge is to find cost-effective ways of improving the standards, in terms of both performance and reporting, of the large numbers of MFIs that are not currently operating on a sound basis. In those countries with second tier microfinance institutions, these institutions can play a very important role in developing standards for the microfinance sector. Such institutions have an effective mechanism through their lending programs for enforcing any standards that they develop. Standards should be based on results achieved rather than the model used, have a proactive role in facilitating improvement in the performance of the microfinance sector over time, and be developed through a process of wide consultation with MFIs. There is a broad range of experience that second tier institutions can draw on in establishing standards.

Another approach to establishing performance and reporting standards for MFIs is through self-regulation. In this regard, the Philippine Coalition for Microfinance Standards is the most important initiative in Asia at present. At this stage, however, it is doubtful that any country has an apex body for MFIs with the necessary resources or authority to monitor and enforce a comprehensive system of self-regulation. Hence, self-regulation may need to be reinforced with some legal or quasi-legal system of incentives or compulsion.

In general, MFIs are not permitted to accept deposits from the general public unless they establish regulated banks. In terms of mobilising savings from members, in most countries the situation is somewhat ambiguous. Generally, regulatory authorities tend not to intervene so long as MFIs mobilise savings from members only, but MFIs do not have a clear legal basis for doing so.

Laws should be clarified to make it clear that MFIs are permitted to require loan-linked deposits or compulsory savings as a condition to receiving a loan, and to use them in their lending programs. Some MFIs also offer voluntary savings facilities. It would generally not seem appropriate to permit MFIs to use voluntary savings in their lending programs unless effective protections are in place. One option is to permit MFIs to mobilise voluntary savings from members if they establish an earmarked account with a regulated financial institution.

Regulation of banks

There is considerable scope for regulated banks to become involved in microfinance. Some specialist MFIs may wish to establish regulated banks, and some traditional banks may wish to become involved in microfinance. The particular combination of supportive policy and regulatory environment and political leadership which underlies the success of Bank Rakyat Indonesia deserves close study throughout the region.

One critical factor affecting the extent to which regulated banks become involved in microfinance is the scope for the establishment of small banks. Of the countries in the study, only Indonesia and the Philippines have a permissive policy environment for the establishment of small banks. Governments in other countries should ensure that the minimum capital requirements for establishing banks are realistic for small banks operating at the local level, and that there are no other restrictions preventing the establishment of small banks. Another critical factor is interest rates. Interest rate ceilings on small loans by banks should be removed, or at the very least set at levels that are sufficient to enable banks to operate microfinance programs sustainably.

Capital adequacy ratios should be higher for small microfinance banks than for standard commercial banks, reflecting higher risk and other factors. Microfinance banks should also provision their overdue loans, based on time overdue, more aggressively than conventional banks, but provisioning requirements must accept that microfinance loans are generally unsecured. There are a number of other prudential standards sometimes applied to commercial banks that may not be appropriate for small microfinance banks.

References

ADB. 1997a. *Microenterprise Development: Not by Credit Alone.* Asian Development Bank, Manila.

ADB. 1997b. *Asian Development Bank Outlook 1997 and 1998*, Asian Development Bank, Oxford University Press, Hong Kong.

Baydas, Mayada, Graham, Douglas H. & Valenzuela, Liza. 1997. *Commercial Banks in Microfinance: New Actors in the Microfinance World.* Rural Finance Program, Ohio State University.

Berenbach, Shari & Churchill, Craig. 1997. 'Regulation and supervision of microfinance institutions: Experience from Latin America, Asia and Africa'. Occasional paper no.1, The Microfinance Network, Washington D.C.

CGAP. 1995. 'The Consultative Group to Assist the Poorest: A microfinance program'. Focus note no.1.

CGAP. 1996. 'Regulation and supervision of microfinance institutions: Stabilising a new financial market'. Focus note no.4.

CGAP. 1997a. Format for appraisal of microfinance institutions. Mimeo, Washington D.C.

CGAP. 1997b. 'Tools for practitioners'. *CGAP Newsletter*, no.4 (July).

Chaves, Rodrigo A. & Gonzalez-Vega, Claudio. 1994. 'Principles of regulation and prudential supervision and their relevance for microenterprise finance organisations'. In *The New World of Microenterprise Finance Organisations,* eds Maria Otero & Elisabeth Rhyne, Kumarian Press, West Hartford.

Christen, Robert Peck. 1997. 'Issues in the regulation and supervision of microfinance'. In *From Margin to Mainstream: The Regulation and Supervision of Microfinance,* eds Rachel Rock & Maria Otero. Monograph series no.11, ACCION International.

Christen, Robert Peck, Rhyne, Elisabeth, Vogel, Robert C. & McKean, Cressida. 1994. *Maximising the Outreach of Microenterprise Finance: The Emerging Lessons of Successful Programs.* IMCC, Arlington.

Churchill, Craig (ed.). 1997. 'Regulation and supervision of microfinance institutions: Case studies'. Occasional paper no.2, The Microfinance Network, Washington D.C.

Committee of Donor Agencies. 1995. *Micro and Small Enterprise Finance: Guiding Principles for Selecting and Supporting Intermediaries.* Committee of Donor Agencies for Small Enterprise Development and Donors' Working Group on Financial Sector Development.

Cuevas, Carlos E. 1996. 'Enabling environment and microfinance institutions: lessons from Latin America'. *Journal of International Development*, vol.8, no.2, pp.195–209.

FDC. 1992. *Banking with the Poor.* Foundation for Development Cooperation, Brisbane.

FDC. 1995. *Best Practice of Banking with the Poor.* Foundation for Development Cooperation, Brisbane.

Fruman, Cecile & Goldberg, Mike. 1997. *Microfinance Practical Guide.* World Bank, Washington D.C.

Gallardo, Joselito S., Randhawa, Bikki K. & Sacay, Orlando J. 1997. 'A commercial bank's microfinance program: the case of Hatton National Bank in Sri Lanka'. Discussion paper no.369, World Bank, Washington D.C.

Getubig, I., Remenyi, J. & Quinones, B. (eds). 1997. *Creating the Vision: Microfinancing the Poor in Asia-Pacific.* Asian and Pacific Development Centre, Kuala Lumpur.

Goodwin-Groen, Ruth. (forthcoming). *The Role of Commercial Banks in Microfinance.* Foundation for Development Cooperation, Brisbane.

Hulme, David & Mosley, Paul. 1996. *Finance against Poverty.* Routledge, London.

Jansson, Tor & Wenner, Mark D. 1997. *Financial Regulation and its Significance for Microfinance in Latin America and the Caribbean.* Microenterprise Unit, Sustainable Development Department, Inter-American Development Bank, Washington D.C.

Llanto, Gilberto M., Garcia, Edgardo & Callanta, Ruth. 1996. 'An Assessment of the Capacity and Financial Performance of Microfinance Institutions: The Philippine Case'. Discussion paper no.96–12, Philippine Institute for Development Studies.

McGuire, Paul B. & Conroy, John D. 1997. 'Bank-NGO linkages and the transaction costs of lending to the poor through groups'. *Small Enterprise Development,* vol.8, no.1, pp.4–15.

Microcredit Summit. 1997. *Declaration and Plan of Action.*

Microfinance Coalition for Standards. 1997. NGO microfinance standards: A conceptual framework. Preliminary draft, September.

Reserve Bank of India. 1995. Expert Committee on Integrated Rural Development Programme: Interim report. Reserve Bank of India, Mumbai.

Rhyne, Elisabeth & Otero, Maria. 1994, 'Financial services for microenterprises: principles and institutions'. In *The New World of Microenterprise Finance,* eds Maria Otero & Elisabeth Rhyne. Kumarian Press, West Hartford.

Rock, Rachel & Otero, Maria (eds). 1997. *From Margin to Mainstream: The Regulation and Supervision of Microfinance.* Monograph series no.11, ACCION International, Washington D.C.

Saltzman, Sonia B., Rock, Rachel & Salinger, Darcy. 1998. 'Performance and Standards in Microfinance: ACCION's Experience with the CAMEL Instrument'. Discussion paper no.7, ACCION International, Washington D.C.

Sustainable Banking with the Poor. 1996. *A Worldwide Inventory of Microfinance Institutions.* World Bank, Washington D.C.

Sustainable Banking with the Poor. 1997a. *An Inventory of Microfinance Institutions in East Asia and the Pacific*. World Bank, Washington D.C.

Sustainable Banking with the Poor. 1997b. *An Inventory of Microfinance Institutions in South Asia*. World Bank, Washington D.C.

Trigo Loubiere, Jacques. 1996. 'Supervising and regulating microfinance institutions: the Bolivian experience'. *Small Enterprise Development*, vol.7, no.3, pp.51–55.

UNDP. 1997. *Human Development Report.* United Nations Development Programme, Oxford University Press, New York.

Women's World Banking. 1995. *The Missing Links: Financial Systems That Work for the Majority*. Women's World Banking, New York.

World Bank. 1990. *World Development Report*. Oxford University Press, New York.

World Bank. 1996. *Staff Appraisal Report: Bangladesh Poverty Alleviation Microfinance Project*. Report no.15431-BD, World Bank, Washington D.C.

World Bank. 1997a. *World Development Indicators*. World Bank, Washington D.C.

World Bank. 1997b. *World Development Report.* Oxford University Press, New York.

Bangladesh

1 Introduction and background

1.1 Key demographic and economic data

Bangladesh is located in South Asia, bounded by the Bay of Bengal to the south, Myanmar to the south-east, and India to the east, north and west. In 1995 it had a population of 119.8 million people, packed into an area of only 144,000 square kilometres. The resulting population density of 832 people per square kilometre is one of the highest in the world. While population growth has slowed considerably in recent years, it remains relatively high at around 1.6 per cent per year between 1990 and 1995, with the total fertility rate in 1995 of 3.5 births per woman well above replacement level.

High population densities have placed considerable strain on resources and contributed to severe economic and environmental problems. Bangladesh is one of the poorest countries in the world, with an annual per capita income estimated at $240 in 1995. Only Nepal and a handful of African countries have lower per capita incomes. Bangladesh also performs poorly in terms of indicators of human development, such as life expectancy, infant mortality and educational attainment. The UNDP human development report for 1997 ranked Bangladesh 143rd out of 174 countries, with Nepal, Cambodia, Bhutan and Afghanistan the only countries outside Africa to rank lower. In 1995, life expectancy at birth was only 58 years, and only 38 per cent of adults were literate.

Bangladesh is still predominantly a rural society, with only 18 per cent of the population living in urban areas in 1995. This is lower than for all other countries included in this study except Nepal. Nevertheless, the structure of production has changed considerably in recent years, in both rural and urban areas. While the share of agriculture in GDP stood at 50 per cent in 1980, by 1995 it had declined to 31 per cent. This was matched by an increase in the share of services from 34 to 52 per cent, partly reflecting population pressure in the rural areas and the need to find alternative sources of income to agriculture. Microfinance is particularly important to many such microenterprises in the service sector. The share of industry increased only marginally from 16 to 18 per cent.

1.2 Poverty

Estimates of poverty

Given the above, it is not surprising that poverty is pervasive, with nearly half the population living in absolute poverty. Official estimates of the number of people in poverty are available from the Bangladesh Bureau of Statistics (1995), based on the periodic household expenditure survey (HES). The HES has been conducted in 1981–82, 1983–84, 1985–86, 1988–89, 1991–92 and 1995–96, but data from the most recent survey are not yet available. Estimates of poverty are based on the food-energy intake method of setting poverty lines. By this method, separate poverty lines for rural and urban areas are obtained by estimating the expenditure level at which the benchmark calorie intake equals the predetermined food-energy requirement.

It is estimated that in 1991–92, 47.5 per cent of the population lived below the absolute poverty line, set at a direct calorie intake of 2,122 calories per day. Based on population data for 1995, this equates to around 57 million people. The incidence of poverty was broadly similar in rural (47.6 per cent) and urban (46.7 per cent) areas. Poverty was only slightly lower than in the 1988–89 survey (47.8 per cent), but well below the level recorded in 1983–84 (62.6 per cent). The 1991–92 survey also included estimates of the hard-core poor (28.0 per cent), based on a poverty line equivalent to a direct calorie intake of 1,805 calories per day, and the ultra-poor (17.8 per cent), based on a poverty line equivalent to a direct calorie intake of 1,600 calories per day.

Some independent researchers have criticised the official estimates, questioning the comparability of the surveys, the methodologies used in deriving the poverty lines, and their consistency with other poverty data. There have also been other estimates of poverty, some of which are based on work carried out by the Bangladesh Institute of Development Studies. These have generally been based on the cost-of-basic-needs method, by which the poverty line is set as the cost in each sector of a 'basic needs' bundle of goods.

An important such study by Ravallion and Sen (1996) estimated that in 1991–92, 49.7 per cent of the population were below the poverty line, comprising 52.9 per cent of the rural population and 33.6 per cent of the urban population. Unlike the official estimates, Ravallion and Sen found that the proportion of people living in poverty was much higher in rural than in urban areas. Moreover, they found little evidence that poverty had fallen in the 1980s. While poverty had fallen from 52.3 per cent in 1983–84 to 43.9 per cent in 1985–86, it had risen consistently since that time. Indeed, the World Bank (1996) has argued that poverty has got worse in the last decade, primarily due to the rapid increase in the working age population, increasing landlessness, and slow growth in non-farm employment. Moreover, the burden of poverty falls disproportionately on women, with the incomes of female-headed households 40 per cent lower than for male-headed households.

Hence, while there is debate as to precise estimates, it is clear that widespread absolute poverty remains a major and intractable problem in Bangladesh. It is evident that a major policy focus on poverty will be necessary if poverty is to be reduced and eradicated.

Policies for poverty reduction

As noted by Hossain and Sakhawat (1996) policies for poverty reduction in Bangladesh, as in other countries, can generally be divided into three broad strategies:

(1) policies to encourage higher economic growth and employment
(2) policies to encourage higher investment in physical and social infrastructure, such as roads, water supply, sanitation, health and education, especially in poor and rural areas
(3) targeted programs to promote employment and income-generating activities among the poor who may otherwise be left out of the development process.

While this discussion focuses on the third category, it should be noted that sustainable poverty reduction is unlikely to be achieved in the absence of effective policies to promote economic growth and human development. This is especially true in Bangladesh, where the low per capita incomes and sheer numbers of the poor make it impossible to eliminate poverty simply by redistributing existing resources. Clearly, an integrated approach combining all aspects of government policy will be necessary to ensure substantial and sustainable reductions in poverty.

In terms of targeted programs to reduce poverty, the main emphasis of the government has been to target the rural poor, with particular reference to unemployed youth and disadvantaged women. There have also been some programs for the urban poor. The most important are those administered by the Bangladesh Rural Development Board (BRDB). The BRDB is a specialised public agency within the jurisdiction of the Ministry of Local Government and Rural Development, charged with promoting rural development and the government's programs for alleviating poverty. It has designed and implemented a series of rural development projects, generally funded by donors, under its Rural Poor Program. There are currently eight such projects operating. Projects are designed to motivate and organise landless men and women into small productive groups, and to provide them with skills, technology, credit and extension services. By mid-1996, more than one million men and women had participated in these projects.

In addition, the Department of Youth Development within the Ministry of Youth and Sports provides a number of training programs and projects for poor and unemployed youth aged between 15 and 30. These include skills development training, the self-employment program for the unemployed, youth leadership and human relations development, programs for the involvement of youth organisations in community development activities, participation of youth in conservation of resources, and poverty alleviation programs. Around 300,000 youths have participated in these programs since 1981, a small number in relation to the 30 million people falling within the relevant age group.

The Ministry of Women's Affairs has been the main vehicle for government programs targeting poor women. The main programs undertaken by the ministry have been skills development, the women's credit program, support services and special women's programs. In many cases these are integrated programs involving other ministries. Again, the cumulative outreach has been limited, with about 200,000 women participating in these programs since 1984.

A number of food aid development programs have also been implemented, through the Ministry of Women's Affairs and the Ministry of Relief and Rehabilitation. The food for work program provides food to landless people in exchange for work on infrastructure projects. The vulnerable groups development program provides food to destitute women, giving preference to poor women with young children who are heads of households. This program has collaborated with the Bangladesh Rural Advancement Committee (BRAC), a leading microfinance non-governmental organisation (NGO), to provide training and microcredit in addition to food.

Hence, the government has implemented a number of targeted programs designed to reduce poverty through employment and income generation, and many of these have included a microfinance component. The programs of the BRDB have been the most important of these. Nevertheless, outreach of these programs has been very limited in relation to the total number of people living below the poverty line.

1.3 Overview of the financial system

The formal financial system in Bangladesh consists of four nationalised commercial banks, three specialised development banks (including two specialised agricultural banks), 18 private commercial banks and ten foreign banks. These banks are subject to regulation by the central bank, the Bangladesh Bank, under the Banking Companies Act 1991. In addition, there are two cooperative networks. Unlike many other countries in the region, Bangladesh does not have a substructure of small banks operating at the local level. The government has been giving some preliminary consideration to the establishment of a network of regional rural development banks. However, it has not taken any firm decisions at this stage, and it is not clear how such banks would operate.

There has been considerable reform of the financial system in recent years. The Financial Sector Reform Program was launched in 1990, with support from the World Bank. The main objectives of the program were to liberalise interest rates and credit allocation, introduce indirect but more effective monetary control, improve debt recovery, strengthen prudential regulation and supervision by the Bangladesh Bank, improve the operations and capital position of the nationalised commercial banks, and assist the development of the capital market.

In the past, interest rates for both deposits and loans were determined by the Bangladesh Bank. In April 1992, interest rate controls were abolished for most lending categories, but were maintained for agriculture, exports and small-scale cottage industries. The current ceilings are 14 per cent for agricultural loans, 10 per cent for export loans, and 12 per cent for loans to small-scale cottage industries. Loans in these categories are eligible for an interest subsidy from the government or refinancing by the Bangladesh Bank. In addition, a floor rate of 5 per cent has been retained for savings and fixed deposits. Requirements to lend to particular priority sectors were also abolished under the Financial Sector Reform Program, with banks now free to allocate credit as they wish. In this respect Bangladesh is slightly unusual, with Bangladesh and Sri Lanka the only countries included in this study to have abolished all priority-sector lending requirements for commercial banks.

Despite these changes, the financial system remains relatively undeveloped. In 1995, the ratio of money and quasi money to GDP, a measure of financial depth, was only 35.6 per cent. This is comparable to most other countries in South Asia, but well below the 46.0 per cent recorded in India. Bank interest rates were positive in real terms reflecting liberalisation. Nevertheless, the 8 percentage point spread between interest rates for deposits (6 per cent) and loans (14 per cent) was the highest for any country in this study for which data were available, indicating a lack of competition in the banking sector.

Apart from the Grameen Bank itself, which is regarded as a specialised development bank, the banks do not tend to lend to the poor. The private commercial banks and foreign banks have largely stayed away from the rural credit sector. By contrast, the nationalised commercial banks and specialised agricultural banks have extensive branch networks in the rural areas, and have lent extensively in these areas. Nevertheless, their total rural lending is now less than that of the specialist microfinance institutions (MFIs). For instance, the World Bank (1996) notes that in 1994–95, the agricultural banks and nationalised commercial banks provided only Tk11 billion ($263 million) of rural credit, compared with around Tk17 billion ($407 million) provided by Grameen Bank and other specialist MFIs. Further, the banks engage in little if any lending that could properly be considered microfinance. Their rural credit programs are generally not targeted to the poor, and do not reach the poor. Moreover, the programs have been unsuccessful and are subject to high default.

1.4 Overview of microfinance

While the commercial banks have largely ignored the poor, a plethora of specialist MFIs has arisen to fill the need and provide financial services to this group. Indeed, the rapid growth of specialist MFIs may partly reflect the absence of small banks operating at the local level.

Microfinance largely originated in Bangladesh, and still operates on a vastly different scale there to anywhere else in the world. Of an estimated 10 million microfinance clients in the world today, no fewer than 6 million are in Bangladesh, representing not less than one in four rural households in the country. Many of the principles and techniques of microfinance that have now become standard throughout the world were pioneered by the now famous Grameen Bank, a Bangladeshi institution which remains the largest MFI in the world. Moreover, Bangladesh boasts a number of other MFIs which are among the largest and most successful worldwide. Indeed, the huge success of microfinance and MFIs in Bangladesh, and the debt owed to the Grameen Bank by the rest of the world, makes Bangladesh the logical starting point for any study of microfinance.

There are three main types of institutions engaged in microfinance. First, there is Grameen Bank itself, the pioneer of microfinance and the largest MFI in the world, with 2.1 million members as at June 1996. The Grameen Bank began as an experimental project of the University of Chittagong in 1976, and was established as a specialised bank under its own ordinance in 1983. The bank has developed highly effective methods for lending to the poor, based on techniques such as taking services to the village level, promoting and motivating self-help groups of the poor, use of group guarantees, compulsory savings mobilisation, transparency of credit transactions, intensive supervision of borrowers, and decentralised and cost-effective operations. Many of these features have become hallmarks of most successful microfinance programs throughout the world. While the Grameen Bank has expanded very rapidly in recent years it has now entered a consolidation phase, and is not currently opening any new branches.

Second, there are numerous NGOs providing credit and savings facilities. These include some of the largest microfinance programs in the world, such as BRAC (1.7 million members as at June 1996), Swanirvar Bangladesh (655,000 members as at March 1997) and Association for Social Advancement (ASA) with 575,000 members as at March 1997. In addition, there is a large number of small NGOs. The Credit and Development Forum (CDF), the apex body for microfinance NGOs, has 662 members, and there are perhaps 1,000 NGOs altogether that provide microfinance services. These NGOs employ a variety of approaches and lending methodologies. For instance, ASA follows a Grameen-style approach, although it is understood that it is presently considering some significant changes to its methodology. By contrast, BRAC and Swanirvar Bangladesh are multi-purpose NGOs concentrating on social development as well as savings and credit.

Third, there are a number of government programs providing microfinance. Foremost among these is the BRDB, which is involved both in lending directly to groups of poor borrowers from revolving funds provided by the government and donor agencies, and in linking groups of poor borrowers to nationalised commercial banks. The largest credit program, RD-12, had some 445,000 members as at October 1996. Some other ministries, such as the Ministry of Youth and Sport and the Ministry of Women's Affairs, also operate small credit programs.

Hence, there is a very large number of MFIs operating in Bangladesh, serving between them around 6 million clients. Nevertheless, around 90 per cent of the market is served by the five largest institutions, namely Grameen Bank, BRAC, ASA, Swanirvar Bangladesh and BRDB.

Some of these institutions are among the most efficient MFIs in the world. While historically some commentators had questioned the sustainability of the Grameen Bank, a recent World Bank study (Khandker, Khalily & Khan 1995a) has shown that the bank has steadily reduced its dependence on subsidies, and is very close to being fully financially self-sufficient. Based on 1994 data, the study estimated that the bank could self-sustain its operations either by increasing its average on-lending rate from 16.5 to 20 per cent (it has since increased its standard lending rate from 16 to 20 per cent), or simply by continuing to expand its membership and loan disbursements. At least one other MFI in Bangladesh has achieved even better financial performance. Of 57 leading MFIs in the Asia-Pacific region that were studied in detail for Bank Poor '96, ASA was the only one that had both attained 'full organisational self-sufficiency' and was reaching a large number of poor people. Grameen Bank was one of six institutions at or near financial self-sufficiency and reaching a sizeable number of poor people. Institutions such as Grameen Bank and ASA are therefore clearly world leaders in terms of sustainability, as well as in terms of outreach.

On the other hand, as in other countries, many of the smaller NGOs and government programs are not nearly as efficient or cost-effective in their operations, and rely heavily on subsidies from government or donor agencies to meet their administrative and other expenses.

2 Arrangements for direct support

2.1 Support for specialised microfinance institutions

Support for Grameen Bank and other microfinance institutions

Microfinance in Bangladesh developed initially because of the initiative of Professor Muhammad Yunus of the University of Chittagong, and remains primarily the preserve of NGOs and private activity. Nevertheless, the industry has relied heavily on support from the government and donor agencies. Without this support, it is highly unlikely that the industry could have developed to anything like its current size.

The Grameen Bank itself has received considerable support from government, Bangladesh Bank and donor agencies. Following the success of the initial experimental project by the University of Chittagong, the Grameen Bank project was established in 1979 with support from Bangladesh Bank and later from nationalised commercial banks. This support enabled the rapid expansion of the project. The bank has received support from a wide variety of donor agencies, and by end-1995 had received donor grants amounting to Tk3.5 billion ($84 million) for its revolving loan fund, nearly as much as its deposit base of Tk3.6 billion ($86 million).

It has also continued to receive support from the government and government agencies. For instance, Bangladesh Bank provided a line of credit of Tk6 billion ($145 million) in 1993–94 at an interest rate of 6 per cent, although less than half of this was drawn down. Since 1994, Grameen Bank has issued bonds guaranteed by the government. Moreover, the nationalised commercial banks purchased around Tk15 billion ($360 million) of such bonds in early 1995, with the encouragement of the government and because such bonds were eligible for statutory liquidity requirements. The bank has recently received a loan of $30 million at 1 per cent for 30 years from Japan's Overseas Economic Cooperation Fund (OECF).

Many other microfinance institutions (MFIs) have also relied on donor funds, especially during establishment phase, with around 250 MFIs currently receiving foreign donations for both operational costs and loan capital. Large inflows of subsidised donor capital have been instrumental in the proliferation and expansion of MFIs. Nevertheless, since the late

1980s and early 1990s, donor funds have become harder to come by. This has mainly affected the smaller MFIs, but has also made it more difficult for larger MFIs to expand their outreach.

Taken together, these arrangements for direct support have clearly been successful. They have contributed importantly to the establishment of a microfinance sector with unparallelled outreach and sustainability in global terms. Institutions such as Grameen Bank and ASA in particular have made very effective use of the available resources to create massive MFIs that have achieved or are fast approaching full financial self-sufficiency. Nevertheless, it is probably fair to say that these successes owe more to the vision and technical competence of the founders and management of these organisations rather than to particular modalities of government and donor support. Support has been essentially ad hoc in nature, and has generally not been explicitly designed to maximise the twin objectives of outreach and sustainability in the most cost-effective manner.

Given the general tightening in development assistance budgets, and the high demand for donor funds to expand microfinance activities in other countries, the availability of government and donor funds to expand the scale of microfinance in Bangladesh further may be somewhat limited. And impressive as the current outreach is, there is still a need for further growth. Given the high incidence of poverty in Bangladesh, there are still many poor households without access to financial services. Moreover, many poor households still only have access to a limited range of financial services. For instance, the vast majority of MFIs do not offer voluntary savings facilities. This suggests that there is a need to target future support more explicitly to increasing outreach and sustainability.

In this context, the Guiding Principles for Selecting and Supporting Intermediaries, agreed by major donor agencies in October 1995, provide a number of suggestions as to how support by donors and government can best be directed to maximising outreach and sustainability (Committee of Donor Agencies 1995). It would be appropriate for all donor agencies to ensure that their support for MFIs is consistent with these principles. In broad terms, the Guiding Principles argue that:

(1) Support for institutional development is appropriate at all stages of an institution's life, but should become more selective and specialised as institutions evolve.

(2) Grants for equity can be of strategic importance in enabling MFIs to build a capital base. A sound equity position is important to generate investment income, build the loan portfolio, and leverage funds from commercial banks and capital markets. As such, they can be a catalyst and complement to domestic mobilisation of funds. Grants for equity can also help MFIs seeking to become formal financial institutions to meet minimum capital requirements.

(3) Grants should only be given to cover operating losses during a clear, time-limited, start-up or expansion phase.

(4) Support through soft loans for on-lending is appropriate for MFIs that meet performance standards. However, it is also important that MFIs seek loan capital from commercial sources.

Palli Karma Sahayak Foundation

A major source of support to the MFIs is the Palli Karma Sahayak Foundation (PKSF), an apex financing institution established in 1990. While until recently PKSF has received all its funding, a total of Tk750 million ($17.9 million), from the government, it is registered as a private non-profit organisation. It is governed by a general body of fifteen people, the majority of whom are from outside government. Its main objective is to provide financial support, institutional support, advice and training to NGOs and other bodies involved in microfinance.

By December 1996, PKSF had provided loans of Tk 1.32 billion ($31.6 million) to 135 MFIs with a demonstrated capacity or potential capacity in microfinance, for on-lending to final borrowers. A total of 546,000 borrowers had obtained loans through these facilities. The World Bank (1996) found that its operating policies and procedures were quite satisfactory, with sound and conservative credit approval policies, intensive credit supervision, and comprehensive external audit.

The role of PKSF is set to expand significantly. The recent World Bank poverty alleviation microfinance project provides for a line of credit of $109 million for MFIs. The funds are on-lent from the government to PKSF at an interest rate of 1 per cent over twenty years, with a five-year grace period. PKSF then on-lends to MFIs that meet various criteria, at interest rates ranging from 3 to 5 per cent. About 60 per cent of the line of credit is earmarked for small and medium MFIs, with the remaining 40 per cent earmarked for large MFIs. To qualify, MFIs will have to meet a number of criteria similar to those already imposed by PKSF, relating to demonstrated or potential capacity, minimum loan recovery rate of 95 per cent, and sound management and accounting. Large MFIs have to meet some additional criteria, including at least Tk10 million ($240,000) of equity and a debt-equity ratio that does not exceed 2.5 to 1.

PKSF has also provided technical support to MFIs, in the form of institutional strengthening, research and dissemination, and developing management information systems. This role is also very likely to expand. The World Bank poverty alleviation microfinance project provides $6 million for technical assistance for capacity and institution building for MFIs, PKSF and the Bangladesh Bank. This will include a number of elements, including the establishment of a training unit which will develop and undertake a greatly expanded range of training programs for MFI staff.

The increasing role of PKSF is a very positive development. By all accounts, PKSF is operating very successfully. It is a well-managed organisation with professional staff. A number of NGOs commented that it operates in a thoroughly independent and business-like manner, with a minimum of government interference. The World Bank has recently expressed its confidence in PKSF by providing it with $115 million through the poverty alleviation microfinance project. It would appear desirable for other bilateral and multilateral donor agencies to also channel their support for microfinance through PKSF as much as possible. This could have a number of advantages:

- It would ensure that different forms of support to a particular MFI are complementary and directed to the same objectives rather than differing and inconsistent objectives as is sometimes the case at present.
- It would ensure that all MFIs face a level playing field, with support available to all MFIs meeting predetermined standards on the same terms and conditions.
- It would mean that MFIs would face one set of performance criteria, reporting standards and operational procedures, rather than a number of different sets as is often the case at present.

If PKSF is to take on this role, however, it would be desirable for it to broaden the range of activities that it is prepared to fund. At present, it only provides soft loans to MFIs for on-lending to final borrowers. It does not provide funds, whether in the form of grants or soft loans, for scaling-up operations, institutional development or increasing equity. In fact, it was suggested that in Bangladesh as in other countries, there is a general shortage of funds for these purposes. As noted above, support for these activities can be important in enabling MFIs to increase their scale of operations and enhance their sustainability. If sufficient funds can be made available, it would appear desirable for PKSF to expand the range of support that it provides. Clearly, appropriate criteria would need to be established for accessing support for each of these activities.

2.2 Support through the banking system

Directed credit schemes and programs channelled through the banking system

As noted above, requirements to lend to particular priority sectors were abolished under the Financial Sector Reform Program, and banks are free to allocate credit as they wish. There are also no significant microfinance programs in which government funds are channelled through the banking system. This absence of government programs for banks to lend to the poor is unique among the nine countries included in this study. Among these countries Bangladesh and Sri Lanka are the only ones to have abolished all priority-sector lending requirements for commercial banks. However, in Sri Lanka (as well as in a number of other countries), the government provides special funds for lending to the poor which are administered by the banks.

In general, directed credit schemes and government programs channelled through the banking system have been very costly, and have not been successful in reaching the poor. The experience of Bangladesh shows that supporting specialist MFIs is a much more effective means of providing financial services to the poor.

Linkages between banks and microfinance institutions

The Bangladesh Bank has offered some support for linkages between commercial banks and NGOs. In 1994 it conducted a seminar on this issue, and it has issued a number of circulars to commercial banks encouraging them to establish linkages with NGOs for lending to the poor.

Such linkages may take a variety of forms. For instance, banks may provide loans to MFIs that lend to the poor on their own account, such as the Bangladesh Rural Advancement Committee (BRAC), ASA and the Shakti Foundation. Alternatively, banks may establish relationships with NGOs such as Swanirvar Bangladesh, which establishes, trains and motivates self-help groups of the poor but does not directly provide loans itself. In this case, the loan contract is between the bank and the final borrower. The number and extent of linkages is gradually expanding. To date, however, no private commercial banks have established linkages with MFIs.

While Bangladesh Bank commented that commercial banks are permitted to make loans without collateral, the banks are still very reluctant to do so, and even suggested that the position of Bangladesh Bank is ambiguous in this regard. The banks also commented that it was necessary for the Bangladesh Bank to take a more proactive role by issuing clear instructions regarding collateral, as well as guidelines that the banks could follow in establishing linkages.

The impediments to linkages reside primarily in the attitudes of the commercial banks, rather than in the prudential or regulatory system. Nevertheless, it would be appropriate for the Bangladesh Bank to take a more active role in encouraging linkages, by issuing clear guidelines that the banks could follow. In this regard, the guidelines issued by the National Bank for Agriculture and Rural Development (NABARD) in India may be a useful starting point (see the India country study), although it is likely that they would need to be adapted considerably to suit the institutional framework in Bangladesh. The interest rate ceiling of 12 per cent on loans by banks to small-scale cottage industries may also discourage banks from establishing linkages with MFIs, although such loans are eligible for refinancing by the Bangladesh Bank.

2.3 Government microfinance programs

While the major focus has been on non-government initiatives, donors and government have also provided support to direct government microfinance programs. As noted above, the largest of these is the RD-12 project of the Bangladesh Rural Development Board (BRDB). This project, funded by the Canadian International Development Agency (CIDA), had some 328,000 borrowers as at December 1995.

BRDB is a semi-autonomous government agency with its own board of directors. In addition, the RD-12 project has a central coordinating committee, including representatives from CIDA, which meets once every six months to decide on overall policy matters relating to the project. The total cost of the project is estimated at Tk1.08 billion ($25.8 million), with an additional TK480 million ($11.5 million) for establishing the revolving loan fund. The project borrows heavily from the experience of NGOs involved in microfinance, including Grameen Bank and BRAC, with the lending methodology based on the Grameen model.

The project has performed very well compared with other most other government microfinance programs both in Bangladesh and in other countries. Khandker, Khan & Khalily (1995b) found that the recovery rate was 77 per cent in 1989 and increased to 91 per cent by 1993, much higher than for most government programs. They also found that it had effectively delivered credit and ancillary inputs to the rural poor, and that the administration and incentive system was less rigid than other government agencies. While sustainability was not emphasised in the initial project design, project management increased interest rates to a flat 15 per cent in 1994, in order to recover a higher proportion of operational costs.

The success of the RD-12 project demonstrates that by using best practice techniques (developed by NGOs) and ensuring relatively independent management free from political interference, it is possible for government agencies to establish effective microfinance programs. Nevertheless, the repayment rates achieved by RD-12, while much higher than those achieved by most other programs, are still well below those achieved by Grameen Bank, BRAC, ASA and other leading MFIs. RD-12 has also not been under as much pressure as the NGO programs to minimise costs and become sustainable. Moreover, other government programs have not been as effective as RD-12. As a general rule, it would appear unlikely that channelling funds through government programs is as cost-effective, in terms of maximising outreach and sustainability, as channelling funds through well-managed MFIs.

2.4 Other issues

While this study focuses on those policies and regulations directly related to microfinance, there is clearly a very wide range of policies that affect the overall environment for microfinance. For instance, a number of commentators noted that to maximise the opportunities for microfinance clients, more effective economic, infrastructure and social policies were also needed. However, it is not possible to consider these issues in this study.

More directly related to microfinance, however, a number of commentators criticised the decision by the government in 1991 to forgive all agricultural loans up to Tk5,000 ($120). This decision created major problems for the Grameen Bank and other MFIs who did not forgive their loans. Clearly, failure to ensure high repayment rates in other parts of the financial system reduces overall borrower discipline and makes it much harder for MFIs to maintain high repayment rates. The government should avoid debt forgiveness for small loans as well as other policies which have unintended adverse effects on MFIs.

3 Regulation of non-bank microfinance institutions

3.1 The broad regulatory framework

The Grameen Bank

The regulatory framework facing the Grameen Bank is different to that facing other MFIs. The Grameen Bank is regulated under its own ordinance, the Grameen Bank Ordinance 1983. The ordinance specifically provides that the Banking Companies Ordinance 1962 and other laws relating to banking shall not apply to the Grameen Bank. The ordinance is administered by the Ministry of Finance, which also has a representative on the board of directors. The general direction and superintendence of the affairs and business of the Grameen Bank is entrusted to a board of directors, which consists of three persons appointed by the government and nine elected by the borrower-shareholders. The term of office for elected directors is three years.

The ordinance provides that the function of the bank will be to provide credit, with or without collateral security, to landless persons for all kinds of economic activities including housing. The ordinance specifies a range of activities that the bank may undertake, including accepting money on deposit. The bank is not permitted to transact any kind of business other than those authorised. For instance, it is not permitted to engage in foreign exchange transactions.

The ordinance provides scope for the Grameen Bank to accept deposits from the general public as well as from its members. To date, however, the bank has not done so. The ordinance also enables the bank to issue bonds and debentures, with prior approval by the government and subject to government guarantee. In the past, the government has approved and guaranteed bonds issued by the bank. However, it is intended to remove this requirement from the Act. This will increase the autonomy of the bank, and enable it to issue bonds without the prior approval of and guarantee by the government. Until now, the Grameen Bank has been exempt from business income tax under a sunset clause in the legislation.

Other microfinance institutions

The regulatory framework facing other MFIs is quite different from that facing the

Grameen Bank. As long as such MFIs do not accept deposits from the public, they are not regarded as financial institutions and are not regulated by Bangladesh Bank. Like other NGOs, they are required to be registered under one or more Acts of Parliament. These provisions apply to NGOs in general, and are not designed specifically for those involved in microfinance. While there has been some discussion about establishing a single, integrated Act under which all NGOs would be registered, this has not occurred to date.

Most NGOs are registered under the Societies Registration Act 1860, administered by the Department of Social Welfare. However, some are registered as non-profit companies under the Companies Act 1913, or under other legislation such as the Trusts Act 1882, the Charitable and Religious Trust Act 1920, or the Cooperative Societies Ordinance 1984. To be registered under the Societies Registration Act, an NGO must have a memorandum of association and rules and regulations, covering such matters as the name of the organisation, objectives, membership, managing committee and organisational structure. Registered NGOs are also required to provide an annual report and financial statements to the department. NGOs commented that these requirements are simple to fulfil and do not place any unreasonable burden on them. Requirements under the other Acts listed above are broadly similar.

Indeed, it is arguable that some of these requirements have not been administered as rigorously as they might. In particular, it was reported that there have been a number of examples of fraud by MFIs. Some MFIs have set up and obtained compulsory savings from members by promising to give them loans. However, the loans have not been forthcoming and the MFIs have absconded with members' savings. While this has not been all that widespread, a number of poor clients have lost their money. Moreover, such fraud has the potential to undermine the confidence of borrowers in the vast majority of MFIs that are operating legitimately. It is not clear if these cases could have been avoided through a stronger regulatory framework for NGOs.

In addition, all NGOs which receive foreign donations are required to be registered with the NGO Affairs Bureau, pursuant to the Foreign Donations (Voluntary Activities) Regulation Ordinance 1978. To be registered with the NGO Affairs Bureau, an NGO must provide a letter of intent from a foreign donor that it intends to provide a donation. It must also have a constitution and by-laws, and an executive committee. After the application is submitted to the NGO Affairs Bureau, the bureau must circulate it to relevant ministries, and approve or reject the application within 90 days. There are a number of forms that have to be completed, and some small NGOs may have some difficulties. However, the NGO Affairs Bureau reported that the vast majority of applications are approved.

NGOs registered under the Societies Registration Act are also required to seek approval each time before they can receive a foreign donation, including providing detailed budgets of how the funds are to be used. These applications are also circulated to relevant ministries. Relevant ministries are required to report to the NGO Affairs Bureau within 21 days, and the NGO Affairs Bureau is required to report to the NGO within 45 days of receiving the application. NGOs are also required to provide acquittals specifying the use of funds annually and when the project is completed. The larger NGOs considered that this system was relatively efficient, although some NGOs commented that the procedures could be cumbersome and bureaucratic. Where possible, these should be simplified.

Moreover, some NGOs reported that the NGO Affairs Bureau and other ministries have wide powers to regulate their activities through these approvals. Most NGOs felt that the bureau operates in a relatively flexible manner, and seeks to solve problems through discussion and negotiation rather than through arbitrary rulings. Nevertheless, it was felt that there is not always a level playing field between NGOs, and that some NGOs are able to influence the NGO Affairs Bureau to restrict the operations of their competitors.

One area of some concern is interest rates, discussed below. Another concern that was raised relates to the geographical area of operations. Some NGOs have been required to liaise with other NGOs and NGO bodies as to the coverage of their operations, or have been asked not to provide services in some areas. The NGO Affairs Bureau appears to be trying to coordinate the activities of NGOs and prevent too many MFIs from operating in the same area. While it can be argued that this reduces duplication, it also reduces competition among MFIs, the level of service provided by MFIs, and the range of options available to borrowers. Competition is a powerful incentive to ensure that MFIs meet the needs of their clients in the most cost-effective manner, and should be encouraged. The NGO Affairs Bureau should allow MFIs to operate in any area they choose.

More generally, the discretion granted to the NGO Affairs Bureau and other ministries leads to some uncertainty. It is not clear why this discretion is needed. It would appear desirable that all regulatory and prudential standards be set out clearly and transparently, and that any MFI that meets them should be free to operate without restriction.

Savings mobilisation

As noted above, the Grameen Bank is permitted to accept deposits from the general public, although to date it has not done so. Financial cooperatives are also permitted under the Cooperative Societies Ordinance of 1984 to mobilise deposits from the general public as well as members. These cooperatives are regulated by the Registrar of Cooperatives, although Carpenter (1997) notes that the registrar has little preventative or protective regulation, and conducts minimal to no supervision.

Other MFIs are not permitted to accept savings from the general public though they are allowed to accept compulsory savings from members. Carpenter (1997) reports that most MFIs hold member savings in low-risk investments, but that several large MFIs, including ASA, Buro Tangail and BRAC, use member savings to fund their lending activity.

As well, ASA, Buro Tangail and BRAC all offer facilities for voluntary savings to members. Indeed, ASA has recently started raising deposits from 'associate members', who are not group members. This facility has proved very popular. By June 1997 total voluntary savings stood at Tk11.15 million ($267,000), consisting of Tk6.37 million ($152,000) voluntary savings by group members and Tk 4.78 million ($114,000) by associate members.

3.2 Interest rates

In the case of the Grameen Bank, interest rates paid on savings and charged on loans are not regulated. There are also no general restrictions on the interest rates that other MFIs can charge. However, some NGOs reported that the NGO Affairs Bureau and other ministries have sought to influence their interest rates when approving foreign donations. The NGO Affairs Bureau does not impose any general ceiling on the interest rates that NGOs can charge. However, one NGO reported that a particular ministry had sought to impose an unrealistic interest rate ceiling on its loans, as a condition of its approval to receive foreign donations. After discussions, this condition was removed. Similar discussions have taken place with other NGOs, and in some cases NGOs have agreed to reduce their interest rates. In no case, however, has an application to receive a foreign donation been refused because the NGO in question charges an interest rate that is considered too high. Recently, the NGO Affairs Bureau has held informal discussions with some of the larger NGOs about the possibility of an overall interest rate ceiling to apply to all NGOs. However, no decision has been taken in this regard.

If there are to be ceilings on the interest rates that MFIs can charge, these should apply equally to all MFIs, should be established through consultation, and most importantly, should be sufficient to enable MFIs to operate in a sustainable manner. It is also not apparent that the NGO Affairs Bureau is the most appropriate body to administer interest rate ceilings. Moreover, it is not clear if any ceilings are necessary. Given the outreach of microfinance and large number of MFIs in Bangladesh, there is much greater scope than in other countries for competition between MFIs to keep interest rates down.

3.3 Prudential regulation and supervision

The Grameen Bank is subject to very little prudential regulation. Its regulating ordinance specifies that the authorised capital of the bank shall be Tk100 million ($2.4 million). However, decisions on capital and liquidity ratios, and loan loss provisioning, are matters for its board, and do not involve regulatory requirements. There are no reserve requirements, nor are there any regulations covering matters such as loan documentation.

Neither are reporting requirements rigorous. Under the ordinance, the bank is required to maintain proper accounts and prepare an annual statement of accounts, including a profit and loss statement and balance sheet. The accounts are required to be audited by approved auditors and must be provided to the government, together with an annual report, within three months of the end of the financial year. While the ordinance does not require the bank to provide more frequent information, it also provides monthly reports to Bangladesh Bank on disbursements, repayments, arrears and savings. It does not provide full balance sheet data as generally required of financial institutions.

There is also very little prudential regulation and supervision of other MFIs. There are no capital or liquidity requirements, or rules regarding loan loss provisioning. Nor are there any reserve requirements. Reporting requirements relate primarily to the provision of information about the use of foreign donations, although NGOs are also required to submit annual financial statements, in some cases audited by an approved auditor, to the various registering agencies and the NGO Affairs Bureau. These statements are not scrutinised with a view to the sustainability or risk of the NGOs' operations. As noted above, cooperatives are regulated by the Registrar of Cooperatives, but the registrar has little preventative or protective regulation, and conducts minimal to no supervision.

This lack of prudential and regulatory control has provided considerable scope for MFIs to develop. As noted by Carpenter (1997, p.15):

> In Bangladesh, the unique circumstances of no regulatory oversight and a large, well-funded non-governmental organisation (NGO) community have resulted in the ad hoc evolution of sophisticated and innovative MFIs seeking to alleviate poverty.

There are currently some initiatives to strengthen the regulatory framework. The World Bank poverty alleviation microfinance project provides $150,000 to the Bangladesh Bank to undertake two studies, in collaboration with the Palli Karma Sahayak Foundation (PKSF) and the MFIs. The first would look at regulatory reforms and proactive measures to enhance the linkage of MFIs with the formal financial sector. The second would study the appropriate regulatory framework and institutions for regulating and monitoring MFIs engaged in deposit taking. It would recognise the special nature of these institutions, and the fact that depositors of MFIs are usually net borrowers, which reduces the need for depositor protection.

As noted by the World Bank (1996), the accounting, management information systems and external audit policies and standards followed by the large MFIs are good and comprehensive. However, for the most part, the standards adopted by the small and medium MFIs need to be substantially upgraded. Inadequate standards are likely to threaten the long-term viability of such MFIs, potentially leading to reduced confidence in the sector as a whole. For this reason, most commentators considered that some prudential and reporting standards for MFIs are necessary. This is a more pressing issue in Bangladesh than in most other countries, given the very large number of MFIs and the scale of their operations.

There are a number of options for establishing prudential and reporting standards. One option is full prudential regulation and supervision by the Bangladesh Bank. Nevertheless, most academic commentators argue that it is unnecessary and may even be counter-productive to subject MFIs which do not accept deposits from the general public to full prudential regulation and supervision.

There would also be practical difficulties in subjecting MFIs to regulation and supervision by the Bangladesh Bank or some other regulatory agency. As noted by Carpenter:

> Bangladesh has a unique set of market conditions: the MFI industry is large, diverse and has many sophisticated institutions, and the regulatory environment and capacity are relatively weak (p.32).

There is no unit within the bank responsible for microfinance, and it is clear that the bank currently does not have a sound knowledge and understanding of the requirements of MFIs. A number of commentators argued that placing MFIs under the supervision of the bank would be likely to stifle them. Moreover, given the very large number of MFIs in Bangladesh, it would be very costly for the bank to regulate and supervise them in the same way that it regulates and supervises other financial institutions. It would have to develop very different approaches if it were to regulate and supervise MFIs in an effective manner. It would therefore seem appropriate to consider alternative means of ensuring that MFIs maintain high standards in their operations.

3.4 Performance and reporting standards of PKSF

One possibility for ensuring that MFIs operate on a sound basis is through the lending policies of PKSF. PKSF requires MFIs that borrow from it to meet certain performance and reporting standards. While there is no requirement on MFIs to adopt these standards, the opportunity to borrow from PKSF is clearly a powerful incentive for them to do so. At present, the main standards are as follows:

- It encourages MFIs to recover at least their recurring administrative and funding costs from interest income.
- It imposes a minimum lending rate of 16 per cent to ensure that MFIs do not lend below commercial bank rates, and to promote cost recovery from operations.
- It encourages MFIs with outside sources of income to set aside a portion of interest income as reserves.

- It requires all MFIs to have a savings program for members, and generally requires that these savings be kept in a bank. Only those MFIs with a good track record and high standards of financial accounting are allowed to use savings in credit programs.

In addition, it imposes a number of requirements in terms of the type of loan program that MFIs must offer to be eligible for funding. Loans must be targeted to the poor as measured by an assets test based primarily on land ownership. Borrowers must be organised into groups comprising not fewer than five members and meeting certain other criteria. And the length of loans must be one year. While these requirements are based on the experience of many successful programs, they limit the scope for flexibility and innovation in microfinance programs. PKSF should only impose standards relating to outreach to poor borrowers and standards of a prudential nature. MFIs able to meet these standards should be free to determine their own lending procedures.

PKSF also requires monthly reports from all MFIs borrowing from it, covering information on the number of loans, disbursements, loans outstanding, recovery of principal and interest, and repayment rates. It monitors repayment rates (measured as repayments collected as a percentage of repayments due), and seeks to ensure that repayment rates remain above 98 per cent. NGOs borrowing from PKSF reported that PKSF is active in following up on these reports. It visits all borrowing MFIs at least four times a year for on-site inspections. NGOs reported that these inspections were very rigorous, although PKSF itself reported that some small borrowers did not currently meet all its requirements to its satisfaction. It audits each borrower MFI once a year, and in addition PKSF's external auditor audits one third of these MFIs each year.

The World Bank poverty alleviation microfinance project provides for further refinement of these standards, and it is envisaged that MFIs will only be eligible for support if they meet these criteria. In particular, PKSF is to receive technical assistance to establish:

- Standards for loan classification and provisioning. Draft standards were released in early 1997. Broadly, the draft standards provide for a provision of 50 per cent of the outstanding balance for doubtful loans (all loans past expiry which have not been paid off), and 100 per cent of the outstanding balance for bad loans (all loans one year or more past expiry which have not been paid off).
- Standards for savings facilities. Draft standards were expected to be released in 1997.
- Uniform accounting policies in respect of reporting repayment rates, arrears, rescheduling, portfolio quality, etc., and audit standards.
- Standards for measuring MFIs' progress in terms of sustainability.
- In the case of multi-purpose NGOs, guidelines for measuring and separating the costs of delivering financial and non-financial services.

These are all critical areas, and the standards being developed will provide an important benchmark for MFIs in Bangladesh. Moreover, since Bangladesh is at the forefront in developing standards in these areas, the results of the project will be of considerable interest in other countries. PKSF should consult widely with both MFIs and technical experts in developing these and other performance and reporting standards, to ensure that they are appropriate to the needs and circumstances of MFIs, and that they are accepted as such by the MFIs. It is also important that regulatory approaches be coordinated. Any moves to establish legally binding prudential standards, or standards for self-regulation, should be carefully coordinated and consistent with the standards currently being developed by PKSF.

3.5 Self-regulation

Coordination between MFIs is important for a number of reasons, including information exchange, training, research, and policy dialogue with government and donor agencies. Where there are effective mechanisms for coordination, it may also be possible to establish a system of self-regulation. Self-regulation may take a wide variety of forms, ranging from a voluntary code of conduct to which MFIs agree to adhere, to a rigorous licensing system administered by an apex body and backed by the force of law. In between, there is a wide variety of possibilities with varying degrees of monitoring and compulsion. The feasibility of various forms of self-regulation depends on a range of factors, including the extent to which there is an apex body that can represent MFIs as a whole, the amount of resources available for monitoring and supervision, and the availability of incentives and/or sanctions to enforce compliance. Self-regulation could be an alternative to, or could supplement and support, performance and reporting standards established by a second tier institution such as PKSF.

The major networking organisation for MFIs in Bangladesh is the Credit and Development Forum (CDF), which was established in 1992. It has a number of objectives including:

- developing effective savings and credit management systems for MFIs
- providing training and technical assistance for the improvement of savings and credit management, and monitoring and evaluation systems
- developing a data bank and resource centre for savings- and credit-related information
- developing linkages between NGOs, donor agencies and government institutions
- working as a networking and policy advocacy forum
- holding seminars and workshops
- undertaking operational research on savings and credit activities.

CDF currently has 662 members. It includes most major MFIs, excluding Grameen Bank itself (which is not an NGO) and Swanirvar Bangladesh. BRAC, ASA and Proshika are all members. It has nine staff, and administrative costs are funded through the Swiss Development Cooperation (although CDF levies small membership fees and user charges). To date, its main function has been to provide training courses. Nevertheless, it has held discussions with Bangladesh Bank on policy issues, and has also held discussions with Sonali Bank and Bangladesh Krishi Bank about establishing linkages with MFIs. It has also received funding from the Consultative Group to Assist the Poorest (CGAP) to undertake ten case studies concerning different aspects of microfinance.

CDF is making significant progress in a number of important areas. Nevertheless, there is clearly no consensus on policy and other issues among the major MFIs operating in Bangladesh, and this limits the ability of CDF to serve as an apex body for the industry in policy dialogue with government, Bangladesh Bank and other bodies. To date, CDF has not been actively involved in trying to establish standards for self-regulation of the microfinance sector. While it could play a useful role in developing a voluntary code of conduct or similar mechanism for self-regulation, it would not appear at this stage to have the resources or the authority to enforce a more rigorous model of self-regulation based on compulsion.

There would be major advantages in strengthening CDF to become an apex body able to effectively represent all the MFIs in the country. This is especially important now that issues such as policy dialogue and prudential and reporting standards are coming increasingly to the fore. While the current divisions may be difficult to overcome, it is important that every effort be made to do so. Those MFIs that are not currently members of CDF or actively involved in its activities should be encouraged to increase their involvement.

4 Regulation of banks

4.1 Licensing and minimum capital requirements

Microfinance institutions (MFIs) are free to operate in a relatively unregulated environment so long as they do not accept deposits from the general public. However, the Banking Companies Act 1991 provides that in order to accept deposits from the general public, an institution must be registered with Bangladesh Bank as a banking institution. Hence, other than the Grameen Bank, which is established as a specialised development bank, MFIs are not allowed to mobilise deposits from the general public.

To obtain a licence as a commercial bank under the Banking Companies Act, it is necessary to have a minimum paid-up capital of Tk200 million ($4.8 million) and meet certain other criteria. Moreover, even if an institution meets all of these criteria, it will not necessarily be able to obtain a banking licence. For instance, BRAC has been trying to obtain a banking licence for some time, but has not been able to obtain one as yet. It is understood that this reflects a desire to limit the number of banks, rather than any deficiencies in BRAC's application. Unlike the situation in most other countries included in this study, there is also no substructure of small regulated banks such as rural banks operating in localised areas at the grassroots level.

These factors may help to explain why regulated banks in Bangladesh have very little involvement in microfinance compared to most other countries in the study. The high minimum capital requirement and other restrictions make it very difficult both for MFIs to establish banks in order to offer full deposit services and increase their access to funds, and for other parties to establish small microfinance banks to operate in localised areas. Experience in other countries suggests that small banks are much more likely to become involved in microfinance than large banks, and that if banks are to play an active role in microfinance it is essential that there be some mechanism to enable small banks to be licensed.

It would therefore be appropriate to establish a framework for licensing small banks, with realistic minimum capital requirements and without other restrictions which may prevent their establishment. In this regard, the experience of countries such as Indonesia and the Philippines may be instructive (see the Indonesia and Philippines country studies).

4.2 Interest rates

As noted above, loans by banks to small-scale cottage industries are subject to an interest rate ceiling of 12 per cent. While such loans are eligible for an interest subsidy from the government or refinancing by the Bangladesh Bank, this does not compensate them for the high administrative costs inherent in small loans to poor borrowers. This ceiling would make it extremely difficult if not impossible for any MFI which established a regulated bank to cover its costs. It would also make it almost impossible for any existing commercial bank to provide loans to poor borrowers on a commercial basis.

In addition to the minimum capital requirement and other restrictions discussed above, these ceilings are a major barrier to regulated banks becoming involved in microfinance. It would be appropriate to remove the interest rate ceiling on loans to small-scale cottage industries and the other remaining ceilings on the interest rates that commercial banks are permitted to charge.

4.3 Prudential regulation and supervision

Commercial banks are subject to a capital adequacy ratio of 8 per cent of risk-weighted assets, and a liquidity ratio of 20 per cent of total demand and time liabilities, including a cash reserve requirement of 5 per cent. Banks are also subject to frequent reporting requirements, as frequent as fortnightly in some cases, and to rules on loan loss provisioning, although the latter are not as strict as those recommended in the Basle Accord. There are no regulations affecting banks in terms of the loan documentation that they maintain, or what they may accept as collateral/security. These requirements would not appear to impose any undue restrictions on small banks or banks engaged in microfinance, although it would be appropriate to review them if more permissive rules for licensing small banks were introduced.

5 Summary and recommendations

Bangladesh is one of the poorest countries in the world, with an annual per capita income estimated at $240 in 1995. Bangladesh also performs poorly in terms of indicators of human development, such as life expectancy, infant mortality and educational attainment. Poverty is pervasive, with an estimated 47.5 per cent of the population below the absolute poverty line in 1991–92.

The commercial banks engage in little if any lending that could properly be considered microfinance. However, specialist microfinance institutions (MFIs) operate on a huge scale in Bangladesh. Of an estimated 10 million microfinance clients in the world today, no fewer than 6 million are in Bangladesh, representing not less than one in four rural households in the country. Many of the principles and techniques of microfinance that have become standard throughout the world were pioneered by the Grameen Bank. These factors make Bangladesh the logical starting point for any study of microfinance.

Arrangements for direct support

Target MFI support for increased outreach and sustainability

The government of Bangladesh and various donor agencies have provided considerable direct support to microfinance. In the past, the government and donor agencies have supported individual MFIs, largely on an ad hoc basis. While this support has generally been effective, it would be appropriate to target future support more explicitly to increasing outreach and sustainability. Donor agencies should ensure that their support for MFIs is consistent with the Guiding Principles for Selecting and Supporting Intermediaries, agreed by major donor agencies in October 1995 (Committee of Donor Agencies 1995).

Channel support for microfinance through PKSF

Much support is now being channelled through the Palli Karma Sahayak Foundation (PKSF), which then on-lends to individual MFIs at concessional interest rates. The increasing role of the PKSF is a very positive development, enabling support for MFIs to be based on a consistent set of standards and procedures. Bilateral and multilateral donor agencies should channel their support for microfinance through PKSF as much as possible. At present, PKSF only provides soft loans to MFIs for on-lending to final borrowers. If sufficient funds can be made available, it should expand the range of support that it provides to include grants and soft loans for scaling-up operations, institutional strengthening and increasing equity, based on appropriate criteria.

Phase out government-administered microfinance programs

The government has itself administered a number of microfinance projects, most notably through the Bangladesh Rural Development Board (BRDB). While some of these programs have been quite successful, microfinance programs administered directly by government agencies are unlikely to be as cost-effective as those administered by non-government MFIs. They should be phased out unless it can be shown that they are as cost-effective, in terms of maximising outreach and sustainability, as programs of well-managed MFIs.

Issue clear guidelines for bank-MFI linkages

Bangladesh is unusual in that it does not have any directed credit schemes or significant government programs for microfinance channelled through the banking system. Such schemes have not been successful in other countries. Supporting specialist MFIs is a much more effective means of providing financial services to the poor. On the other hand, one potential avenue for MFIs to access loanable funds is to obtain loans or lines of credit from commercial banks. The Bangladesh Bank should issue clear guidelines that the banks can follow to encourage linkages between banks and MFIs.

Avoid debt forgiveness

The decision by the government in 1991 to forgive all agricultural loans up to Tk5,000 ($120) created major problems for the Grameen Bank and other MFIs who did not forgive their loans. The government should avoid debt forgiveness for small loans and any other policies which may have unintended adverse effects on MFIs.

Regulation of non-bank microfinance institutions

Avoid unnecessary restriction of MFIs

Non-governmental organisations (NGOs) engaged in microfinance are subject to a number of regulatory requirements of a non-prudential nature. In most cases, these are relatively simple to fulfil. However, the process for approving foreign donations gives the NGO Affairs Bureau and other ministries wide powers to regulate the activities of MFIs seeking foreign donations. In general, these powers have not been used in a restrictive manner, but there are some areas of concern.

The NGO Affairs Bureau should not try to coordinate the geographical coverage of MFIs, but should allow MFIs to operate in any area they choose. The discretionary power of the NGO Affairs Bureau and other ministries should also be limited. All regulatory and prudential standards should be set out clearly and transparently, and all MFIs that meet these standards should be free to operate without restriction.

Avoid interest rate restriction

While there are no general restrictions on the interest rates that MFIs can charge, the NGO Affairs Bureau and other ministries have on some occasions sought to influence interest rates through the foreign donations approval process. Any ceilings should apply equally to all MFIs, should be established through consultation, and should be sufficient to enable

MFIs to operate in a sustainable manner. It is also not clear if ceilings are necessary, given the large number of MFIs in Bangladesh and the scope for competition.

Neither the Grameen Bank nor other MFIs are subject to any real prudential supervision. There are no requirements for minimum paid-up capital, nor any required capital adequacy ratio. MFIs are not required to maintain reserves with any regulatory agency, nor are there any regulations concerning matters such as liquidity or loan loss provisioning. While there are some reporting requirements, these relate solely to the preparation of annual financial statements and are not specifically designed for NGOs engaged in microfinance.

Develop appropriate benchmark standards for MFIs

This unregulated environment has contributed to the development of microfinance. Some standards are now necessary, given the very large number of MFIs in Bangladesh and the scale of their operations. However, full prudential regulation and supervision by the Bangladesh Bank would not be appropriate or practical.

A more promising mechanism for ensuring that MFIs operate on a sound basis is through the lending policies of PKSF. PKSF already requires MFIs that borrow from it to meet certain performance and reporting standards, and the World Bank poverty alleviation microfinance project provides for further development and refinement of these standards. The standards being developed will provide an important benchmark for MFIs in Bangladesh, and PKSF should consult widely with both MFIs and technical experts in developing them. PKSF should only impose standards relating to outreach to poor borrowers and standards of a prudential nature, with MFIs able to meet these standards free to determine their own lending procedures.

Strengthen CDF to become national apex body

Coordination between MFIs is important for a number of reasons, including information exchange, training, research, policy dialogue with government and donor agencies, and self-regulation. While the Credit and Development Forum (CDF) is making significant progress in a number of important areas, there is currently no consensus on key issues among the major MFIs. There would be major advantages in strengthening CDF to become an apex body able to effectively represent all the MFIs in the country. Those MFIs that are not currently members of CDF or actively involved in its activities should increase their involvement.

Ensure consistency between CDF and PKSF standards

It is also important that regulatory approaches be coordinated. Any moves to establish legally binding prudential standards, or moves by CDF or some other body to establish standards for self-regulation, should be carefully coordinated and consistent with the standards currently being developed by PKSF.

Regulation of banks

The Banking Companies Act 1991 provides that in order to accept deposits from the general public, an institution must be registered with Bangladesh Bank as a banking institution. Hence, other than the Grameen Bank, which is established as a specialised development bank, MFIs are not allowed to mobilise deposits from the general public.

Establish framework for licensing small banks

High minimum capital requirements and other restrictions make it very difficult both for MFIs to establish regulated banks in order to offer full deposit services and increase their access to funds, and for other parties to establish small microfinance banks to operate in localised areas. This is a major impediment to regulated banks engaging in microfinance. The government should establish a framework for licensing small banks, specifying realistic minimum capital requirements and removing other restrictions which may prevent their establishment. In this regard, the experiences of countries such as Indonesia and the Philippines may be instructive.

Remove interest rate ceilings for commercial banks

The 12 per cent interest rate ceiling on loans by banks to small-scale cottage industries also makes it extremely difficult if not impossible for regulated banks to provide loans to poor borrowers on a commercial basis. The government should remove this ceiling and the other remaining ceilings on the interest rates that commercial banks can charge.

References

Bangladesh Bureau of Statistics. 1995. *Report on the Household Expenditure Survey, 1991–92*. Dhaka, Bangladesh Bureau of Statistics.

Carpenter, Janney. 1997. 'Bangladesh'. In *Regulation and Supervision of Microfinance Institutions: Case Studies*, ed. Craig Churchill. Occasional paper no.2, The Microfinance Network, Washington D.C.

Hossain, Iftekhar & Sakhawat, Javed. 1996. *Microfinance Capacity Assessment Study: Bangladesh*. Asian and Pacific Development Centre, Kuala Lumpur.

Khandker, Shahidur R., Khalily, Baqui & Khan, Zahed. 1995a. *Grameen Bank: Performance and Sustainability*. Discussion paper no.306, World Bank, Washington D.C.

Khandker, Shahidur R., Khan, Zahed & Khalily, Baqui. 1995b. *Sustainability of a Government Targeted Credit Program: Evidence from Bangladesh*. Discussion paper no.316, World Bank, Washington D.C.

Khandker, Shahidur R. & Khalily, Baqui. 1996, *The Bangladesh Rural Advancement Committee's Credit Programs: Performance and Sustainability*. Discussion paper no.324, World Bank, Washington D.C.

Rahman, Pk Md Motiur. 1995. Poverty alleviation: Government and non-government organisational interventions. Unpublished paper, 49pp.

Ravallion, Martin & Sen, Binayak. 1996, 'When method matters: monitoring poverty in Bangladesh'. *Economic Development and Cultural Change*, pp.761–792.

Rutherford, Stuart. 1997. 'Executive summary of microfinance capacity assessment in Bangladesh'. In *Creating the Vision: Microfinancing the Poor in Asia-Pacific: Issues, Constraints and Capacity-Building*, eds I. Getubig, J. Remenyi & B. Quinones. Asian and Pacific Development Centre, Kuala Lumpur.

Shand, Ric & Alauddin, Mohammad. 1997. *Economic Profiles in South Asia: Bangladesh*. Australia South Asia Research Centre, Australian National University, Canberra.

World Bank. 1996. *Staff Appraisal Report: Bangladesh Poverty Alleviation Microfinance Project*. Report no.15431–BD, World Bank, Washington D.C.

Persons consulted

Dr Rushidan Rahman	Senior Research Fellow Bangladesh Institute of Development Studies
Dr Binayak Sen	Research Fellow Bangladesh Institute of Development Studies
Mr Aminul Alam	Director, Rural Development Program Bangladesh Rural Advancement Committee
Mr Md Atiqun Nabi	Program Manager, Rural Development Program Bangladesh Rural Advancement Committee
Mr Md Khalid Shams	Deputy Managing Director Grameen Bank
Mr Mufazzel Hossain	Director General Bangladesh Rural Development Board
Mr Charles Stuart	High Commissioner Australian High Commission, Dhaka
Ms Roushan Akhter	Senior Development Officer Australian Agency for International Development
Dr Humaira Islam	Executive Director Shakti Foundation
Professor Syed M. Hashemi	Project Director, Programme for Research on Poverty Alleviation, Grameen Trust
Mr Md S. H. Choudhury	Chief Executive Association for Social Advancement
Mr K. Javed Sakhawat	Managing Director Associates for Development Initiatives
Mr S. M Al-Husainy	Chairman Swanirvar Bangladesh
Mr Salah Uddin Ahmed	Secretary General Swanirvar Bangladesh
Mr A. B. M. G. Kibria	Member, Executive Committee Swanirvar Bangladesh
Mr Humayun Kabir	Member, Executive Committee Swanirvar Bangladesh
Dr Tarafder R. Islam	Member, Executive Committee Swanirvar Bangladesh
Mr Md Moksud Alam	Chief Executive Swanirvar Bangladesh
Mr Azharul Huq Chowdhury	Project Coordinator Swanirvar Bangladesh
Dr Md Youssuf Ali	Project Director, Small Holder Livestock Development Project, Swanirvar Bangladesh
Mr Humayun Kabir	Project Secretary, Credit Programme Swanirvar Bangladesh
Mr Md Shafiqul Haque	Administrative Officer Swanirvar Bangladesh

Mr Md Mosharrof Hossain	Secretary Swanirvar Workers' Trust
Mr Mahbubur Rahman Khan	Training Coordinator Swanirvar Bangladesh
Ms Shebika Sarkar	Coordinator, Management Information Systems Swanirvar Bangladesh
Mr Suhel Ahmed Choudhury	Director General NGO Affairs Bureau
Mr Iftekhar Hossain	Partner Acnabin & Co
Mr Sukhendra K. Sarkar	Chairman Credit and Development Forum
Mr P. K. Bagchi	Program Coordinator Credit and Development Forum
Mr Lutfar Rahman Sarkar	Governor Bangladesh Bank
Dr Sohrab Uddin	Deputy Governor Bangladesh Bank
Mr Md Buzruch Meher	General Manager, Agricultural Credit Department Bangladesh Bank
Mr Md Hafizuddin	Deputy General Manager, Agricultural Credit Project Department, Bangladesh Bank
Mr Owaise Saadat	The World Bank
Dr Francis B. Narayan	Senior Programs Officer Asian Development Bank
Mr Rezaul Karim Khan	Economist Asian Development Bank
Mr A. B. M. Mahbubul A. Khan	Former Deputy Governor Bangladesh Bank
Syed Amirul Mulk	Secretary, Banking Division Ministry of Finance
Dr Salehuddin Ahmed	Managing Director Palli Karma Sahayak Foundation
Mr Khondkar I. Khaled	Managing Director Sonali Bank
Mr Golam Mustafa	Managing Director Janata Bank
Mr Md Shamsuzzoha	General Manager Janata Bank
Mr A. H. M. Helaluddin	Assistant General Manager, Rural Credit Division Janata Bank
Mr Md Masuduzzaman	Senior Principal Officer, Rural Credit Division Janata Bank

India

1 Introduction and background

1.1 Key demographic and economic data

India is the largest country in South Asia covering an area of some 3.288 million square kilometres. Southern India is surrounded by the Arabian Sea and Indian Ocean, whereas the northern part shares borders with Pakistan, China, Nepal, Bhutan, Myanmar and Bangladesh. With a population of 929.4 million in 1995, it is the second most populated country in the world. It accounts for around 60 per cent of the total population of the nine countries in this study and 16 per cent of the world's population. The population density is 283 people per square kilometre, the second highest of the nine countries included in this study, although it has only one third the population density of Bangladesh. Population growth has slowed considerably in recent years, averaging 1.8 per cent per year between 1990 and 1995. Nevertheless, the total fertility rate at 3.2 births per woman in 1995 remains well above replacement.

Income per capita stood at $340 in 1995, above Bangladesh and Nepal but well below the other countries included in the study. After relatively slow growth over much of the period since 1950, India has achieved respectable economic growth in recent years, with income per capita increasing by 3.2 per cent per year between 1985 and 1995. This is the highest growth rate in South Asia but well below the dynamic Southeast Asian countries of Indonesia, Malaysia and Thailand. The structure of production has changed somewhat with economic growth, with the share of agriculture in GDP falling from 38 per cent in 1980 to 29 per cent in 1995, and the shares of industry and services increasing modestly.

Social indicators of development also remain poor, with India classified as a low human development country by UNDP. In 1995 life expectancy at birth was 62 years and the infant mortality rate was 68 per 1,000 live births, similar to the average for all low-income countries. Only 52 per cent of adults were literate. Moreover, there is a significant gender gap with respect to many indicators, particularly those relating to education and employment.

1.2 Poverty

Estimates of poverty

Poverty reduction has been a major concern of the government since independence, and India has one of the longest series of national household surveys for tracking the living conditions of the poor. Official estimates of poverty are produced by the Planning Commission, based on regular surveys of household consumption expenditure carried out by the National Sample Survey Organisation. A recent World Bank research project (World Bank 1997) assembled and analysed 35 rounds of the survey, covering the period from 1951 to 1993–94.

The official poverty line has been established on the basis of consumption data from the 1973–74 household survey. It is based on a daily calorie intake of 2,400 calories per capita in rural areas, and 2,100 calories per capita in urban areas. The poverty line was set equal to the level of total expenditure, on both food and non-food items, at which this daily minimum was just met. Since 1973–74, the poverty lines so derived have been indexed by movements in the consumer price index, disaggregated by rural and urban sectors.

In 1993, the Planning Commission established the Expert Group on Estimation of Proportion and Number of Poor, which recommended two broad sets of changes to the methodology used for estimating the number of people in poverty. First, it recommended that the poverty line should be adjusted to take account of differences in the cost of living in each state. Second, it noted there has long been a discrepancy between the estimates of consumption in the household survey and in the national accounts, with the national accounts consistently showing a higher level of consumption. Moreover, the gap has been increasing over time. In the past, when estimating the incidence of poverty, the Planning Commission would adjust upwards the estimates of consumption in the household survey proportionately for all consumption classes, so that total consumption was consistent with the national accounts estimate. Using this method, it was estimated that only 16.8 per cent of the population was below the poverty line in 1993–94. The Expert Group found that this adjustment was arbitrary and led to poverty being significantly understated, and recommended that it be discontinued.

The Planning Commission has recently adopted the Expert Group's recommendations. Based on the new methodology, it is estimated that 35.0 per cent of the population was below the poverty line in 1993–94. The incidence of poverty was slightly higher in the rural areas (36.7 per cent) than in the urban areas (30.5 per cent).

The percentage incidence of poverty has declined significantly since the 1950s. The World Bank (1997) notes three phases in the evolution of poverty:

(1) From the early 1950s to the early 1970s there were fluctuations in the incidence of poverty, but no clear trend in either direction. The percentage of people in poverty was around 53 per cent between 1951 and 1955, and about the same percentage between 1970 and 1974.

(2) From 1971 to 1986–87 the incidence of poverty declined steadily, from around 53 per cent in 1971 to around 38 per cent by 1986–87.

(3) Poverty appears to have entered a new phase of fluctuations since 1986–87, with the incidence of poverty varying between 34 and 41 per cent, but with no clear trend.

While the incidence of poverty has clearly declined over the longer term, the recent stabilisation at 35 to 40 per cent is a cause for concern. Moreover, the decline in the proportion of people living in poverty has been slow, and has been insufficient to prevent large increases in the absolute number of people in poverty. The World Bank notes that the absolute number of poor has increased from around 200 million in the 1950s to 312 million in 1993–94, by far the largest number in any country in the world. The huge number of people in poverty increases the urgency of ensuring an effective policy framework for poverty reduction.

The incidence of poverty differs significantly by state. In Bihar, 63.5 per cent of the rural population was below the poverty line in 1993–94. Other states with high incidences of poverty include Orissa, Assam, Uttar Pradesh and Madhya Pradesh, and there are also major differences between regions within states. A survey by the National Council of

Applied Economic Research also found that rural poverty is much higher among the landless (52 per cent) than among landowners (31 per cent), with 68 per cent of landless wage earners below the poverty line. Other groups with high rates of poverty include scheduled castes and tribes (50 per cent) and households in which all members are illiterate (45 per cent).

Policies for poverty reduction

India has a three-pronged strategy for poverty eradication. First, the strategy emphasises economic growth. India's experience between the early 1950s and early 1970s, when GDP per capita increased by around 1.5 per cent per annum but the incidence of poverty remained constant, led to widespread scepticism regarding the role of economic growth in reducing poverty. However, it is now considered that economic growth can contribute to lasting poverty reduction so long as it is combined with effective policies in other areas. Second, policies for human development play a critical role, with an emphasis on health, education and minimum needs. Third, there are a number of directly targeted programs for poverty alleviation. This brief description focuses on these programs.

The World Bank (1997) notes that there is a wide range of programs financed through the central and state budgets. The share of the central budget devoted to anti-poverty programs increased from around 5.4 per cent in 1990–91 to 7.7 per cent in 1995–96, with spending by state governments contributing an additional 25 to 50 per cent of the amount spent from the central budget. The main types of programs are food subsidies, wage employment and infrastructure development programs, self-employment and income-generation programs, social welfare and nutrition programs, and programs for the welfare of scheduled castes and scheduled tribes.

The major food subsidy program is the Public Distribution System (PDS), which distributes rice, wheat, edible oil, kerosene and sugar at subsidised prices through a network of 400,000 fair price shops throughout India. Subsidies in the PDS represent around 0.5 per cent of GDP. The program is available to anyone with a ration card, and there is evidence that the poor are no more likely to benefit from the PDS than middle class consumers. The government has recently announced reforms to the PDS to ensure that a higher proportion of benefits go to the poor.

The main program for wage employment and infrastructure development is Jawahar Rozgar Yojana (JRY), which has been in operation since 1989. Its primary objective is the creation of additional gainful employment for the unemployed and underemployed in the rural areas. The secondary objective is the creation of rural infrastructure and assets in favour of the rural poor. It is a self-targeting program, based on the premise that only the poor will come forward for manual work at the minimum wage for agricultural labourers. Nevertheless, preference is given to scheduled castes and tribes, freed bonded labour and women. JRY has a number of elements, including the Indira Awaas Yojana for the provision of rural housing free of cost to the shelterless poor, the Million Wells Scheme which provides open irrigation wells free of cost to poor, small and marginal farmers, and the Employment Assurance Scheme which provides additional resources in areas with a high concentration of poverty and underemployment. Recent studies have pointed to a number of problems with the JRY, including poor targeting and a bias in favour of male employment.

Special programs for self-employment and income generation have been an integral part of the government's strategy for poverty alleviation since the sixth five-year plan, which began in 1982. During the eighth five-year plan from April 1992 to March 1997, more than Rs300 billion ($8.3 billion) was earmarked for self-employment schemes. This money has been used both for financing the grant element in government microfinance schemes such as the Integrated Rural Development Programme (IRDP), and for providing training and other support services for people below the poverty line. The IRDP is described in more detail in the section on direct support for microfinance.

1.3 Overview of the financial system

As at March 1996, the banking sector in India included some 27 nationalised commercial banks, 35 domestic private commercial banks and 29 foreign banks, with a combined total of nearly 33,000 branches. Most of these were branches of the nationalised commercial banks, which have by far the largest outreach in the rural areas.

In addition, there were 196 regional rural banks with nearly 15,000 branches. These were established in the late 1970s as subsidiaries of the public sector commercial banks, specifically to meet the credit requirements of the poor, such as small and marginal farmers, landless workers, artisans and small entrepreneurs. There is also a network of cooperative banks. There are 28 state cooperative banks with around 650 branches and 361 district cooperative banks with nearly 11,000 branches, as well as urban cooperative banks operating in the urban areas.

All of these institutions are subject to prudential regulation by the Reserve Bank of India under the Banking Regulation Act of 1949. In the case of commercial banks and urban cooperative banks, supervision is carried out directly by the Reserve Bank. In the case of regional rural banks and rural cooperative banks, supervision is carried out by the National Bank for Agriculture and Rural Development (NABARD), which was established by the Reserve Bank in 1982 as an apex body for rural credit.

In recent years, there has been considerable reform and deregulation of the financial system. Reserve and liquidity requirements, which were previously extremely high, have been reduced significantly since 1991. In the past interest rates were highly regulated, but they have now been largely deregulated. Commercial banks are subject to interest rate ceilings of 12.0 per cent on loans below Rs25,000 ($690), and 13.5 per cent on loans between Rs25,000 ($690) and Rs200,000 ($5,560). Larger loans are not subject to interest rate ceilings. In 1995 interest rates on loans averaged 16.3 per cent, about 4 percentage points above the inflation rate. No interest rate ceilings apply to loans by regional rural banks or cooperative banks. In the case of deposits, term deposits of between 30 days and one year are subject to a minimum interest rate of 2 per cent below the bank rate. Interest rates on other deposits are deregulated. The Reserve Bank has also introduced prudential norms and regulations relating to income recognition, asset classification, provisioning for bad and doubtful debts, and capital adequacy.

Nevertheless, in some respects the system remains highly regulated. The nationalised commercial banks, regional rural banks and most cooperative banks remain under government ownership and control. There is also considerable reliance on directed credit, with all commercial banks and regional rural banks required to lend 40 per cent of net bank credit to priority sectors. On balance, however, macroeconomic data indicate that the financial system is reasonably well developed, with a ratio of money and quasi money to GDP of 46.0 per cent in 1995. This is significantly higher than for any other country in South Asia, but well below the levels in Malaysia and Thailand.

1.4 Overview of microfinance

The government has expressed a strong commitment to microfinance as a means of reducing poverty. At the Microcredit Summit in February 1997, it announced that India could easily have a share of 25 million in the overall target of 100 million poor families to be reached by microfinance by 2005. It estimated that this would require credit of Rs150 billion ($4.2 billion) over nine years. It also commented that while no difficulty was envisaged in finding resources of this order, the availability of NGOs capable of delivering microfinance successfully was likely to pose a major challenge. It called for support for donor agencies in meeting this challenge. The government also announced that it would set up a Policy Advisory Group, headed by the founder of SEWA Bank, Ms Ela Bhatt, to advise the Ministry of Industry on how to create a conducive policy framework for microfinance.

By far the largest microfinance program in India is the IRDP. The scheme involves loans to poor borrowers through the banking system, with a subsidy paid to the borrowers by the government. To date, the program has provided loans to over 49 million families, with between 2 and 2.5 million loans provided annually in recent years. The program has been criticised for poor targeting of borrowers, and suffers from very low repayment rates in the region of 30 per cent.

In addition, there are three major types of institutions devoted specifically to providing microfinance to the poor. The most important in terms of numbers of the poor reached are self-help groups (SHGs). SHGs are based primarily on the principle of lending their members' savings, but they also seek external financing to augment the savings of their members. An important source of such financing is through linkages between banks and SHGs under the NABARD pilot program launched in 1992. Other government agencies, such as Rashtriya Mahila Kosh (RMK) and the Small Industries Development Bank of India (SIDBI), have established programs for lending to non-governmental organisations (NGOs) for on-lending to SHGs. To date, these three programs have provided loans to SHGs with a total membership of around 370,000 households. In all of these programs, NGOs play an active role either as direct financial intermediaries, or as non-financial intermediaries that promote and train the SHGs.

The cooperative movement contributes a second category of MFIs. Around 90,000 primary agricultural credit societies operate at the village level and advance loans for productive purposes. They receive loan funds from the district central cooperative banks, which in turn are supported by the state cooperative banks. In addition, there are urban cooperative banks which operate in urban areas. Most of the primary agricultural credit societies are reported to be non-functional, due to financial mismanagement, failure to mobilise village-level savings and inability to recover dues (EDA Rural Systems 1996b). Even where they are functional, management is dominated by rural elites in collusion with local government officials, with funds allocated on the basis of patronage rather than needs. EDA Rural Systems (1996b) report that in 1991–92 the poor (that is, tenant farmers, share croppers and landless workers) received only 5.1 per cent of all loans advanced by the primary agricultural cooperative societies. Nevertheless, there is a small number of highly successful cooperative banks and societies which are devoted specifically to providing financial services to the poor, such as SEWA Bank and Working Women's Forum.

Third, there are a number of Grameen Bank replications following the methodology developed by the Grameen Bank in Bangladesh, based on individual lending but with group guarantees. Grameen Bank replications are not as widespread as in some other countries, with no more than eight to ten NGOs in India known to be following this model.

The overall outreach of microfinance remains very low compared to the number of people living in poverty. As noted above, around 2 million to 2.5 million borrowers per year are assisted under the IRDP. Because of the nature of the program and the very low repayment rates, the program operates essentially as a one-off grant rather than as a mechanism to provide financial services to the poor over an extended period of time. While the overall outreach of the NGOs, SHGs and cooperatives is not known, it is unlikely that the total outreach of genuine microfinance programs to poor borrowers is significantly more than 500,000. Hence, there remains a huge unmet demand for microfinance. Expanding outreach dramatically is clearly the major challenge facing the sector.

This, in turn, requires microfinance programs to operate on a more sustainable basis than they do at present. Currently, most microfinance programs operate with a large degree of subsidy and do not have definite plans for achieving self-sufficiency. Most notably, the IRDP is clearly not financially viable, imposing heavy costs on the government and on the banking system. Even the programs operated by apex bodies such as NABARD and RMK are not sustainable in their current form. In particular, the mark-ups under these programs do not provide a sufficient margin for NGOs to recover the costs of forming and motivating SHGs, and NGOs are only able to participate in the programs where they obtain donor funds to subsidise these activities. On the other hand a small number of institutions, such as SEWA Bank and some of the Grameen Bank replicators, are close to self-sufficiency or have plans for attaining self-sufficiency.

2 Arrangements for direct support

2.1 Support for specialised microfinance institutions

The government has provided considerable support to specialised MFIs through the second tier microfinance institutions. Essentially, these institutions channel funds to specialised MFIs at concessional interest rates. The three major second tier institutions are Rashtriya Mahila Kosh (RMK), the Small Industries Development Bank of India (SIDBI) and NABARD.

Rashtriya Mahila Kosh

The largest of the three programs is that operated by RMK. RMK was established by the government in 1993 with a corpus fund of Rs310 million ($8.6 million), and is registered as a society in Delhi. It is managed by a governing board appointed by the government, consisting of ten government officials and seven representatives from the NGO community. In addition the general body, which includes all the NGO partner organisations, meets once a year to exchange experiences and advise on policy matters.

RMK provides loans to NGOs for on-lending to poor women. It also channels funds through women's development corporations and cooperative societies. In most cases, these partner organisations lend to SHGs, although in a small number of cases they lend direct to final borrowers. Loans must be means tested, with borrowers in rural areas required to have a family income of Rs11,000 ($310) per annum or less, and borrowers in urban areas required to have a family income of Rs11,800 ($330) or less. Loans must be provided for income-generating activities, to a maximum of Rs4,000 ($110) for short-term loans (6 to 15 months) and Rs6,000 ($170) for medium-term loans (2 to 5 years).

The interest rate charged by RMK to partner organisations is 8 per cent, and they are required to lend to SHGs at 12 per cent. SHGs must lend to members at no more than the unsecured lending rate charged by state commercial banks, currently 18.75 per cent. Hence, the margin available to partner organisations is only 4 percentage points. However, they are able to obtain some interest rate relief from RMK. If they disburse loans to final borrowers within 30 days of receiving the funds from RMK, they receive relief of 1 per cent of the loan amount. If they repay their loan to RMK on time, they receive relief of a further 0.5 per cent of the loan amount. They are also eligible for a subsidy of 1 per cent of the loan amount for training SHGs. Hence, if they meet these conditions, the effective interest rate from RMK to partner organisations is 5.5 per cent, providing a margin of 6.5 percentage points to the partner organisation.

By March 1997, RMK had sanctioned loans of Rs351 million ($9.8 million) to 170 NGOs. These credit facilities are expected to benefit 190,000 women. Rs205 million ($5.7 million) had already been disbursed. RMK plans to reach 1 million borrowers during the ninth plan period from 1997 to 2002. The cumulative repayment rate on loans from RMK to partner organisations is currently 95.0 per cent. RMK does not monitor repayment rates on loans by partners to SHGs or individuals.

RMK also provides support to microfinance in other ways. It offers interest-free loans to NGOs who are already partners or who have the potential to become partners for the formation, promotion and development of SHGs. These loans are convertible into grants if certain conditions are fulfilled. It also conducts exposure workshops for NGOs.

Small Industries Development Bank of India

SIDBI has also operated a microcredit scheme since 1994. The objective is to support well-managed NGOs for on-lending to the rural poor (individuals and groups), especially women, for taking up industrial activities at the micro level. The scheme provides loans to NGOs for on-lending to SHGs or individuals. SIDBI lends to NGOs at 9 per cent, and the NGOs are required to on-lend to SHGs at a rate not higher than 15 per cent. The maximum amount that an NGO is permitted to lend to an individual borrower is Rs10,000 ($280), with most loans in the range Rs2,000 ($55) to Rs5,000 ($140). By March 1997 SIDBI had provided loans of Rs101.7 million ($2.8 million) to 79 NGOs with a combined membership of around 61,600. The repayment rate to SIDBI was around 92 per cent. SIDBI has also provided a total of Rs6.3 million ($180,000) in capacity building grants to 47 NGOs for managerial salaries, strengthening accounting and managerial capabilities, and training SHGs, as well as supporting training programs for NGOs.

National Bank for Agriculture and Rural Development

In addition to the much larger linkage program discussed below, NABARD provides a small amount of revolving fund assistance to NGOs for on-lending to SHGs. This is seen as a transitional measure and stepping stone for linking SHGs to banks. To date, NABARD has provided revolving fund assistance to 13 NGOs. This assistance falls into two broad categories:

(1) NABARD provides assistance to select NGOs, such as Friends of Women's World Banking and Rashtriya Gramin Vikas Nidhi, which work as financial intermediaries

and network with smaller NGOs. Such assistance is provided at an interest rate of 6.5 per cent, and the NGOs who receive it are free to determine their own rates for on-lending to smaller NGOs.

(2) Assistance has been provided to three Grameen Bank replicators. This assistance has been provided at a 9 per cent interest rate, and again the NGOs concerned are free to determine their own on-lending rate.

NABARD has also provided grant assistance to selected NGOs and federations of SHGs for capacity building in areas such as promotion, strengthening and monitoring of SHGs, training and computerisation.

Comment

The model used by RMK, SIDBI and NABARD, whereby a second tier institution channels funds to specialist MFIs that meet certain criteria, offers a number of advantages. Most importantly, it takes account of the particular strengths that specialist MFIs have in reaching poor borrowers, such as their proximity, trust, commitment, flexibility and responsiveness. It can also ensure that MFIs face a level playing field, with support available to all MFIs meeting predetermined standards. And it can ensure that MFIs face one set of performance and reporting standards. The data that are available indicate that the three institutions have been quite successful in expanding the outreach of microfinance in a cost-effective manner, with RMK in particular reaching a substantial number of borrowers and achieving reasonably high repayment rates on loans to MFIs. Nevertheless, total outreach of the three programs is not much more than 200,000 — a very small number in relation to the 60 million poor households in India.

There are a number of ways in which the current arrangements could be strengthened, to increase the overall outreach and sustainability of microfinance in India. First and most important, the interest rate policies of RMK and SIDBI make it very difficult, if not impossible, for their partner organisations to be truly self-sufficient:

(1) The interest rate charged by RMK to partner organisations is 8 per cent, and they are required to lend to SHGs at 12 per cent, a margin of only 4 percentage points. While MFIs can obtain some interest rate relief from RMK, this only enables them to increase the margin to 6.5 percentage points. Moreover, the interest rate charged by SHGs to members is also restricted.

(2) SIDBI lends to MFIs at 9 per cent, and the MFIs are required to on-lend to SHGs at a rate not higher than 15 per cent, a mark-up of 6 percentage points.

(3) On the other hand, NABARD does not impose any interest rate restrictions in its small program of direct lending to NGOs (this is not the case under its much larger linkage program, discussed below).

The margins permitted by RMK and SIDBI are not enough to enable MFIs to cover their costs. Microfinance is a costly activity. Effective microfinance programs require intensive inputs in motivating and training borrowers and in follow-up, with regular monitoring and frequent loan repayments. All of these factors add to costs. Currently, MFIs participating in the RMK and SIDBI programs are only able to operate through grants from donor agencies and other sources, which meet a large proportion of their costs. A recent evaluation of five NGOs borrowing under the SIDBI program by Professional Assistance for Development Action (PRADAN), a leading NGO, found that the interest spread presently available to NGOs is rather tight for meeting operational costs and creating provision for risks. This greatly inhibits their ability to expand, and reduces the scope for new MFIs to be established.

This is a major constraint, possibly the major constraint, to increasing the outreach of microfinance in India. As noted above, at the Microcredit Summit the government commented that the availability of NGOs capable of delivering microfinance successfully was likely to pose a major challenge to India in meeting its target of reaching 25 million poor families with microfinance by 2005. Clearly, this constraint could be eased significantly if MFIs were permitted to cover more of their costs through interest income, and thus operate on a more sustainable basis. It would be appropriate for RMK and SIDBI to remove all restrictions on the interest rates that partner MFIs can charge. At the very least, the margins should be increased significantly to enable MFIs to recover all of their costs, on the basis of a careful study of the cost structures of successful MFIs.

In the case of RMK, ten members of the governing board are government bureaucrats and the remaining seven are from among the NGOs and nominated by the government as members. While the board appears to have operated with a reasonable degree of independence, there remains considerable scope for political interference. It may therefore be appropriate to take additional measures to safeguard the independence of the board. Possible ways of achieving this may be to reduce the number of public sector representatives, to provide for fixed-term appointments, and to enable various private and non-government bodies to appoint representatives to the board directly. The institution of a general body, which includes all NGO partner organisations and meets once a year to exchange experiences and advise on policy matters, is a positive initiative which should be continued.

It is also important that the various second tier institutions establish and enforce appropriate performance and reporting standards for the MFIs that they fund, to ensure that they operate soundly. As far as possible, the standards of the different second tier institutions should be consistent so as to reduce the administrative burden on MFIs and ensure a level playing field between them. These issues are discussed in more detail below in the section on regulation and supervision by second tier institutions.

One very positive feature of all three programs is the availability of capacity building funds to enable MFIs to strengthen their capabilities and scale up their operations. This is in contrast to the situation in some other countries, where second tier institutions provide funds for on-lending to final borrowers, but not for capacity building. It may be useful for the three programs to establish appropriate criteria for grants and/or soft loans jointly, for activities such as scaling-up operations, institutional development and increasing equity. This would enable a consistent approach that is clearly directed to assisting MFIs to become sustainable.

2.2 Support through the banking system

Priority-sector lending requirements

India has much more detailed priority-sector lending requirements than most other countries in the study. Commercial banks and regional rural banks are required to lend 40 per cent of net bank credit to priority sectors, while in the case of foreign banks the requirement is 32 per cent. In broad terms, at least 18 per cent of lending must be to agriculture. In addition, 10 per cent must be to weaker sections, such as small and marginal farmers, rural artisans and agricultural labourers. The remaining 12 per cent is unmarked, and can be for either of the above categories or for small-scale industry. Of the lending to small-scale industry, 40 per cent must be for tiny industry.

At the end of December 1996, total outstanding priority-sector advances of state banks alone aggregated Rs736 billion ($20.4 billion), or 41 per cent of their net credit. Private banks' total advances amounted to Rs63 billion ($1.75 billion) or 34 per cent of their net credit, lower than the prescribed minimum of 40 per cent. Advances by foreign banks were Rs54 billion ($1.5 billion) or 39 per cent of net credit, higher than the prescribed target of 32 per cent applying to foreign banks. Advances to weaker sections as at 31 March 1996 constituted 8.7 per cent of net credit for state banks and only 2.1 per cent for private banks, well below the requirement of 10 per cent.

Clearly, very large amounts of the banks' loanable resources have been set aside for priority-sector lending, which covers the whole spectrum of disadvantaged persons and disadvantaged industries. It is clear that the scheme is not commercially viable. It was reported that the repayment rate on priority-sector lending is generally low, in the range of 60 to 65 per cent. Moreover, smaller loans made by commercial banks under the scheme are subject to interest rate ceilings. As noted previously, commercial banks are subject to interest rate ceilings of 12.0 per cent on loans below Rs25,000 ($690), and 13.5 per cent on loans between Rs25,000 ($690) and Rs200,000 ($5,560). These ceilings are lower than market rates for larger loans, even though small loans are more costly for the banks to administer. Hence, the scheme imposes very large costs on the banks, especially in the case of the smaller loans to weaker sections and tiny industry.

The banks are able to pass some of these costs on to NABARD. Most lending to priority sectors is eligible for refinancing from NABARD, with refinancing of between 50 and 100 per cent available at interest rates of between 6.5 and 14 per cent, depending on the interest rate charged by the bank. While this is insufficient to compensate for all of the losses from low repayment rates, interest rate ceilings and high administrative costs, it means that the costs are shared between the banks and NABARD.

As such, the total cost to the community is high. Moreover, the scheme does not specifically target the poor. While some of the allocations for weaker sections and tiny industry may filter down to the poor, it is likely that the vast majority of borrowers under the scheme are not poor. While the scheme has other objectives as well, it is clearly a very inefficient means of providing access to financial services for the poor.

Integrated Rural Development Programme

The IRDP is by far the largest microfinance program in India, and one of the largest in the world. The scheme involves the provision of credit by banks, with a cash subsidy provided to borrowers by the government. Beneficiaries are selected by the village assembly on the basis of a survey by local officials of households below the poverty line, and are then screened by the banks. It is designed to assist the poorest of the poor with household incomes below Rs11,000 ($305) per year, with reservations for scheduled castes and tribes (50 per cent), women (40 per cent) and the physically handicapped (3 per cent). Priority is also given to the families belonging to the assignees of ceiling surplus land, women-headed households, freed bonded labourers and those who accept the small family norm.

There is no specific interest rate set under the program, but where loans are made by commercial banks they are subject to the general 12 per cent ceiling for small loans. The maximum loan under the IRDP is Rs25,000 ($690), with the average loan size in 1995–96 around Rs8,150 ($230). The repayment period is three years. Lending by banks under the IRDP, along with other lending to priority sectors, is eligible for refinancing from NABARD. Between 20 and 33 per cent of NABARD's annual refinancing has been disbursed for refinancing IRDP. The cash subsidy is equal to 25 per cent of the total cost of the project for small farmers, 33.3 per cent for agricultural labourers, marginal farmers and rural artisans, and 50 per cent for scheduled castes and tribes and the physically handicapped.

As at August 1996, over 49 million loans had been advanced under the program since its beginning in 1978. The banks had disbursed credit of around Rs166 billion ($4.6 billion) and the direct budgetary cost to government had been around Rs105 billion ($2.9 billion). In recent years, between 2 and 2.5 million households have been assisted each year.

Numerous evaluation studies have shown that the IRDP has not met its objectives. For instance, the Interim Report of the Expert Committee on the IRDP, constituted by the Reserve Bank (1995), found the following shortcomings:

(1) There was inappropriate identification of borrowers, with the subsidies often being captured by households which are better off.

(2) The provision of the subsidy at the beginning of the loan had caused leakages and malpractices, such as encouraging beneficiaries to dispose of the assets purchased with the loan and simply pocket the subsidy.

(3) Repayment rates were very low, with the cumulative repayment rate having declined to 30.9 per cent by end-June 1993.

It should also be noted that the program focuses exclusively on credit, rather than on savings. Moreover, given the nature of the program and the very low repayment rates, it operates essentially as a one-off grant rather than as a mechanism to provide financial services to poor households over an extended period of time.

Recently, some changes have been made to the operation of the scheme, in response to the report of the Expert Committee. Most significantly, the government subsidy element has been made back-ended, rather than being received at the commencement of the loan. It remains to be seen to what extent these changes will lead to an improvement in the performance of the program. Nevertheless, it is fair to say that most government microfinance programs implemented through commercial banks have been unsuccessful. Most banks have not made the thoroughgoing changes in organisational design and financial technologies that are necessary to operate successful microfinance programs. Moreover, participation in government microfinance programs such as the IRDP, which is seen as marginal to their overall operations and where some of the losses are borne by government, is unlikely to induce them to make these changes.

The government has devoted a great deal of resources to the IRDP, both directly through the budget and through refinancing loans made under the program. But the program appears to have contributed relatively little in terms of providing financial services to the poor on an ongoing basis. While there may be some scope to improve the program through reforms such as those recommended by the Expert Committee, it is very unlikely that such reforms can effectively address all of the issues identified above. It would therefore appear appropriate to abolish the IRDP and to reallocate the funds to supporting microfinance in more effective ways, such as by channelling them through second tier microfinance institutions and specialist MFIs.

NABARD program for linking banks with self-help groups

As noted above, NABARD was established by the Reserve Bank in 1982 as the apex body for rural credit. NABARD has provided considerable support to microfinance. In 1992 it launched a pilot project for linking SHGs to banks, including commercial banks, regional rural banks and cooperative banks. The project has now moved beyond pilot phase and become a full program of the bank. Its objectives are as follows:

(1) To evolve supplementary credit strategies for meeting the credit needs of the poor by combining the flexibility, sensitivity and responsiveness of the informal credit system with the technical and administrative capabilities and financial resources of the banks.

(2) To build mutual trust and confidence between the bankers and the rural poor.

(3) To encourage banking activity, on the thrift as well as credit side, in a segment of the population that the formal financial institutions usually find difficult to reach.

(4) To improve the flow of credit to the rural poor with reduced transaction cost, both for the financing bank and the borrower.

The main features of the program are as follows:

(1) The banks extend loans to SHGs either directly or through NGOs. In around 94 per cent of cases, the SHGs have been initiated and promoted by NGOs. In around two-thirds of these cases the NGOs have acted as non-financial intermediaries, and the loan contract has been between the bank and SHG. This is NABARD's preferred model. In around one-third of cases, the NGOs have acted as financial intermediaries, and have borrowed from banks and on-lent to the SHGs. NABARD, however, has sought to discourage this model.

(2) The banks lend at an interest rate of 10.5 per cent if lending through an NGO, or at 12 per cent if lending directly to an SHG. Where the bank lends to an NGO, the NGO on-lends to SHGs at 12 per cent. The banks receive refinancing from NABARD at 6.5 per cent.

(3) Loans from banks to NGOs and SHGs are generally for three years, but loans from SHGs to members are flexible, with terms determined by the members. SHGs normally charge interest rates of between 24 and 36 per cent.

NABARD has set out a number of criteria for banks and NGOs to use in selecting SHGs. A group should have between 10 and 20 members of homogeneous background. It should have been in active existence for at least six months, and should have successfully undertaken savings and credit operations from its own resources. It should maintain proper accounts and records. And the amount of credit given by the bank should be in proportion to the savings of the group, with the proportion of savings to loan varying from 1:1 to 1:4 depending on the assessment of the SHG by the bank. NABARD also suggests that the group should prepare a simple credit plan for its members and the group as a whole, and submit this to the bank. The documentation to be submitted by the group to the bank is decided by the bank, but should be simple and kept to a minimum.

As of March 1997, a total of 8,546 SHGs, with a total membership of more than 150,000, had been linked to banks. Banks had lent Rs111 million ($3.1 million) to these groups, and had received refinancing from NABARD of Rs103 million ($2.9 million). Twenty-six (26) state commercial banks, two private commercial banks, 67 regional rural banks, seven cooperative banks and 166 NGOs had been involved in the program.

As well as providing refinancing, NABARD has also supported linkages between banks and SHGs in a variety of other ways. For instance, it has funded exposure and training to commercial bank staff to enable them to understand the program and the advantages that it offers to banks. Training is normally provided by NGOs and training institutes. By September 1996, around 2,200 bank officers had received training and exposure.

The program has also received support and encouragement from the Reserve Bank. For instance, in April 1996 the Reserve Bank issued a circular to all commercial banks endorsing NABARD's operational guidelines and advising the banks to initiate 'necessary action. . .to step up their credit to the rural poor by extensively utilising the SHG route'. The circular pointed to a number of advantages of the linkage approach, including reduced transaction costs, high repayment rates and gradual improvements in incomes for SHG members. The circular also included lending under the program as an additional segment of lending to the weaker sections under the priority-sector lending requirements, irrespective of the purposes for which loans are used. It also encouraged banks to identify branches having potential for linkages, and to provide necessary support services to such branches.

The program is clearly a very positive initiative, with India one of only two countries in this study with an active program for supporting linkages between banks and specialised MFIs. The linkage approach offers a number of advantages as a model for the delivery of microfinance services. First, it combines the financial strength and resources of the formal banking system with the advantages of community-based MFIs in reaching the poor. Second, it provides specialised MFIs with what is potentially an almost unlimited source of funds with which to expand their operations. Third, it provides for an integrated financial system, rather than separate financial systems for poor and non-poor clients.

Nevertheless, the program as currently implemented suffers from a number of drawbacks which hinder its expansion. Most importantly, it is not sustainable in its current form. In particular, the mark-ups do not provide anywhere near a sufficient margin for NGOs to recover the costs of forming and motivating SHGs. Where NGOs act as non-financial intermediaries, banks receive refinancing from NABARD at 6.5 per cent and lend to SHGs at 12 per cent. Hence, the mark-up between bank and SHG is only 5.5 percentage points. In practice, banks retain this margin and do not reimburse the NGOs for their costs, which in any case are likely to be well above 5.5 percentage points. Where NGOs act as financial intermediaries, the mark-up is only 1.5 percentage points. Hence, the margins available to NGOs under the linkage program are even less than those available under the programs operated by RMK and SIDBI, and NGOs are only able to participate in the program if they can obtain donor funds to subsidise their activities.

Clearly, this is a major impediment to the expansion of the program. It would be appropriate to remove the restrictions on the interest rates that both banks and NGOs can charge to SHGs. This would permit NGOs to recover their costs, and enable the program to operate on a much more sustainable basis. Where NGOs act as financial intermediaries, they could directly increase the interest rate that they charge SHGs. Where NGOs act as non-financial intermediaries, it would enable banks and NGOs to establish a contractual relationship, whereby banks charge a higher interest rate to SHGs and reimburse the NGOs for the costs of promoting the groups.

It should also be noted that the program encourages NGOs to operate as non-financial intermediaries, rather than as financial intermediaries. While NABARD has a preference for NGOs as non-financial intermediaries, the rationale for this is not clear. In some countries many microfinance NGOs are financial intermediaries, making loans to individual borrowers or groups of borrowers in their own name, and it is clear that this can be a highly successful model of microfinance. While there are some NGOs that operate very successfully as non-financial intermediaries, this model is less common, especially outside India and to a lesser extent Indonesia. It would be appropriate for the linkage program to treat financial and non-financial intermediaries equally.

The program has been dominated by state banks, with only two private commercial banks participating in it to date. It is not clear why this should be the case. The 5.5 percentage point mark-up available to banks would appear more than sufficient to enable them to recover their costs, given that most of the costs of promoting SHGs and follow-up are borne by the NGOs. It would be appropriate for NABARD to undertake a study to determine why private commercial banks have been reluctant to participate in the program. (The forthcoming study by Goodwin-Groen on the role of commercial banks in microfinance is relevant to these issues.)

Another disadvantage of the program is that it is not means tested. While some commentators suggested that most members of SHGs involved in the program are poor, there does not appear to be any rigorous research on this issue. Given that the program relies on considerable funding from the government in the form of refinancing, and from donor agencies in the form of support for NGOs, it would be appropriate to ensure that it is targeted solely at the poor. It would therefore be appropriate to make access to refinancing dependent on banks and NGOs applying a means test for the selection of borrowers.

3 Regulation of non-bank microfinance institutions

3.1 The broad regulatory framework

There are no specific regulatory provisions relating to MFIs which do not accept deposits from the general public. They are regulated under the various provisions relating generally to NGOs. In broad terms, the regulatory framework is relatively relaxed. In practice, MFIs are permitted to accept savings and make loans so long as all clients are 'members' of the organisation and the term 'interest' is not applied directly to the benefits paid and charges imposed, although some commentators suggested that, technically, they should be registered under state moneylending Acts.

Registration

There are a number of options available to MFIs in terms of registration. The most common and generally simplest options are to be registered as a society or as a public charitable trust. Alternatives may be registration as a cooperative, as a trade union, or as a non-profit company. In general, registration is a responsibility of the state governments, rather than the government of India. Hence, regulations differ from state to state.

The registration of societies is governed by the Indian Societies Registration Act of 1860. This Act is now administered by the state governments and various states have passed amendments, so the precise rules differ from state to state. In general, forming a society requires seven or more people associated with a literary, scientific or charitable purpose. To be registered, it is necessary to file a memorandum of association with the state or district registrar of societies, including the name, objectives, details of the governing body, and rules and regulations. In some states registration needs to be renewed every five years or so. Registration of public charitable trusts is covered by the Indian Trusts Act of 1882. Again, different states have passed different amendments. In general, the application for registration must contain various details about the membership, and include the memorandum of association and by-laws of the trust. NGOs commented that the administrative requirements for registration as a society or trust are simple to fulfil and do not place any burden on them.

Cooperative societies are also regulated by state governments. In general, they must have at least ten members, be non-discriminatory in membership and have a democratic structure, with all members having equal voting rights. They are also required to submit by-laws with the application, covering name and objectives, membership rules, power and functions of the general body, frequency of meetings, and the size and composition of the board of directors.

In addition to these requirements, cooperatives are subject to considerable administrative control by state governments. It was commented that in most cases, cooperatives are not financially self-sufficient and rely heavily on government funds (although this is less so in some states such as Maharashtra and Gujarat, where cooperatives tend to be stronger and more independent). Because of the reliance on government funds, they are largely owned and controlled by the state government. State cooperative departments have the right to be represented on the board of directors, and can therefore exert considerable influence on the management of cooperatives. They often have the right to decide on the timing of elections for the board, and this may result in delays. Permission may also be needed to invest funds, change their area of operations, use funds from their reserves, and similar matters. A number of commentators stated that these procedures are very bureaucratic and often result in considerable delays.

The state of Andhra Pradesh has recently passed the Mutually Aided Cooperative Societies Act of 1995, designed to remove cooperatives from many of the administrative controls of the state and make them more self reliant and autonomous. This is giving rise to some transitional difficulties in converting existing cooperatives, which currently rely heavily on government funds and have large debts to the government, into member-funded institutions. Nevertheless, it is clearly a positive development. It is understood that the states have given in-principle agreement to the government of India to pass a similar law at the national level, which would apply throughout India. This should provide the opportunity to streamline the regulatory requirements facing cooperatives and remove unnecessary requirements. It would be desirable to set out the regulatory requirements facing cooperatives as clearly as possible, and to minimise government involvement in their day-to-day operations.

Self-help groups (SHGs) are generally not registered. However, if they have more than twenty members, the Companies Act of 1949 requires that they be registered. It is not necessary that they be registered as a company; it is sufficient that they register under state law as a society, trust or cooperative. In general, registering as a society is the simplest form of registration. However, some of the requirements for registration as a society may be onerous and unnecessary for a small SHG. For this reason, many SHGs restrict their membership to twenty persons or less. It is also understood that some larger SHGs operate informally and are not registered.

Foreign contributions

All NGOs receiving grants from foreign sources are subject to registration and reporting requirements under the Foreign Contributions Regulation Act. They are required to establish a separate bank account for all transactions relating to foreign contributions, and to provide the account number to the Ministry of Home Affairs. At the end of each financial year they are required to report to the Ministry of Home Affairs on how much they received, for what purpose, and how much they spent. NGOs commented that it is sometimes difficult to get initial registration under the Act, but that once this is achieved, the procedure is not onerous. However, if not all of the grant is spent, approval from the Ministry of Finance is necessary to return the unspent portion to the donor, and this can take some time.

In the case of loans from foreign sources, there are further complications. Approval from the Ministry of Finance is needed before any loan can be received from foreign sources, and such approval can be difficult to obtain. For instance, EDA Rural Systems (1996b) reports that the Society for Helping and Awakening Rural Poor through Education (SHARE), a Grameen Bank replicator, had to engage in lengthy discussions to obtain permission to receive recoverable grants and soft loans from the Grameen Trust. Other NGOs reported similar experiences, with one NGO having to wait two years for approval. Moreover, it is necessary to obtain approval from the Reserve Bank every time a repayment is made. This requires a detailed utilisation report, and NGOs commented that this report is quite onerous to complete. While the requirement for approval can be waived by the Reserve Bank, it is still necessary to complete the utilisation report.

Clearly, these restrictions primarily reflect a desire on the part of the authorities to conserve foreign exchange, and are not designed specifically with MFIs in mind. Nevertheless, the procedures are cumbersome, and can place a significant administrative burden on MFIs. It is likely that in the future, more and more donor agencies will provide support to MFIs in the form of concessional loans rather than grants. It would therefore be appropriate for the Ministry of Finance to review the procedures so as to minimise the administrative burden as far as possible. It is also possible that further deregulation of the foreign exchange market in the future may remove the need for such approvals.

3.2 Interest rates

There are no legal restrictions on the interest rates that NGOs, cooperatives or SHGs can charge borrowers. Nevertheless, while state governments do not have the legal power to regulate interest rates charged by cooperatives, it was suggested that in many cases they control the interest rates that cooperatives can charge through their ownership of shares in them. This may make it difficult for cooperatives to cover their costs and operate on a commercial basis, in turn increasing the extent to which they are reliant on government. In drafting the proposed law to govern cooperatives, it would be appropriate to spell out the right of cooperatives to set their own interest rates based on commercial considerations, and to remove as far as possible the scope for state governments to influence interest rates.

3.3 Prudential regulation and supervision

There are no regulations of a prudential nature governing MFIs, whether registered as societies, public charitable trusts, cooperatives or as some other legal form. There is no minimum capital requirement, and no regulations covering matters such as capital adequacy, reserves, liquidity or loan loss provisioning.

Reporting requirements are also relatively modest, and are designed for NGOs in general rather than for MFIs. There are no requirements for the provision of monthly portfolio reports and balance sheets, as regulatory agencies would normally require of financial institutions. Societies and trusts are generally required to maintain regular accounts, have their accounts audited annually, and provide a copy of the accounts to the relevant registrar. Requirements on cooperatives are slightly more onerous. They are generally required to provide regular statements of income and expenses and balance sheets to the State Cooperatives Department. Accounts are generally required to be audited annually, in many cases by an auditor from the State Cooperatives Department. SHGs are not registered, and are therefore not subject to any reporting requirements.

Nevertheless, it would probably not be appropriate to introduce a legal framework for prudential regulation and supervision for MFIs. While MFIs provide savings facilities and loans to their members, they are not permitted to accept deposits from the general public. Most commentators argue that it is unnecessary and may even be counter-productive to subject MFIs which do not accept deposits from the general public to full prudential regulation and supervision. In any case, such a framework would not be cost-effective, given the large number of MFIs in India (including NGOs, cooperatives and SHGs, all with very different characteristics), the size of the country, and the federal system of government with overlapping responsibilities between the government of India and state governments. Clearly, it would not be realistic for the Reserve Bank or some other regulatory agency to regulate and supervise these MFIs, or even just NGOs and cooperatives, in the same way as a central bank would normally regulate and supervise financial institutions. It is therefore necessary to consider alternative ways to ensure that MFIs maintain high standards in their operations.

3.4 Performance and reporting standards of second tier institutions

A more cost-effective way of seeking to ensure that MFIs operate in a financially sound and sustainable manner is through the policies of the various second tier institutions which lend to them. These institutions impose a number of conditions on their partner MFIs.

Rashtriya Mahila Kosh

For a partner organisation to borrow from Rashtriya Mahila Kosh (RMK), it must satisfy a number of conditions:

(1) It should have at least three years' experience in thrift and credit administration.

(2) It should have about 90 per cent recovery performance during the last three years (in practice, RMK generally accepts a recovery rate in the range of 80 to 90 per cent).

(3) It should have satisfactory funds management and financial performance.

(4) It should have a good track record of work in the socioeconomic field.

There are also a number of requirements on loans by the partner organisations to individual borrowers and SHGs covering matters such as means testing, size and duration of loans, interest rates charged and a requirement that loans should generally be for income-generating activities. Moreover, partner organisations have to maintain 10 per cent of the credit availed from RMK as reserves, although this is not strictly enforced. Ultimate borrowers are required to save at the rate of 10 per cent of the amount that they borrow.

Partner organisations are required to submit monthly and quarterly reports to RMK, but these deal with the utilisation of the loan from RMK and do not cover data necessary for monitoring their overall financial performance. They are also required to submit annual financial statements covering income and expenses and balance sheet data, which must be audited by a registered chartered accountant. RMK staff try to visit each partner once a year.

Small Industries Development Bank of India

The Small Industries Development Bank of India (SIDBI) is a specialised development bank, and while it provides loans to NGOs engaged in microfinance, this is only one, relatively minor, part of its overall operations. As such, it has not developed criteria for loans to MFIs that are as detailed as those developed by RMK. To qualify for a loan from SIDBI, NGOs must be well managed, have been in existence for at least five years, have a good track record and an established network, and have experience in small savings and credit programs with SHGs or individuals.

National Bank for Agriculture and Rural Development

The National Bank for Agriculture and Rural Development (NABARD) does not generally lend to NGOs. As noted above, it has only lent to a small number of NGOs as a transitional measure, and these tend to be large and well-established NGOs. It uses the following four criteria for selecting NGO partners:

(1) They must have a good track record, and must be successfully undertaking savings and credit operations with the poor, whether individually or in small groups, with very high recovery rates.

(2) They must have a proper system of maintaining accounts/records, and be audited regularly.

(3) They must have adequate financial management capability for enlarged operations.

(4) They must have adequate trained and motivated field staff for close observance and monitoring.

NABARD does not subject the NGOs to which it lends to any rigorous reporting requirements. NGOs are required to provide a quarterly report to NABARD, covering details of the revolving fund assistance, and some very basic data on loans disbursed by the NGO. These cover number of SHGs and individuals assisted, amount of loans disbursed and outstanding, one-line recovery rate, and basic data on savings mobilised. The report is very simple, and does not provide a basis for monitoring the financial performance of the NGO.

Comment

There is considerable scope for the performance and reporting standards set by these second tier institutions to become general throughout the microfinance sector. Between them, the three institutions lend to many of the more prominent MFIs in India. There is a powerful incentive for MFIs who do not currently borrow from them to meet the standards they set if they wish to access funding at concessional interest rates from such institutions in the future. As such, these institutions are very well placed to shape the development of the microfinance sector in general. For this to happen, however, the performance and reporting standards applied by the three institutions would need to be strengthened considerably. It would also be appropriate for them to adopt a common set of standards, or at least a consistent set of standards. In developing such standards it would be useful to study the experiences of second tier institutions in other countries, particularly Palli Karma Sahayak Foundation (PKSF) in Bangladesh, which has played an active role in developing standards for microfinance in that country (see the Bangladesh country study).

3.5 Self-regulation

Another possibility for establishing performance and reporting standards for MFIs is through self-regulation. Developing standards for self-regulation requires an effective apex body, and until recently there has not been an apex body for MFIs in India. At present, however, an attempt is being made to establish such a body. The major impetus is coming from the Evangelical Fellowship of India Commission on Relief (EFICOR), a multi-purpose NGO engaged in microfinance. The proposed apex body, the All India Association of Micro Enterprises Development (AIAMED) Network was registered as a trust under the Indian Trusts Act in February 1997. Its vision is to make microenterprise development/microfinance a significant national strategy for enabling the poor to become self-employed and contribute with dignity to nation building.

The first major activity was to conduct seven regional coordination consultations in different regions in India between June and November 1997. Some 400 MFIs expressed an interest in attending these consultations, including the most prominent MFIs such as SEWA Bank, the Mysore Resettlement and Development Agency (MYRADA), Working Women's Forum, Friends of Women's World Banking and the Grameen Bank replicators. The consultations were to address the five key themes of outreach, viability, resource mobilisation, the policy environment and capacity building, with presentations on each by major MFIs. Following these consultations, it was intended to establish a national council with key MFIs from each region as well as donor agencies, policy and regulatory agencies, and possibly some institutions from other countries.

While the activities of the AIAMED Network have not yet been developed in detail, it is intended that it will not operate its own microfinance program, nor will it directly provide funding to MFIs. Major activities are expected to include designing and conducting a national microfinance survey, training MFIs, sharing information, developing and promoting microfinance standards, and policy dialogue and advocacy. It is also understood that the establishment of an Indian collective for microfinance was discussed at a meeting in Delhi hosted by RMK and ActionAid in December 1997.

The establishment of the AIAMED Network is a very positive development. While it is obviously still at an early stage of development, it has the potential over time to become a focal point for the establishment of performance standards within the MFI sector, and for dialogue on policy issues between MFIs on the one hand and government bodies, donor agencies and second tier institutions on the other. It would be appropriate for all MFIs to join the Network and to become active in its affairs, to ensure that it is fully representative of the microfinance sector.

4 Regulation of banks

4.1 Licensing and minimum capital requirements

As noted previously, non-bank microfinance institutions (MFIs) are not permitted to accept deposits from the general public. Only institutions licensed as banks pursuant to the Banking Regulation Act of 1949 and regulated by the Reserve Bank are permitted to offer the full range of depository services to poor clients. Hence, specialist MFIs are only able to expand their sources of funds and provide a full range of services to poor clients if they are licensed as a bank.

One critical factor affecting the extent to which regulated banks become involved in microfinance is the scope for the establishment of small banks. Small banks operate in more localised areas than larger banks, and are more likely to engage in microfinance. Moreover, the scope for establishing small banks is also of critical importance to specialist MFIs wishing to establish regulated banks. Unless there is provision to establish smaller banks, it is generally not feasible for specialist MFIs to become regulated financial institutions.

In India, minimum capital requirements differ for different types of banks. In the case of private commercial banks, the minimum capital requirement is Rs1 billion ($27.8 million). Hence, there is no scope to establish a small commercial bank. Recently, the Reserve Bank has created special provisions for the establishment of local area banks. Such banks face a minimum capital requirement of Rs50 million ($1.4 million). They are permitted to offer the full range of banking services, but their operations are limited to three geographically contiguous districts. While this makes it easier to establish new banks, the minimum capital requirement is still likely to be too high for small microfinance banks operating in a localised area. It is also understood that there has been pressure from some commercial banks against these provisions, and that in practice it is difficult to obtain a licence to establish a local area bank.

There may be some scope to establish small urban cooperative banks. Minimum capital requirements for urban cooperative banks vary by locality, with the minimum set at Rs5 million ($139,000) in large metropolitan areas, Rs1 million ($28,000) in other metropolitan areas, Rs100,000 ($2,800) in urban areas, and Rs10,000 ($280) in semi-urban areas. In the past, urban cooperative banks have been allowed to operate only in one urban area, and have not been allowed to operate in rural areas. However, one specialist MFI that has been established as an urban cooperative bank, SEWA Bank, has recently been permitted to operate in certain rural areas. It is understood that other urban cooperative banks may also be permitted to establish rural branches in the future. Nevertheless, the establishment of new branches requires approval from the Reserve Bank, and this may be difficult to obtain. Moreover, it is not clear to what extent it is possible to establish new urban cooperative banks, or for specialist MFIs to transform themselves into urban cooperative banks, especially if they wish to operate in predominantly rural areas.

As noted above, the regulated banking system also comprises regional rural banks and rural cooperative banks. Regional rural banks are owned by the state commercial banks, while rural cooperative banks are largely under the control of state governments. To a limited extent, some of these banks do provide microfinance to the poor. However, they have been established to cover a particular geographical area, and it is not expected that new regional rural banks or rural cooperative banks will be licensed in the future. Hence, the legislation covering these types of banks does not appear to offer a mechanism for the establishment of small microfinance banks, or for MFIs to convert themselves into banks.

If regulated banks are to play an active role in microfinance, it is important that there be a more effective mechanism to enable small private banks to be licensed. It would be appropriate for the government to provide a framework for the establishment of small banks at the local level with a realistic minimum capital requirement, and to minimise any other restrictions which may discourage the establishment of small banks. In this respect it may be appropriate to consider the policy regimes in Indonesia and the Philippines, where there is considerable scope to establish small banks (see the Indonesia and Philippines country studies). Banks in those countries are much more active in microfinance than in India and the other countries in this study.

4.2 Interest rates

Until recently, the Reserve Bank imposed extensive interest rate ceilings on bank loans. As noted above, most of these have been removed. However, commercial banks are still subject to interest rate ceilings of 12.0 per cent on loans below Rs25,000 ($690), and 13.5 per cent on loans between Rs25,000 ($690) and Rs200,000 ($5,560). Local area banks, regional rural banks and cooperative banks are not subject to any interest rate regulation.

Microfinance is a costly activity, and to operate successful microfinance programs it is necessary to charge higher rates of interest than those charged on other loans. While commercial banks do not often lend successfully to poor borrowers even where interest rates are deregulated, the interest rate ceilings currently in place prevent any possibility of their covering their costs on small loans, and further discourage them from establishing microfinance programs. It would be appropriate to remove the ceilings, or at the very least to increase them to levels which would enable commercial banks to cover their costs on such loans.

4.3 Prudential regulation and supervision

The prudential requirements facing commercial banks, local area banks, regional rural banks and cooperative banks are broadly the same.

All banks except cooperative banks are subject to a capital adequacy ratio of 8 per cent of risk-weighted assets, as recommended under the Basle Accord. In the case of cooperative banks there is an in-built mechanism for share capital to increase as loans increase, and it is estimated that these provisions are equivalent to a capital adequacy ratio of around 7.5 per cent. These requirements do not appear to impede small microfinance banks in any way. In fact, the standard in the Basle Accord may be too low for small banks such as regional rural banks and cooperative banks, with most commentators suggesting that capital adequacy ratios should be higher for small microfinance banks than for other banks because of higher risk and other factors.

All banks are required to maintain a cash reserve ratio with the Reserve Bank. For local area banks, regional rural banks and cooperative banks, the requirement is for 3 per cent of their net demand and time liabilities. As at April 1997 commercial banks were subject to a ratio of 10 per cent, but this is gradually being reduced. In addition, all banks are subject to a statutory liquidity ratio, over and above the cash reserve ratio, of 25 per cent of net demand and time liabilities. While this requirement is the same for all banks, this statutory liquidity ratio is high by international standards. This reduces the extent to which banks can provide credit and, to the extent that banks are engaged in microfinance, limits their ability to provide loans to poor borrowers. It may also act as a disincentive to MFIs seeking to establish banks. It would be appropriate for the Reserve Bank to review the level of the statutory liquidity ratio.

All banks face the same requirements for income recognition and loan loss provisioning, based on the Basle Accord. In terms of reporting, the requirements are the same for commercial banks, local area banks and regional rural banks. Broadly, these involve a series of fortnightly, monthly, quarterly and annual reports. The requirements are similar for cooperative banks but slightly less onerous, reflecting their more limited range of activities. One urban cooperative bank involved in microfinance commented that the reporting requirements were rigorous but realistic. It also commented that a two-person team from the Reserve Bank carries out an on-site inspection once every two years for one week. It found the officers cooperative and positive, and considers that the visits are useful.

It should also be noted that under the NABARD linkage program, the Reserve Bank has encouraged banks not to seek physical collateral on microfinance loans to self-help groups (SHGs), but to rely on group guarantees and peer pressure. This has encouraged banks to become involved in the program and provided a boost to microfinance, and it would be appropriate if central banks in other countries were to issue similar explicit guidelines on the use of collateral substitutes.

5 Summary and recommendations

With a per capita income of $340 in 1995 and generally poor social indicators of development, India is classified as a low-income country by the World Bank and a low human development country by UNDP. The most recent estimates suggest that 35 per cent of the population was below the poverty line in 1993–94. While the proportion of the population in poverty has declined significantly since the 1950s this has been insufficient to prevent large increases in the absolute number of people in poverty, with a massive 312 million people living below the poverty line in 1993–94.

By far the largest microfinance program in India is the Integrated Rural Development Programme (IRDP), a subsidised program which provides loans to poor borrowers through the banking system. In addition, there are three major types of institutions devoted specifically to providing microfinance to the poor. These are non-governmental organisations (NGOs), self-help groups (SHGs) and cooperatives. Nevertheless, outreach remains very low compared to the number of people living in poverty, with the total outreach of genuine microfinance programs to poor borrowers not much more than 500,000. Hence, there remains a huge unmet demand for microfinance. The government has expressed a strong commitment to microfinance as a means of reducing poverty, and at the Microcredit Summit in February 1997 it set a target to reach 25 million poor families with microfinance by 2005.

Arrangements for direct support

The government has supported microfinance in a number of ways. First, it has provided considerable support to specialised microfinance institutions (MFIs) through a number of second tier microfinance institutions, which channel funds to MFIs at concessional interest rates. The three major second tier institutions are Rashtriya Mahila Kosh (RMK), the Small Industries Development Bank of India (SIDBI) and the National Bank for Agriculture and Rural Development (NABARD).

Remove restrictions on interest rates charged by MFIs

While this model has been quite successful, there are a number of ways in which the current arrangements could be strengthened. Most importantly, the interest rate restrictions imposed by RMK and SIDBI make it very difficult, if not impossible, for their partner MFIs to operate in a sustainable manner. RMK and SIDBI should remove all restrictions on the interest rates that partner MFIs can charge or, at the very least, increase the margins significantly to enable MFIs to recover all of their costs. The government should also take additional measures to safeguard the independence of RMK.

Establish consistent criteria for grants/soft loans

One very positive feature of all three programs is the availability of capacity building funds to enable MFIs to strengthen their capabilities and scale up their operations. The three programs should establish consistent criteria for grants and/or soft loans for activities such as scaling-up operations, institutional development and increasing equity.

The government has also sought to support microfinance through the banking system. Commercial banks and regional rural banks are required to lend 40 per cent of net bank credit to priority sectors, including the poor. This scheme imposes large costs on the banks and the community in general, and is unlikely to reach many poor borrowers. While the scheme may have other objectives, it is a very inefficient means of providing financial services to the poor.

Reallocate IRDP funds for better support for microfinance

The IRDP involves the provision of credit to poor borrowers by banks, with a cash subsidy provided to borrowers by the government. Numerous evaluation studies have shown that the IRDP has not met its objectives. While it has recently undergone some changes, it is unlikely that these will overcome the fundamental problems. The government should abolish the IRDP, and reallocate the funds to supporting microfinance in more effective ways, such as by channelling them through second tier microfinance institutions and specialist MFIs.

Remove interest-rate restrictions under the linkage program

Another program supported by the government is the NABARD program for linking banks and SHGs. The program is a very positive initiative, combining the financial strength and resources of the formal banking system with the advantages of community-based MFIs in reaching the poor. Nevertheless, the program as implemented suffers from a number of drawbacks. Most importantly, interest rate restrictions imposed by NABARD do not provide anywhere near a sufficient margin for NGOs to recover the costs of forming and motivating SHGs. NABARD should remove the restrictions on the interest rates that both banks and NGOs can charge to SHGs. NABARD should also offer greater encouragement to NGOs to act as financial intermediaries, and ensure that the program is means tested.

Regulation of non-bank microfinance institutions

While there are no specific regulatory provisions relating to MFIs as such, there are a number of options for registration. The most common options are to be registered as a society, public charitable trust or cooperative. While regulations differ from state to state, the administrative requirements for societies and trusts are generally simple to fulfil. On the other hand, cooperatives are subject to considerable administrative control by state governments. Governments should streamline the regulatory requirements facing cooperatives and remove any unnecessary requirements. SHGs are generally not registered. However, if they have more than twenty members, they are legally required to be registered as a society, trust or cooperative.

Review procedures to minimise administrative burden

All NGOs receiving grants from foreign sources are subject to registration and reporting requirements under the Foreign Contributions Regulation Act. In the case of loans from foreign sources there are further complications. The Ministry of Finance should review these procedures to minimise the administrative burden as much as possible.

Ensure cooperatives can set adequate interest rates

There are no legal restrictions on the interest rates that NGOs, cooperatives or SHGs can charge borrowers. Nevertheless, while state governments do not have the legal power to regulate interest rates charged by cooperatives, they sometimes control the interest rates that cooperatives can charge through their ownership of shares in them. Governments should ensure that cooperatives are able to set their own interest rates based on commercial considerations.

There are no regulations of a prudential nature governing MFIs, whether registered as societies, public charitable trusts, cooperatives or in some other legal form. There is no minimum capital requirement, and no regulations covering matters such as capital adequacy, reserves, liquidity or loan loss provisioning. Reporting requirements are also relatively modest, with no requirements for the provision of monthly portfolio reports or balance sheets as generally required by regulators of financial institutions. While this environment may seem permissive, most commentators argue that it is unnecessary and even counter-productive to subject MFIs that do not accept deposits from the general public to full prudential regulation and supervision. In any case, such a framework would not be cost-effective, given the large number of MFIs in India, the size of the country, and the federal system of government.

Strengthen performance and reporting standards for MFIs

A more cost-effective way of seeking to ensure that MFIs operate in a financially sound and sustainable manner is through the policies of the various second tier institutions which lend to them, particularly RMK, SIDBI and NABARD. Between them, these three institutions lend to many of the more prominent MFIs in India. There is also an incentive for MFIs who do not currently borrow from them to meet the standards they set if they wish to access funding from them in the future. The three second tier institutions should strengthen their performance and reporting standards considerably. They should adopt a consistent set of standards, achieved through consultation with the MFIs themselves.

Another possibility for establishing performance and reporting standards for MFIs is through self-regulation. In this context, the establishment of the All India Association of Micro Enterprises Development (AIAMED) Network as an apex body for MFIs is a very positive development. While it is obviously still at a very early stage of development, the network has the potential to become a focal point for the establishment of performance standards and for policy dialogue. All MFIs should join the network to ensure that it is fully representative of the microfinance sector.

Regulation of banks

Non-bank MFIs are not permitted to accept deposits from the general public. Only institutions licensed as banks and regulated by the Reserve Bank are permitted to offer the full range of depository services to poor clients.

Provide framework for establishing small banks

There are no clear provisions enabling the establishment of small private banks in India, and there is no scope to establish a small commercial bank. While the Reserve Bank has created special provisions for the establishment of local area banks, the minimum capital requirement is still likely to be too high for small microfinance banks. There may be some scope for urban cooperative banks to expand into rural areas, but it is not clear to what extent it is possible to establish new urban cooperative banks. And while there is a network of regional rural banks and rural cooperative banks, these are largely under government control, and it is not expected that new banks in these categories will be licensed in the future. The government should provide a framework for the establishment of small banks at the local level with a realistic minimum capital requirement, and should minimise any other restrictions which may discourage the establishment of small banks.

Remove interest rate ceilings on small loans

While most interest rate restrictions have been removed, commercial banks are still subject to ceilings of 12.0 per cent on loans below Rs25,000 ($690), and 13.5 per cent on loans between Rs25,000 ($690) and Rs200,000 ($5,560). While commercial banks do not often lend directly to poor borrowers even where interest rates are deregulated, these ceilings prevent them from covering their costs on small loans. The government should remove them or, at the very least, increase them to levels which would enable commercial banks to cover their costs on such loans.

Review statutory liquidity requirement

Prudential requirements such as capital adequacy ratios, reserve and liquidity requirements, loan loss provisioning and reporting requirements are broadly the same for all banks. In general, these do not impose any undue restrictions on small banks or banks involved in microfinance. However, all banks are subject to a statutory liquidity ratio, over and above the cash reserve ratio, of 25 per cent of net demand and time liabilities. This is high by international standards, and may limit the ability and willingness of banks to provide loans to poor borrowers. The Reserve Bank should review the level of the statutory liquidity requirement.

References

EDA Rural Systems. 1996a. *India: Microenterprise Country Paper*. Study prepared for the Asian Development Bank, Manila.

EDA Rural Systems. 1996b. *India: Microfinance for the Poor: An Assessment of the Status and Efficacy of Microfinance Institutions and Programmes*. Study prepared for the Asian and Pacific Development Centre, Kuala Lumpur.

Ghate, Prabhu. 1997. Enhancing the contribution of the informal financial sector: Proposals for some policy and regulatory changes, and a pilot project. Rural Financial Reform Program, mimeo.

Mahajan, Vijay & Ramola, Bharti Gupta. 1996. 'Financial services for the rural poor in India: Access and sustainability'. *Journal of International Development*, vol.8, no.2, pp.211–224.

NABARD. 1989. *Studies on Self-Help Groups of the Rural Poor*. National Bank for Agriculture and Rural Development, Mumbai.

NABARD. 1995. *Linking Self-Help Groups: An Indian Experience*. National Bank for Agriculture and Rural Development, Mumbai.

NABARD. 1996a. *Linkage Banking in India: An Overview.* National Bank for Agriculture and Rural Development, Mumbai.

NABARD. 1996b. *Microfinance Innovations and NABARD*. National Bank for Agriculture and Rural Development, Mumbai.

Reserve Bank of India. 1995. *Expert Committee on Integrated Rural Development Programme*: Interim Report. Reserve Bank of India, Mumbai.

World Bank. 1997. *India: Achievements and Challenges in Reducing Poverty.* World Bank, Washington D.C.

Persons consulted

Mr P. Kotaiah	Chairman National Bank for Agriculture and Rural Development
Mr Y. C. Nanda	Executive Director National Bank for Agriculture and Rural Development
Mr G. K. Agrawal	Chief General Manager National Bank for Agriculture and Rural Development
Mr S. M. Sheokand	General Manager National Bank for Agriculture and Rural Development
Mr S. Santhanam	Deputy General Manager National Bank for Agriculture and Rural Development
Mr Y. G. Milton	Assistant General Manager National Bank for Agriculture and Rural Development
Mr B. R. K. Kamath	Executive, Banking Operations Indian Banks' Association
Mr Bandi Ram Prasad	Chief Economist Indian Banks Association
Ms Vijayalakshmi Das	Chief Executive Friends of Women's World Banking
Ms Anjali Mahajan	Senior Credit Officer Friends of Women's World Banking
Ms Jayshree Vyas	Managing Director Shri Mahila Sewa Sahkari Bank
Dr Dinesh N. Awasthi	Senior Faculty Entrepreneurship Development Institute of India

Dr Naresh Singh	Associate Faculty Entrepreneurship Development Institute of India
Mr R. Ramanujan	Chief General Manager Reserve Bank of India
Mr Y. S. P. Thorat	Additional Chief General Manager Reserve Bank of India
Mr T. K. E. Das	General Manager Reserve Bank of India
Ms Mangala Vaidyanathan	Assistant General Manager Reserve Bank of India
Mr Swarn Singh Boparai	Secretary Dep't of Small Scale Industries & Agro & Rural Industries
Mr Rashid Jilani	Chairman and Managing Director Punjab National Bank
Mr Rajan Samuel	National Coordinator AIAMED
Mr Manoj Lakhanpal	Senior Officer, MEDU Evangelical Fellowship of India Commission on Relief
Mr V. B. Tulasidhar	Economist Asian Development Bank
Dr M. Balasubramanian	Senior Agriculturist The World Bank
Dr Indira Misra	Executive Director Rashtriya Mahila Kosh
Mr Kashmirilal	General Manager Rashtriya Mahila Kosh
Mr S. S. Sharma	Manager Rashtriya Mahila Kosh
Mr M. S. Malek	Manager Rashtriya Mahila Kosh
Dr Pronab Sen	Adviser Planning Commission
Dr Jane Lake	First Secretary (Development Cooperation) Australian Agency for International Development
Mr Tony Liston	Second Secretary (Development Cooperation) Australian Agency for International Development
Ms Bharti Gupta Ramola	Senior Director Price Waterhouse
Mr P. M. Tripathi	President Association of Voluntary Agencies for Rural Development

Indonesia

1 Introduction and background

1.1 Key demographic and economic data

The Indonesian people live in an archipelago of more than 13,000 islands extending over some 40 degrees of longitude along the Equator, a span not much less than that of the continental United States. With a population of some 193 million in 1995, Indonesia is the fourth most populous nation (after China, India and the United States). With a total land area of 1.905 million square kilometres, Indonesia's population density is a relatively modest 100 persons per square kilometre. However, there is great internal variation; the three smaller islands of Java, Bali and Madura with some 7 per cent of the nation's land area support around 60 per cent of its population.

Much analysis of Indonesia's economic and administrative problems hinges on this distinction between the 'Inner Islands' of Java, Bali and Madura, and the 'Outer Islands' which have much lower population densities and greater difficulties of transport and communications. These characteristics pose problems for the provision of all services in the Outer Islands, including microfinance.

The rate of growth of population in Indonesia has been falling in a sustained manner since the 1970s. At 1.6 per cent per annum between 1990 and 1995, this growth was significantly lower than the rates in Malaysia and the Philippines and was, indeed, below those in all countries in this study other than Sri Lanka and Thailand. The rate of population growth in the Inner Islands is only around 1 per cent — another facet of the Inner/Outer contrast noted above. Indonesia is not yet a highly urbanised society; the urban proportion, at 34 per cent, is below that of other Southeast Asian states discussed here, in particular Malaysia and the Philippines (both above 50 per cent).

With GNP per capita of $980 in 1995, Indonesia was classified as a lower middle-income economy by the World Bank. It had experienced quite sustained economic growth since the early 1970s, with per capita GNP growing at an annual 6 per cent over the period 1985–95. Income distribution (with a Gini coefficient of 0.317) was notably more even than in any of the other Southeast Asian countries in this study, and was broadly comparable with the distributions observed in the lower growth environment of South Asia.

Commencing in the second half of 1997, and in common with other economies in East Asia, Indonesia has experienced a currency and banking crisis resulting in substantial loss of production, severe open unemployment and rapid inflation. At the time of writing it is becoming clear Indonesia has been much more adversely affected than any other country in the region, and that these events represent a decisive break (or at the least a severe check) in the long-term pattern of growth, with little prospect of its early resumption.

Indonesia's robust growth to 1997 had been accompanied by marked structural change. Agriculture now contributes only 17 per cent of GDP, while industry accounts for some 42 per cent. Agriculture has by no means been stagnant, however; vigorous growth of agricultural productivity has created many opportunities for informal off-farm economic activities with consequent burgeoning demand for microfinance services in the rural economy, especially on Java and Bali.

In terms of social development, life expectancy (at 64 years) and the infant mortality rate (at 51 per 1,000) compare somewhat unfavourably with indicators in the other Southeast Asian countries in this study, as well as with Sri Lanka. The adult literacy rate is 84 per cent, and the Human Development Index, at 0.668, is at much the same level as in the Philippines, although well below the levels of Malaysia and Thailand, and slightly below Sri Lanka.

1.2 Poverty

Estimates of poverty

At the Microcredit Summit in February 1997, the Indonesian Minister of State for National Development Planning tabled figures showing a decline in the proportion of the Indonesian population living in poverty from 60 per cent in 1970 to below 12 per cent in 1996. Some 70 million Indonesians were said to be living below the poverty line in 1970; in 1996 the number was estimated at only 22.6 million. On the face of it, this was a remarkable achievement.

The primary data source for measurement of poverty is the periodic national household expenditure survey known as *Susenas*, conducted since 1964. Since 1976, these data have been used by the Central Bureau of Statistics to calculate urban and rural poverty lines for Indonesia. These are based on estimates of calorific requirements and minimum basic needs for non-food items. An earlier attempt to relate the estimate of poverty to minimum consumption requirements was the poverty line calculated by Professor Sajogyo, dating from 1975 and based on rice consumption per capita. It is still employed in some studies. The World Bank has also estimated the incidence of poverty in Indonesia at intervals since the 1970s.

Observers note that despite different estimates of the incidence of poverty at any one time, there is consensus that the trend over time had been for poverty to decline nationally from the late 1960s to 1996. Moreover, the proportion of the population living below the poverty line had declined in both urban and rural areas. Over the thirty years to 1996, while poverty had declined everywhere in Indonesia, the rate of decline was much faster in Java, especially urban Java. The trends were such that by the early years of the next century, the majority of the poor seemed likely to be found in rural areas outside Java.

However, the estimate was quite sensitive to the poverty line chosen; raising the poverty line slightly would make a substantial difference to the numbers defined as poor. Thus, despite the remarkable achievements of the New Order government of Soeharto, the 1996 *Susenas*, which provided an estimate of poverty at less than 12 per cent overall, also showed that between 130 and 140 million people (that is, up to 70 per cent of the total population) spent less than a dollar a day. (For comparison, the urban poverty line was set at Rp1300 (56 cents) per capita per day, and the rural level at Rp900 (38 cents).

Moreover, while all deciles of the income distribution had become better off over time, and while the evidence of the Gini coefficient, cited above, indicated a relatively equitable distribution of income by the standards of the region, *absolute* disparities of income (and hence the perception of *relative* poverty) had tended to increase. This, together with concerns about the distribution of income and wealth between ethnic groups and between regions of the country, had forced poverty close to the top of the political agenda.

Given the vulnerability of that substantial group close to the poverty line, there can be little doubt that the current economic crisis, with its consequences of inflation and unemployment exacerbated by widespread losses of agricultural production due to drought, is leading to marked increases in the incidence of poverty. Income disparities are now an even more pressing political issue, and the likelihood of political, rather than economic, solutions being applied is correspondingly greater.

Policies for poverty reduction

Indonesia's primary policy to secure the reduction of poverty has been the achievement of rapid economic growth. A noted observer of the Indonesia economy has commented on the remarkable transformation of the Indonesian economy during the 30-year period to 1995, during which:

> . . . sustained economic growth at an average rate of more than 6 per cent has more than trebled per-capita income. From near the bottom of the World Bank listing of 'low-income' countries, Indonesia has become one of the booming, industrialising 'middle income' countries. The proportion of the Indonesian people living in poverty has declined from over 70 to well under 20 per cent. There have been striking improvements in almost every sector of the economy . . . Rapid rise in rice yields has made it possible to reconcile greatly improved standards with food self-sufficiency. . . Remarkable improvements in the literacy and infant mortality rates reflect expansion in health and education services. Rising levels of income and education, reinforced by the effort that has gone into family planning, have yielded a significant decline in the birth rate. Rapid growth of industry and services has created enough jobs for a workforce increasing by more than two million a year without a serious rise in unemployment or underemployment (Arndt 1996).

Arndt points to two pieces of good luck enjoyed by the New Order government from the 1970s: the 'green revolution' enabling Indonesia to move towards self-sufficiency in rice, and the OPEC oil boom. But other countries experienced green revolutions and/or oil booms, without necessarily handling them well. Arndt believes that:

> Indonesia's outstanding economic performance is due to good economic management, prudent macroeconomic policies and, especially during the 1980s, major microeconomic reforms which in successive packages substantially deregulated the banking system and capital market, liberalised trade, facilitated direct foreign investment and reformed the tax system. Indonesia turned its back on the inward-looking strategy of industrial development based on import substitution by highly protected industries and opened its economy to international markets and competition.[1]

This is not to say that Indonesia had relied exclusively on 'trickle down' mechanisms to achieve the reduction of poverty. Major initiatives included the Transmigration Program under which more than 3.6 million people have been resettled by government from Java to the Outer Islands. The Kampung (urban village) Improvement Program is another long-running social program improving the provision of social services and infrastructure to the

---

1 It is fair (in the light of Indonesia's current financial crisis) to note that Arndt also referred in 1995 to 'some falling off in performance', noting the growth of Indonesia's foreign debt, some weaknesses in the deregulated banking system and some evidence of the growing influence of vested economic interests. These elements are essential to an understanding of the crisis as it has been revealed.

urban poor. Indonesia's national family planning program and associated infant and maternal health programs are world leaders in the field. And, as noted above, the New Order government has made substantial investments in education, commencing with the elementary schools.

Poverty alleviation became a more explicit element in national development planning during Repelita VI (the sixth five-year development plan, 1993–1998). This reflected growing political concern about regional disparities in income distribution in Indonesia. A special program directed at 'backward' village communities (the Inpres Desa Tertinggal, or IDT, program) was launched. It combines grants for the provision of infrastructure for more than 20,000 villages, with grants for microcredit to stimulate economic activities. These are targeted at the poorest one-third of all villages in Indonesia and are designed to address issues of regional, as well as inter-personal, distribution of income.

The 'mass movement' character of the IDT program is echoed by a somewhat similar program launched in 1996 in response to current political concerns about inequality. Whereas the IDT program is coordinated by BAPPENAS (the national development planning agency) the 'Prosperous Family' program is based on infrastructure already in place for the national family planning program and implemented by the National Family Planning Coordinating Board. The initiative is unusual in being conducted outside the framework of the five-year planning process, and in being based on a levy collected outside the framework of the tax code. The Prosperous Family program also employs microcredit as a tool, and is discussed below.

The World Bank World Development Report (1997b) noted that it was Indonesian government policy to eradicate absolute poverty within a decade. The Bank suggested that this posed a challenge since the remaining poor 'are concentrated in isolated pockets of poverty with poor natural resource endowments, low population densities, and other socioeconomic characteristics that make them difficult to reach', these 'pockets' being mostly located in the Outer Islands. However, the priority accorded this goal was indicated by the fact that the former President Soeharto himself chaired a special ministerial-level committee to oversee the national poverty eradication program.

1.3 Overview of the financial system

This overview is concerned principally with the banking system, and with the extensive network of small financial institutions supervised by Bank Indonesia, the central bank. It is also necessary to say something about the Indonesian cooperative movement, which occupies an important place in the national ideology. This account reflects the situation in mid-1997 when fieldwork was conducted; substantial structural change in the sector is, however, an inevitable consequence of the economic crisis underway as this study goes to press.

Banks within the Indonesian financial system are regulated by Bank Indonesia (although the licensing of banks is the responsibility of the Ministry of Finance, acting under recommendation from Bank Indonesia). All non-bank financial institutions, with the exception of finance companies which are under the supervision of Bank Indonesia, are the direct responsibility of the Ministry of Finance.

Under the Banking Act of 1992, there are broadly two kinds of banks in Indonesia. These are the commercial banks and the Bank Perkreditan Rakyat (BPR: literally, 'people's credit banks', more usually translated as 'rural banks'). Commercial banks 'provide general banking services with access to the payments system and may also provide foreign exchange services (in fact, about one half of these banks provide foreign exchange services; these are the larger private banks with much more extensive branch networks). The rural banks (or BPRs) do not offer cheque or foreign exchange facilities. Cole and Slade (1996, p.128) describe them as:

> . . . basically small-scale savings banks; they are limited in terms of location, function, and portfolio composition. They are precluded from taking demand deposits and participating in the payments system. Their main role is to take time and savings deposits and to extend credit.

In February 1997 there were 237 commercial banks in Indonesia, with 7,342 branches. Seven state banks had some 1,700 branches between them and there were also 27 commercial banks owned by provincial governments with around 750 branches. Seventy-nine private commercial banks authorised to conduct foreign exchange transactions had some 4,000 branches, while 83 private commercial banks not offering foreign exchange services had some 800 branches. There were in addition 31 joint venture banks and 10 foreign banks. The latter two categories are restricted to locations in a small number of major cities.

At the same time, there were in operation some 2,000 rural banks (BPRs) and around 7,300 other rural financial institutions. This latter group consisted of institutions established prior to 1988, when significant changes (described below) occurred in the policy framework for banking. A range of rural financial agencies had developed throughout Indonesia during the Dutch colonial period, and more after Independence; these small financial institutions date from these earlier periods. They go by a variety of names depending on the province where they are located (for example, the Badan Kredit Desa (or village credit institution) dates back to 1898 and there are some 5,300 of these still active and operating in rural Java). Many have a close association with their respective provincial governments and have become self-sustaining rural financial institutions.

The seven state banks, among them Bank Rakyat Indonesia (BRI) which was given special responsibility for the rural agricultural sector, also date from colonial times and dominated the financial system until the commencement of financial sector liberalisation in 1983. The removal of restrictions on interest rates for deposits and loans at that time freed the private banks to compete with the state banks and began a shift in their relative importance which has continued until today. Thus, in 1982 the private domestic banks owned slightly less than 10 per cent of all bank assets, while the major state banks controlled almost 80 per cent. By 1988, the private banks' share of total bank assets had risen to more than 22 per cent and the major state banks held around 69 per cent.

Another consequence of the financial sector reforms of 1983 was the commencement of BRI's small deposit and loan programs, *Simpedes* and *Kupedes*, which have subsequently achieved international recognition for their outreach and effectiveness. They were constructed upon the failure of BRI's earlier programs of rural financing, which had been designed to stimulate rice production, and for which purpose an infrastructure of 3,600 *unit desa* (village units) had been created. These were deployed to deliver rural financial services in which, following the freeing up of interest levels, rates paid on savings were sufficient to attract deposits while those charged on loans were high enough to cover costs. Over time this rural financial revolution was to transform BRI from a loss-making institution to a profitable one; thus in 1993, *Simpedes* and *Kupedes* accounted for about one-sixth of BRI's balance sheet, but were the principal source of its profits (Cole & Slade, p.109).

The trend of relative growth of the private sector was accelerated by further banking sector reforms in 1988. These significantly reduced barriers to the entry of new private banks to the system, as well as facilitating the expansion of existing branch networks. State-owned enterprises were permitted to deposit funds with private banks while the reserve requirements imposed on all banks were substantially reduced, permitting an expansion of bank lending. The number of branches of the major state banks rose from around 850 in 1988 to almost 1,200 in 1994. The number of private banks rose from 63 to 166 over the same period, while the number of their branches rose from around 560 to more than 3,200. By 1994, the private domestic banks controlled more than 44 per cent of all bank assets, while the share of the seven major state banks had fallen to just 43 per cent (Cole & Slade, tables 5.4, 5.5).

Central bank officials regard the period from 1988 to 1991 as one of 'acceleration' of the liberalisation process, while more recent years have been a period of 'consolidation'. Several bank crises contributed to a reassessment of policy and the emergence of some re-regulation was a result. A new Banking Act was passed in 1992; this enshrined the basic division of the banking sector between commercial banks and rural banks (BPRs). The latter had also been subject to some liberalisation in the 1988 reforms, which set a minimum capital requirement of Rp50 million as an incentive for small-scale indigenous entrepreneurs to set up these small banks. This stimulated rapid growth in their numbers.

By 1992, when the Banking Act was passed, some 850 new rural banks had been established in addition to the thousands of pre-existing rural financial institutions. This law envisaged these institutions upgrading themselves ultimately to meet rural bank standards. A subsequent directive required institutions to conform by October 1997 or cease operations. The law also approved the provision of financial services by BPRs to small urban entrepreneurs; this led to the growth of 'rural' banks in urban areas. There are now more than 300 in Jakarta alone. By early 1997, there were some 1,350 of the 'new' rural banks and about 650 'old' rural banks from the pre-1988 period.

With the rapid growth of bank assets since 1983, and particularly since 1988, the ratio between broad money (M2) and GDP rose from less than 19 per cent in 1983 to more than 46 per cent in 1994. While well below the levels of Malaysia and Thailand, this measure of financial development is comparable with that achieved in the Philippines and higher than in most of the South Asian countries considered in this study. With inflation at 9.4 per cent in 1995, the real rate of interest on short-term deposits was between 5 and 6 per cent. This is a substantial real return to domestic savers and creates an environment conducive to savings mobilisation.

Turning briefly to the cooperative system, it is notable that cooperation has a special place in the Indonesian national ideology of *Pancasila*. The New Order government has promoted cooperatives as a vehicle for government programs since 1967, especially in the agricultural sector, and has directed substantial resources to them. While subsidised credits channelled through the central bank and the state banks have been substantially reduced, the government-sponsored agricultural cooperatives benefit from those that remain. Neither the central bank nor the Ministry of Finance has authority over the credit activities of cooperatives, which are the domain of the Ministry of Cooperatives. Private cooperatives have been discouraged, but some independent credit cooperatives exist, coordinated by

CUCO (the Indonesian Credit Union Coordinating Office), an affiliate of the world credit union movement.

The 1992 Cooperatives Law entrenches the role of the 34,000 officially supported cooperatives (the Koperasi Unit Desa, village cooperative units, or KUD) and their continuing claim on government resources. Bank Indonesia data (cited in Cole & Slade, p.307) suggest that total credit extended to cooperatives from all sources may have been as much as 12.3 per cent of all credit outstanding as at March 1994. They cite one observer's comment that the official cooperatives are 'largely viewed as inefficient, corrupt and smothered by central government bureaucracy'.

Notwithstanding this, Cole and Slade sum up the transformation of the financial sector as follows:

> During the period 1984–1994 the financial system expanded rapidly and became much more diversified and sophisticated. The number of enterprises engaged primarily in financial business quadrupled, and the ratio of total financial assets to the gross national product (GNP) nearly tripled.

The lessons they draw are that:

> The Indonesian experience with implementing policies for the banking sector demonstrates that freeing up direct controls over price allocation and entry of new institutions . . . can result in reasonably healthy growth, expanded services and improved efficiency. It also demonstrates that both small, locally owned limited activity banks and widely dispersed units of a large state-owned bank can provide needed financial services and operate profitably in rural areas of a relatively poor country.

The reference here is to the effective and sustainable operations of small, locally owned rural banks and of Bank Rakyat Indonesia, both of which are discussed in greater detail below.

1.4 Overview of microfinance

An overview of microfinance in Indonesia must necessarily take a rather different form from the overviews presented in a number of the other country studies. There are two major reasons for this. The first of these is that certain formal financial institutions in Indonesia have been successful in extending sustainable financial services deep into the countryside, and that a wide range of small financial institutions exists which effectively provide financial services to rural populations, including many of the poor. They are not microfinance institutions per se, but rather financial institutions, both large and small, which have succeeded in incorporating elements of microfinance into their range of activities.

The second element of difference concerns the role and status of NGOs, which in other countries underpin much microfinance activity. In Indonesia, an effective system of local administration under the Department of Home Affairs, together with widespread networks of cadres employed by line agencies (health, family planning, family welfare, agriculture) gives the central government considerable capacity to implement its policies and programs in the provinces. Coupled with some reserve felt by officials at all levels towards NGOs (which, despite their undoubted capacity to respond to local needs are also viewed as alternative foci of political energy and influence), this means that there has been less scope in Indonesia for the spontaneous emergence of private NGO initiatives than in, say, India or the Philippines. Many community-based structures exist for the implementation of government policies and programs, but these are closely associated with the system of village administration and do not have the character of NGOs. Indeed, NGOs do exist, but the climate is not conducive to their proliferation, by comparison with a number of other countries included in these country studies.

For both the reasons outlined above, there is little direct support provided by the government for independent microfinance activities in Indonesia. Some individual NGOs have links with international NGOs which have brought limited funding and know-how from overseas. The Grameen Bank approach to microfinance is practised in Indonesia, but to a quite limited degree.

It is estimated that there are rather more than 5,000 NGOs operating in Indonesia. They have a wide range of involvement, ranging from education and health services, cooperatives and rural community development, legal aid and human rights, to environment preservation and customer protection activities (Bambang 1997b). Relatively few are involved in microfinance, and very few exclusively so. One of the most important NGOs with multiple activities is Bina Swadaya. It was founded in 1967 and now has more than 700 staff and a multi-faceted program, which includes microenterprise development and microfinance. Besides being a leading player in the PHBK (Bank/SHG linkage program) where it specialises in developing the capacities of self-help groups, Bina Swadaya also owns five rural banks. The tendency for NGOs engaged in microfinance to create or acquire BPRs as vehicles for providing microfinance services is an interesting development in Indonesia. At least one NGO has taken the further step of establishing a commercial bank, Bank Purba Danarta, with initial capital of $5 million (Seibel 1997).

The limited role of NGOs in microfinance does not mean that private initiative is lacking in Indonesia to promote this approach to poverty alleviation. As evidence of this, it is only necessary to mention again the proliferation of small, locally based financial institutions, totalling some 7,300 separate entities which serve the needs of lower income groups, including some of the poor. However, it is also necessary to recall that these small institutions are heavily concentrated in the Inner Islands; this suggests the need to establish microfinance institutions more widely throughout the country. In this process there is great scope for NGOs to contribute. The existence of many self-help groups in Indonesia, often based on traditional or customary arrangements, also suggests greater scope for NGO involvement than is presently occurring.

Hans Dieter Seibel, a well-informed observer of microfinance in Indonesia, has calculated the volume of lending by microfinance institutions as at end-1995 (table 2). Total lending by BRI's Unit Desa totalled more than twice as much as was lent by BPRs, while the lending of BPRs was, in turn, nearly five times as great as that of the small financial institutions. Strictly speaking, the table exaggerates the value of microfinance lending in Indonesia. It is stretching the definition of microfinance too far to include all the loans of BPRs and the other institutions under the heading of microfinance. Nonetheless, some idea of the relative importance of BRI, BPRs, and the other small lenders can be gained from these data.

Seibel also points out that in Indonesia, as elsewhere, this subsector is minute in relation to the financial system as a whole. The loans recorded in table 2 account for only 2.2 per cent of those advanced by the commercial banking sector. The disparity in savings is even greater; the savings deposits held by the MFI sector as he defines it equal only 0.7 per cent of commercial bank deposits. However, Seibel estimates that in terms of outreach the institutions with which we are concerned serve around 8 or 9 per cent of all borrowers and depositors in the Indonesian financial system. This is a more relevant statistic.

Table 2 BRI Unit Desa, rural banks and small financial institutions (December 1995)

Type of financial institution	Number	Credit		Funds mobilised		Total financial services	
		Accounts (' 000)	Amount (Rp bn)	Accounts (' 000)	Amount (Rp bn)	Accounts (' 000)	Amount (Rp bn)
1 BPRs (rural credit banks) and secondary banks	1,948	1,232	1,566	2,969	1,226	4,252	2,792
2 Small financial institutions (LKPD and BKDs)	7,313	1,216	317	1,632	181	2,846	498
Sub-total MFIs	9,261	2,448	1,883	4,601	1,447	7,098	3,290
3 BRI Unit Desa	3,482	2,264	3,194	14,483	6,016	16,747	9,210
TOTAL	12,743	4,712	5,077	19,084	7,463	23,845	12,500
4 Commercial banks	240	91,168	234,611	49,904	214,764	141,072	449,375

Source Adapted from Seibel 1997

Most surveys of microfinance activity focus on the supply side, considering the range of microfinance institutions serving the market, and their sustainability. This account of microfinance in Indonesia reports much achievement in terms of the supply side. It also records the impressive record of macroeconomic growth which has contributed to a burgeoning demand for microfinance services in Indonesia. However, at the microeconomic level, observers point out that there are many examples of rent-seeking behaviour by particular economic interest groups which constrain output and income in particular sectors and subsectors of the economy. Some of these situations are addressed in the World Bank's 1997 Report on Indonesia. Such circumstances constrain the demand for microfinance in many respects, particularly in rural areas and with respect to agricultural products.

2 Arrangements for direct support

Aside from the work of Bank Indonesia in promoting and supervising rural banks, in the interests of financial sector development, the government does not provide direct support to microfinance institutions per se. It does give support to MFIs when they play the role of agent for government in one or another of the several poverty alleviation programs employing credit. These are described below. Nor does the government support the establishment or operation of 'second tier' institutions, such as Palli Karma Sahayak Foundation (PKSF) in Bangladesh or the People's Credit and Finance Corporation (PCFC) in the Philippines. These have no direct equivalents in Indonesia, although BRI functions in some contexts as a second tier organisation.

For the most part, the provision of microfinance is simply one aspect of the operation of certain formal financial institutions in Indonesia. To the extent that they provide financial services to the poor, they do so by virtue of their effectiveness in serving populations, especially rural populations, with appropriate financial products in a commercially viable manner.

This brings us again to Bank Rakyat Indonesia (BRI), a state-owned financial institution which does not have the provision of microfinance services (at least as they are understood in this study) as a primary goal. Nonetheless, by virtue of its outreach and efficiency in the provision of financial services to low-income people, BRI succeeds in encompassing microfinance to some considerable degree. As mentioned in the overview of the Indonesian financial system in section 1.3, BRI is a world leader in the field of rural financing in low-income countries.

2.1 Bank Rakyat Indonesia: a rural financial institution encompassing microfinance

Bank Rakyat is one of the largest banks in Indonesia. It had more than 300 branch offices, mainly in provincial and district centres, and $12 billion in assets at the end of 1996. Its rural operations are conducted through some 3,600 village banking units (Unit Desa), but it also provides a broad range of services including corporate and commercial banking (CGAP 1997). CGAP also reports that at end-1996 some 2.5 million loans were outstanding from Unit Desa, with a total value of $1.7 billion. These rural banking units also held some 16 million savings accounts totalling $2.6 billion.

CGAP notes that the average loan balance outstanding is $680, which represents 65 per cent of annual per capita income in Indonesia, while the average savings balance, at $163, is around 16 per cent of average income. Some evidence concerning the distribution of loan sizes comes from a sample survey made in January 1995, at which time 14.6 per cent of *Kupedes* credits consisted of loans below Rp500,000 ($215) per individual. However, average loan size has been increasing, and in order to improve its service to small borrowers, BRI is now offering a smaller scale *Kupedes* product, granting loans up to Rp500,000 ($215). It is hoped that this will more effectively meet the credit needs of the poor in rural areas. However, all BRI loans are collateralised, even if (at the lower end of the scale) 'collateral' is interpreted generously to include household removables. Nonetheless, this requirement is a barrier to the bank's reaching the poorest.

The importance of the financial sector liberalisation measures of 1983, which freed BRI and other banks to set interest rates adequate to mobilise savings and cover the costs of lending, has been mentioned. In addition, CGAP cited the stable macroeconomic environment, strong political leadership and substantial investment in professionalising BRI's human resource base as factors in its success. When an additional factor cited by CGAP ('clear and transparent financial reporting and accountability') is taken into account, it is instructive to compare BRI's market-oriented Unit Desa system of financial outreach with the subsidised activities of the Koperasi Unit Desa (village cooperative units). The lessons of BRI's success should be studied carefully by all state agricultural banks in the region, to consider how they may be applied in support of sustainable rural financial (and especially microfinancial) services.

2.2 Support through the banking system

Directed credit schemes

Kredit Usaha Kecil (KUK): Small Scale Business Credit

The most important instance of directed credit in Indonesia is the Kredit Usaha Kecil (credit for small activities or KUK). This commenced in 1990 as a political response to the reduction of Bank Indonesia's subsidised refinancing of a range of economic activities (discussed above in connection with the cooperatives). All banks were required to extend at least 20 per cent of their total loans to small and medium enterprises, originally defined as firms with assets of less than Rp600 million ($257,000) (not including land and buildings). Considering that the maximum amount of such loans was to be Rp200 million ($85,000), it will be clear that this was not primarily directed to the microenterprise sector. It is principally concerned with supporting the development of indigenous small business, in the face of ethnic Chinese dominance of larger scale enterprise.

Bank Indonesia estimates that there are some 30 million small-scale enterprises in Indonesia. Requiring relatively low capital, using simple technology and having the potential for substantial employment generation, small-scale enterprises are an important objective of government policy. However, the relevance of the KUK for microfinance is limited to the fact that any credits extended by the banks for genuine microfinancing may be counted towards the 20 per cent requirement. A directive from Bank Indonesia dated April 1997 redefines the maximum net worth of small-scale entrepreneurs eligible for KUK credits at Rp200 million (not including land and buildings) or around $85,000. The maximum credit allowable under the scheme is now Rp350 million (or around $145,000) (Bank Indonesia, 1997a).

It is understandable that many of the private commercial banks in Indonesia have had difficulty in meeting the 20 per cent requirement for loans to small enterprise. Those which are focused on corporate lending and which lack extensive branch networks have been particularly affected. One response has been for these banks to channel funds through the rural banking system (BPRs) in partial satisfaction of the requirement. This arrangement has become institutionalised with the creation of a foundation, DABANAS, as a joint enterprise of Perbanas (the Association of Indonesian National Private Banks) and Perbarindo (the Association of Indonesian Rural Banks). The DABANAS Foundation will be funded by a spread of 1 per cent between the rate at which it receives money from the commercial banks (16.5 per cent) and the rate at which it on-lends to the rural banks. It will also provide technical assistance to the rural banks. Given that they have outreach to lower income sections of the population, the increasing involvement of BPRs in handling small-scale business credits for the commercial banks is likely to have some benefit for the microenterprise sector. DABANAS also has the potential to exercise some of the regulatory and supervisory functions of a second tier organisation, with respect to rural banks. This could be a valuable service, especially in regard to smaller rural banks which have access to poorer sections of the population.

Programs channelled through the banking system

Bank Indonesia liquidity credits

As described in section 1.3, the village cooperative units (Koperasi Unit Desa, or KUD) are among the beneficiaries of the remaining 'liquidity credits', or subsidised refinancing, available from Bank Indonesia and channelled via commercial banks. The persistence of this financing for KUDs in the face of the more general move away from subsidised credit reflects the special role accorded to the official cooperatives in the state ideology. The credits are designed to support food self-sufficiency, small-scale enterprise in the agricultural sector and the viability of the cooperatives themselves. Schemes include the KKUD, which funds village cooperative units to purchase *padi*, food crops, and other agriculture output from farmer members, and also to purchase agricultural inputs for sale to their members. The average loan size to members is between Rp200,000 and Rp400,000 ($85 to $170). It is funded 75 per cent by the central bank's liquidity credit at an interest rate of 14 per cent, with 25 per cent supplied by commercial banks at market rates of 18 to 20 per cent. Another program is the KKPA, which grants credit facilities to members of cooperatives for small business development up to a maximum of Rp50 million ($20,000). The financing arrangements are similar to those of the KKUD.

The scheme of most general application is the KUT (farming activities credit) for which Bank Indonesia provides 100 per cent funding at 14 per cent interest, 5 per cent of which goes to the cooperative unit as the executing agent. Although sometimes described as microcredit, these lending arrangements are directed to landowners and to the support of the cooperative movement itself, and do not benefit the very poor to any significant extent. A somewhat similar comment can be made with respect to another Bank Indonesia program sometimes described as 'microfinance', the Small Enterprise Development Project, which is not discussed in this survey.

Bank Indonesia's Microcredit Project

Bank Indonesia is responsible for implementing two projects which have explicit microfinance elements; these are the Microcredit Project and the Project Linking Banks with Self Help Groups. The latter is described below. The microcredit project is funded by a loan of $25.5 million from the Asian Development Bank, with $17 million counterpart funding from Bank Indonesia. It will extend over the period 1995–2000 with the objective of reaching 300,000 borrowers in five of the provinces of Indonesia. It is located so as not to overlap with the IDT program described below.

Loanable funds are disbursed by Bank Indonesia to BPDs (the provincial government commercial banks) and BPRs. BPRs on-lend directly to microentrepreneurs, while BPDs lend to small financial institutions. Bank Indonesia lends the funds at 16.5 per cent and these are on-lent at market rates of 2 to 3 per cent flat per month. NGOs do not play a financial intermediary role but are involved in organising self-help groups. BPDs receive a spread of 2 per cent for providing technical assistance to rural banks and small financial institutions.

Apart from the objectives of income and employment generation, the project is also directed to the development of small financial institutions and NGOs dealing with microfinance. The belief is that if they are sufficiently strengthened, these institutions can continue to serve microentrepreneurs by accessing normal commercial funding sources. Many of the small financial institutions are already doing so, but one of the objectives of the project is to encourage these institutions to redirect credit to lower income people. The project is preparing to define its own poverty line. It will target one third of its loans to people below this line, and two thirds to the 'nearly poor' just above the line.

However, while the project has some poverty focus, its other objective is to encourage financial development through further outreach by the existing rural banks and small financial institutions. This is what Bank Indonesia feels to be its primary function. In fact, the central bank does not have explicit policies in regard to microfinance per se, and poverty is seen as a broader government responsibility, for which mass campaigns such as the IDT and Prosperous Family programs are seen as more appropriate responses. The former Governor of Bank Indonesia recently acknowledged that the central bank's policies in regard to 'financial aspects of poverty alleviation' have relevance to 'national efforts to alleviate poverty' but emphasised that these must be seen 'within the scope of its role as a central bank'. He described the bank's 'core functions' as monetary management, guardianship of the payments system and banking supervision (Soedradjad Djiwandono 1996).

This description by the former governor of Bank Indonesia's core functions is accurate and appropriate; current events indicate the importance of central banks in the region giving priority to traditional central bank functions. Nonetheless, Bank Indonesia has taken a strong incidental interest in microfinance development and its leadership, expressed through programs such as the PHBK and microcredit project, has sent valuable signals to the banking sector as a whole. Bank Indonesia should maintain this leadership, although pressing concerns arising from the crisis in Indonesia's formal banking sector, commencing in the second half of 1997, will make it difficult for the central bank to do so.

Income Generating Project for Marginal Farmers and Landless (P4K)

The P4K project is conducted by the Ministry of Agriculture and is a multifaceted set of activities targeted at groups of the rural poor whose family income is below the Sajogyo poverty line, equivalent to 320 kg of rice per capita per year. It differs from all the other programs discussed above by reason of this exclusive poverty focus. The participants in P4K include small farmers, the landless, farm labourers, sharecroppers, marginal farmers and small fishermen who are organised in 'small farmer groups'.

Groups range in size from eight to sixteen persons and operate on the principles of homogeneous membership, group decision making, progress towards self-reliance, and learning by doing. Extension workers from the Ministry of Agriculture and other agencies provide support and training activities. NGO involvement is extremely limited. Groups undertake a range of training activities before the option of credit is introduced.

Microfinance is a major component of the P4K, and the microfinance component is conducted for the Ministry of Agriculture by Bank Rakyat Indonesia. When P4K commenced in 1979, BRI acted simply as a channelling bank for loan funds in keeping with the operating methods common to that period. It had two elements: conventional credits repaid to the bank and also revolving funds. The former had much better results because of BRI's supervision, with the result that the revolving funds were dropped from the second phase of the project. Also, over time the improvement in BRI's general operating methods was reflected in its conduct of the P4K project, including greater emphasis on savings as a precondition for credit. In the second phase BRI became the executing, rather than simply the channelling, bank. Loans to groups were made by BRI branches, with repayments by individuals made to the Unit Desa. Loanable funds came from IFAD and Bank Indonesia at a mean cost of 6.3 per cent, and were on-lent to small farmer groups (SFGs) at 12 per cent flat (22.15 per cent effective annual). The BRI margin was 1 to 2 per cent after costs, which put the scheme on a commercial basis.

So far, some 47,000 self-help groups (SHGs) have been formed with over half a million members below the poverty line. More than a third of groups are exclusively for women, a similar proportion exclusively for men, and around one quarter are mixed. Some

80 per cent of all groups have so far borrowed from the program in the second phase. Arrears in mid-1997 were about 3.6 per cent, with cumulative arrears as a proportion of current outstanding credit at 12 per cent. IFAD is said to regard this as the best performance of any project it supports in Asia, and to consider any cumulative repayment figure of 95 per cent or more as very good. All credit has been non-collateralised. Since the beginning P4K has employed only 'social collateral', with group guarantees, while group savings are blocked for the duration of the loan.

A third phase of P4K is under negotiation, to commence from 1998 with IFAD and ADB support. It is proposed to increase the number of groups to 85,000. Whereas during the current phase credits to individuals have had an upper limit of Rp100,000 ($430) for first loans, rising to a maximum of Rp300,000 ($1,280) for the fourth loan cycle, in the next phase the maximum for individual loans will be raised to Rp500,000 ($2,140). It is hoped that, after individuals have received three successive loans at that level, it will be possible for them to graduate to standard BRI Unit Desa loans. There they will face collateral requirements and the higher interest rates applicable to *Kupedes*. However, it is hoped that persons graduating from the scheme will have an excellent chance of succeeding with *Kupedes* loans, because they will have been identified by officers of BRI's Unit Desa responsible for the P4K lending.

The Ministry of Agriculture claims that evaluations of P4K activities indicate benefits in productivity, employment, social and community life, and the status of women. The project claims increases in the volume of production in 80 per cent of groups and qualitative improvements in 65 per cent. Perhaps equally significant are changes in the 'relations of production' with many beneficiaries graduating to self-employment. The project claims increased working hours in two-thirds of groups, with an average of 27 hours additional gainful work per week per household.

Benefits are seen in social and community life through the improvement in self-confidence of beneficiaries and in their social standing. The organisation of women in groups (with 35 per cent of all groups being exclusively for women and 40 per cent of all beneficiaries being women) is regarded as an achievement. The most common activity funded for women is petty trading (in 38 per cent of cases). While cautioning against the too ready acceptance of these kind of survey data, Hans Dieter Seibel (1997) describes the impact of the project as 'remarkable'. He notes, however, that despite the 'spectacular' growth of P4K's outreach it still has reached fewer than 10 per cent of the population below the official poverty line. In regard to the prominent role played by women in P4K, Seibel comments that:

> Special programs focussing solely on the poor like P4K made the experience that a strong though not necessarily exclusive focus on women will greatly contribute to the viability of the program and also be more effective in poverty alleviation in terms of donor investment (p. 12).

Seibel believes this suggests the need for a special effort to transform the P4K program, and others of similar nature, by creating 'large numbers of autonomous local MFIs owned and run by women'. We endorse this view.

Linkages between banks and specialised microfinance institutions

PHBK: Linking Banks and Self-Help Groups

In Asia, the initial impetus for financial linkages between banks and self-help groups (SHGs) came from APRACA (the Asia Pacific Rural and Agricultural Credit Association) which recommended that its member institutions should trial such linkages to improve access for the poor to financial services. Bank Indonesia was the first APRACA member to take up this challenge, and in 1989 in partnership with the German aid agency GTZ launched the PHBK program (project linking banks and self-help groups) in four provinces of Indonesia. By 1992 this project had gone beyond the pilot phase and had spread to twelve provinces.

To seek to use self-help groups as intermediaries for microfinance raises the question of how such groups are to be established. In other countries, and in Indonesia initially, NGOs were regarded as the logical institutions to create and prepare SHGs for microfinance. Informal savings and credit groups, suitable for organisation as self-help groups and appropriate for participation in such programs as PHBK, P4K and the Microcredit Project, are described by Seibel (1997) as 'ubiquitous' in Indonesia.

A number of leading Indonesian NGOs participate in the PHBK program, but the NGO movement has not shown the capacity to meet the targets for expansion of PHBK outreach. Efforts to establish an umbrella organisation for NGOs engaged in the PHBK program, which might facilitate improved performance by them, have also languished. Much work in group formation has also been done by other agencies and community groups linked with government programs; these groups and the NGOs collectively are known in Indonesia as self-help promoting institutions. Quite recently, the PHBK has tapped the energies of Indonesia's rural banks, which has enabled more rapid expansion of the program's outreach.

In September 1996 the PHBK program involved 410 banks, 183 NGOs and some 6,800 SHGs in 16 provinces. Total savings mobilised had reached Rp8,625 million ($3.7 million), while the cumulative total of credit extended was Rp44,808 million ($19.2 million) (with current outstandings of Rp19,625 million [$8.4 million]). The cumulative repayment rate was said to be 96.4 per cent. A flexible savings to credit ratio which typically ranges from 1:3 to 1:6 determines the size of the loan. Interest rates are market based and transaction costs are covered by interest margins.

As its operational methods have evolved, the PHBK has tended to discourage 'self-help promoting institutions' from acting as financial intermediaries, in favour of a model of 'social' intermediation in which training and guidance for the SHG are provided by NGOs and other community-based groups. However, since 1995 a third path has rapidly come into use, with a dramatic increase in the involvement of rural banks in the PHBK program. Small rural banks and even commercial banks which have local branch networks close to the target group are encouraged to establish their own direct linkages with self-help groups, and to take the initiative to form such groups themselves if necessary, a process which will be facilitated by the operations of the new DABANAS Foundation, discussed above. Other commercial banks are encouraged to create indirect linkages with the poor by providing refinancing to BPRs. Such lending counts towards these commercial banks' requirement to support small enterprise under the 20 per cent KUK rule, and is a convenient way of discharging the obligation. Since the decision to concentrate the expansion of the program on rural banks, the numbers of groups and loans outstanding are reported to have been growing at a compound rate of 10 per cent per month.

While the rural banks have shown the capacity to develop and manage SHGs for themselves, NGOs and other 'self-help promoting institutions' will continue to have a role, especially in the Outer Islands where BPRs are much less common. One of the themes which emerges from this survey is the need to allow NGOs in Indonesia a greater role in microfinance provision, principally through their support of the self-help group movement. The resistances to this arise partly from the limitations of NGOs themselves but also from political factors.

The PHBK has proved a significant mechanism to serve the credit needs of those who are generally bypassed by formal banking institutions. However, it does not specifically target those below the poverty line. Intensive technical inputs, training and guidance provided by GTZ have contributed greatly towards the introduction and strengthening of the PHBK program in Indonesia. Present plans call for the expansion of the PHBK mechanism to all 27 provinces of Indonesia by the year 2000, but the program of technical assistance provided by GTZ will cease in 1999, so that sustainability will become an important issue at that time.

Both the PHBK and the P4K programs are carefully crafted models of sustainable microfinance service delivery, with the former operating since 1987 and the latter since 1979. P4K, as we have seen, has reached about 10 per cent of the eligible population in the social groups which it targets. It is perhaps understandable, therefore, that given the large absolute number of the poor remaining (some 22.5 million in 1996) that larger scale, more 'broad brush' approaches to the eradication of poverty have emerged in recent years. In the process, considerations of financial institution development, sustainability and the like are being given much less priority than mass outreach. However, the value of continued expansion of sustainable programs such as P4K and PHBK should be recognised.

2.3 Other major programs

Reflecting political concern with the problem of the hardcore poor, the Government of Indonesia has introduced two mass programs during the current Repelita (1993–1998). The first of these is the Inpres Desa Tertinggal (IDT) which was a scheduled program of Repelita VI and commenced in 1993. The second major campaign, the Prosperous Family Program, was introduced as an emergency measure in 1996. Both programs reflected a decision that direct intervention was necessary to overcome problems of residual poverty in Indonesia. In previous Repelitas the government had made considerable progress in meeting basic needs in education and health, in the development of rural financial services, and in maintaining an overall rate of economic growth which distributed benefits to all income classes. However, issues of relative poverty, and the persistence of regional and subregional concentrations of poverty, were felt to call for a more direct approach.

Inpres Desa Tertinggal (IDT)

Inpres Desa Tertinggal means 'presidential instruction relating to backward villages'. As a presidential program, the IDT calls upon an interdepartmental effort, coordinated by BAPPENAS, the national development coordination authority. The program commenced with the identification of some 28,000 backward (literally, 'left behind') villages. While the chosen villages represent 44 per cent of the national total, only 26 per cent of villages on Java were chosen for the program, whereas 68 per cent of villages on the Outer Islands other than Java and Sumatra qualified for assistance. This indicates the thrust to redress regional income inequalities.

The assistance to these villages under the IDT contains three basic components:

- a capital injection of Rp20 million ($8,500) per year to each village for up to three years to fund income-generating activities of the poor, organised in groups

- the provision of 'facilitators' to assist these self-help groups of the poor in each village become economically active. The facilitators include teachers, health workers, social workers and young college graduates assigned to the program
- the provision of rural physical infrastructure (roads, bridges, jetties, water supply and sanitation) to the value of Rp100 to 130 million ($43,000 to $56,000) per village (Gunawan 1997).

The capital injection of $600 million was spread over three years (1994–97) to stimulate economic activity in the chosen villages. The program of infrastructure development is phased over a longer period, and involves multilateral loans as well as Indonesian government funding. In the previous Repelita, the thrust of central government programs to reduce regional inequalities had been very largely towards physical infrastructure development, a process to which the World Bank and other agencies had contributed. The new thrust is designed to be more direct, providing village people with the financial resources and technical assistance to increase their productivity and earnings. Infrastructure provision is a secondary measure.

The capital injections for income generation have been allocated to self-help groups (*Kelompok Masyarakat* or 'people's groups') in the chosen villages as outright grants. Groups are free to decide the terms on which this capital will be loaned to members. This is essentially a revolving fund scheme, although the longer run objective is for the SHGs in villages to be linked with BPRs, small financial institutions and other sources of commercial funds.

The outreach of the IDT has been impressive. At the end of 1996 some 107,000 self-help groups had been created, involving almost 2.9 million people. By March 1997 this number was reported to have grown to more than 120,000 groups and 3.3 million persons. A high degree of freedom has been given in relation to the use of funds, which are employed as seed capital for ventures in agriculture, horticulture, livestock rearing, fisheries, artisanal trades, and petty trading. Approximately 3 million poor households had received seed capital averaging $85 per household by mid-1997.

An evaluation of groups in eleven provinces, conducted in 1996, came to the conclusion that after three years of IDT funding some 31. 6 per cent, or almost one third, were adequately prepared for entry to the Bank Indonesia linkage project, the PHBK (Sajogyo 1997). This is another alternative under consideration. Although it would require a substantial increase in the resources allocated by Bank Indonesia for technical assistance under the PHBK, such an increase appears justified. This may be an opportunity for external assistance; such assistance should focus on achieving transition to commercial operation by groups which, under present IDT operating practices, benefit from substantial subsidies.

The Prosperous Family program

As mentioned in section 1.2, a second mass program was launched by the government in 1996 as an emergency response to political concerns about income inequality. Apart from its having been launched outside the framework of Repelita VI, it has several other unusual features. It is financed by a levy of 2 per cent on the incomes of persons and corporations in excess of Rp100 million ($42,700) per year. This levy is collected and administered by a foundation created by the former President Soeharto. The levy raises revenue outside the normal taxation framework and gives the impression of being a populist response to resentment of the wealth of the 'conglomerates'.

The Prosperous Family Program is implemented by BKKBN (the National Family Planning Coordination Board). BKKBN is an agency of the government of Indonesia with an international reputation for the sustained effectiveness of its family planning program, which is credited with substantially reducing the rate of population growth over the past quarter century. In the process, it has built up an infrastructure in practically every village in Indonesia, giving it almost unrivalled outreach. This capacity has been deployed in disseminating contraceptive knowledge and supplies, and in influencing the attitudes of two generations of Indonesians.

Women's groups set up as the vehicles for these activities enrol a high proportion of the cohort of Indonesian women of child-bearing age. They provide a ready-made organisational structure for the Prosperous Family program. The program is directed by State Minister for Population Haryono Suyono who is quoted (*Kompas*, 28 June 1997) as stating that up to April 1997 some 9.8 million Indonesian families had received funding. This is an extraordinary administrative and logistic achievement, accomplished in just 12 months. Funds are channelled to the groups via Bank Negara Indonesia, a state bank, or via post offices where there are no bank branches, and administered on the ground by government field staff.

Beneficiaries of the program are women. They are divided into classes according to their economic status. The poorest groups are enrolled initially in the *Takesra* (Prosperous Family savings scheme). Each woman receives a tiny initial grant of Rp2,000 (85 cents) to commence a savings account. She is encouraged to put aside Rp100 (4 cents) each month for 6 months, at which time she receives a bonus of Rp2,000 in the account. If these women can accumulate Rp25,000 ($11), they then become eligible for loans under the *Kukesra* (Prosperous Family credit scheme) which also has a savings component. Much criticism has been directed at the small size of the initial loan under this scheme, Rp20,000 ($9), which is loaned at a concessional rate of 6 per cent. In press interviews Haryono has defended the scheme on the basis that it is designed to effect social change, and that the poorest of the poor lack confidence to handle larger sums; they must be brought up to the point where they are capable of managing their finances.

The program is undoubtedly huge and operates on a subsidised interest rate indicating that financing under the program is not sustainable. Secondly, doubts remain whether the groups of family planning acceptors, accustomed to outright grants and organised originally with quite different objectives, will be able to convert themselves into successful savings and credit groups. Similar doubts must be raised about the capacity of family planning and family health field staff to implement an essentially economic or 'livelihood' program.

Comment

Considering the IDT and Prosperous Family programs, it is clear that both represent a substantial break from the pattern of careful expansion of sustainable financial activity in rural Indonesia. The IDT provides outright grants which initiate revolving funds. Groups are not required to set terms of lending which would cover costs and compensate for inflation. The Prosperous Family program provides credit in amounts which might be thought too small to finance significant economic activities for borrowers, at the highly concessional interest rate of 6 per cent. Both programs depend on intensive inputs from government field staff, and there are real questions concerning the capacities of the staff concerned to nurture economic, as distinct from social, activities. Finally, although IDT and Prosperous Family are not supposed to overlap geographically, in some cases they do, as well as coinciding to some degree with P4K which is attempting to cover costs with an effective interest rate of 22 per cent. The expansion of small commercial financial institutions such as the rural banks could also be inhibited to the extent there is an overlap with their potential client base. Such distortions should be avoided so far as possible.

For both IDT and Prosperous Family it is intended that groups will graduate to relationships with commercial funding sources (be they rural banks, the PHBK program, or small financial institutions). The success of these programs, in terms of substantial expansion of access of the poor to microfinance, will only be assured if this loop can be closed. The judgement of Hans Dieter Seibel (1977), made with respect to the IDT, could equally well apply to both of these mass campaigns: '. . . IDT will only be successful to the extent that concerns for institutional viability and sustainability will outweigh the concern for short-term political gains from liberal disbursement of funds'.

The 'graduation' of the best groups emerging from the IDT and Prosperous Family programs to a more rigorous commercial environment along the lines of programs such as PHBK and P4K should be encouraged, but will need resources for technical assistance. This is an area where NGOs are capable of making a greater contribution than at present.

Bambang Ismawan has attempted to calculate the human resource and financial requirements necessary to achieve Indonesia's share of global targets set at the Microcredit Summit in Washington in February 1997. Of a global target of one hundred million families to be provided with sustainable microfinance services by the year 2005, Bambang estimated Indonesia's share at seven million families or approximately thirty million people. (Bambang 1997a). This would ultimately require the formation of 280,000 SHGs and the services of 11,200 'facilitators', together with coordinators and administrative staff employed in 2,240 SHG facilitation centres. He estimated the annual operational expenses of these centres at Rp138 billion ($59 million) and saw a major role for NGOs in the process.

3 Regulation of non-bank microfinance institutions

3.1 The broad regulatory framework

This survey of microfinance in Indonesia has emphasised the importance of small financial institutions which provide microfinance services to the poor as part of their more general outreach. These include the Unit Desa of BRI, BPRs and a range of 'small financial institutions'. Our approach has been to describe institutions which provide microfinance, without necessarily describing them as microfinance institutions. BRI is a very clear case of a banking institution which provides microfinance services; the regulatory environment in which it operates is described under section 4 below. The other category of regulated bank in Indonesia is the BPRs or rural banks. The regulatory framework for BPRs is also described in section 4.

It will be useful at this point to distinguish between BPRs and the generic category of 'rural banks' of which they are a part. These consist of:

- *functioning rural banks (BPRs)*: there were some 2,000 of these in February 1997, of which around 1,350 are 'new' BPRs established under the reforms of 1988. There are around 650 'old' BPRs, dating from before 1988. Both categories are regulated banks under the 1992 Banking Act and are supervised by Bank Indonesia.

- *BKDs (rural credit agencies)*: there are around 5,350 of these very small local institutions exclusively on Java and the island of Madura. This category of institution originated under a Dutch ordinance. They are now licensed by the Ministry of Finance as BPRs, although for the time being they are not fully functioning as such.
- *LDKPs (rural fund and credit institutions)*: there were almost 2,000 of these early in 1997, licensed by provincial and local governments to mobilise savings and to lend. They are supervised by the provincial governments and BPDs (provincial government banks). They were mandated to upgrade to BPR status, supposedly by October 1997, although relatively few have done so.

All three categories (BPRs, LDKPs and BKDs) provide microfinance services to a greater or lesser extent. The functioning BPRs are regulated banks while LDKPs and BKDs are regarded for our purposes as non-bank MFIs and are therefore discussed in this section of the Indonesia survey. These latter institutions and their transition to BPR status are comprehended in the 1992 Banking Act.

As we have seen, NGOs play a relatively subdued role in the provision of microfinance in Indonesia, whereas in other countries they underpin much of the microfinance sector. As explained in section 1.4, effective local administration in Indonesia and the widespread networks of cadres employed by line agencies give government considerable capacity to implement policies and programs. When combined with reservations held by officials towards NGOs, particularly at the local level, this can lead to programs being conducted without them. For example, while it is IDT policy to involve NGOs so far as possible in the preparation of self-help groups, local-level officials charged with implementing the program are sometimes less willing to involve the NGOs from their districts.

The procedures for creating and registering an NGO are simple and straightforward. NGOs take the form of a *Yayasan*, a legal entity similar to a foundation. *Yayasan* are established for social objectives, and may conduct economic activities in pursuit of those objectives. A great many *Yayasan* are established in Indonesia for a wide range of purposes, such as Yayasan Dana Sejahtera Mandiri set up by the former President Soeharto to collect the levy on high-income earners and operate the Prosperous Family program. Some *Yayasan* control assets worth hundreds of millions of dollars and their activities can only be described as opaque. There are no reporting requirements, nor any provision for the taxation of the income of a *Yayasan*, although taxation liability on income derived from the business activities of a *Yayasan* is a grey area.

To form a *Yayasan*/NGO requires the services of a notary and the drafting of Articles of Association and rules. The *Yayasan* is established by a letter from the notary certifying it. It is apparently advisable to register the *Yayasan* with the Directorate General of Social and Political Affairs within the Department of Home Affairs, but not obligatory. Registration with the Directorate General, at a cost of Rp25,000 ($11), will establish that the objectives and activities of the *Yayasan* are consistent with *Pancasila*, the state ideology. An NGO intending to conduct lending activities does not require permission to do so; however, it is forbidden to mobilise savings from its members, other than by placing deposits on their behalf in a regulated financial institution. In fact, some savings mobilisation by NGOs appears to be tolerated, so long as the volume is small. This limitation on their capacity to mobilise resources for lending from their membership is one factor driving NGOs to consider creating rural banks. The situation of microfinance NGOs would be improved if ambiguities were removed concerning their right to collect compulsory savings from clients in connection with the provision of other microfinance services. NGOs should be free to do so.

Self-help groups are completely informal organisations in Indonesia. Seibel (1997) notes that hundreds of thousands of informal SHGs with savings and credit activities exist in Indonesia. Many are spontaneous groupings, based on traditional forms of association. Many others have been founded by government and community organisations in connection with government programs, or have been created by NGOs. The expansion and capacity building of self-help groups is a field which could benefit from greater involvement of NGOs, if a more positive attitude to their involvement were adopted by officials, especially at the local level.

Cooperatives are regulated by the Ministry of Cooperatives and can accept the savings of members. Because of their functions, cooperatives are perceived more as agents of the government than as people's institutions. As suggested in section 1.3, they are of relatively little significance for microfinance.

3.2 Interest rates

MFIs in Indonesia are free to set interest rates on deposits and loans. It is interesting to note that even before 1983 the myriad of small financial institutions in rural areas had been able to operate largely without restraint on their interest rates. This was a factor in establishing this system even before the liberalisation of 1983.

Where MFIs operate within the framework of a government program they may be constrained by the policies of that program in regard to maximum lending rates. In some cases also, the availability of subsidised credit from the Koperasi Unit Desa, the IDT or the Prosperous Family program can affect the ability of MFIs to charge full cost interest rates. Such distortions inhibit private responses to the need for microfinance. The overlap of programs which leads to such distortions should be avoided.

3.3 Prudential regulation and supervision

NGOs engaged in lending are subject to no external prudential regulation or supervision. When engaged on one or another of the government microfinance programs (for example, P4K or PHBK) they are subject to supervision by the relevant agency in each case. However, in the great majority of cases NGOs do not conduct financial intermediation, but instead serve as social intermediaries, working with self-help groups to prepare them for microfinance.

BKDs, as mentioned, now have BPR status under licence from the Ministry of Finance. As such, they are subject to the supervision of Bank Indonesia. They are continuing to function as rural credit agencies under the field supervision of officers of BRI. They have not yet commenced mobilising savings, although in principle they are entitled to do so. BRI staff visit BKDs on a weekly basis and assist management to compile weekly reports on the volume of credit outstanding and the quality of credit, applying BRI criteria. These reports are compiled at BRI branches, and aggregated reports are filed quarterly with Bank Indonesia. These institutions will make the transition to full operation as BPRs in due course.

LDKPs (rural fund and credit institutions) are in a different situation, having been established by decision of various provincial governments, by which they are registered.

Responsibility for their supervision is not as clear-cut as in the case of the BKDs above; the provincial government banks (BPD) provide technical assistance and collect some data on their operations. This is not forwarded to Bank Indonesia, nor does Bank Indonesia have the authority to require reporting.

Since the expiry of the October 1997 deadline to upgrade to BPR status, those institutions remaining are no longer entitled to mobilise savings. They must upgrade or wither away; stronger institutions with the necessary capital, office premises and appropriate leadership will become BPRs. One path to this could involve LDKPs using their capital base to establish a 'new' BPR (as permitted under the 1988 reforms) and then to go into liquidation. These 2,000 institutions are a resource for microfinance, especially since some are located outside Java. Every effort should be made to bring them up to the standards required for operation as BPRs.

3.4 Performance and reporting standards of second tier institutions

There are no second tier institutions in Indonesia equivalent to PKSF in Bangladesh or PCFC in the Philippines. However, BRI has responsibility for field supervision of BKDs, the rural banks which are not yet functioning as such. It can play a very important role in advancing BKDs to full operational status as rural banks. BRI is also the channelling bank for government microcredit programs, including the P4K. It is thus in a strategic position to set performance and reporting standards for the institutions with which it works. The new DABANAS Foundation will provide technical assistance to rural banks as well as loanable funds; to the extent it accepts the development of microfinance as an appropriate goal for the rural banks it could grow to exercise second tier functions also.

3.5 Self-regulation

With respect to NGOs, attempts have been made to achieve an organisational framework for those NGOs involved in Bank Indonesia's PHBK project. Since 1994, several meetings have been held, to form an organisation (given the acronym ALTRPAKU) which might provide a forum for communication between NGOs, and between them as a group and Bank Indonesia. The association has not yet functioned. Grameen replicators in Indonesia are associated with the Grameen Trust and CASHPOR, the network of replicators, which fulfils self-regulatory functions. BKDs, while not yet functioning as rural banks, will be eligible to join Perbarindo, the Association of Indonesian Rural Banks. Although it is not clear to what extent this organisation sees itself as responsible for self-regulation, the potential exists.

4 Regulation of banks

Some elements of the regulatory environment for banks have already been discussed in section 1.3 and elsewhere. Banks within the Indonesian financial system are regulated by Bank Indonesia, while the licensing of banks is done by the Ministry of Finance, acting under recommendation from the central bank. The current legislation is the Banking Act of 1992 which defines two categories of banks in Indonesia: commercial banks and rural banks. It is worth noting that the Act (Article 12) mandates all banks to support government programs; this is potentially a very significant obligation.

4.1 Licensing and minimum capital requirements

Banking licences are issued in consideration of an application satisfying certain criteria. These are described by Bank Indonesia as:

- the acumen and character of the prospective owners and managers
- the ability to provide the required resources for the bank's capital base
- the capacities of the bank owners and managers to conduct banking operations.

Bank Indonesia judges applications according to these criteria and recommends accordingly to the Minister of Finance (Bank Indonesia 1996). The minimum capital requirements are currently Rp50 billion ($21.4 million) for a commercial bank and Rp100 billion ($42.7) for a joint venture bank (with maximum 85 per cent foreign ownership). Minimum capital required for a rural bank is only Rp50 million ($21,000).

Under the 1992 Banking Act, rural banks are permitted to accept deposits only in the form of time deposits and savings. The category includes both the 'new' rural banks registered after the reform package of 1988 (of which there were around 1,350 in March 1997) and those registered before the 1988 reforms (of which there were some 640 in March 1997). The Act recognises the existence of the array of small rural financial organisations (of which as mentioned in section 3.1 there are currently somewhat more than 7,300) subdivided between LDKPs (rural fund and credit institutions) and BKDs (rural credit agencies). The Act empowers the government to set rules for changing their status. It provides for these small institutions ultimately to upgrade to meet the requirements for licensing as rural banks (Cole & Slade, p.129).

Cole and Slade note a number of key differences between commercial banks and rural banks. The latter are restricted both in their scope of operations and where they may locate. Rural banks are not part of the payments system, neither can they offer cheque accounts, or deal in foreign exchange. They must be wholly 'Indonesian owned' by individuals or an Indonesian legal entity. Cole and Slade comment that:

> . . . the Law actually changed the original expected role of these new BPRs from providing just rural finance to also 'providing services to economically weak groups and small-scale businessmen in urban areas'. The Law broadened the location opportunities for BPRs . . . New BPRs located outside cities could open branches in capital cities of districts, municipalities, provinces and in Jakarta . . .

The low minimum capital requirements and the relaxation of restrictions on location of BPRs have contributed to their flexibility and capacity to provide microfinance services. Their ability to operate in cities has spurred substantial growth in their activities in major urban areas. Jakarta alone now has more than 300 BPRs. It should be noted, however, that the current financial crisis has led to the closure of a number of rural banks, and may also lead to a tightening of the requirements for the establishment of rural banks.

4.2 Interest rates

The financial reforms of 1983, as described in section 1.3, included the freeing of interest rates on deposits and loans throughout the banking system. Since then real interest rates in the banking system (adjusted for inflation) have been strongly positive. This has stimulated a surge in savings mobilisation which contributed to shifting the balance between private and state banks in Indonesia. Seibel notes that the effect of deregulating interest rates 'has been more pronounced on savings proper, an instrument of the poorer sections of the population, than on time deposits, an instrument of the non-poor' (1997, p.21). BRI's capacity to set interest rates on advances high enough to cover the costs of lending underpinned the expansion of rural credit (including microfinance) through the Unit Desa system of BRI. Substantial increases in both interest rates and inflation are now occurring in Indonesia, however, and it is difficult to judge their impact at the time of writing.

BRI has a standard 1.5 per cent monthly flat rate on the smaller *Kupedes* loans which are relevant to microfinance. However, an additional flat 0.5 per cent monthly is added to each payment. If repayment obligations are met in timely fashion over a six-month period, this additional interest charged is returned to the borrower. However, if one or more loan payments is late, the additional charge is forfeited and the annual effective interest rate can exceed 40 per cent. Rural banks charge monthly flat interest rates which can be as high as 3 or 4 per cent. For example, rural banks involved in the PHBK typically charge 2.5 to 3 per cent per month flat.

4.3 Prudential regulation and supervision

Prudential requirements are broadly the same for commercial banks and rural banks. The capital adequacy ratio is set at a minimum 8 per cent of risk-weighted assets, following the standards established by the Bank for International Settlements. The reserve requirement imposed by Bank Indonesia applies only to commercial banks which are required to deposit a minimum reserve of at least 3 per cent of 'third party funds' in an account with the central bank. Rural banks have no such obligation.

The Banking Act does not require that loans be secured against collateral; this has significance for microfinance since there is no legal impediment to non-collateralised lending. However, the required provisioning for loan losses is greater in the case of loans without collateral, since the lending bank is entitled to deduct the value of collateral held from the outstanding balance before making provision.

Certain requirements apply to members of the board of directors of a bank. These relate partly to character and reputation, and partly to banking experience. At least 50 per cent of board members must have not less than three years banking experience (for commercial banks) or one year experience (for rural banks). Quite apart from problems of capitalisation, this requirement of banking operational experience is a hurdle for many small financial institutions which might seek to upgrade to rural bank status.

Banks are rated by Bank Indonesia as part of the supervisory process. The rating system, which is the same for commercial banks and rural banks, is a qualitative appraisal of various factors which affect the 'health' and growth of a bank. It assesses the CAMEL factors, as well as compliance with certain banking regulations. For rural banks this latter evaluation covers only the legal lending limit provision; for commercial banks it is more demanding. In the field of prudential regulation, Bank Indonesia is increasingly emphasising self-regulatory banking principles. Banks are required to have their own written credit policy guidelines; these must be sound and the banks must comply with them once they are established.

The reporting requirements of Bank Indonesia are somewhat less onerous for rural banks than for commercial banks. The latter must report weekly in relation to their mandatory reserve requirements and certain foreign exchange transactions. Monthly reporting for all banks includes a balance sheet for each office and reports of any legal lending limit violations. Financial statements are required on a semi-annual and annual basis, together with an annual auditor's report (from which the smallest rural banks are exempt). There are also some suggestions that the supervision of banks has not always been as rigorous as it could have been, and that this may have contributed to some of the problems currently facing the banking sector.

Bank Indonesia's Banking Regulation and Development Department comments that a more appropriate and helpful system of supervision and reporting needs to be developed for the rural banks. Issues of regulation, supervision and developing the capacity of the rural banking system are being actively considered. Considering the potential for rural banks to expand the availability of microfinance services, such reforms could be helpful.

5 Summary and recommendations

With GNP per capita of $980 in 1995, and after experiencing economic growth at an average 6 per cent annually for some thirty years, Indonesia was classified as a lower middle-income economy. This economic growth performance had been accompanied by a rapid decline in the proportion of the Indonesian population living in poverty, from 60 per cent in 1970 to below 12 per cent in 1996. Nevertheless, poverty in its inter-ethnic, interpersonal and inter-regional aspects had become a sensitive political issue in recent years. Moreover, the current economic crisis is likely to lead to a marked increase in the incidence of poverty, at least in the short term.

Indonesia has achieved substantial outreach of financial services to the poor through the medium of regulated financial institutions, including Bank Rakyat Indonesia and the rural banks. Together with a myriad of other small financial institutions which are in transition to rural bank status, they have succeeded in providing microfinance services to many of the rural poor in a sustainable manner. A generally favourable policy environment has supported these developments.

A number of innovative government programs of microfinance have been conducted with the organisation of borrowers into groups and the involvement of commercial and rural banks. By comparison with many other countries in the region, the role of NGOs in microfinance provision in Indonesia has been relatively limited. More recently, the government has felt the need to respond to concerns about poverty by launching two mass poverty eradication campaigns which focus more on outreach than on capacity building and which are not designed for sustainability.

Maintain active role of Bank Indonesia

Bank Indonesia does not have policies in regard to microfinance per se, and poverty is seen as a broader government responsibility. The bank sees its core functions as monetary management, guardianship of the payments system and banking supervision. Recent events in Indonesia and the region point to this as an appropriate role for the bank. However, Bank Indonesia has taken a strong incidental interest in microfinance development, considered as an aspect of the broader issue of financial sector development. Its leadership, expressed through programs such as the PHBK and the Microcredit Project, has sent valuable signals to the banking sector as a whole. Bank Indonesia should maintain this position of leadership with respect to microfinance, although current circumstances increase the difficulty of playing such a role.

Study success of Bank Rakyat Indonesia

The achievements of Bank Rakyat Indonesia in providing rural financial services which encompass substantial numbers of the poor in a professional and sustainable manner is well known. Factors supporting this achievement (at least until the second half of 1997) have been a stable macroeconomic environment, strong leadership, substantial investment in professionalising BRI's human resource base, clear and transparent financial reporting and accountability. While replicating this success in different political and institutional contexts is difficult, all countries in the region need to consider to what extent and how they may apply the experience of BRI in support of sustainable microfinance services.

Arrangements for direct support

Expand the role of NGOs

There is very little direct support provided for independent microfinance institutions in Indonesia, and the role of NGOs as the operators of independent MFIs is accordingly limited. The limited role of NGOs in microfinance does not mean that private initiative is lacking to promote this approach to poverty alleviation. The proliferation of rural banks, which are small, locally based financial institutions serving the needs of lower income groups, is evidence of a wealth of private initiative, at least in the Inner Islands where these small institutions are concentrated.

There is great scope for NGOs to contribute to the extension of microfinance services in other parts of Indonesia, where the rural banks have been slower to become established. And, in all parts of Indonesia, there is scope for NGOs to contribute to the expansion of microfinance by facilitating the formation, training and operation of self-help groups of the poor, which are a culturally congenial form of social organisation. This is shown by the existence of many self-help groups in Indonesia engaged in savings and credit, often informal and based on traditional patterns of behaviour. Reservations are held about NGOs by many officials; suffice to say that one of the costs of this is the failure to maximise the contribution to the Indonesian society and economy of a potentially creative social force.

Expand the role of the DABANAS Foundation

Even though directed credit schemes are not the best way to secure resources for microfinance, the requirement that 20 per cent of all commercial bank advances must be made to the small industry sector (the KUK scheme) can work to the advantage of MFIs. When commercial banks choose to discharge their obligations under the KUK by funding the lending activities of rural banks, this makes funds available for microfinance to a certain degree. The channelling and rationalisation of this flow through the newly created DABANAS Foundation could increase the loanable funds of rural banks with a microfinance mission, such as are now being established by some NGOs. These NGOs would do well to press their claims to these resources, and Bank Indonesia should exert influence to see that the funding of microfinance is among the new foundation's priorities.

Develop P4K and PHBK programs

In terms of programs channelled through the banking system, two programs, the P4K and the PHBK, are of particular significance. Both are carefully crafted models of microfinance service delivery working with SHGs of the poor.

The success of the P4K microfinance program in creating successful self-help groups for women suggests the possibility that this program and others could work towards the creation of autonomous local MFIs owned and run by women. Technical assistance and the involvement of Indonesian NGOs will be necessary to achieve this goal.

The recent rapid growth of linkages between small rural banks and self-help groups under the auspices of the PHBK linkage program conducted by Bank Indonesia indicates the potential for Indonesia's rural banks to expand microfinance in direct partnership with SHGs. This approach should be developed further. Bank Indonesia has responsibility for the supervision and development of the rural banking subsector; this potential to develop microfinance as a market niche should be considered in designing a more appropriate and helpful system of supervision and reporting for the rural banks, as suggested below.

Make mass government programs more sustainable

Unfortunately, the PHBK and P4K have been slow to achieve the necessary outreach. As a consequence, mass campaigns of group-based microfinance (the IDT and Prosperous Family programs) have been commenced in recent years. In the process it appears that considerations of institutional development and sustainability may be given less priority than mass outreach, although both programs share the objective of preparing group members to participate in more orthodox microfinance programs in due course.

One aspect of the mass campaigns, which may have negative consequences for microfinance more generally, concerns interest rate subsidies. IDT loanable funds are given to groups as a grant, with the group itself determining the terms of on-lending. Prosperous Family loanable funds are available to borrowers at a highly concessional interest rate of 6 per cent. These two programs overlap geographically to an extent, as well as serving the same populations as P4K in some cases. The P4K program is attempting to cover costs with an effective interest rate of 22 per cent. Furthermore, the expansion of small commercial financial institutions such as the rural banks could also be inhibited, to the extent that the mass campaigns overlap with these banks' potential client base. Such distortions should be avoided so far as possible.

Channel IDT groups into PHBK linkage project

As against this, an evaluation of the IDT program suggests that some 30 per cent of groups are adequately prepared to enter the PHBK linkage project. Although it would require a substantial increase in the resources needed by Bank Indonesia for technical assistance under the PHBK, such an increase appears justified if the initial benefits flowing from the IDT campaign are to be translated into continuing poverty reduction. The 'graduation' of the best groups emerging from the IDT and Prosperous Family programs to a more rigorous commercial environment should be encouraged. The success of these mass programs will only be assured if this loop can be closed. This is another area where NGOs are capable of making a greater contribution than at present. However, the capacity of the banking system to accept this challenge, and Bank Indonesia's capacity to support any expansion, must both be doubted in the light of events since this judgement was made.

The regulatory framework for non-bank MFIs

Permit NGOs to collect compulsory savings

In principle, the requirements for establishing an NGO are simple to satisfy, and NGOs may freely enter into microcredit activities. Limitations on their capacity to mobilise resources for lending from clients are a constraint on their expansion. The situation of microfinance NGOs would be improved if ambiguities were removed concerning their right to collect compulsory savings from clients. They should be free to do so.

Encourage establishment of MFI networks

The role of NGOs in microfinance in Indonesia will be strengthened if they are able to organise for purposes of communication, coordination and self-regulation. Efforts to establish an association of NGOs involved in the PHBK linkage program under the sponsorship of Bank Indonesia have so far proved fruitless. This initiative deserves the continuing support of Bank Indonesia.

The BKDs (village credit bodies) while not yet functioning as rural banks, will in time be eligible to join the Association of Indonesian Rural Banks (Perbarindo). The potential for this body to act as a mechanism for self-regulation of the rural banks needs to be developed. The expiry of the October 1997 deadline for LDKPs (rural fund and credit institutions) to upgrade to the status of BPRs has left many of these institutions in an ambiguous position. Established by provincial governments and local communities, they have a strong basis of support in a number of provinces, including several outside Java and Bali. Because of their continuing potential to provide microfinance services every effort should be made to bring them up to the standard required for operation as BPRs, rather than allowing them to wither away.

The regulatory framework for banks

Maintain flexible arrangements for establishment of small banks

The regulatory environment permitting the establishment of small banks in Indonesia is a model for other countries in the region. The prudential regulation, supervision and reporting requirements for rural banks are essentially similar to those for commercial banks. However, Bank Indonesia's Banking Regulation and Development Department believes that a more appropriate and helpful system of supervision and reporting needs to be developed for these smaller banks. The potential for rural banks to develop microfinance as a market should be recognised and facilitated in the process of revising their regulatory environment. The impact of the current banking crisis on the rural bank subsector is unclear at the time of writing. It would be unfortunate if suggestions to raise the minimum capital requirements of banks were applied in an inappropriate way to the rural banks.

The DABANAS Foundation has been set up jointly by the associations of private commercial banks and rural banks. It will channel funds to rural banks from those commercial banks which experience difficulty in meeting the 20 per cent small loan obligation. It will also provide technical assistance to the rural banks and has the potential to exercise some of the regulatory and supervisory functions of a second tier organisation. This could be a valuable service, to the extent it accepts the goal of encouraging rural banks to engage in microfinance.

References

Arndt, Heinz. 1996. 'Opening address'. In *Indonesia Assessment* 1995, eds Colin Barlow & Joan Hardjono. Institute of South East Asian Studies, Singapore.

Bambang Ismawan. 1997a. Poverty eradication through self-help group promotion and microcredit. Paper presented at the UNDP Regional Conference on Poverty Eradication, Vietnam, June.

Bambang Ismawan. 1997b. Exposure programme on people's economy development activities: Bina Swadaya experience. Paper prepared for the conference 'Envisioning the Future: International Cooperation among Asian Foundations and Organisations', Tokyo, February.

Bank Indonesia. 1996. *The Banking System in Indonesia*. Bank Indonesia, Banking Regulation and Development Department, Jakarta, March.

Bank Indonesia. 1997a. *Surat Keputusan Direksi Bank Indonesia Tentang Pemberian Kredit Usaha Kecil*, Jakarta, April.

Bank Indonesia. 1997b. *Innovation in Microfinance: Linking Banks and Self-Help Groups in Indonesia*. Bank Indonesia/GTZ, Jakarta.

CGAP. 1997. *State-owned Development Banks in Microfinance*. Focus note no.10, August.

Cole, David & Slade, Betty. 1996. *Building a Modern Financial System: The Indonesian Experience*. Cambridge University Press, Cambridge.

Gunawan Sumodiningrat. 1997. Poverty alleviation in Indonesia, 1997: An overview. Paper presented at the Regional Expert Group Meeting on Rural Poverty Alleviation, Beijing, March.

Kompas. 1997. *Membangkitkan mereka dari kemiskinan*. 28 June.

P4K. 1997. *Indonesia's Poverty Eradication Methodology*. Income Generating Project for Marginal Farmers and Landless, September 1996–1997, Ministry of Agriculture, Jakarta.

P4K. 1997. *Monthly Report March 1997*. Income Generating Project for Marginal Farmers and Landless, Ministry of Agriculture, Jakarta.

Sajogyo (ed.) 1997. *Pokmas IDT: Menuju Kelompok Swadaya Masyarakat Mandiri*. Puspa Swara, Jakarta.

Siebel, Hans Dieter. 1997. *Microfinance in Indonesia: An Assessment of Microfinance Institutions Banking with the Poor*. Occasional paper no.2365, Rural Finance Program, Department of Agricultural Economics, Ohio State University, March.

Soedradjad Djiwandono, J. 1996. Towards a more favourable policy environment for microfinance. Address to Bank Poor '96, Kuala Lumpur, 10 December.

Persons consulted

Mr Bishnu P. Shrestha	Managing Director APRACA Consultancy Services
Mr Moh Said Paggo	Deputy Manager APRACA Consultancy Services
Mr Dwi Pranoto	Credit Research and Regulation Division Bank Indonesia
Mr Eddie Setiadi	Credit Research and Regulation Division Bank Indonesia
Mr Sumantoro Martowijoyo	Project Manager Microcredit Project Bank Indonesia
Mr M. Jarot Eko Winarno	Manager, Product Management BRI Unit Division Bank Rakyat Indonesia

Ms Patricia A. Markovich	Project Assistant Harvard Institute for International Development
Mr Kadhim A. Al-Eyd	Senior Resident Representative International Monetary Fund
Mr Dominique Gallman	Technical Advisor GTZ
Mr Pachji Araspradja	Deputy Manager Bank Indonesia Head, PHBK Team
Mr G. Ravi Rajan	Resident Coordinator of UN Operational Activities in Indonesia, United Nations Development Programme
Ms H. P. Bonaria Siahaan	Programme Manager United Nations Development Programme
Mr Kunikazu Nate	Programme Officer United Nations Development Programme
Mr Toga Ritonga	Consultant, UNDP Rural Banking Specialist Department of Agriculture P4K Project Office
Mr M. Makbul	Participatory Development Specialist, UNDP Department of Agriculture P4K Project Office
Mr Richard Beresford	Senior Planning Advisor, UNDP Department of Agriculture P4K Project Office
Mr Mukhlis Rasyid	Managing Director Bank Indonesia
Mr Abdul Salam	Director Credit Department Bank Indonesia
Mr Emri	Deputy Director Rural Bank Supervisory Division Bank Indonesia
Ms Variani Selvini	Bank Supervisor Rural Bank Supervisory Division Bank Indonesia
Ms Dewi W. Budimulia	Bank Supervisor Rural Bank Supervisory Division Bank Indonesia
Ms Endah S. Enarianto	Manager Credit Division II Credit Department Bank Indonesia
Ir Ratna Tjiptopranoto Pardede	Deputy Manager Credit Division II Bank Indonesia

Mr Jorge Garcia Garcia	Senior Economist The World Bank Jakarta Resident Office
Mr R. P. Soeroto	Secretary General Perbarindo Indonesian Association of Rural Banks
Mr Wikono Wongsodirdjo	Manager Bank Pasar Puspita Sari
Prof Dr Mubyarto	Assistant Minister for Poverty Eradication The National Development Planning Agency
Mr St. Notobudhiharjo	Chief of Finance and Small Enterprise Program Bina Swadaya
Mr B. S. Soesapto	Bina Swadaya
Dr Gunawan Sumodinigrat	Head Bureau of Regional and Rural Development

Malaysia

1 Introduction and background

1.1 Key demographic and economic data

Malaysia covers an area of some 330,000 square kilometres in Southeast Asia. Peninsular Malaysia forms the southern portion of mainland Southeast Asia, with Thailand to the north and the island of Singapore to the south. The East Malaysian states of Sabah and Sarawak constitute the northern part of the island of Borneo. Malaysia is a multi-racial society following large-scale immigration of Chinese and Indians from the nineteenth century. In 1995, the population of 20.1 million included 58 per cent *Bumiputera* (ethnic Malays and indigenous people), 26 per cent Chinese, 7 per cent Indians and 3 per cent others. The remaining 6 per cent were non-citizens, primarily foreign workers brought in because of labour shortages.

The population density is around 61 people per square kilometre, the lowest for any country in this study. The total fertility rate remains relatively high at 3.4 births per woman in 1995. This, combined with substantial immigration of foreign workers from neighbouring countries, contributed to robust population growth of 2.4 per cent per year between 1990 and 1995.

Malaysia is by far the wealthiest country included in the study, and is the only one classified as an upper middle income country by the World Bank. GNP per capita was $3,890 in 1995, 40 per cent higher than that of Thailand and nearly four times that of any other country in the study. Economic growth has been rapid in recent years with per capita income increasing by 5.7 per cent per year between 1985 and 1995, although the current financial crisis in Southeast Asia has led to a marked slowdown in growth in the short term. The structure of the economy reflects Malaysia's status as a newly industrialising country, with industry constituting 43 per cent of GDP in 1995 and agriculture having only a 13 per cent share. Fifty-four (54) per cent of the population lived in urban areas, the highest for any country in the study.

Performance in terms of human development is also generally good. Life expectancy at birth was 71 in 1995, slightly below Sri Lanka but higher than for any other country in the study. The infant mortality rate was 12 per thousand live births, the lowest for any country studied. On the other hand, the adult literacy rate was only 83 per cent, below the levels recorded in the Philippines, Thailand, Sri Lanka and Indonesia. While this may partly reflect measurement factors, it would appear to be a cause for some concern. Malaysia was classified as a high human development country under the UNDP human development index for 1994, scoring fractionally lower than Thailand because of the lower literacy rate but well above any other country included in the study.

1.2 Poverty

Estimates of poverty

The official poverty line in Malaysia has been calculated since 1976. The original poverty line was based on three components. First, household food requirements were derived by the Institute of Medical Research by estimating the daily minimum calorie requirement (set at 9,910 calories per household), and establishing a basket of food items based on the usual consumption patterns that just met this daily minimum. This basket was then costed by the Department of Statistics. Second, household clothing requirements were derived in a similar manner by the Ministry of Welfare. And third, requirements for items other than food and clothing were estimated using the household expenditure survey conducted by the Department of Statistics in 1973. The poverty line level of expenditure on these items was set equal to the average actual household expenditure on items other than food and clothing by those households who just met the poverty line levels of expenditure on food and clothing. Since the initial poverty line was established in 1976, each of these three components has been indexed by movements in the relevant groups of the consumer price index. One poverty line has been established for the whole of peninsular Malaysia, with separate poverty lines for Sabah and Sarawak.

The most recent estimates for 1995 put the poverty line at RM425 ($170) per month per household for peninsular Malaysia, with higher poverty lines of RM601 ($240) for Sabah and RM582 ($233) for Sarawak. Based on these poverty lines, the incidence of poverty has fallen significantly in Malaysia over the last two decades. In 1976, an estimated 42.4 per cent of households were below the poverty line. This percentage has fallen consistently to 20.7 per cent in 1984, 17.1 per cent in 1990, and 9.6 per cent or 417,200 households in 1995.

The incidence of poverty in 1995 was much higher in rural areas (16.1 per cent) than in urban areas (4.1 per cent). However, it should be noted that the poverty line is the same in both urban and rural areas. Some commentators noted that this is unrealistic. Given the much higher living costs in the Kuala Lumpur region, for instance, it was argued that a higher poverty line is necessary for urban areas. One commentator suggested that an appropriate poverty line for Kuala Lumpur would be monthly household income of RM1,000 ($400) or even higher. This suggests that the official statistics understate poverty in the urban areas. Recently, the Department of Statistics has started collecting separate price data for urban and rural areas, and the Economic Planning Unit is considering establishing separate poverty lines for urban and rural areas.

The government has not published estimates of the incidence of poverty by ethnic group or state. It is understood that the great majority of poor households are *Bumiputera*, although there are also pockets of poverty among the Indian community. It is also understood that the incidence of poverty is higher than the national average in the East Malaysian states of Sabah and Sarawak, the northern states of Perlis and Kedah, and the east coast states of Kelantan and Terengganu.

The government also publishes estimates of hard-core poverty, defined as those households with incomes of less than half the poverty line. In 1995, 2.2 per cent of households, or 93,500 households, were in hard-core poverty. Hard-core poverty has fallen even more sharply than overall poverty, falling from 17.0 per cent of households in 1976 to 6.9 per cent in 1984, 4.0 per cent in 1990 and 2.2 per cent in 1995.

The Seventh Malaysia Plan projects that the incidence of poverty will fall to 6.0 per cent of households by the year 2000. However, this projection is likely to prove optimistic in light of the current recession.

Policies for poverty reduction

Poverty eradication has been the major objective of government policy since the commencement of the New Economic Policy in 1971. The main policy for reducing poverty has been rapid economic growth and employment creation. Nevertheless, the government has also recognised the importance of specific policies directed to the poor. This has enabled rapid economic growth to be combined with an improving distribution of income and sharper reductions in the incidence of poverty than would otherwise have been possible.

During the period of the New Economic Policy from 1971 to 1990, there was a major focus on reducing poverty and income disparities between ethnic groups, particularly by elevating the position of *Bumiputera*. This included a range of programs to increase the incomes and productivity of agricultural producers, and to improve access to basic amenities and the quality of life of low-income households. Both of these groups consist predominantly of *Bumiputera*. Since the Third Malaysia Plan covering the period 1976 to 1980, plans have had explicit targets for poverty reduction. They have also identified specific programs for poverty reduction, directed to specific target groups such as *padi* farmers, rubber smallholders, coconut smallholders, fishermen, estate workers, agricultural labourers and indigenous groups.

As incomes have increased and absolute poverty has declined, the focus of government policy has shifted somewhat from broad-based policies to reduce poverty in general to a greater focus on eradicating poverty among the hard-core poor. Under the National Development Policy which commenced in 1991, the government has established a special development program which incorporates economic and social programs to assist the hard-core poor. This package includes a number of elements:

(1) Income-generating projects, primarily for cash crop cultivation, livestock rearing, aquaculture, petty trading and cottage industries. During the Sixth Malaysia Plan covering the period 1991 to 1995, 16,740 hard-core poor households benefited from such projects.

(2) Programs to provide and upgrade low-cost housing, and to provide basic amenities and facilities such as electricity, safe drinking water and health facilities.

(3) Direct welfare assistance and attitudinal change programmes. During the Sixth Malaysia Plan, 37,200 hard-core poor households received welfare assistance, while 39,060 participated in attitudinal change programs.

(4) Programs to meet the food and nutritional requirements of undernourished children, and to assist school children from hard-core poor families.

(5) The Amanah Saham Bumiputera scheme, a special investment scheme which enables hard-core poor *Bumiputera* households to obtain an interest-free loan of RM5,000 ($2,000) to invest in a unit trust program.

The government has also recognised the importance of non-governmental organisations (NGOs) in the overall policy framework to eradicate poverty. In particular, it has supported the microfinance activities of Amanah Ikhtiar Malaysia (AIM) as an integral part of its poverty programs.

1.3 Overview of the financial system

The financial system in Malaysia includes 37 commercial banks, of which 23 are domestic and 14 are foreign. While most of these commercial banks are owned by private interests, the two largest, Maybank and Bank Bumiputra, have majority shareholding by the government. The commercial banks have a combined total of 1,569 branches, disbursed widely throughout the country. In addition, Bank Islam Malaysia provides Islamic banking services throughout the country. There are also 40 finance companies, 12 merchant banks and seven discount houses. All of these institutions are supervised by the central bank, Bank Negara Malaysia.

In addition, there are seven development finance institutions owned by the government which are registered with, but not supervised by, Bank Negara. These include the Development Bank of Malaysia, the Industrial Bank of Malaysia and the Agriculture Bank of Malaysia (Bank Pertanian). There are also a number of savings institutions, including the National Savings Bank, as well as the credit cooperatives and various other non-bank financial intermediaries, all of which are outside the scope of Bank Negara supervision.

The financial system has been subject to a process of gradual liberalisation since around 1987, when interest rates on deposits were deregulated. Interest rates on loans were partially deregulated in 1991, when each commercial bank was permitted to establish its own base lending rate according to its cost of funds. In 1995 the average bank lending rate was substantially positive in real terms at 7.6 per cent, well above the inflation rate of 3.4 per cent. Exchange controls have also been liberalised since 1987. In 1994 a two-tier regulatory system was introduced for commercial banks, allowing greater freedom to well-managed banks with strong financial standing. This system has now been extended to finance companies and merchant banks, which have also been given greater freedom to accept deposits. Malaysia has the greatest financial depth of any country in this study with a ratio of money and quasi-money to GDP of 85.0 per cent in 1995, no doubt reflecting its greater economic development.

Nevertheless, a number of regulatory requirements remain. Bank Negara has three lending guidelines requiring banks to lend to particular priority sectors of the economy. None of these directly targets poor borrowers. Interest rates also remain regulated by Bank Negara. Each bank must establish a base lending rate, based on the Kuala Lumpur inter-bank offer rate (KLIBOR), its cost of funds and its cost structure. The base lending rate for each bank must be approved by Bank Negara, and the maximum lending rate for any loan is set at the base lending rate plus 4 per cent. Some specific categories of loans face lower ceilings.

1.4 Overview of microfinance

The only institutions that engage in microfinance to a significant degree are a handful of NGOs. Of these, by far the largest is Amanah Ikhtiar Malaysia (AIM). AIM was established in 1987 and is modelled on the Grameen Bank. Loans are provided for any type of legal income-generating activity. As in the Grameen Bank, poor borrowers form themselves into groups of five who guarantee each other's loans. There is also compulsory group training, and a compulsory savings component. In the past loans were provided interest free with a small administrative charge, but from 1997 new loans are subject to an interest rate of 19 per cent. AIM offers a number of loan products.

(1) Ikhtiar Loan Scheme 1 provides loans to poor households with average monthly incomes of not more than RM270 ($108). Initial loans are for a maximum of RM500

($200), increasing to RM2,000 ($800) for the fourth and subsequent loans. Loans are provided for a period of 50 weeks, with weekly repayments.

(2) Ikhtiar Loan Scheme 2 provides loans of between RM1,500 ($600) and RM5,000 ($2,000) to borrowers who have graduated from scheme 1 and have increased their monthly household incomes to at least RM405 ($162). The repayment period is between 50 and 100 weeks.

(3) Ikhtiar Loan Scheme 3 provides loans of between RM5,000 ($2,000) and RM10,000 ($4,000) to borrowers with a good track record under the other schemes and monthly household incomes of at least RM600 ($240). These loans have a longer repayment period, up to five years.

(4) In addition, special education loans up to RM500 ($200) and special housing loans up to RM2,000 ($800) are available to borrowers who have completed some loans under scheme 1.

As at 30 April 1997, AIM had 30,029 current borrowers under schemes 1, 2 and 3, including 18,613 under scheme 1. In addition, there were 9,312 education loans and 3,900 housing loans with outstanding balances. AIM is currently operating in nine states of Malaysia, and it is understood that the vast majority of borrowers are ethnic Malays. Repayment rates were reported to be 99.9 per cent.

There are several other NGOs involved in microfinance, but they operate on a much smaller scale than AIM. Yayasan Usahamaju is a Grameen Bank replicator operating in Sabah, with around 5,000 borrowers. Another NGO using the Grameen Bank approach is Partners in Enterprise, which has recently started lending in the Batu Caves area near Kuala Lumpur. Another program which provides individual loans to poor borrowers is the Projek Tekun pilot project of the Centre for Policy Research at the Malaysian University of Science (Universiti Sains Malaysia), which operates in the states of Penang, Kelantan and Terengganu. It is also understood that a number of the state governments operate foundations to alleviate poverty and that some of these incorporate microfinance components, although in most cases these are grants rather than loans.

Other institutions do not appear to be actively involved in microfinance. Commercial banks are involved in microfinance through extending lines of credit to AIM, and as a conduit for schemes such as the loan fund for hawkers and petty traders operated by the Credit Guarantee Corporation (CGC), although the schemes do not generally reach poor borrowers. Some commercial banks have very small programs for individual lending to poor borrowers. The financial system also includes a number of urban and rural credit cooperatives which provide savings and credit facilities for their members. The urban credit cooperatives have a combined membership of around 40,000, but these are predominantly relatively well-off wage and salary earners. The rural credit cooperatives have much lower outreach of around 2,000. While they are not targeted at the poor, it is understood that some of their members are low-paid workers in the estate sector.

AIM has received large volumes of grants and soft loans from government and from government-related agencies. This relatively easy access to funds has enabled it to expand outreach much more rapidly than would otherwise have been possible, with AIM now the largest Grameen Bank replication outside of Bangladesh. Given the relatively small number of poor households in Malaysia and the widespread opportunities for wage employment which reduce the need for poor households to rely on self-employment, the outreach of AIM and the other small programs is reasonably high in relation to demand. Nevertheless, there is some scope for expansion, and AIM is currently seeking to move into new areas. For instance, it has recently expanded its operations to Sarawak in East Malaysia. AIM and Yayasan Usahamaju could also increase their numbers of clients by relaxing their means tests. For instance, AIM currently uses a means test for monthly household income of only RM270 ($108) per month, above the hard-core poverty line of RM212 per month but well below the overall poverty line of RM425 ($170) per month.

Ready access to cheap funds has reduced the pressure on AIM to operate on a self-sufficient basis. In the past, it charged borrowers a modest administrative charge, equivalent to an effective interest rate of around 5 per cent. However, grants for operational expenses have been reduced considerably, and AIM is now focusing much more strongly on sustainability. It has recently increased its interest rates to 19 per cent, and hopes to be able to cover all of its operational expenses from interest earnings by the end of 1997. The other NGOs are still relatively new and are operating on a small scale, and are not able to cover their operational expenses from interest earnings at this stage. Yayasan Usahamaju has received grants from the Sabah state government, while Partners in Enterprise has received donations from the private sector and from foreign donors.

2 Arrangements for direct support

2.1 Support for specialised microfinance institutions

Both the government of Malaysia and the state governments have provided considerable support for AIM, while the smaller microfinance institutions (MFIs) have also received funding from government and/or donor agencies. Between 1989 and 1995, the government of Malaysia gave AIM an annual grant from the budget, equivalent to around 60 per cent of its operational costs. These grants have now been terminated. AIM has also received grants from state governments, ranging from around 10 to 40 per cent of operational costs in those states in which it operates, with the amount depending on the particular state government. These grants are continuing.

AIM has also received grants and soft loans from the government for loan capital. These funds have been channelled through the Foundation for Islamic Economic Development (YPEIM). The Sixth Malaysia Plan covering the period 1991 to 1995 allocated RM18.2 million ($7.3 million) as a grant to AIM for its revolving fund. YPEIM is providing this amount to AIM over a 30-year period from 1991 to 2020. The Seventh Malaysia Plan covering the period 1996 to 2000 provides for an interest-free loan to AIM of RM200 million ($80 million). The loan will be disbursed over the period 1996 to 2000, and AIM will not have to start repaying it until 2006.

AIM has also received soft loans from the Credit Guarantee Corporation (CGC) and from some of the commercial banks. In 1992 CGC allocated an initial sum of RM2 million ($800,000) from its own resources as a revolving fund for on-lending by AIM. In 1995 the revolving fund was increased to RM5 million ($2 million). In 1996 CGC organised another revolving fund for AIM, with 15 financial institutions contributing a total of RM13 million ($5.2 million). Both of these revolving funds are provided to AIM at a highly concessional interest rate of 1 per cent. AIM has received further soft loans at 1 per cent interest from the two commercial banks with majority government shareholding, namely Bank Bumiputra (RM4 million or $1.6 million) and Maybank (RM5 million or

$2 million), as well as a grant of RM750,000 ($300,000) and soft loan of RM300,000 ($120,000) from Bank Islam Malaysia.

Hence, AIM has received large volumes of grants and soft loans from government and from government-related agencies. These funds have reduced the pressure on AIM to operate on a self-sufficient basis, and have clearly enabled it to expand its outreach much more rapidly than would otherwise have been possible. In this respect Malaysia is very different to any other country included in the study. The incidence of poverty is much lower, while per capita incomes are much higher. It is therefore possible to access far more public resources, relative to the number of poor households, for programs to reduce poverty. The experience of AIM has shown that in Malaysia there are sufficient public resources for an institution like AIM, with relatively low levels of self-sufficiency, to reach a significant proportion of poor households by relying heavily on government funding.

Reflecting this relative abundance of public resources and to the extent that microfinance is an effective strategy for reducing poverty, there is a strong case for the government of Malaysia to subsidise it as part of its overall policy strategy for poverty reduction. Anecdotal evidence suggests that AIM has indeed contributed to significant improvements in the lives of many borrowers, although it would be appropriate to conduct a more rigorous study of the impact of the program. In the meantime, it would appear appropriate for governments to continue to subsidise AIM as an effective strategy for poverty reduction.

Given the concessional loans currently being disbursed, it is not necessary for AIM to achieve full financial self-sufficiency, at least in the short term. This enables it to continue to concentrate primarily on increasing outreach. While AIM already has significant outreach, there is still considerable scope for it to expand by widening its geographic base and relaxing its means test to cover slightly less poor households. It may also be appropriate for it to consider deepening its activities by offering its clients a wider range of services, such as more flexible savings products.

At the same time, the recent increase in the interest rate charged by AIM is to be welcomed. As noted above, the increase is expected to enable AIM to attain operational self-sufficiency. Access to public resources is not unlimited, as demonstrated by the fact that the government of Malaysia has recently replaced grant assistance with soft loans. The current financial crisis is also giving rise to cuts in government spending in a number of areas. Increasing self-sufficiency will ensure that the program can be sustained over the medium term, and will also enable greater AIM to achieve greater outreach for a given call on public resources.

2.2 Support through the banking system

Directed credit schemes

Bank Negara has three lending guidelines requiring banks to lend to particular priority sectors of the economy. First, commercial banks and finance companies are required to maintain loans to *Bumiputera* at 30 per cent of total loans outstanding. Base figures for loans outstanding are revised periodically, and the current requirement is for loans to *Bumiputera* to be at least 30 per cent of loans outstanding as at 31 December 1995.

Second, banks and finance companies are required to set aside a certain amount for financing low- and medium-cost housing (that is, housing units costing less than RM100,000 or $40,000). Targets for low- and medium-cost housing are determined in the

Malaysia national plans, and quotas are then allocated to individual commercial banks and finance companies based on their assets, capital base and other criteria. The global allocation for all banks is currently around RM10 billion ($4 billion), equivalent to around 4 to 5 per cent of total loans outstanding.

Third, banks and finance companies are required to provide loans to small business without good security or established track record under the New Principal Guarantee Scheme of the CGC. At present, commercial banks are required to provide a total of RM1 billion ($400 million) under this scheme, around 0.5 per cent of their loans outstanding. Again, the allocation is divided between banks based on their assets, capital base and other criteria. Individual loans under the scheme must be RM500,000 ($200,000) or less, and are partially guaranteed by CGC. Of the total allocation for each bank, at least 50 per cent must be provided to *Bumiputera*.

None of these guidelines directly targets poor borrowers. Given the relatively large loan sizes and the fact that the banks will tend to lend to households within the target groups which are better off, it is unlikely that these requirements benefit the poor to any significant extent.

Microfinance activities of the Credit Guarantee Corporation

CGC was established in 1972 with Bank Negara and the commercial banks as its shareholders. It is currently owned as to 20 per cent by Bank Negara, 50 per cent by the 37 commercial banks, and 30 per cent by the 40 finance companies operating in Malaysia. Its main function is to guarantee loans by banks to small and medium enterprises, especially those with inadequate collateral or without collateral or track record, who would otherwise not have access to credit. While most of its activities are beyond the scope of microfinance, it also provides some support to microfinance loans.

One scheme is the loan fund for hawkers and petty traders, which provides loan funds and 100 per cent guarantee for loans up to RM10,000 ($4,000) to eligible businesses by commercial banks and finance companies. Eligible businesses are: permanent and market stalls selling groceries, food, handicrafts, etc; mobile stalls with a specific place of business; and stalls and shops providing services such as tailoring, barber, welding, motor repairs, etc. To participate in the scheme, borrowers must be Malaysian, above 18 years of age, have a valid licence to trade, be directly involved in the business, and have a specific place of business. Borrowers with existing business loans in excess of RM10,000 ($4,000) or with an adverse borrowing record are ineligible. Loans must have terms ranging from 42 weeks to 138 weeks, with weekly repayments.

A closely related scheme is the Association Special Loan Scheme. Conditions under this scheme are essentially the same as under the loan fund for hawkers and petty traders, except that borrowers apply for a loan through their trade association. The trade association then processes, evaluates and approves the application and applies to CGC for guarantee cover. CGC then issues a letter of agreement to the participating bank or finance company, which releases the loan.

These schemes are funded through a one-off soft loan from the government to CGC of RM120 million ($48 million). This money is on-lent to commercial banks and finance companies free of interest, and banks lend to final borrowers at an interest rate of 4 per cent to cover administrative costs. Repayment rates under the scheme are reported to be high, with only around 6 per cent of loans classified as non-performing (in the early 1990s, however, non-performing loans were up to 40 per cent of loans granted under the schemes). In 1996, 6,079 loans were granted under the loan fund for hawkers and petty traders, and a further 291 under the association special loan scheme. Nevertheless, CGC reported that banks generally follow their usual credit practices in approving loans under the schemes. While this no doubt accounts for the high repayment rates, it also means that the schemes do not generally reach poor borrowers.

As noted above, CGC has also provided support for AIM in its microfinance activities, through a revolving fund from its own resources of RM5 million ($2 million) and by organising an additional revolving fund of RM13 million ($5.2 million) with contributions from 15 financial institutions. In 1996, 8,407 loans were approved under these revolving funds. In addition, CGC has allocated RM6 million ($2.4 million) to support the Projek Tekun scheme operated by the Centre for Policy Research at the Malaysian University of Science, with 449 loans supported in 1996.

3 Regulation of non-bank microfinance institutions

3.1 The broad regulatory framework

Registration

There are number of options for registration for NGOs. AIM and Yayasan Usahamaju are registered as trusts, pursuant to the Trustee Act 1949 and Trustees (Incorporation) Act 1952. As trusts, they are required to file an instrument of trust with the Attorney-General's Office, covering matters such as the objectives of the trust, appointment of trustees, rules and functions of the board of trustees, arrangements for meetings, maintenance of annual accounts, responsibilities of the management committee, and detailed rules and regulations. They are required to submit their annual report, audited financial statements and any amendments to the instrument of trust to the Attorney-General's Office.

Partners in Enterprise, by contrast, is registered under the Companies Act 1965 as a non-profit company limited by guarantee. To be registered as a company, two or more persons must lodge a memorandum and articles of association, outlining the name and objectives of the company, with the Registrar of Companies. Companies are required to maintain regular accounts, and to provide their audited annual financial statements to the registrar. The Act also sets out various requirements concerning the office and name, directors and officers, and meetings and proceedings. It is understood that these requirements are generally quite straightforward.

Many NGOs are registered as societies with the Registrar of Societies, pursuant to the Societies Act 1966, although it is not known if any MFIs have registered under these provisions. To apply for registration as a society, it is necessary to complete an application providing details of the name, address, purpose and office-bearers of the society, as well as the rules. It is also necessary to have an annual general meeting, and to provide details of the office-bearers and the financial statements to the registrar on an annual basis.

All of these provisions are designed for NGOs in general, rather than for MFIs. Indeed, registration under one of these Acts does not permit an NGO to engage in microfinance. Under Malaysian law, only specified institutions such as banks, cooperative societies and licensed moneylenders are permitted to lend money in consideration of a larger sum being repaid. Trusts, non-profit companies and societies are generally not permitted to make loans. If such bodies are to operate as MFIs and make loans, they need to obtain a specific exemption from the provisions of the Moneylenders Act 1951.

Such exemption must be obtained on a one-off basis from the Minister of Housing and Local Government, and is generally granted for a period of three to four years. AIM, Yayasan Usahamaju and Partners in Enterprise have all obtained exemptions under this provision. The ministry requires NGOs who have received this exemption to provide their annual report and audited financial statements on an annual basis, and portfolio data once every six months. However, there are no clear criteria for obtaining an exemption, and some commentators stated that it may be difficult for smaller NGOs without connections to obtain an exemption. It would be appropriate for the government to establish a transparent framework for the registration of MFIs based on a clearly established set of guidelines, rather than requiring them to seek exemption from the Moneylenders Act.

There are no requirements on NGOs which receive foreign donations to seek prior approval from any government agency, or even to report that they have received such donations. Any profits from interest or other income earned by MFIs are subject to income tax, but to date no MFIs have made a profit. At present, donations to MFIs are not eligible for income tax deduction. It is understood that it would be difficult to obtain exempt status for such donations, on the grounds that MFIs are engaged in lending money for interest. Given the focus of MFIs on poverty reduction, it would be appropriate to allow donations to them to be income tax deductible.

Savings mobilisation

The Backing and Financial Institutions Act 1989 provides that no person shall carry on banking business, including receiving deposits on current account, deposit account, savings account or other similar account, without a licence as a bank or financial institution. Hence, it is clear that NGOs are not permitted to accept deposits from the general public. While it is not clear if this provision also covers compulsory and/or other savings by members of MFIs, it is understood that Bank Negara has determined that NGOs can accept compulsory savings at least, so long as these compulsory savings are put into a trust account and not used as loanable funds. AIM and Yayasan Usahamaju keep their borrowers' savings in separate bank accounts in the names of the borrowers.

This would appear to be unnecessarily restrictive. Under the Grameen Bank model used by AIM and Yayasan Usahamaju, almost all members are net borrowers, with the outstanding balance on their loans greater than the balance of compulsory savings. Clearly, such members are not at risk of losing their savings if the institution fails. For these reasons, the Consultative Group to Assist the Poorest (CGAP) has argued that compulsory savings should probably be thought of as part of the cost of the loan, rather than as true financial intermediation requiring public intervention to protect depositors. Most countries in this study allow MFIs to use the compulsory savings of members as loanable funds. It would be appropriate for the government to permit MFIs to use the compulsory savings of their members in their lending programs. This would increase their access to loanable funds and reduce administrative costs.

3.2 Interest rates

There are no regulations on MFIs concerning the interest rates that they can charge borrowers. In practice, MFIs have tended to maintain interest rates and charges at low levels, reflecting community expectations and relatively easy access to funds from government and donor agencies. As noted above, AIM in 1997 moved from a flat administrative charge to an interest rate of 19 per cent. While this is below the level charged by successful MFIs in most other countries and below the level necessary for full financial self-sufficiency, it is estimated that it will be sufficient for AIM to cover all of its operational expenses.

3.3 Prudential regulation and supervision

There is no prudential regulation and supervision of MFIs, in terms of matters such as minimum capital requirements, capital adequacy ratios, reserve or liquidity requirements, or loan loss provisioning requirements. Reporting requirements are also limited to the provision of annual accounts to the various bodies that regulate NGOs, and do not relate to the specific needs of MFIs. However, AIM provides its annual report, audited annual financial statements and annual portfolio data to Bank Negara on the basis that the banks from which it obtains funds are required to report to Bank Negara. When requested, AIM provides more frequent data to Bank Negara.

It is generally considered that it is not appropriate to subject MFIs which do not accept deposits from the public to prudential regulation and supervision. Systems used by regulatory agencies to supervise financial institutions are generally not appropriate to the needs of MFIs. In most countries there is a large number of small MFIs, and it would not be feasible for regulators to monitor their activities properly. And in most cases there is scope for other, more cost-effective approaches to ensuring that MFIs operate at a high standard, such as through the policies of second tier microfinance institutions or through self-regulation.

However, it is not clear if these considerations apply in the case of Malaysia. Given the very small number of MFIs, it would not be onerous for Bank Negara or some other regulatory agency to establish some system for monitoring them. Moreover, as discussed below, there would not appear to be much scope for monitoring through a second tier microfinance institution or through a system of self-regulation.

It would therefore be appropriate for the government to establish a small cell of one or two people within Bank Negara or some other regulatory agency to monitor and supervise MFIs. The same body could also be responsible for registering MFIs, as discussed above (it should be noted that if Bank Negara were to undertake this role some change in focus would be required, as it has had little involvement with microfinance to date). It would be necessary to develop performance and reporting standards that are appropriate to the needs of MFIs, covering matters such as loan classification and provisioning, savings facilities, accounting and audit standards, progress towards self-sufficiency, etc. Such standards should be developed in consultation with the MFIs themselves. Experience in developing performance and reporting standards for MFIs in other countries, such as through the Palli Karma Sahayak Foundation in Bangladesh and the Coalition to Develop Standards for Microfinance in the Philippines may also be useful (see the Bangladesh and Philippines country studies).

3.4 Performance and reporting standards of second tier institutions

In many countries, second tier microfinance institutions have been established to channel funds to specialised MFIs. Often, performance and reporting standards established by such institutions become norms for the microfinance sector. There is no such second tier institution in Malaysia (although to a limited extent the Credit Guarantee Corporation (CGC) has channelled funds to MFIs as an adjunct to its primary responsibilities). Given the very small number of NGOs and the relatively small size of the potential market for microfinance, there is little reason to establish a specialist second tier institution. Hence, this approach to establishing standards for microfinance does not appear to be an option in the case of Malaysia.

3.5 Self-regulation

There are no formal arrangements for self-regulation or coordination among the MFIs operating in Malaysia. Given the small number of MFIs and the dominant position of AIM, this is perhaps not surprising. It is understood that one of the smaller NGOs has expressed interest in establishing a national network of microfinance NGOs, but there has been no further progress to date. Nevertheless, both AIM and Yayasan Usahamaju are members of the international Credit and Savings for the Hardcore Poor (CASHPOR) network of Grameen Bank replicators, and there have been some informal contacts between these organisations and Partners in Enterprise. In terms of policy dialogue, AIM commented that it has a very good relationship with government, and is able to engage in constructive policy dialogue on issues relating to microfinance. It would nevertheless be appropriate at least to establish an informal network of MFIs to exchange information and to ensure that the views of all MFIs are taken into account in discussions with government.

4 Regulation of banks

4.1 Licensing and minimum capital requirements

As noted above, the Banking and Financial Institutions Act 1989 provides that no person shall accept deposits without a licence as a bank or financial institution. Unlike many other countries included in this study, there is no network of small banks in Malaysia. The minimum capital requirement to establish a commercial bank is RM20 million ($8 million). This is likely to be too high for an MFI wishing to establish a bank, or a body wishing to establish a small bank at the local level. While the minimum capital needed to establish a finance company is less at RM5 million ($2 million), finance companies are not allowed to accept deposits on current account. Moreover, Bank Negara considers that there are already too many financial institutions in Malaysia, and is currently not issuing any new licences for the establishment of either banks or finance companies. In fact, it is seeking to encourage existing banks and finance companies to amalgamate.

Experience in other countries suggests that small banks are much more likely to become involved in microfinance than large banks. Hence, if banks are to play an active role in microfinance, it is important that there be some mechanism to enable small banks to be licensed. Such banks would also tend to serve small entrepreneurs who in many cases have only limited access to financial services at present. It would therefore be appropriate for the government to establish a framework for licensing small banks, by setting a realistic minimum capital requirement and removing any other restrictions which prevent the establishment of small banks. In this regard, it may be useful to examine the experiences of countries such as Indonesia and the Philippines (see the Indonesia and Philippines country studies).

4.2 Interest rates

As noted above, the maximum lending rate for any bank loan is set at the base lending rate for the particular bank plus 4 per cent. In addition, some specific loans face lower ceilings. For instance, loans for low- and medium-cost housing are subject to a ceiling of the base lending rate plus 1.75 per cent or 9 per cent, whichever is lower. Loans of less than RM500,000 ($200,000) guaranteed by the Credit Guarantee Corporation (CGC) under the new principal guarantee scheme face an interest rate ceiling of base lending rate plus 2 per cent. Banks are also required to lend at below market interest rates under various other schemes where they are able to obtain refinancing or soft loans from Bank Negara.

Small loans to poor borrowers inevitably incur high administrative costs. The interest rate ceiling of base lending rate plus 4 per cent would make it very difficult if not impossible for any bank to cover the costs of small loans to poor borrowers. In addition to the minimum capital requirements and other restrictions discussed above, this ceiling further discourages regulated banks from becoming involved in microfinance. It is also perhaps surprising that Malaysia retains interest rate controls when a number of other countries included in this study with less developed financial systems — namely Indonesia, the Philippines, Sri Lanka and Thailand — have removed them. It would be appropriate for the government to remove interest rate ceilings applying to loans by regulated banks, or at least review the spreads applicable to small and very small loans.

4.3 Prudential regulation and supervision

Commercial banks are subject to a capital adequacy ratio of 8 per cent of risk-weighted assets in line with the Basle Accord. There is a statutory reserve requirement of 13.5 per cent of net eligible liabilities, to be held as an interest-free deposit with Bank Negara. In addition, commercial banks are required to maintain liquid assets equal to 17 per cent of liabilities. In terms of loan loss provisioning, commercial banks are required to maintain a general provision of 1.5 per cent of loans outstanding, plus specific provisions of 100 per cent for bad debts and 50 per cent for doubtful debts. Banks are also required to provide a series of reports to Bank Negara on a weekly, fortnightly, monthly, quarterly and annual basis. These requirements would not appear to impose any undue restrictions on small banks or banks involved in microfinance. This is largely academic at this stage, as there is no scope for the establishment of small banks in any case.

There are no restrictions preventing commercial banks from establishing linkages with MFIs by extending loans for on-lending to poor borrowers. As noted above, a number of commercial banks have provided loans to AIM, albeit not on a commercial basis.

5 Summary and recommendations

With GNP per capita of $3,890 in 1995, Malaysia is by far the wealthiest country included in the study and is classified as an upper middle income country by the World Bank.

Performance in terms of human development is also generally good. The incidence of poverty was estimated at 9.6 per cent of households in 1995, the lowest for any country in the study.

The only institutions in Malaysia that engage in microfinance to a significant degree are a handful of non-governmental organisations (NGOs). Of these, by far the largest is Amanah Ikhtiar Malaysia (AIM), the largest Grameen Bank replicator outside of Bangladesh with around 30,000 borrowers. There are several other much smaller NGOs involved in microfinance. While total outreach is small it is reasonably high in relation to demand, given the relatively small number of poor households in Malaysia and the widespread opportunities for wage employment which reduce the need for poor households to rely on self-employment.

Arrangements for direct support

Both the government of Malaysia and the state governments have provided considerable support to AIM, for both operational expenses and loanable funds. The smaller microfinance institutions (MFIs) have also received funding from government and/or donor agencies.

Continue to subsidise AIM

These funds have reduced the pressure to operate on a self-sufficient basis, and have enabled AIM in particular to expand its outreach much more rapidly than would otherwise have been possible. Malaysia is very different to any other country included in the study, in that it is possible to obtain quite large amounts of public resources, relative to the number of poor households, for programs to reduce poverty. Governments should continue to subsidise AIM as an effective strategy for poverty reduction. This will enable AIM to concentrate primarily at increasing its outreach, and possibly offering a wider range of services to its clients. Nevertheless, access to public resources is not unlimited, and AIM's recent decision to increase interest rates and strive for operational self-sufficiency is to be welcomed.

While some support to small borrowers is provided through the banking system, it is unlikely that much of this reaches the poor. None of Bank Negara's lending guidelines for banks targets poor borrowers. The various schemes of the Credit Guarantee Corporation (CGC) also do not reach poor borrowers.

Regulation of non-bank microfinance institutions

Establish transparent framework for registering NGOs

The registration procedures for NGOs are not designed with microfinance in mind, and NGOs wishing to engage in microfinance must obtain a specific exemption from the provisions of the Moneylenders Act 1951. While a number of institutions have obtained an exemption, there are no clear criteria. The government should establish a transparent framework for the registration of MFIs, based on a clearly established set of guidelines and outside the ambit of the Moneylenders Act. The government should also allow donations to MFIs to be tax deductible.

Permit MFIs to use members' savings in lending programs

At present, Bank Negara only permits MFIs to accept compulsory savings if they are put into a trust account and not used as loanable funds. This is unnecessarily restrictive. The government should permit MFIs to use at least the compulsory savings of their members in their lending programs.

There are no regulations on MFIs concerning the interest rates that they can charge borrowers. There is also no prudential regulation and supervision of MFIs, in terms of matters such as minimum capital requirements, capital adequacy ratios, reserve or liquidity requirements, or loan loss provisioning requirements.

Develop performance and reporting standards

While it is generally considered that it is not appropriate to subject non-depository MFIs to prudential regulation and supervision, it is not clear if the usual considerations apply in the case of Malaysia. Given the very small number of MFIs, it would not be onerous to establish some system for monitoring them. And while in some countries second tier microfinance institutions have developed performance and reporting standards for MFIs, there is no such institution in Malaysia. The government should consider establishing a small cell within Bank Negara or some other regulatory agency to monitor and supervise MFIs. This body could develop performance and reporting standards that are appropriate to the needs of MFIs, in consultation with the MFIs themselves and drawing on experience from countries such as Bangladesh and the Philippines.

Establish informal MFI network

There are no clear arrangements for self-regulation or coordination among the MFIs operating in Malaysia. The major MFIs should establish an informal network to exchange information and for policy dialogue with government.

Regulation of banks

Establish framework to license small banks

The minimum capital requirement to establish a commercial bank is too high for an MFI wishing to establish a bank, or for a body wishing to establish a small bank at the local level. Moreover, Bank Negara is currently not issuing any licences for the establishment of new banks. Experience in other countries suggests that if banks are to play an active role in microfinance, it is important that there be some mechanism for the establishment of small banks. Such banks also tend to serve small entrepreneurs who do not have access to financial services. The government should establish a framework for licensing small banks, by setting a realistic minimum capital requirement and removing any other restrictions which prevent the establishment of such banks.

Remove interest rate ceilings

The maximum lending rate for any bank loan is set at the base lending rate for the particular bank plus 4 per cent. This ceiling makes it very difficult if not impossible for any bank to cover the costs of small loans to poor borrowers, and further discourages banks from becoming involved in microfinance. It is also perhaps surprising that Malaysia retains interest rate controls when other countries with less developed financial systems have removed them. The government should remove the interest rate ceilings applying to loans by regulated banks, or at least review the spreads applicable to small and very small loans.

There are no restrictions preventing commercial banks from establishing linkages with MFIs. A number of commercial banks have provided loans to AIM, albeit not on a commercial basis.

References

Government of Malaysia. 1996. *Seventh Malaysia Plan* 1996–2000. Economic Planning Unit, Kuala Lumpur.

Singh, Avtar. 1995. 'Poverty eradication: The role of government, NGOs and SHGs in Malaysia'. In *Papers Presented at the International Seminar on Development of Rural Poor Through Self-Help Groups*, National Bank for Agriculture and Rural Development, Bangalore.

Siwar, Chamhuri. 1996. *Microfinance Capacity Assessment Study: The Malaysian Case*. Asia-Pacific Development Centre, Kuala Lumpur.

Persons consulted

Mr Wan Azhar Wan Ahmad	Acting General Manager Credit Guarantee Corporation
Mr Rusdi Hj Ibrahim	Manager, Guarantee II Credit Guarantee Corporation
Mr Hj Mohd Arif Hj Azhari	Assistant Manager, Guarantee II Credit Guarantee Corporation
Mr Mohd Asri Abdul	Director, Loan and Finance Amanah Ikhtiar Malaysia
Ms Zalmah Mahusin	Deputy Director, Finance and Planning Amanah Ikhtiar Malaysia
Ms Norbaiti Haji Rahmat	Deputy Director, Loan Division Amanah Ikhtiar Malaysia
Ms Nor Fazidah Kadri	Deputy Director, Administration Amanah Ikhtiar Malaysia
Dato' Ahmad Tajudin Abdul Rahman	Managing Director Bank Islam Malaysia
Mr Ismail Mahayudin	Senior General Manager, Retail Banking Bank Islam Malaysia
Associate Professor Sukor Kasim	Senior Research Fellow Universiti Sains Malaysia
Dr Denison Jayasooria	Executive Director Partners in Enterprise
Mr Nik Hassan Nik Mohd Amin	Senior General Manager Corporate Planning and Research Division Bank Bumiputra
Mr Ch'ng Soo Keong	General Manager, Commercial and Domestic Banking Oriental Bank
Mr Zainul Akbar Mohd Nor	Assistant General Manager Planning, Research and Support Centre Sime Bank
Ms Azizah Talib	Senior Assistant Manager Economics Department Bank Negara Malaysia

Mr Muhammad Kamil	Senior Executive, Bank Regulation Department Bank Negara Malaysia
Mr Md Khairuddin bin Hj Arshad	Bank Regulation Department Bank Negara Malaysia
Ms Catherine Abigail Ridu	Assistant Director, Women's Affairs Division Ministry of National Unity and Social Development
Mr Mat Noor Nawi	Principal Assistant Director, Distribution Section Economic Planning Unit
Professor Chamhuri Siwar	Faculty of Economics Universiti Kebangsaan Malaysia
Dr Abdul Ghafar Ismail	Faculty of Economics Universiti Kebangsaan Malaysia

Nepal

1 Introduction and background

1.1 Key demographic and economic data

Nepal is a landlocked country and one of the least developed countries of the world. It has borders with India in the west, south and east, and with the Tibet Autonomous Region of the People's Republic of China in the north. The nearest sea coast is 1,120 km away in India. Nepal is mainly a hilly country with about one-fourth of its total land area falling in the Terai region which has a 26–32 km wide fertile plain contiguous with India. The remainder of the land area consists of hills and the Himalayas. There are 250 peaks of which 22 peaks exceed 7,600 m in altitude including the world's highest peak, Mt Everest (8,848 m). Only 17 per cent of the land is arable. However, Nepal is endowed with abundant water resources. Its main nine rivers are estimated to have the potential to generate 83,000 MW hydropower, about 2.27 per cent of the world's total estimated hydropower potentiality. The actual production of electricity only amounts to 237 MW or less than 1 per cent of its potential.

Nepal is estimated to have a population of 21.5 million as at end-1995, and its population growth rate of 2.5 per cent between 1990 and 1995 was higher than most South and Southeast Asian countries and second only to Pakistan. The total fertility rate in 1995, at 5.3 per cent births per woman, was the highest among all the countries under study. The population density in the same year was 152 persons per square kilometre. The Himalayan region in the north has virtually no human habitation because of perpetual snow, and population density increases as one descends into the hilly and Terai regions. The country is largely rural, with only about 14 per cent of the population living in urban areas in 1995.

Nepal is still at a very low level of development, with a per capita income of only $200 in 1995, lowest among all the countries studied. It ranks 151 out of 175 countries on the human development index. Gross national product (GNP) per capita growth rate between 1965 and 1995 was 2.4. In the last three years, however, the growth rate has been about 4.6 per cent. The structure of production has changed with economic growth, with the share of agriculture falling from 50 per cent in the late 1980s to 42 per cent in 1995. The share of industry and particularly of the services sector has increased at a rapid pace.

1.2 Poverty

Estimates of poverty

Estimates of the poverty line or of the incidence of poverty have been made by some agencies in the past. The first of such estimates was by the National Planning Commission in 1976–77. This concluded that based on the 'minimum income angle', 36.2 per cent of the total population were below absolute poverty, and from the 'minimum consumption angle', 31.54 per cent of the total population were below the absolute poverty line. The Multi-Purpose Household Budget Survey (MPHBS) of 1984–85 (published in 1989) conducted by Nepal Rastra Bank concluded that, based on the consumption of Nepal households of both food and non-food items, the poverty line for the country was 42.6 per cent. This was taken as a guide until the National Planning Commission in its Eighth Plan (1992–97) estimated the poverty line as 49 per cent of population or about 9.2 million persons in 1992. The total population of Nepal at that time was close to 20 million.

In determining the incidence of poverty, the Eighth Plan adopted calorie consumption as the basis. Accordingly, the calorie-based national poverty line was estimated at 2,250 calories per capita: 2,300 for the hills area and 2,000 for the Terai region. It was termed a Basic Need Approach (BNA). (According to FAO, the basic minimum daily human need of a person is 2,256 calories.) Nepal's current average consumption is estimated at 2,078 calories. Due to the insufficient calorie energy available, the death rate of children at birth has exceeded 20 per cent, and nearly one million persons are rendered blind. About 60 per cent of the population are illiterate, and 62 per cent of the school age children cannot go to school due to severe poverty. It is true that sampling and methodological differences between the survey of 1984–85 and that of the Eighth Plan in 1992 do make the comparison difficult. But the estimate of the Eighth Plan (a five-year plan) is the latest authoritative estimate available.

Recently, the Central Bureau of Statistics of the government of Nepal with the assistance of the World Bank launched a national survey entitled Nepal Living Standards Survey (NLSS) in July 1994. The survey was completed in July 1996 and states:

> On the basis of the poverty line which we have developed for Nepal, the incidence of poverty in the country as a whole is 42 per cent. In urban areas the rate is 23 per cent while in rural areas it is 44 per cent. Given that about 90 per cent of the population resides in rural areas, it is clear that poverty is overwhelmingly a rural phenomenon . . . rural poverty is both deeper and more severe than urban poverty . . . And the mountain region as a whole is poorer than the hills and Terai.

In monetary terms, the survey determined Rs4500 ($82) per capita per annum as the poverty line.

Regardless of the outcome of past surveys and their findings, if we were to estimate the population below the poverty line by adopting the commonly agreed upon international standard of $150 as the threshold, nearly 71 per cent of Nepal's population would fall below the poverty line. It is difficult, however, to compare Nepal's situation with other countries and it is safer to judge the prevalence of poverty on the most recent and reliable estimates made at the national level by the responsible institution — in this case, the Central Bureau of Statistics.

Policies for poverty reduction

Being one of the poorest countries in the world, the government has always placed a high priority on poverty alleviation. Among the programs implemented in the past were:

(1) the Tribhuwan Village Development program (1950s)

(2) declaration of the land reform program (1960s)

(3) the cooperative movement (1960s and 1970s)

(4) an integrated rural development program launched in the 1980s for the overall development of the rural sector

(5) establishment of the Nepal Food Corporation to provide food security at subsidised rates to remote parts of the country (1960s)
(6) price and transport subsidies on fertiliser and agricultural inputs provided through the Agricultural Inputs Corporation
(7) interest and capital subsidies provided to poor farmers through the Agricultural Development Bank and two commercial banks for cash crops, livestock and irrigation since the late 1980s
(8) the WFD-supported food-for-work program since the early 1970s.

The above and many other schemes launched in the past have typically suffered from implementation weaknesses. In fact, over the years poverty may have increased both in terms of absolute numbers and as a percentage.

The Eighth Plan (1992–1997)

The Eighth Plan had targeted that, as a result of various programs envisaged for addressing poverty, the number of absolute poor would have been reduced to 8.7 million from the 9.2 million at the beginning of the plan period — a reduction by 1.4 million or 7 per cent during the period of the plan.

The Eighth Plan included several programs ensuring that the poor would have access to social and economic sources and employment opportunities. However, realising that absence of targeting has been a shortcoming in the past, the plan for the first time proposed targeting poverty specifically. In respect of credit for poverty alleviation, the plan specifically mentioned the Small Farmers Development Program (SFDP) of the Agricultural Development Bank and the Production Credit for Rural Women (PCRW) implemented by the Ministry of Local Development and involving two large banks, the Nepal Bank Ltd and the Rastriya Banijya Bank.

No evaluation of the outcome of the Eighth Plan is available so far, and so it is not yet possible to assess its impact on poverty in concrete, quantifiable terms. However, compared to the period 1987–92 during which annual GDP growth rate remained 2–3 per cent, the period of the Eighth Plan (1992–97) witnessed a GDP growth of 4–5 per cent. As such, the overall growth rate of about 3.5 per cent in the last decade must have had a positive impact on poverty reduction. However, in the absence of an impact study, this cannot be stated conclusively.

In 1994 Nepal joined other SAARC (South Asian Association for Regional Cooperation) countries, namely Bangladesh, Bhutan, India, Maldives, Pakistan and Sri Lanka, in declaring its commitment to poverty alleviation in this region by adopting a strategy which lays stress on social mobilisation of the poor by providing them with:

- skill generation
- organisation
- savings mobilisation.

Based on these three themes, Nepal conducted pilot testing of the concept in the district of Syangjha. The result so far has been quite encouraging according to the National Planning Commission.

The government has adopted a basic document outlining the Ninth Plan beginning the fiscal year 1997–98. This provides a perspective of twenty years of development and again, poverty alleviation is a priority goal. The plan targets that in twenty years or by 2017, poverty would have reduced from the present level of 42 to 10 per cent. The reduction will be progressive in successive five-year plans as follows:

- end of the Ninth Plan: population below the poverty line to be reduced to 32.5 per cent
- end of the Tenth Plan: population below the poverty line to be reduced to 22 per cent
- end of the Eleventh Plan: population below the poverty line to be reduced to 15 per cent
- end of the Twelfth Plan: population below the poverty line to be reduced to 10 per cent.

The specified targets are to be achieved through the implementation of various sectoral plans of line ministries and the work of specialised financial institutions such as the regional rural development banks and the microfinance programs of NGOs and international NGOs operating in the country. The recently adopted 20-year Prospective Agricultural Development Plan, Land Redistribution Plan, and the Development of Backward Classes, Skill and Employment Generation programs will play a contributing role.

1.3 Overview of financial system

Nine private commercial banks, two state-owned commercial banks, two development banks, five regional rural development banks (RRDBs), 37 finance companies and about 17 non-bank financial institutions together with the Nepal Rastra Bank, the central bank of the country, constitute the core of the institutional financial system. They are regulated by Nepal Rastra Bank (NRB) under the NRB Act 1956 and the Commercial Bank Act 1984. In the case of RRDBs they are regulated under the Development Bank Act enacted in 1996. Among them, two state-owned commercial banks (the Nepal Bank Ltd and the Rastriya Banijya Bank) and the Agricultural Development Bank of Nepal (ADB/N) together share about two-thirds of loans and investment and 55 per cent of total deposits of all banks and finance companies. The two state-owned commercial banks also have the most extensive outreach in terms of branch network. The eleven commercial banks and the Agricultural Development Bank have a total of 700 branches all over the country providing banking services. The majority of these branches are located in rural and semi-urban centres.

Additionally, 16 credit cooperatives and 23 NGOs undertake limited banking activities, mainly loans and deposits. They are licensed to undertake limited banking activities under the NRB Act 1956.

Until 1984, no foreign banks were allowed to open branches and engage in banking activities in Nepal. Since 1985, as part of the open policy and to attract modern technology and management into the banking industry, foreign banks were allowed as joint ventures with local promoters on an equity-sharing basis to the extent of 50 per cent. The remaining 50 per cent of equity capital had to be owned by nationals. So far, foreign commercial banks, mostly from the neighbouring SAARC countries as well as one each from France and Australia have established themselves as joint ventures. Foreign capital investment has also gone into finance companies, a phenomenon witnessed for most of the last three years. A separate Act, the Finance Company Act 1985, regulates their operation. Despite the fact that foreign capital and management have been imported into the commercial banking field, financing of the poverty sector remains outside the consideration of joint-venture banks except where, by regulation, they are compelled to set aside a certain percentage of their loan portfolio for the priority sector (including the 'deprived' or hard-core poor).

Commercial banks are obliged to allocate 12 per cent of their total loan portfolio to the priority sector (including the 'deprived' or hard-core poor). Of the 12 per cent meant for the priority sector, 0.25 per cent (in the case of newly established banks) to 3 per cent (in the case of two large state-owned commercial banks) must be lent to the 'deprived' or hard-core poor. Commercial banks are, however, entitled to refinance 11 per cent from NRB if they achieve a minimum of 12 per cent fixed for priority sector lending. 'Deprived' sector lendings are those which fall within the range Rs5,000–Rs15,000 ($91–$272) per loanee: assets, landholdings or income are not guiding factors. Whereas normal commercial interest rates for loans range from 19 to 24 per cent at present, loans for the priority sector have been between 13 and 15 per cent. This is a voluntary decision on the part of the commercial banks and without any regulatory compulsion. In so doing, commercial banks are guided more by social considerations than commercial. It is also possible that they (commercial banks) intend to achieve the 12 per cent obligatory target as soon as possible, even by lowering interest rates.

In the recent past, NRB has introduced a number of changes aimed primarily at encouraging private initiative and more prudent monetary measures in the financial market, which may help achieve this objective.

1.4 Overview of microfinance

The government's commitment to microfinance is reflected in the declaration through the five-year development plans. In particular, the following programs illustrate these commitments:

- IBP (Intensive Banking Program) initiated by NRB in the early 1970s requires that the commercial banks set aside 12 per cent of their loan portfolio for the priority sector, inclusive of 3 per cent which should go to the 'deprived' or hard-core poor.
- SFDP (Small Farmers Development Program) launched by the Agricultural Development Bank of Nepal in the early 1970s is meant to meet the credit needs of small farmers in the rural areas.
- PCRW (Production Credit for Rural Women) introduced in the early 1980s and implemented by the Local Development Ministry of the government of Nepal. The International Fund for Agricultural Development (IFAD) is the main donor of this program.
- MCPW (Micro Credit Project for Women) an ADB-assisted project which is coordinated by NRB and implemented through commercial banks, using NGOs as intermediaries.
- RRDBs (regional rural development banks), also known as Grameen Bikas banks and established under the Development Bank Act 1996, replicating the Grameen Bank model. There are five such banks in five development regions of the country.
- Nirdhan and the Center for Self-Help Development (CSD) are NGOs replicating the Grameen model.

Twenty credit cooperatives have so far been permitted by NRB to provide microfinance services in the rural areas.

The Agricultural Development Bank of Nepal (ADB/N) has been the single largest formal credit institution in the agricultural and rural sector. Its main credit program is designed to lend to farmers, tenants and landless with per capita income of Rs2,500 ($45) under the Small Farmers Development Program (SFDP) which now operates through 322 Sub-Project Offices (SPOs) of the bank. As of mid-July 1996, it had 26,743 groups, consisting of 189,061 members (146,589 males and 42,472 females).

The Intensive Banking Program (IBP) which focuses on the priority sector as defined by the Nepal Rastra Bank (that is, cottage industries, agricultural activities and the services sector) had by mid-July 1996 disbursed a cumulative total of Rs4,056 million ($74 million) to 246,439 borrowers through the network of 338 branches — Rastriya Banijya Bank (164), Nepal Bank Ltd (172) and Nepal Arab Bank Ltd (2) — in 74 out of the 75 districts of the country. The borrowers under this program consist of both poor and non-poor individuals. The poor segment within IBP are those whose maximum borrowing limit is Rs30,000 ($544) per person. No separate statistics are available for the poor categories.

Production Credit for Rural Women (PCRW) under the Ministry of Local Development operates through 139 branches of Nepal Bank Ltd (NBL), Rastriya Banijya Bank (RBB) and ADB/N spread over 55 districts covering a total of 13,181 credit groups with 64,724 women members. Of these, 35,017 had borrowed Rs230 million ($4.2 million) up to mid-July 1996. The average loan size was Rs8,050 ($146).

As of mid-January 1997, MCPW was operating through 31 branches of two participating banks, Nepal Bank Ltd and Rastriya Banijya Bank, covering 93 village development committees (VDCs) and ten municipalities. There were 1,885 SHGs with 11,591 women members. Rural or urban women belonging to a household with a per capita income of less than or equal to Rs2,511 ($46) are eligible to join a group. Between July 1994 and January 1997, a total of Rs69 million ($45.6 million) was disbursed to 5,708 women borrowers. Recovery so far has been nearly 100 per cent. The groups have also collected total savings of Rs37 million ($0.7 million) up to January 1997. The Banking with the Poor (BWTP) program of The Foundation for Development Cooperation has been implemented by RBB since 1992. It now covers a number of selected villages of 15 districts and is expanding gradually.

All in all, 522,000 persons have received microfinance services under the poverty-focused credit programs. As has been explained, except in the case of SFDP, PCRW, MCPW and BWTP where the target groups are defined as poor, the Intensive Banking Program (IBP) does not necessarily target the poor. IBP is especially for small sectors, and only an insignificant part is devoted to those below the poverty line.

The government of Nepal introduced the Rural Self-Reliance Fund in March 1991 to supplement NGO funding for rural lending. The fund started as a pilot project with a one-time contribution of Rs20 million ($0.4 million), and 45 NGOs (mostly saving and credit associations) have been given Rs15 million ($0.3 million) as loans out of the fund at 8 per cent interest. NGOs with a satisfactory performance are also given 6 per cent rebate for administrative support. Until now 3,194 families have received loans from 45 NGOs, with a repayment rate of 84.12 per cent.

With regard to cooperatives, Nepal Rastra Bank estimates that there are about 3,132 cooperatives registered under the Cooperative Act 1992. Of these, 343 are savings and credit cooperatives, the others being multi-purpose. Out of these 343 savings and credit cooperatives, 214 have formed a national-level federation named Nepal Federation of

Saving and Credit Cooperatives Union (NEFSCUN). With a total membership of 16,041 persons, their total cumulative savings is Rs74 million ($1.3 million) and their disbursement Rs59 million ($1.1 million). As of January 1997 their deposit was Rs203 million ($3.7 million), with loans and advances of Rs299 million ($5.4 million). According to NRB, the average loan size per borrower of the 16 cooperatives is higher than that of the cooperatives collecting savings from their members only.

With the enactment of the Cooperative Act 1992, there was an upsurge of community-based informal savings and credit organisations (SCOs) trying to get themselves registered as primary societies under the Act. As of April 1995, 158 community-based SCOs were formally registered as cooperatives. It is estimated that there may be in excess of 12,158 such community-based savings and credit groups (CECI 1996). Their sources of fund are members' share contributions, deposits from members and external borrowings. On average, an SCO has Rs58,076 ($1054) as deposits, Rs28,115 ($510) as share and Rs32,187 ($584) as loans. Their loans are for a smaller amount (less than Rs2,000) and the recovery rate is 100 per cent. All of them are operationally viable, enjoying surplus over expenditure by an average of Rs5,282 ($96). This is due to the voluntary nature of their workers with their economical operation.

The Social Welfare Council estimates that about 18,000 NGOs are operating in Nepal. They are categorised mainly into three types:

(1) those with credit supply as the main objective

(2) those with community or social development as the major objective, and income generation or credit supply as a minor activity

(3) those not having income generation or credit supply as either a major or minor activity (Sharma & Acharya 1995).

Four thousand (4,000) of them are registered under the Society Registration Act 1978 as non-profit social welfare organisations.

About 24 such NGOs have gained the permission of NRB to engage in limited banking activities. Of these, two — Nirdhan and CSD — are active in the rural finance market and replicate the Grameen Bank model. They have formed 2,332 groups in seven districts and 102 village development committees (VDCs) with 11,037 members (women). By January 1997, they had disbursed Rs73 million ($1.3 million) to 10,050 borrowers, with an average loan size of Rs7,230 ($131) and with 100 per cent recovery. The total savings mobilised amounts to Rs7 million ($0.1 million).

With about 8 per cent cost of funds and 11 per cent service delivery cost, the total operating cost of CSD is 19 per cent against a lending rate of 20 per cent. Nirdhan has incurred an operating cost of 24 per cent (delivery cost 15 per cent and cost of funds 8 per cent). CSD has attained sustainability because of its larger outreach (CSD has 6,431 borrowers as against Nirdhan's 3,619) and fewer staff (CSD's 42 compared to Nirdhan's 96). Both enjoy 100 per cent repayment with zero overdue. Both NGOs have been able to attract commercial bank loans. Nirdhan has borrowed a total of Rs2.5 million ($45,400) from five commercial banks, and CSD Rs0.7 million ($12,700) from three commercial banks.

By 1996 five regional rural development banks (RRDBs) had been established in five regional development centres of the country to provide easy access to credit to 'deprived' sections of the society, especially women from poor rural households. These banks are capitalised by the government and NRB up to 75 per cent of the paid-up capital of Rs60 million ($1.09 million) each, the balance being subscribed by other banks and financial institutions. RRDBs replicate the Grameen Bank model. They have extended operations to 19 districts and 332 VDCs, formed 9,520 groups with 47,780 members and disbursed Rs652 million ($11.8 million) to 45,352 borrowers. They have attained 100 per cent repayment rate (as of January 1997).

The Micro Credit Project for Women (MCPW) is a microcredit program funded by the Asian Development Bank (ADB) and initiated in 1994 by the Ministry of Local Development in coordination with two large commercial banks, the Nepal Bank Ltd (NBL) and Rastriya Banijya Bank (RBB). It is committed to developing and involving NGOs as financial intermediaries, and serves both urban and rural women. At present 80 per cent of the loan funds provided by ADB are channelled through NBL and RBB, 10 per cent from the two participating banks and 10 per cent by the beneficiaries of the program. The project also involves grant assistance from the Japanese Special Fund and government of Norway for institutional support to NGOs.

How NGOs in Nepal can intermediate between banks and SHGs promoted by them is a subject currently under discussion. The ADB-assisted MCPW program has engaged the Canadian Center for International Studies and Cooperation (CECI) to conduct a study of issues which has produced draft legislation entitled the 'Financial Intermediation Act'. The draft envisages a financial intermediary being licensed by a registrar specially created for this purpose. The relevant functions of the financial intermediary are to:

- evaluate loan applications
- determine whether the loan is meant for microenterprise
- supply microcredit to the groups without tangible collateral
- mobilise savings and manage them
- obtain loans and grants from donor and financial agencies
- monitor and follow-up loan repayments.

Other provisions of the proposed draft relate to record keeping, accounting, audit, reporting and compliance with the Act, etc. In short, the draft legislation creates an opportunity for NGOs and MFIs to act as intermediaries without being subject to the other prevailing banking and financial regulations of the NRB which are stringent. It is still in draft form and may have to undergo a range of scrutiny before it is finally enacted.

2 Arrangement for direct support

2.1 Support for specialised microfinance institutions

Rural Self-Reliance Fund (RSRF)

The establishment of the Rural Self-Reliance Fund (RSRF) in 1991 was a step in the right direction. It can be compared with the Palli Karma Sahayak Foundation (PKSF) of Bangladesh. The fund was established to lend to NGOs and MFIs that have otherwise had difficulty in accessing financial institutions and banks. RSRF received initial funding of Rs20 million ($0.4 million) in 1991 from government budgetary resources, but has not received additional funds since then. Up to January 1997, about 54 NGOs (mostly SCOs) had borrowed Rs17 million ($0.3 million) for on-lending to members from deprived families.

Eligible NGOs are those that are registered with the relevant government body and are permitted by Nepal Rastra Bank to engage in banking transactions. Activities that can be supported by the fund are agriculture and horticulture, livestock farming, cottage industries, services and other income- and employment-generating activities. The loan conditions are:

- rate of interest of 8 per cent
- rebate of 6 per cent for proper utilisation of loan fund and on-time repayment
- repeat loan guaranteed
- loans to individual borrowers not to exceed Rs15,000 ($272)
- regular savings among the groups is encouraged
- skill and training are imparted.

The fund is being managed by Nepal Rastra Bank. NGOs are further required to submit to NRB returns concerning: (a) sources of income and list of assets; (b) operational results; (c) audit reports on an annual basis; (d) operational and loan procedures; (e) provision for monitoring and inspection; and (f) social mobilisation activities benefiting the targeted groups.

The fund has attained a repayment rate of 84 per cent. In the past, the repayment rate has ranged from 67 to 85 per cent, indicating the weakness in supervision, monitoring and follow-up. Though it is designed to target the poorest, it has not achieved the purpose of meeting the credit needs of the poor since the lending operations of savings and credit associations in Nepal are not, in practice, poverty focused. Nevertheless, the fund has the potential to support a large number of NGOs, if it is properly managed and better resourced.

Regional rural development banks (RRDBs)

As noted above, five regional rural development banks (RRDBs) were established by 1996 to provide credit to 'deprived' sections of the society, especially poor rural women. They are owned primarily by the government, and replicate the Grameen Bank model.

One of the five RRDBs, the Eastern Region Development Bank (ERDB) was the first to attain operational self-sufficiency by 1996 based upon its operating cost of 18 per cent (delivery cost 10 per cent plus cost of funds of 8 per cent, and a loan loss zero per cent) against its lending rate of 20 per cent. The other four RRDBs are yet to attain sustainability, mainly because their outreach is far below that of ERDB.

RRDBs initially established under the Commercial Bank Act have now been registered under the Development Bank Act 1996 which is more appropriate for poverty-focused microfinance institutions like RRDBs.

Of late, RRDBs are being increasingly plagued by political pressure and interference in their operation. Having achieved so much in such a short period of time, it is unthinkable that RRDBs may be facing a similar fate to other government-run credit programs for the poor. One way of diluting undesirable pressure from 'above' would be to divest the shareholdings of government, NRB and government-owned banks to borrowers and savers in the program as well as to the public generally.

The total outreach of five RRDBs is 9,520 groups with 47,780 members, ERDB's share being nearly 70 per cent of the total. Sources of lending funds are mainly equity capital, group funds and borrowings from NRB and commercial banks. Shortage of loanable funds has been a problem as the group fund and equity cannot meet the growing needs of this expanding program. NRB recently extended a line of credit of Rs100 million ($1.8 million) to ERDB to overcome its funding problem. As yet, it has not been utilised. However, the line of credit promised by NRB indicates the willingness of the central bank to fill the void created by the funds shortage and to see that a successful RRDB does not have to suffer for want of loanable funds. However, RRDBs could also mobilise deposits from the public, borrow from banks, and even try for external assistance to augment their resources, if they pay the prevailing interest rates. At this stage of their operation, RRDBs have obviously not been able to explore other potential avenues for resource augmentation.

2.2 Support through the banking system

Small Farmers Development Program (SFDP)

The government of Nepal has played an important role in seeing that the rural poor and those below the poverty line are given credit for income and employment generation. The move for the provision of microcredit started first in the early 1970s with the introduction of the Small Farmers Development Program (SFDP) implemented by the Agricultural Development Bank of Nepal (ADB/N) which is owned by the government. SFDP is now the single largest microcredit program encompassing about 190,000 small farmers in 74 out of the 75 districts of the country. It targets those below the per capita income of Rs2,511 ($46) per year. It should be noted, however, that the poverty line of Rs2,511 ($45.6) was fixed at the beginning of the sixth five-year development plan, or about ten years ago. It is likely to be revised shortly, to reflect inflation and exchange rate changes since then. It is possible that the revised poverty line may be fixed at or around Rs5,000 ($90).

SFDP, an ongoing program, has witnessed deterioration over time in terms of its effectiveness. This is reflected in its loan repayment rates which have now fallen to 58 per cent (1995–96). Starting in the early years at subsidised interest rates, the program is not yet operationally viable despite the fact that since 1988, applicable interest rates have been near market rates which range between 16 and 18 per cent. Some grant element is provided by bilateral donors and IFAD for social mobilisation and development. However, SFDP's transaction costs of 11 per cent combined with nearly 10 per cent of cost of funds totalling 21 per cent is far above its interest income of 16 to 18 per cent. Coupled with the program's recovery rate of only 58 per cent, SFDP is unsustainable.

Several factors account for this state of affairs. Bureaucratic handling of the program by state-owned development banks, lack of supervision, lack of motivation and training of the field staff, and interferences from above have compounded to affect SFDP adversely.

Since the early 1990s, GTZ has been assisting ADB/N to restructure SFDP and salvage the once well-known microcredit program which is of far-reaching importance to Nepal's agriculture-based economy. Accordingly, in selected districts on a pilot basis, groups of small farmers are being linked with what is now known as Small Farmers Cooperatives Ltd, owned and managed by the members themselves. ADB/N plays a supportive role. Assets and liabilities of small-farmer groups are transferred to this newly created organisation which, in turn, continues to be linked with ADB/N for funding and training inputs. So far, results are reported to be quite satisfactory. Ownership and autonomy in decision making have encouraged the active participation of members, recovery rates have improved, and some of the small-farmer cooperatives are already operationally self-sustainable.

Production Credit for Rural Women (PCRW)

PCRW was launched by the Ministry of Local Development in 1982 in collaboration with three public-sector banks (Nepal Bank Limited, Rastriya Banijya Bank and the Agricultural Bank of Nepal) and UNICEF. In this program, the Women Development Section (WDS) of the ministry acts as social intermediary and the participating banks provide loans directly to the group members who are developed and promoted by WDS staff. The program focuses at improving the socioeconomic status of rural women. Since 1988, 90 per cent of the loan funds have come from IFAD and been channelled through the two commercial banks and ADB/N. Participant banks contribute 10 per cent. Technical input is provided by IFAD and UNICEF on a grant basis, so that there is no cost to banks for social preparation.

PCRW has been a reasonably successful program with a repayment rate of 81.85 per cent as of 1995–96. However, being a socioeconomic program, its delivery cost has been rather high at 42 per cent. With the added funds cost and bad debt cost, it will be quite high, compared to its income of 15–16 per cent interest.

In the past 14 years, about 35,000 rural women have received loans and since the staff members of WDS are temporary, the program has lacked the necessary motivation to organise groups. In its present form, it is not a sustainable program, but its contribution in terms of women's awakening has been valuable. To make the program self-sustainable, a move similar to that taken by ADB/N for SFDP under GTZ technical assistance, might be appropriate for PCRW.

Micro Credit Project for Women (MCPW)

The Micro Credit Project for Women (MCPW) was initiated by the government under ADB assistance in 1994, and is the second in a series of credit programs with a focus on women. The project is designed to provide three components:

(1) group formation and training of women

(2) institutional support to NGOs

(3) provision of credit to women.

The loan component consists of $4 million and technical assistance of $9 million by bilateral donors. It is committed to involving NGOs as service delivery agents in the first phase and as financial intermediaries in the second phase which is due to begin soon.

Nepal Rastra Bank is the executing agency for the credit, with Nepal Bank Ltd and Rastriya Banijya Bank as participant banks. It is the first government credit program which is committed to involving NGOs as an alternative mechanism for service delivery in a cost-effective manner. MCPW serves mostly the poorest, as only women with incomes less than or equal to Rs2,511 ($45) are eligible to join a group. A mid-term review of the project is under way at present and more about its implementation will be known after the review. Available information indicates that the project has experienced 100 per cent repayment so far.

Intensive Banking Program (IBP)

Initiated in October 1981, IBP has been recognised as one of the poverty-focused microcredit programs. The program follows an area approach, each IBP branch covering

250 to 400 households and concentrating on loan operations within this given area. Households are categorised as 'high income' and 'low income' families. Viable projects are financed with adequate collateral for high-income families and without collateral for low-income families under group guarantee schemes. The maximum individual loan size is determined at Rs30,000 ($544) and loans are granted on an individual as well as a group basis.

Commercial banks are obliged to lend 12 per cent of their loan portfolio to the priority sector. Loan sizes of Rs5,000 ($91) ranging up to Rs15,000 ($272) to individual borrowers are regarded as loans given to hard-core poor. The initiation of priority-sector lending has been the sole factor in drawing commercial banks to microfinance activities. The commercial banks are still very hesitant, and the repayment performance under IBP has declined to less than 50 per cent indicating poor loan management, political pressure on banks and lack of motivation. NRB has eased the obligation of commercial banks to some extent by allowing their loans to MFIs, two Grameen replicators and five regional rural development banks (also Grameen replicators) to be considered as part of their mandatory 12 per cent lending to the priority sector.

IBP has proved non-viable commercially. The World Bank in 1993 estimated that in order for IBP to be viable, it needed to be able to charge an interest rate of 30.3 per cent against the banks' then lending rate of 15.50 per cent. The situation in 1997 is not very different.

Commercial banks perceive that lending small sums to large numbers of borrowers scattered over distant geographic areas is not operationally cost-effective, and their staff members do not possess the kind of orientation to deal with poor clients. Moreover, they argue that microfinance requires a different kind of institutional set-up, one for which commercial banks are inherently unsuitable. This may be the reason why the commercial banks' priority sector credit as against their total loan portfolio has remained below 8 per cent. As recommended by the Nepal Rural Credit Review Report (ADB/NRB 1994), a fresh look into the future of IBP seems urgent. In its present form IBP has not well served the needs of the weaker sections. The objective can be better attained either by creating an autonomous entity or a fund which will support the activities of microfinance institutions (MFIs) which are successful in poverty lending.

3 Regulation of non-bank microfinance institutions

There are no specific regulations applicable to MFIs. NGOs are normally registered as non-profit organisations under the Society Registration Act 1978 and do not have a capital base. A large number of small NGOs undertaking lending programs depend on external donor funding. To a limited extent, they also mobilise savings of the group members, although under the Nepal Rastra Bank Act 1956, no institution can engage in credit and savings activities without NRB's prior approval. NRB has tolerated it, considering these transactions as being insignificant at this stage.

Limited banking

In the last three years NRB has granted 'limited banking' authority to 24 NGOs. This was a much discussed subject in 'Bank Poor 1996' in Kuala Lumpur in December 1996, and is a practice which has no parallel in other Asian countries. Under the 'limited banking' arrangement, NGOs/MFIs are permitted to accept savings deposits, but are not allowed to engage in other banking activities such as overdrafts, bills and foreign exchange transactions, issuance of bonds etc.

NRB has issued two types of limited banking permission. In the first category, only two large NGOs, namely Nirdhan and the Center for Self-help Development (CSD), both Grameen Bank replicators, have been authorised to accept deposits from members as well as from non-members and also to lend to non-members. The second category is where NGOs have authority only to accept deposits from and lend to members. There are 380 NGOs given such authority.

Nepal Rastra Bank has imposed reserve requirements similar to banks to the first category of NGOs. No such requirements exist for the second category. NRB expects that the first category of NGOs will gradually make a move towards converting themselves into a development bank where the capitalisation requirement is Rs10 million ($0.2 million) as against Rs500 million ($9.1 million) for opening a commercial bank. Nirdhan is reported to have applied to NRB for such a licence. As a development bank Nirdhan will have much more flexibility and opportunity to mobilise untapped and potential savings in the rural areas and to achieve financial self-sustainability in a relatively short period of time.

Financial Intermediation Act

Another new aspect of microfinance operations in Nepal is a piece of draft legislation, the Financial Intermediation Act proposed by Nepal Rastra Bank to the government for enactment. When adopted, it will legally empower qualified NGOs to act as financial intermediaries between banks and SHGs of the poor.

The draft defines a financial intermediary as a society which has obtained a certificate of permission to perform the functions of financial intermediation — financial intermediation meaning 'anything done in playing the role of an intermediary in the supply of microcredit'.

Certificates of financial intermediation are to be issued by a registrar specially created for this purpose under the Act. The registrar will decide on NGO qualifications for obtaining such a licence, and strict criteria and standards are expected to be applied. Non-compliance will be subject to penalties including cancellation of the certificate. The registrar is also empowered to carry out inspections from time to time and receive reports, as well as returning to ensure compliance. It is expected that NRB itself might be designated as the registrar. The functions of the intermediary under the proposed Act include:

(1) to supply microcredit for the operation of micro or small enterprises with or without collateral

(2) to supply microcredit up to the prescribed amounts on an individual or group basis to members of such groups without collateral

(3) to activate groups to mobilise savings, and manage such savings as prescribed

(4) to obtain loans or grants from donors and use them for microcredit.

The intermediary is prohibited from performing any function with a commercial or profit motive. Interest rates to be charged will be decided by the intermediary itself.

The above are some glimpses from the proposed Act, but it remains to be seen whether the final adoption will follow the proposed course. It is an attempt born out of the special requirements of the MCPW program, rather than an independent initiative of NRB. Its objective is to facilitate intermediation by NGOs under the MCPW program assisted by

ADB. Nevertheless, it is possible that the proposed Financial Intermediation Act may eventually prove an instrument in strengthening NGOs/MFIs as effective microfinance institutions. It may be noted that the Act does not require any capitalisation for NGOs acting as intermediaries.

3.1 The broad regulatory framework

Licensing

Institutions engaged in microfinance are required to obtain a licence as follows.

Commercial banks

- under Commercial Bank Act, by NRB

Agricultural Development Bank

- under its own charter, Agricultural Development Bank, by the Government Bank of Nepal
- under Nepal Rastra Bank Act 1956 by NRB (to engage in deposit taking and other commercial banking activities)

Cooperatives

- under the Co-operative Act 1989
- under Nepal Rastra Bank Act 1956 (to engage in deposit taking)

NGOs

- under Society Registration Act 1978
- under Nepal Rastra Bank Act 1956 (to engage in deposit taking)
- under the Social Welfare Act 1991

RRDBs

- registered under Development Bank Act 1996

It should be noted that the Agricultural Development Bank and cooperatives are subject to registration under two pieces of legislation and the NGOs under three different pieces of legislation. There are numerous savings and credit groups and their associations all over the country, most of which operate informally. Some are incorporated under the Cooperative Act 1992. However, no statistics of their operation are readily available.

According to Nepal Rastra Bank, it has so far given permission to 128 cooperatives and 20 NGOs to engage in limited banking activities, especially deposits. Generally speaking, NGOs and cooperatives which are given such authority for deposits are limited to accepting deposits from members only. Moreover, such licensed NGOs and cooperatives are subject to the following:

- Deposit accepting is not to exceed 10 per cent of paid-up capital in the case of cooperatives.
- Loans are not to exceed Rs100,000 ($1815) per individual in the case of NGOs.
- In the case of cooperatives, there is a liquidity requirement of 10 per cent of total deposit liabilities.
- NGOs are required to set aside 10 per cent of their net profit to the risk fund.
- NGOs are not to exceed more than 3 per cent as fees for other services.
- Cooperatives are subject to loan provisioning according to four types of loan classification — good, substandard, doubtful and bad loans at the rate of 1, 10, 50 and 100 per cent respectively.

In addition to deposit taking, very few NGOs have asked for authority to engage in other banking activities, that is, letters of credit, foreign exchange transactions, etc.

There are 343 single-purpose savings and credit cooperatives that are registered under the Cooperative Act 1992 which allows them to accept savings and deposits from their members or other persons, and to provide loans to their members. According to Article 26: 'A Society or Union may conduct banking transactions with permission of the Nepal Rastra Bank'. This means some overlap with NRB regulation. Authorities of NRB interpret it differently and believe that all societies engaged in financial intermediation rightfully fall under the regulation of the central bank.

Most savings and credit cooperatives have not bothered to obtain permission from NRB as the issue is still under debate and the scale of their operation is small. On the other hand, some of the savings and credit cooperatives whose financial operations are fairly large and expanding have applied for NRB's permission and 128 of them have been granted such permission. Twenty (20) NGOs have also been given permission by NRB. The feeling on the part of most NGOs and community-based savings and credit organisations (SCOs) is that with formalisation they might be subjected to political and bureaucratic control with consequent loss of autonomy and flexibility. As such, they prefer to operate informally.

3.2 Interest rates and other charges

Non-governmental organisations (NGOs) are restricted to charging a maximum of 15 per cent on loans. They can charge a maximum of an additional 3 per cent as a service charge. Thus, NGOs are limited to charging a maximum of 18 per cent. There is no such restriction on commercial banks and cooperatives, and there is therefore no level playing field between players in poverty lending. Although there does not seem to be any rationale for this regulation, policymakers seem to fear that if NGOs are given full freedom, they might charge an exploitative rate — an apprehension which presently stands in the way of NGOs attaining financial self-sustainability. Selected NGOs, mainly Nirdhan and CSD, have received lines of credit from the commercial banks at 6–8 per cent. The prevailing market rates charged by commercial banks on other commercial loans range between 17 and 20 per cent, though the rates may differ to some extent among institutions.

Loans to individuals by banks, NGOs and cooperatives ranging up to Rs15,000 ($272) are defined as loans given to the 'deprived' sector or 'hard-core' poor, and attract an interest subsidy of 80 per cent up to the loan amount of Rs5,000 ($91) and 33 per cent for up to Rs15,000 ($272). The effective rates of interest for such loans are therefore 3 and 10 per cent respectively. Such low interest rates on small-sized loans have become controversial and it is alleged that members of SHGs and clients of RRDBs pressurise Grameen Bikas banks for loans because of these extremely low effective interest rates. It is feared that this might prove a hurdle to maintaining high loan repayment rates in the future. Observers comment that in the absence of an effective monitoring system, subsidies have led to distortions and should therefore be withdrawn.

A constraining influence for microfinance institutions in attaining operational self-sufficiency has been the two restrictions imposed by NRB regulation: that is, a ceiling of 6 per cent on 'spread' (uniformly applied to banks, finance companies, cooperatives and NGOs) and 15 per cent on loans. The cost of operations of NGOs at this stage is much higher, and successful microfinance institutions might need to charge at least 25 per cent loan rates for break-even. NGOs do enjoy the freedom to charge application and other service fees not exceeding 3 per cent, but the same is not allowed to the cooperatives.

3.3 Prudential regulation and supervision

Capital adequacy

Eight (8) per cent of risk-weighted average assets is required for commercial banks and cooperatives. Guidelines given with regard to calculation of risk are associated with the quality of loan and the assets of the organisation. For NGOs, no capital requirement has been imposed. They are, however, directed by NRB to build a reserve fund to which NGOs have to allocate 10 per cent of their operating profit as provisions for loan loss. In case of RRDBs, the Development Bank Act 1996 gives discretion to NRB to decide on the capital stock to be maintained by them. The five RRDBs now in operation have Rs60 million ($1.1 million) each as their paid-up capital.

NRB regulations presently in force require that commercial banks must have Rs250–500 million ($4.5–9.1 million) as paid-up capital depending on the location of head office and geographic coverage of business, and no capital is fixed for NGOs. For saving and credit cooperatives, the requirement is a minimum of Rs2.5 million ($45,400) to open a branch within the same district and Rs10 million ($181,500) for opening a branch in another district.

Liquidity

For commercial banks the liquidity requirement is 12 per cent of total deposits, while for cooperatives, it is 10 per cent of total deposits. No liquidity requirements have been fixed by NRB for NGOs involved in credit and savings activities focused on the poverty sector.

Limiting deposit as a ratio of share capital

An NRB directive states that a society shall not collect deposits exceeding ten times its paid-up capital. A similar regulation applies to finance companies but not commercial banks. NGOs are exempt as they do not have a capital base. In their case, a loan ceiling of Rs100,000 ($1815) per group or individual has been fixed.

Loan classification and provisioning

An NRB directive provides an operational definition of six categories of loan classification according to which the commercial banks have to make provisions ranging from 1 to 100 per cent, based on the quality and ageing of the loan. Societies have to maintain a reserve account to cover the risk associated with four categories of loans: good (1 per cent), weak (10 per cent), doubtful (50 per cent) and bad (100 per cent). Such provisions are considered normal with the formal financial sector.

With regard to the rationale for minimum capital requirements, they are simply based on policy decisions which followed Basle Accord recommendations concerning prudent banking practices. Despite these, however, the above provisions are subject to debate and interpretation.

Loan documentation

The regulatory authority — in this case, NRB — and the applicable legislation governing microfinance institutions (MFIs) have not laid down specific requirements for loan documentation. These have been left to the discretion of the lending institutions. In practice, the basic information required of the loan applicant generally include project cost, profitability, investment, maturity, loan amount, type of collateral etc. Adherence to documentation by borrowers at the poverty level is often facilitated by the NGO intermediaries assisting them. It is the availability of credit according to the need of such borrowers which is more important and pressing than the formalities. With group guarantees legalised as collateral in the case of low-income families under the Development Bank Act 1996, it is hoped that many of the hurdles concerning loan documentation would have been solved. It must be mentioned, however, that cooperatives, under their law and practice, require adequate collateral, and group guarantees are not applicable in their case.

Rastriya Banijya Bank (RBB) became conscious of the impact of the many and lengthy documentary requirements being applied by their branches while granting loans, and early in 1992 introduced a number of modifications to make them short and simple. In this process, some of the formalities considered not so relevant were also dropped. These actions have helped RBB branches to reduce their transaction costs of lending to the rural poor under their Banking with the Poor Program.

Collateral

In practice in Nepal, group guarantees have been accepted for some years as loan collateral for poverty lending. This is true for all MFIs with a poverty focus. In fact, group guarantees are quite prevalent and even commercial banks involved in group lending have accepted them as a collateral substitute, traditional collateral being land and buildings. Commercial banks have also extended lines of credit to NGOs (Nirdhan and CSD) against collateral of: (a) personal guarantees of chairman and members of the board of directors; (b) physical assets and properties of NGOs; (c) track record of the NGO involved, performance and volume of loans; and (d) trustworthiness of the NGO leadership. For the first time, the Development Bank Act recognised joint liability of the group as sufficient collateral for low-income families up to a specified loan amount (Rs30,000 per borrower) given to them.

Reporting requirements

NGOs and cooperatives as well as MFIs licensed by NRB to accept deposits and carry out limiting banking activities are all obliged to submit data on their financial operation to NRB. In the case of RRDBs, such requirements are specified in detail in the Development Bank Act itself under which RRDBs are incorporated. By separate instructions issued from time to time, NRB has asked MFIs to submit financial information and data relating to the following areas:

- loan terms and conditions
- interest rates
- deposits, terms, maturity and conditions
- balance sheet, profit and loss
- portfolio and outreach
- loan repayment and arrears.

Depending upon the kind of activity, information must be submitted, weekly, monthly and yearly. Returns are monthly, and balance sheet and profit and loan accounts are submitted on a yearly basis.

Auditing

For cooperatives, auditing must take place within five months after the end of the fiscal year. The auditor must hold at least a 'B' class certificate and be approved by NRB. For

NGOs, auditing is required within six months after the end of the fiscal year, and at least a 'C' class auditor is required. NRB approval is not required.

Governance

The Society Registration Act 1978 under which NGOs are registered provides for an annual general meeting, board of management, duties and responsibilities of the board and of the chief executive. The Act also provides strictly for annual audit reports to be submitted to the Chief District Officer. Where such NGOs are licensed by NRB for limited banking activities, they are instructed by NRB to abide by the law strictly. This also applies for cooperatives under the Cooperative Act. As such, internal management, control and supervision are duly provided for in the respective legislation in the case of MFIs.

With regard to ownership, there is no provision for capitalisation under the Society Registration Act, and accordingly NGOs are not based on the principles of ownership. In almost all cases, the private initiative of a few dedicated persons or social workers as promoters have led to the establishment of the NGO. NGOs do not have their own internal rules of governance, and boards of directors are elected from among the promoters. Cooperatives, of course, by the very nature of their operation are owned by members in the private sector. Cooperatives do have a capital structure, and voting rights consist of one vote per member. The term of office of the board varies and is decided by the general body. RRDBs are now licensed under the Development Bank Act 1996 which is quite elaborate in terms of the internal control and management of those institutions set up under it. RRDBs at present are owned by NRB and the government (75 per cent), and by banks and other financial institutions (25 per cent). Political pressure exercised by the government on RRDBs has been a matter of concern of late: chief executives have been subject to frequent transfers and there has also been interference in the appointment of staff members.

Taxation

No tax exemptions of any nature — on income, financial transactions, deposits or payrolls — are extended to MFIs. MFIs which are registered with the government do pay taxes, albeit not regularly. In the case of those operating on an informal basis, the government does not seem to have kept any record of their operation and does not appear to bother about it.

Comment

MFIs in Nepal are at an early stage of development. They do not have adequate administration and trained personnel, except in the case of Nirdhan and CSD, and therefore are not capable of adhering to stringent norms that are normally applied to formal financial institutions. This fact has been recognised by the policymakers and, accordingly, MFIs enjoy specific exemptions to some extent. Nevertheless, ceilings on the level and spread of interest rates, and possibly some reporting requirements need to be relaxed to suit the need of MFIs.

3.4. Self-regulation

The Social Welfare Council estimates that there are about 18,000 NGOs operating in the country. Only 20 have been granted permission to engage in limited banking and two large NGOs, Nirdhan and CSD, have been able to receive lines of credit from commercial banks to a limited extent.

On the national level, the NGO Federation which is a coalition of 800 NGOs charged with the responsibilities of reformation as well as framing and enforcing a code of conduct, capacity building and advocacy has not been effective. It is a federated body of multi-functional NGOs, not only of credit-based NGOs. Of late, it has increasingly been put under political pressure, NGOs being divided on political party loyalties.

The Nepal Federation of Savings and Credit Cooperative Union (NFSCUN) is a national-level federation of credit and savings cooperative societies with a membership of more than 200 cooperatives. It is relatively free from political pressure, but it has not been effective in influencing policymakers towards reform in favour of cooperatives. Hence, at the moment, discussion about the development of a code of conduct and standards for MFIs has not come to the fore. However, credit-based NGOs might rally around to form a platform of their own (similar to CDF of Bangladesh) for developing standards for self-regulation. The initiative to frame new legislation, that is, the Financial Intermediation Act, could potentially lead to such development.

4 Regulation of banks

4.1 Licensing and minimum capital requirements

Official policy permits any number of banks and non-bank financial institutions except that, in order to slow down possible over-expansion, applications for operating such banks are invited by Nepal Rastra Bank only once a year. In 1995, NRB revised the capital requirements for opening a bank, raising it from the previous Rs60 million ($1.1 million) to Rs500 million ($9.1 million) where a bank sets its headquarters in Kathmandu, and to Rs250 million ($4.5 million) if the bank is established in districts outside the valley. As a consequence and mainly because of the raised capital requirement, a recently established joint venture bank with Sri Lanka (Bank of Ceylon) was headquartered in the Lumbini District.

4.2 Interest rates

Interest rates charged by the banks and non-banking finance institutions have been deregulated since 1989 as part of financial-sector reform. However, limited restrictions of a specific nature are in place. Banks and financial institutions may not have more than a 6 per cent margin between the deposit and lending rates. NGO financial intermediaries are subject to a maximum interest rate of 15 per cent in their lending rates. While commercial banks are free to fix their own interest rates, they are obliged to publish such rates and changes therein and are permitted only one percentage point variation, up or down, on these published rates for their depositors. Similarly, on the lending side, banks can deviate by 2 percentage points (positive or negative) on lendings between borrowers for the same purpose. These restrictions, it was explained, were imposed to deter banks from engaging in unhealthy competition with one another through setting arbitrary and large deviations in interest rates to attract customers.

5 Summary and recommendations

With a per capita income of $200, the World Development Report 1996 categorises Nepal as among the poorest one dozen countries of the world, with ten devastated countries of sub-Saharan Africa below it. While estimates vary, the most recent suggest that in 1996, 42 per cent of the population was below the poverty line. Several programs which were launched in the past and aimed at poverty reduction have suffered due to implementation weaknesses. In fact, it is believed that poverty may have increased both in absolute and percentage terms over the years.

Several microfinance programs are in operation among which the Small Farmers Development Programme (SFDP) is the largest. In addition, there are five regional rural development banks specifically catering to the credit needs of the targeted poor. In the private sector, a number of NGOs are dealing in microfinance, though the most prominent are Nirdhan and the Center for Self-help Development (CSD). The total outreach of microfinance services covers 522,000 as against 8.4 million people below the poverty line. The gap is to be met through a combination of efforts in the coming twenty years, so that by 2017, the total number of poor below the poverty line will have been reduced to 10 per cent of the total population.

The government has supported microfinance for a number of years, and the Intensive Banking Program (IBP), Small Farmers Development Program (SFDP), Production Credit for Rural Women (PCRW), Micro Credit Project for Women (MCPW) are examples of such support. However, over the years these programs have lacked drive, reform and effective implementation. Consequently, their repayment rates have declined to an unacceptably low level. Moreover, they are not yet financially self-sustainable. The newly established RRDBs and private sector MFIs have been found more effective.

Review IBP and introduce alternative mechanisms for greater effectiveness

The government has also supported microfinance through IBP which is implemented by commercial banks as directed by Nepal Rastra Bank. However, commercial banks have generally been found reluctant and have not reached the specified target of 12 per cent to the priority sector in their total loan portfolios. There are several reasons for this. There is a need to review IBP and to introduce alternative organisational and operational mechanisms to make it effective.

Policies adopted in respect of interest rates affecting this sector have also not proved helpful. The ceiling of 6 per cent on 'spread' and 15 per cent on loans by NGOs limits the ability of MFIs to reach self-sufficiency since their cost of operation is high especially at the beginning.

Introduce one-window MFI licensing

The system at present fails to provide 'one-window' treatment to MFIs in licensing. NGOs must obtain licenses from three different agencies (the government, NRB and the Social Welfare Council), and the cooperatives from two agencies (the government and NRB). One-window treatment would facilitate the operation of MFIs.

Relax regulations for MFIs

Once MFIs expand outreach and loan volumes and intend to accept deposits, they need to obtain NRB approval and abide by NRB directives for loan provisioning, reserve requirements and reporting requirements. These regulations should be relaxed in the case of MFIs which have relatively limited resources and administrative capability.

References

ADB/NRB (Asian Development Bank & Nepal Rastra Bank). 1994. *Nepal Rural Credit Review: Final Report*, 4 vols. Nepal Rastra Bank, Kathmandu.

CECI. 1996. *Community Based Savings and Credit Organisations in Nepal: Current Status and Future Prospects*. Study funded by the Ford Foundation, Canadian Center for International Studies and Cooperation, January.

Central Bureau of Statistics. 1996. *Estimates of Poverty for Nepal 1996*. Survey by Central Bureau of Statistics with World Bank assistance.

Financial Intermediation Act. 1997. Draft.

ul Haq, Mahbub. 1997. *Human Development in South Asia 1997*. Study published for the Human Development Centre, Islamabad, Pakistan.

Micro Credit Project for Women. 1997. *Micro Credit Project for Women*, Nepal. Mid-term review report.

Nepal Rastra Bank. 1987. *Country Profile of Member States of South Asian Association for Regional Cooperation* (SAARC). Kathmandu.

Nepal Rastra Bank. 1996. *Annual Report*.

Nepal Rastra Bank. 1996. *Development Bank Act 2052 (1996)*. Banking Operations Department.

Nepal Rastra Bank. 1996. *Quarterly Economic Bulletin*, vol. XXX, mid-January 1996 – mid-July.

Panday, Sriram Raj. 1996. *Understanding Poverty and Development*. Study conducted for Action Aid, Nepal.

Sharma, S. R. & Acharya, P. 1995. Improving access of women to formal credit facilities in Nepal. Submitted to Institute for Intergrated Development Studies, Kathmandu.

Sharma, Shalik Ram & Nepal, Vishnu. 1997. Strengthening of credit institutions/programs for rural poverty alleviation in Nepal. Case study submitted to ESCAP, Bangkok.

Persons consulted

Dr K. K. Gurugharana	Member National Planning Commission
Dr P. K. Kafle	Deputy Governor Nepal Rastra Bank
Mr S. G. Sharma	Chief, Development Finance Department Nepal Rastra Bank
Mr R. B. Pant	Chief, Banking Development and Regulation Department Nepal Rastra Bank
Ms Kabita Bhattarai	Canadian Center for International Studies and Cooperation
Mr Cloude Perras	Canadian Center for International Studies and Cooperation
Mr K .B. Tamang	Rastriya Banijya Bank
Dr Shakti Shrestha	Economic and Finance Officer World Bank
Mr Raghu Adhikari	Project Implementation Officer Asian Development Bank

Dr Hari K. Upadhaya	Founder-Chairman CEAPRED (NGO leader)
Mr Shankar M. Shrestha	Ex-Director Center for Self-Help Development
Mr Uttam Dhakwa	GTZ

Pakistan

1 Introduction and background

1.1 Key demographic and economic data

Pakistan is the seventh most populous country in the world, with a population of 129.9 million in 1995. It is located in West Asia bordering onto the Arabian Sea, and its principal neighbours are India to the south, Iran to the west, and Afghanistan to the north. Population growth averaged 2.9 per cent per year between 1990 and 1995, the highest for any of the nine countries included in the study. The total fertility rate was 5.2 births per woman in 1995, very high by Asian standards, and second only to Nepal among the countries included in this study. Nevertheless, population density remains much lower than in most other South Asian countries, with 163 people per square kilometre in 1995.

GNP per capita stood at $460 in 1995, significantly above the levels recorded in Bangladesh, India and Nepal, but well below Sri Lanka and the four Southeast Asian countries included in the study. Pakistan's recent economic performance has been disappointing with income per capita increasing by only 1.2 per cent per year between 1985 and 1995, the lowest growth rate for any of the nine countries studied. Possibly reflecting this relatively slow economic growth, the structure of production has not changed markedly over the last 15 years. The share of agriculture in GDP declined from 30 per cent in 1980 to 26 per cent in 1995, the smallest decline for any country in the study other than the Philippines. There was a corresponding increase in the share of services, from 46 to 50 per cent of GDP. In 1995, 35 per cent of the population lived in urban areas.

Pakistan performs poorly in terms of human development, with most indicators well below those of countries with similar per capita incomes. For instance, while Pakistan has significantly higher per capita income than India, it has lower life expectancy, higher infant mortality and lower adult literacy. More generally, the World Bank (1995) notes that while Pakistan's GNP per capita is higher than the average for all low-income economies:

> Pakistan's total fertility rate is 65 per cent higher than the average for all low-income economies, its infant mortality rate is 30 per cent higher, its adult literacy rate is 25 percentage points lower, and its gross primary and secondary school enrolments are not much more than half the average for all low-income economies. Moreover, the disparities in life expectancy at birth, the under-five mortality rate, the adult literacy rate, and especially school enrolment ratios are wider for females than for males.

1.2 Poverty

Estimates of poverty

The incidence of poverty in Pakistan is estimated at between 30 and 35 per cent of the population. While cross-country comparisons of poverty inevitably suffer from a lack of comparable data, this is broadly similar to the rates of poverty observed in India and the Philippines.

Official estimates of poverty in Pakistan are derived from the Household Income and Expenditure Survey, which has been carried out by the Federal Bureau of Statistics at irregular intervals since 1963–64. The poverty line is set with reference to a daily calorie intake of 2,550 calories per adult, as recommended by the Planning Commission. Poverty lines for both rural and urban areas were established for 1984–85, equal to the total level of expenditure, on both food and non-food items, at which this daily calorie intake was just satisfied. These poverty lines have been adjusted by movements in the consumer price index to obtain poverty lines for more recent years.

Based on this methodology, the incidence of poverty declined from 46.0 per cent of the population in 1984–85 to 37.4 per cent in 1987–88 and 34.0 per cent in 1990–91. Using 1995 population data, this is around 44.2 million people. Indicators of the depth of poverty also fell substantially over the period. In 1990–91, the incidence of poverty was slightly higher in rural areas (36.9 per cent) than in urban areas (28.0 per cent). By province, poverty was highest in North West Frontier Province (NWFP) with 40.0 per cent, followed by Punjab (35.9 per cent), Sindh (27.6 per cent) and Balochistan (22.0 per cent). However, the coverage of the household survey in NWFP and Balochistan is known not to be fully representative.

Another source of poverty data is the Pakistan Integrated Household Survey, conducted by the Federal Bureau of Statistics in 1991 with technical assistance from the World Bank and UNDP. This survey was based on a smaller sample than the household survey, but covered a broader range of topics and was designed to be nationally representative. Based on this survey, the World Bank (1995) established poverty lines based on the cost of a basic needs basket of goods and services. Poverty lines were set at Rs296 ($8.40) for monthly per capita consumption expenditures in rural areas, and Rs334 ($9.50) for monthly per capita consumption expenditures in urban areas.

The broad estimates of poverty based on this method were similar to the official estimates, with 31.6 per cent of the population below the poverty line in 1991. Again, the incidence of poverty was slightly higher in rural areas (33.5 per cent) than in urban areas (27.0 per cent). However, the incidence of poverty by province was very different to that implied by the household survey, with poverty highest in Balochistan (41.2 per cent) and lowest in NWFP (19.7 per cent). This makes it difficult to come to firm conclusions about the regional distribution of poverty.

Policies for poverty reduction

In large part, Pakistan has relied on economic growth as a key means of reducing poverty. Nevertheless, as Amjad and Kemal (1997) have pointed out, the experience of Pakistan illustrates that there is no direct relationship between economic growth and poverty reduction. Over the last three decades, Pakistan has experienced periods of high economic growth and rising poverty, periods of low economic growth and falling poverty, as well as periods when economic growth has contributed positively to poverty reduction.

There have been relatively few programs directly targeted at reducing poverty. The most important has been the income transfer program based on the religious taxes of *Zakat* and *Ushr*. *Zakat* taxes are levied on various financial assets at the rate of 2.5 per cent per annum, while *Ushr* taxes are levied on the produce of landowners in excess of 948 kilograms of wheat or other crops of the same value. These revenues finance income transfers to widows, orphans and disabled individuals not able to support themselves. They receive a monthly subsistence allowance of Rs225 ($6.40) per beneficiary. There is also provision for a one-off rehabilitation grant of up to Rs3,000 ($85).

The program is administered by the central *Zakat* administration within the Ministry of Finance. Local beneficiaries are selected by around 40,000 local *Zakat* committees. However, partly due to avoidance practices, the government has been able to collect only a small amount of *Zakat* revenue, equal to 0.2 per cent of GDP in 1993–94. This has reduced the number of beneficiaries. Local *Zakat* committees have been given a quota of ten beneficiaries, and directed to choose the ten neediest from within the target group. As such, the scheme is limited to around 400,000 beneficiaries. There have also been allegations of abuse and inappropriate selection of beneficiaries.

Another program, Bait-ul-mal, was established in 1992 by the Ministry of Social Welfare. While it has a number of components, the two most important are the individual financial assistance scheme and the food subsidy scheme. The target group for the individual financial assistance scheme is widows, orphans and disabled persons who live in households with a monthly income of Rs1,500 ($43) or less and who do not receive *Zakat* assistance. They are eligible for a monthly grant of Rs500 ($14.30) if they do not own their own shelter and Rs300 ($8.60) if they do, plus Rs50 ($1.40) per child up to a maximum of four. The target group for the food subsidy scheme is other households with a monthly income of Rs1,500 ($43) or less that do not receive Zakat assistance. They are eligible for benefits of Rs150 ($4.30) per month per household. Again, the budgetary allocation for Bait-ul-mal is very small, around 0.05 per cent of GDP in 1994–95. As such, not all eligible persons are able to receive a benefit, especially under the food subsidy scheme.

A more significant program is the Social Action Programme, initiated in 1992–93. While not directly targeted at poverty reduction, it is designed to improve human development on a priority basis. The key objectives are to improve primary education (especially among girls), primary health, nutrition, family planning and rural water supply and sanitation, particularly in the most disadvantaged regions. Public expenditure under the program increased from 1.96 per cent of GDP in 1992–93 to 2.55 per cent of GDP in 1995–96, and there is evidence that it has led to some improvement in a number of social indicators.

1.3 Overview of the financial system

The banking sector in Pakistan includes four state-owned commercial banks (three 'old' banks and the relatively new First Women Bank), two privatised commercial banks, 15 private commercial banks and 21 foreign banks. In addition, there are four specialised banks, all owned by the government. These institutions, plus the investment banks, are supervised by the State Bank of Pakistan. Of these institutions, the three old state commercial banks, the two privatised commercial banks and the Agricultural Development Bank of Pakistan have the most extensive outreach in the rural areas, with around 8,000 branches between them. The ratio of money and quasi-money to GDP (a measure of financial sector development) was 40.9 per cent, higher than Bangladesh, Nepal and Sri Lanka, but lower than India and the three Southeast Asian countries for which data were available. Until recently, non-bank financial institutions such as leasing companies were also supervised by the State Bank, but supervisory responsibility for these bodies has now been transferred to the Corporate Law Authority.

The banking system has traditionally been largely owned and controlled by the government, and has been subject to extensive regulation. Since 1991–92, there has been considerable deregulation. Two of the state-owned commercial banks have been privatised, and new private and foreign commercial banks have been allowed to establish. Restrictions on capital flows and foreign exchange transactions have been liberalised. Nevertheless, there is still considerable regulation. For instance, the State Bank administers a very complex scheme requiring the three old state-owned commercial banks, the two privatised commercial banks and the Agricultural Development Bank to lend a certain proportion of their loans to agriculture. Moreover, three of the largest commercial banks with a combined market share of around 60 per cent remain under government ownership. Legislation passed in May 1997 will reduce administrative control by the government of these state-owned commercial banks.

There has also been considerable emphasis on Islamic banking. Interest rates are generally referred to as mark-ups, and in accordance with Islamic principles some lending and all deposit rates are set on a profit or loss sharing basis. In the past the mark-ups charged by banks were highly regulated, but they have now been largely deregulated. The only requirement is that banks must charge a minimum of 14 per cent for certain loans, and there is no maximum. Small loans are generally charged at the minimum of 14 per cent. While there is no requirement on the banks to lend at this rate, it is understood that they feel under a social obligation to do so. Given the relatively high inflation rate in Pakistan (13.0 per cent in 1995), this suggests that real interest rates on small loans are very low, and would be insufficient to cover costs. Loans to most other borrowers generally attract a higher mark-up.

In addition to the banking system, there is also a system of cooperatives. The State Bank lends to the Federal Bank for Cooperatives (one of the four specialised banks) at a mark-up of 0.5 per cent. These funds are then on-lent to the provincial cooperative banks at 1.8 per cent, which in turn on-lend to some 53,000 primary cooperative societies at the village level. These primary cooperative societies on-lend to final borrowers, with a ceiling of 14 per cent applying to loans from the primary societies to final borrowers. The effective rate of on-lending from the provincial cooperative banks to the primary cooperative societies is based on a profit sharing arrangement, whereby the primary societies retain 70 per cent of the profits and remit 30 per cent to the provincial cooperative banks. The primary societies also raise some funds from members' savings, but it is understood they are not very active in this regard. The cooperative banks are supervised by the Federal Bank for Cooperatives, while the cooperative banks and societies are regulated by the provincial governments. It is understood that the supervisory and regulatory framework is not very rigorous, and the cooperative movement is not generally well regarded. It has suffered from low repayment rates, and many cooperatives are dormant. It is understood that they also tend to be dominated by village elites, and do not tend to provide financial services to the poor.

1.4 Overview of microfinance

Microfinance is much less prominent in Pakistan than in any other country covered in this study. While the government has given some limited emphasis to credit in its policy framework for poverty reduction, most government programs do not in fact reach the poor. Microfinance in Pakistan is almost entirely the preserve of non-governmental organisations (NGOs), and even here, there is only a small number of NGOs operating on a significant scale.

The main government scheme that actually reaches the poor is a small program operated by the First Women Bank and funded by the Ministry of Women's Development. This scheme is discussed in more detail below. Some of the other state commercial banks, such as Habib Bank, also have very small microfinance programs.

The largest NGO program in Pakistan is that operated by the Aga Khan Rural Support Program (AKRSP) in the Northern Areas and Chitral. AKRSP is an integrated development program, providing physical infrastructure, training, and financial and technical services, and has operated since 1982. A key element of the program is institutional development at the village level through the establishment of village organisations and women's organisations. One function of these organisations is to operate credit and savings services. Members of these organisations are required to make a deposit at every meeting (generally fortnightly), and this money is deposited in a profit and loss sharing account (essentially a savings account) at a commercial bank or post office.

Village and women's organisations and individuals can then borrow from AKRSP through certain windows. First, AKRSP provides specific-purpose short- and medium-term loans at a 15 per cent mark-up. Second, village and women's organisation credit programs can borrow up to the value of members' savings from AKRSP at a mark-up of 12 per cent, and in turn approve and issue loans to their members. Individual members can borrow up to the value of their savings, or larger amounts with the approval of two guarantors who have not borrowed up to their limits. Village and women's organisations typically charge a mark-up of 20 per cent on loans to members. Third, AKRSP makes uncollateralised loans direct to individual members of the village and women's organisations, with the consent of the organisation. Loans are between Rs5,000 ($142) and Rs40,000 ($1,140), and attract a mark-up of 20 per cent. This program is funded by a grant from the government of the Netherlands.

A number of other NGOs, which have received support from government or donor agencies, are also providing credit and savings services. Some of these, such as the National Rural Support Program, the Balochistan Rural Support Program and the Sarhad Rural Support Corporation, are based on the AKRSP model. Other prominent NGOs providing credit and savings services include the Orangi Pilot Project, Basic Urban Services for Katchi Abadis (BUSTI) and Sungi.

One specialist microfinance institution (MFI) is the Kashf Foundation, established in Lahore in 1996 as the first Grameen Bank replication in Pakistan. Initial loans are Rs4,000 ($114), with repayments over 13 months and a mark-up of 18 per cent. Subsequent loans rise to Rs8,000 ($228) in the second year and Rs10,000 ($285) in the third year. The Kashf Foundation is currently at an early stage of operation, but plans to expand to cover a minimum of 10,000 borrowers. It is understood that Taraqee Trust in Quetta has also started replicating the Grameen Bank model.

Total membership of these various microfinance programs is small, and does not cover more than a very small fraction of people below the poverty line. There is clearly a need for a dramatic increase in the outreach of microfinance programs. Moreover, the NGO programs are not sustainable at this stage. Almost all of these programs are operated by multi-purpose NGOs which charge relatively low mark-ups and meet most of the costs of their credit and savings activities through donor grants. For instance, the World Bank (1996) found that AKRSP operates efficiently, with operating expenses that are not excessive for an NGO or rural development project. However, at the time it did not cover the cost of its credit operations, and relied on subsidies from donors. It is understood that AKRSP now covers all of its direct operating expenses from its operating income. Other NGOs are understood to be operating well below self-sufficiency, partly reflecting the relative newness and the small scale of their microfinance activities.

2 Arrangements for direct support

2.1 Support for specialised microfinance institutions

Existing schemes by donor agencies

There is currently very little direct support for MFIs from either the government or donor agencies. There has been no systematic attempt by the government to increase access of the poor to microfinance, whether through specialist MFIs or some other avenue. In this regard, Pakistan is unique among the nine countries considered in this study. What little government support there has been for microfinance has been largely incidental, rather than the result of any coherent policy framework. And while there has been some support from donor agencies for microfinance, this has been primarily in the form of small-scale projects to support NGOs through seed capital or revolving funds.

The World Bank microenterprise project has been operating since 1993. One component of the project, funded through a grant of NLG4.8 million ($3 million) from the government of the Netherlands, provides grants for seed capital and institutional strengthening for NGOs engaged in microfinance. Grants for seed capital have been provided to four NGOs, namely Orangi Pilot Project, AKRSP, Balochistan Rural Support Program and Basic Urban Services for Katchi Abadis (BUSTI). A fifth NGO was provided with some funds, but was suspended from the project due to poor performance. The project was intended to provide funds for on-lending to poor borrowers, although there was no specific means test for identifying borrowers. All funds have now been disbursed and the World Bank commented that the project was very successful, with all four NGOs achieving very high repayment rates on loans to final borrowers.

A second, larger component was provided to leasing companies for financing leases to cottage industries, defined as those with less than ten employees (leasing is a popular technique in Islamic banking). The lessee makes a down payment of around 10 per cent, and monthly payments incorporating both principal and mark-up. At the end of the repayment period, the lessee acquires the goods. The project is not directed at poverty alleviation, and it is understood that it does not generally reach poor borrowers. Swiss Development Cooperation has also funded a leasing project.

The International Labour Organization operates two programs which include a microfinance element, broadly defined. One project, funded by the government of the Netherlands, provides grants for revolving funds to groups of 10 to 25 women in the North West Frontier Province and reaches around 5,000 women. The other project, funded by the government of Japan, provides grants for revolving funds to groups of between 25 and 100 members throughout Pakistan, and reaches around 2,000 men and women. These revolving funds are used for projects at the group level, rather than being on-lent to individual borrowers.

Poverty Alleviation Fund

While there is very little direct support for microfinance at present, the government and the World Bank are developing a major new initiative for providing support to MFIs, in the form of the Pakistan Poverty Alleviation Fund. It is understood that the government will provide an initial grant of $100 million to establish the fund, while the World Bank will provide a loan of a further $100 million. The fund will be set up as a joint stock company under the Companies Ordinance of 1984. The board of directors will be chosen by the government, but it is intended that it will include representatives from the private sector and the NGO community.

The fund will not lend directly to individual borrowers but will operate as a second tier microfinance institution, lending to NGOs and possibly other community-based organisations for on-lending to self-help groups or final borrowers. While the policy on mark-ups has not yet been determined, it is envisaged that it would lend to NGOs at slightly concessional rates, and that NGOs would charge full commercial rates to final borrowers. Detailed criteria for the selection of partner NGOs have not yet been developed, but it is understood that the main criteria will include a good governance record, transparency, a strong tradition of accountability and results-oriented arrangements. It is intended that the fund will be available to support a variety of models of microfinance. It is not yet clear whether there will be a specific means test for final borrowers, and if so, how this will be determined.

The proposed establishment of the fund is a very positive development. Similar institutions have been successful in a number of other countries in the region, most particularly Bangladesh but also India, the Philippines, Sri Lanka and Thailand. Experience from these countries suggests that the fund is likely to be most successful if it adopts a number of the following principles.

The fund should be as independent and as free from political interference as possible. The plans to set the fund up as a joint stock company, and to include representatives from the private sector and the NGO community on the board of directors, are encouraging. Nevertheless, these measures may not be enough in themselves. Additional measures may be to enable private and NGO bodies to appoint representatives to the board directly, to provide for fixed-term appointments, and to spell out clearly the objectives of the fund while allowing the board maximum independence to meet these objectives.

It will also be necessary for the fund to set and enforce appropriate performance and reporting standards for the MFIs that it funds. This will mean striking an appropriate balance between the need to increase outreach and the need to strengthen the capabilities of existing MFIs. It would be appropriate to require all partner organisations to meet a set of minimum standards, and to increase these gradually over time. These standards should ensure a level playing field between MFIs, and should not be prescriptive as to the particular lending methodologies adopted by individual MFIs.

The fund should ensure that all MFIs to which it lends target their programs to the poor. MFIs should be required to set appropriate means tests that are transparent and readily enforceable. And it is important that the fund emphasises the need for MFIs to become financially self-sufficient. Given the vast unmet demand for microfinance in Pakistan, the need for self-sufficiency is even more critical than in most other countries. MFIs should be free to charge mark-ups that are sufficient to cover their costs, and should be required to have realistic plans for attaining self-sufficiency.

2.2 Support through the banking system

Directed credit schemes

The State Bank of Pakistan administers a scheme requiring some banks to lend a certain proportion of their loans to agriculture. The scheme applies to the three old state-owned commercial banks, the two privatised commercial banks, the Agricultural Development Bank and the cooperative banks.

There is a complex procedure for determining the allocations for individual banks. First, the government develops an annual credit plan for the economy as a whole, specifying the maximum loans outstanding for the banking system. It then estimates the requirements for agriculture that are expected to come from the formal financial system. The two figures are not directly comparable, because the overall credit plan is expressed in outstandings whereas the allocation for agriculture is expressed in disbursements. This annual requirement for disbursements to agriculture is then allocated to individual banks depending on a range of criteria, including area of operations, deposit ratios, and the particular bank's own plans and projections. For instance, in 1996–97 the global allocation for agriculture was Rs26 billion ($740 million), of which around Rs10 billion ($285 million) was allocated to the commercial banks, around Rs12 billion ($340 million) to the Agricultural Development Bank, and around Rs4 billion ($115 million) to the cooperative banks. In the case of commercial banks, it is understood that the requirements mean that around 5 per cent of the value of loans outstanding are to agriculture.

Within this allocation, commercial banks are required to ensure that 50 per cent of their disbursements to agriculture are for small farmers (this requirement does not apply to the Agricultural Development Bank or the cooperative banks, although it is understood that the cooperative banks probably meet it anyway). Small farmers are defined on the basis of their landholdings, whether as owners or tenants. In more fertile areas with irrigation, small farmers are defined as those with 12.5 acres of land or less. In desert areas with irrigation, the ceiling is higher, ranging from 16 to 32 acres. In rain-fed areas, the ceilings are double those in irrigated areas.

It is unlikely that many poor farmers benefit from this allocation. It is understood that around 70 per cent of farmers fall within the definition of small farmers, and even so, some large farmers have managed to find ways of obtaining loans. Under the supervised credit scheme, the State Bank has required the banks to establish mobile banking units for reaching small borrowers, and has also provided banks with territorial jurisdiction. These measures have led to higher repayment rates on small loans than had previously been the case, with repayment rates now in the 70 to 75 per cent range.

It is understood that the State Bank has been giving preliminary consideration to extending these rules, to require all banks to allocate a part of their loan portfolio to microfinance. Alternatively, banks may be required to reinvest a certain proportion of the resources they raise from a particular village or region back into that village or region. However, no decisions have been taken yet.

Microfinance program of First Women Bank

There are a number of government programs designed to provide finance for small and microenterprise development. However, the only one that appears to reach poor borrowers is a relatively small program operated by the First Women Bank, a state commercial bank established in 1989. In 1993 the Department of Women's Development provided a grant of

Rs48 million ($1.4 million) to establish the program, and it is understood that it is considering a further allocation of Rs19 million ($540,000) to extend it. Under this program, the bank provides loans up to a maximum of Rs25,000 ($712) with a mark-up of 12 per cent to women with household income of less than Rs2,000 ($57) per month.

Loans are generally provided to individual borrowers, although in some cases borrowers organise themselves into groups and provide group guarantees. In addition, 22 NGOs are associated with the program as non-financial intermediaries, in identifying and training borrowers. The bank has also lent to five NGOs as financial intermediaries for on-lending to final borrowers. In some cases, the NGOs themselves use smaller community-based organisations as non-financial intermediaries. The NGOs borrow from the bank at 13 per cent and on-lend to final borrowers at 17 to 18 per cent.

To date, the program has achieved a cumulative repayment rate of around 97 per cent. It has provided loans to around 5,040 borrowers (excluding sub-loans granted by the National Rural Support Program, a large NGO which has received a line of credit under the program). As at May 1997 there were 2,160 current borrowers, again excluding sub-loans by the National Rural Support Program. The program appears to have been quite successful, especially compared to most microfinance programs channelled through commercial banks in other countries. This may reflect the fact that First Women Bank is a relatively small bank with a particular focus on women, and the use of NGOs as financial and non-financial intermediaries.

2.3 Other major programs

The main government agency for lending to small borrowers is the Small Business Finance Corporation (SBFC), established in 1972 under the Ministry of Finance. The National Development Finance Corporation (NDFC) and some other agencies also provide loans to small and microenterprises in addition to their other activities.

The SBFC operates three main loan programs. First, its main program is to provide loans to small businesses. The maximum loan amount is Rs2 million ($57,000), with a mark-up of 15 to 18 per cent. Second, the national self-employment scheme provides loans of between Rs10,000 ($285) and Rs300,000 ($8,550) to self-employed persons, at a mark-up of 14 to 16 per cent. The average loan size is around Rs150,000 ($4,275), with very few loans at the bottom end of the range.

Third, the Youth Investment Promotion Society Scheme provides loans of between Rs10,000 ($285) and Rs200,000 ($5,700) to unemployed high school graduates aged between 18 and 35 for self-employment projects, with a mark-up of 14.5 per cent. This scheme is administered by another government agency, the Youth Investment Promotion Society, which identifies the borrowers and provides technical training. However, loans are disbursed through the SBFC. The nature of the target group means that it does not tend to reach the poor, and most loans are for considerably more than Rs10,000 ($285).

The SBFC currently has around 90,000 borrowers, and loans outstanding of around Rs12 billion ($342 million). As well as not reaching the poor, it has low recovery rates in the range of 30 to 40 per cent. Since March 1996, the SBFC has required collateral in the form of a mortgage equal to at least 50 per cent of the value of the loan, in an effort to increase repayment rates. In the past, the SBFC has been funded mainly through lines of credit from the State Bank of Pakistan, but it has not had access to such funding for the last two years, and is relying on recycling loan repayments to maintain its lending. It is understood that the government is currently considering the future of the SBFC. Given the poor financial performance of the SBFC and the fact that it does not reach poor borrowers, it would be appropriate for the government to consider reallocating some of the its funds to the proposed Poverty Alleviation Fund.

3 Regulation of non-bank microfinance institutions

3.1 The broad regulatory framework

There are no specific provisions relating to NGOs engaged in microfinance. Hence, the regulatory framework for such NGOs is the same as for other NGOs. NGOs do not have to register in order to carry out their work. The NGO Resource Centre (1991) found that many NGOs that have chosen not to register have functioned well, achieved their objectives and gained recognition. However, registration provides a legal status and may facilitate access to financial support.

There are five main avenues for NGOs to seek registration, and all of these could apply to NGOs engaged in microfinance. First, they can register as a non-profit company under the Companies Ordinance of 1984. There are two different avenues for registration under this Ordinance. An NGO can register itself at the provincial level with the Assistant Registrar of Joint Stock Companies, or at the national level with the Corporate Law Authority.

The second avenue is to register with the Registrar of Joint Stock Companies as a society under the Societies Registration Act of 1860. Third, they can register as a cooperative society under the Cooperative Societies Act of 1925. Registration is with the provincial Registrar of Cooperative Societies. The fourth option is registration as a voluntary social welfare agency with the Directorate of Social Welfare, pursuant to the Voluntary Social Welfare Agencies Registration and Control Ordinance of 1961. Finally, they can register as a public charitable trust under the Trust Act of 1882. This is the simplest method and entails no reporting requirements. However, it may be restrictive, as operations must be funded out of earnings and cannot be funded out of the capital of the trust.

In broad terms, the requirements for registration as a non-profit company, a society, a cooperative society or a voluntary social welfare agency are similar. A minimum number of members is required, ranging from around seven to ten. The application must include a constitution or a memorandum and articles of association providing details of the NGO — including name, address, aims and objectives, areas of operation, membership, details of the governing body, organisational structure, arrangements for meetings, and similar matters. Moreover, all of these bodies are required to prepare an annual report, maintain accounts, have the accounts audited annually, and submit these documents to the registration authority.

It was reported that the process of registration under these various Acts can be time-consuming. For instance, the NGO Resource Centre (1991) found that NGOs regarded the procedures for registration as problematic. They cited the lack of clear direction, inadequate guidelines, the time taken in getting the required documents together and the loss of time in making amendments and corrections. However, once they were registered, they generally had no problems. Clearly, it would be desirable to streamline and simplify the procedures for registration where this is possible.

In terms of the reporting requirements, different regulatory agencies enforce them differently. It is understood that the agencies regulating non-profit companies tend to enforce the requirements quite rigorously. Other agencies are less rigorous, and usually do not enforce the requirements that accounts be audited and submitted to them. Some NGOs engaged in microfinance, such as the Aga Khan Rural Support Program (AKRSP) and Kashf Foundation, have registered as non-profit companies because of the added credibility that this brings.

NGOs receiving donations from abroad are required to inform the Economic Affairs Division of the Ministry of Finance. They are required to submit an annual report, providing details of the amount received and the usage of the funds. In practice, however, it is understood that this requirement is rarely enforced.

In 1994, the government introduced a new bill to provide for the registration and regulation of social welfare agencies, to be called the Social Welfare Agencies (Registration and Regulation) Act of 1994. The NGO movement was critical of certain aspects of this bill, and initiated discussions with the government. Following this, the bill was withdrawn and revised, and a new one was introduced in March 1996. The Pakistan NGO Forum argues that the new bill does not take account of the consultative process held during 1994–95.

One concern is that all NGOs would be required to be registered under the new bill, regardless of whether they receive public funds or not. It would also give wide powers to the registration authority, with opportunity for misuse. NGOs also consider that the reporting requirements would be onerous, particularly with respect to the use of foreign donations. Further, there would be considerable scope for NGOs to be dissolved, with inadequate right of appeal.

The bill has been tabled in the Upper House but is still pending, with its current status unclear. It is beyond the scope of this study to analyse the proposed Bill in detail. However, it is important that any legislation strike an appropriate balance between ensuring that NGOs are properly monitored and accountable to their members and third parties, while minimising bureaucratic interference into their affairs. It is also desirable to limit the discretionary power of the regulatory authority as much as possible. Regulatory and prudential requirements should be set out clearly and transparently, with any NGO that meets these standards free to operate without restriction.

3.2 Mark-ups

In general, there are no regulations concerning the mark-ups that NGOs involved in microfinance can charge borrowers. However, mark-ups charged by cooperatives are regulated, with a ceiling of 14 per cent on loans from the primary societies to final borrowers. There also appears to be considerable social and political pressure on financial institutions in general, including microfinance institutions (MFIs), to keep mark-ups low, and this may make it difficult for MFIs to operate on a sustainable basis. It would be appropriate for the government to remove the ceiling on the interest rate that cooperatives can charge, and issue a clear statement that MFIs should charge mark-ups sufficient to cover their costs.

3.3 Prudential regulation and supervision

NGOs engaged in microfinance are not subject to any prudential requirements covering matters such as minimum capital, capital adequacy, reserves, liquidity or loan loss provisioning. Other than the requirements to maintain accounts and have them audited annually, there are also no financial reporting requirements.

Most commentators consider that it is not appropriate for MFIs which do not accept deposits from the general public to be subject to full prudential regulation and supervision. The question of appropriate standards for MFIs is also not as pressing in Pakistan as in some other countries, given the small number and scale of MFIs. Nevertheless, given the risks inherent in providing financial services, some standards would appear appropriate. This is discussed below.

3.4 Performance and reporting standards of second tier institutions

As noted above, there is currently no second tier microfinance institution operating in Pakistan. However, it is proposed to establish the Poverty Alleviation Fund, to lend to NGOs and possibly other district-level organisations for on-lending to self-help groups and final borrowers. It will be necessary for the fund to set and enforce appropriate performance and reporting standards for the MFIs that it funds. The relatively late development of microfinance in Pakistan means that Pakistan can benefit from the experience of other countries, and establish an appropriate policy regime at an early stage in the development of the microfinance sector. It would be useful to study the policies and experiences of second tier institutions in other countries, particularly the Palli Karma Sahayak Foundation in Bangladesh (see the Bangladesh country study).

3.5 Self-regulation

A national microfinance network has recently been established, with the Kashf Foundation taking the lead role. All of the major NGOs involved in microfinance have joined, including the Kashf Foundation, AKRSP, Sungi Development Foundation, Aga Khan Foundation, Orangi Pilot Project and Network Leasing, and the initiative is being supported by the Asia Foundation. The network aims to promote an enabling environment for microfinance by:

- encouraging purposeful networking among microfinance practitioners and organisations supporting microfinance
- supporting best practice research and exchanges of information
- promoting awareness and understanding of microfinance among policymakers and financial institutions in the private sector.

The establishment of this kind of apex body is a positive development. Over time, such a body could perform a number of important roles, including information exchange, training, research, policy dialogue with government and donor agencies, and establishing standards for self-regulation. All microfinance NGOs in Pakistan should be encouraged to play an active role in the new body.

4 Regulation of banks

4.1 Licensing and minimum capital requirements

As in most other countries, MFIs are not permitted to accept deposits from the general public. All institutions which accept deposits of money from the public for the purpose of lending or investing are required to be registered as banks under the Banking Companies Ordinance of 1962.

Unlike most other countries in South Asia, there is no network of small banks operating in the rural areas in Pakistan. Moreover, the regulatory framework precludes the establishment of small banks. The main avenue for establishing a bank is to obtain a licence as a commercial bank. The minimum capital requirement is Rs500 million ($14.2 million), although it has been suggested that this may be increased to Rs1,000 million ($28.5 million). There are also some additional requirements that prevent the establishment of small banks operating at the local level. For instance, it is necessary to establish a branch in each of the four provinces of Pakistan and the disputed territory of Kashmir. It is also necessary to be a publicly listed company with public shareholders to the extent of at least 50 per cent.

The difficulty in establishing a bank is illustrated by the experience of the Aga Khan Rural Support Program (AKRSP), which is currently seeking to establish a bank in northern Pakistan. Because of the restrictions on commercial banks, AKRSP is considering establishing an investment bank. The minimum capital requirement for investment banks is Rs100 million ($2.9 million). While successive governments have agreed in principle to AKRSP's establishing an investment bank, there have been protracted discussions and negotiations over a range of hurdles that need to be overcome. Investment banks are also not allowed to accept short-term deposits or maintain cash counters. This clearly limits the range of deposit services that any MFI established as an investment bank would be able to provide.

Given that small banks are much more likely to provide services to poor borrowers in remote locations than large banks, the restrictions on establishing banks reduce the likelihood that banks will engage in microfinance. They also make it extremely difficult for MFIs to establish banks so that they can accept deposits and offer a wider range of services. It would be appropriate for the government to establish a framework for licensing small banks, by imposing more realistic minimum capital requirements and by removing other restrictions such as the requirement to establish a branch in each province. In this regard, the experiences of countries such as Indonesia and the Philippines may be useful (see the Indonesia and Philippines country studies).

It should be noted that in some cases, it may be possible to establish a small bank in the form of a cooperative bank. Under the Cooperative Societies Act of 1925, the minimum capital requirement for a cooperative bank is only Rs20,000 ($570). However, cooperative banks are not regulated by the State Bank. Moreover, they are generally owned and controlled by the provincial governments, and it is not clear if they would permit the establishment of new cooperative banks. Cooperative banks are subject to little prudential supervision, and generally have low credibility with the public. As such, they have difficulty in attracting deposits from the public and rely on the Federal Bank for Cooperatives for most of their funds. Hence, even it were possible, licensing as a cooperative bank would not provide a sound basis for a microfinance bank.

4.2 Mark-ups

As noted above, the only regulation applying to the mark-ups charged by commercial banks is that they must charge a *minimum* of 14 per cent for certain loans. There is no maximum. Nevertheless, there appears to be considerable pressure on banks to keep mark-ups on small loans low, and small loans are generally charged at the minimum of 14 per cent. Small loans are not commercially viable at this mark-up, and are subsidised by the banks' other operations. Clearly, this situation makes it very difficult for regulated banks to engage in microfinance on a commercial basis. It would be appropriate for the government or central bank to issue a clear statement that regulated banks should set mark-ups on small loans at a level that is sufficient to cover all the costs of making such loans, and to make it clear to the banks that they should not feel under any political pressure to maintain mark-ups on small loans at artificially low levels.

4.3 Prudential regulation and supervision

Commercial banks are required to maintain capital equal to at least 7.5 per cent of total time and demand liabilities, a cash reserve of 5 per cent of deposits, and liquidity of 30 per cent of deposits, including the cash reserve. Under the loan loss provisioning requirements, banks are required to maintain a provision of 2 per cent for other assets especially mentioned, 25 per cent for sub-standard loans, 50 per cent for doubtful loans, and 100 per cent for loss loans. Commercial banks are required to provide weekly position reports to the State Bank, as well as fortnightly, monthly, quarterly and annual reports on various aspects of their operations. The requirements listed above would not appear to impose any undue burdens on banks engaged in microfinance.

However, there are two major restrictions of a prudential nature that make it extremely difficult for banks to establish linkages with NGOs or self-help groups. Among the countries included in this study these restrictions are unique to Pakistan, with no comparable restrictions in any other country.

First, banks are only permitted to make unseccured loans up to Rs100,000 ($2,800). This limit was raised from Rs50,000 ($1,400) in 1996, and even then only for loans of less than three years for trade, commerce or business. For other loans, the clean limit is Rs25,000 ($700). For all loans above these limits, the State Bank requires that the loan be fully collateralised. While loans to individual borrowers of above Rs100,000 ($2,800) could not be considered microfinance, this rule greatly restricts the scope for banks to lend to NGOs, village organisations or self-help groups for on-lending to poor borrowers.

Second, other than individuals, banks are only allowed to lend to structured bodies which meet certain conditions. For instance, structured bodies are required to maintain audited accounts, and are subject to regulations concerning debt-equity ratios and other matters. This makes it very difficult for banks to lend to relatively informal group structures, such as village organisations and self-help groups.

AKRSP is holding discussions with the State Bank to amend these rules or to exempt loans to NGOs and village organisations from these requirements. Nevertheless, as they stand, these restrictions are clearly a major barrier to banks establishing linkages with NGOs and self-help groups of the poor, and it would be appropriate to remove them.

5 Summary and recommendations

GNP per capita in Pakistan stood at $460 in 1995, higher than the levels recorded in Bangladesh, India and Nepal, but lower than for the other countries included in this study. Performance in terms of human development is poor, with most indicators well below those of countries with similar per capita incomes. For instance, while Pakistan has significantly higher per capita income than India, it has lower life expectancy, higher infant mortality and lower adult literacy. The incidence of poverty is estimated at around 34.0 per cent in 1990–91, equivalent to around 44.2 million people.

Microfinance is much less prominent in Pakistan than in any other country covered in this study. While the government has given some limited emphasis to credit in its policy framework for poverty reduction, most government programs do not in fact reach the poor. Microfinance is almost entirely the preserve of NGOs, and even here, there is only a handful of NGOs operating on a significant scale. They do not reach more than a very small fraction of people below the poverty line, and there is clearly a need for a dramatic increase in the outreach of microfinance programs.

Arrangements for direct support

There is currently very little direct support for microfinance institutions (MFIs) from either the government or from donor agencies. There has been no systematic attempt by the government to increase access of the poor to microfinance, whether through specialist MFIs or some other avenue. In this regard, Pakistan is unique among the nine countries considered in this study.

The State Bank of Pakistan administers a complex scheme requiring some banks to lend a certain proportion of their loans to agriculture. It is unlikely that many poor farmers benefit from this allocation, and it is clearly not a cost-effective way of reaching the poor. Similarly, the Small Business Finance Corporation (SBFC) does not reach the poor and has performed poorly. The government should consider reallocating some of its funds to the proposed Pakistan Poverty Alleviation Fund, discussed below. The only government-sponsored program that appears to reach poor borrowers is a relatively small program operated by the First Women Bank, a state commercial bank.

Maximise effectiveness of the Poverty Alleviation Fund

At present, the government and the World Bank are developing a major new initiative for providing support to MFIs, in the form of the Pakistan Poverty Alleviation Fund. It is understood that the government will provide an initial grant of $100 million to establish the fund, while the World Bank will provide a loan of a further $100 million. The fund will lend to NGOs and possibly other community-based organisations for on-lending to self-help groups or final borrowers. This is a very positive development. To maximise its effectiveness, the government should ensure that the fund is as independent and as free from political interference as possible. The fund should set appropriate performance and reporting standards for the MFIs that it finances, ensure that MFIs target their programs to the poor, and require them to have realistic plans for attaining self-sufficiency.

Regulation of non-bank microfinance institutions

Streamline and simplify registration procedures

There are no specific provisions relating to NGOs engaged in microfinance. While NGOs do not have to register in order to carry out their work, registration provides a legal status and may facilitate access to financial support. NGOs can seek registration as a non-profit company, society, cooperative society, voluntary social welfare agency or public charitable trust. It was reported that registration can be a time-consuming process. The government should streamline and simplify the procedures for registration where this is possible.

Provide for appropriate regulation and minimise interference

In 1994, the government introduced a new bill to provide for the registration and regulation of social welfare agencies. The bill has been criticised by the NGO movement, and its current status is unclear. The government should ensure that any new legislation strikes an appropriate balance between making sure that NGOs are properly monitored and accountable to their members and third parties, while minimising bureaucratic interference into their affairs. It should limit the discretionary power of the regulatory authority as much as possible.

Ensure mark-ups sufficient to cover costs

In general, there are no regulations concerning the mark-ups that NGOs involved in microfinance can charge borrowers. However, cooperatives are subject to a ceiling of 14 per cent, and other MFIs seem to be under pressure to keep mark-ups low. The government should remove the ceiling for cooperatives, and issue a clear statement that MFIs should charge mark-ups sufficient to cover their costs.

Establish and enforce appropriate standards

NGOs engaged in microfinance are not subject to any prudential requirements covering matters such as minimum capital, capital adequacy, reserves, liquidity or loan loss provisioning. Reporting requirements are also minimal. Most commentators consider that it is not appropriate for MFIs which do not accept deposits from the general public to be subject to full prudential regulation and supervision. However, the proposed Poverty Alleviation Fund should set and enforce appropriate performance and reporting standards for the MFIs that it funds. It would be useful to study the policies and experiences of second tier institutions in other countries, particularly the Palli Karma Sahayak Foundation in Bangladesh.

Support new apex body for MFIs

The recent establishment of a national microfinance network as an apex body for MFIs in Pakistan is a positive development. Donor agencies should encourage all microfinance NGOs in Pakistan to play an active role in the establishment of the new body.

Regulation of banks

Establish framework for licensing small banks

Unlike most other countries in South Asia, there is no network of small banks operating in the rural areas in Pakistan. Moreover, the regulatory framework precludes the establishment of small banks. Given that small banks are much more likely than large banks to provide services to poor borrowers in remote locations, this reduces the likelihood that banks will engage in microfinance. It also makes it extremely difficult for MFIs to establish banks so that they can accept deposits and offer a wider range of services. The government should establish a framework for licensing small banks, by imposing realistic minimum capital requirements and removing other restrictions, such as the requirement to establish a branch in each province.

Support mark-ups which recover costs

While banks are not subject to a ceiling on the mark-ups they can charge, they appear to be under considerable pressure to keep mark-ups on small loans low. This makes it very difficult for them to engage in microfinance on a commercial basis. The government or central bank should issue a clear statement that regulated banks should set mark-ups on small loans at a level that is sufficient to cover costs.

Abolish prudential restrictions which discourage bank-NGO linkages

There are two major restrictions of a prudential nature that make it extremely difficult for banks to establish linkages with NGOs or self-help groups. First, banks are only permitted to make clean loans up to Rs100,000 ($2,800). Second, other than individuals, banks are only allowed to lend to structured bodies which meet certain conditions. These restrictions make it very difficult for banks to lend to NGOs or self-help groups, and the government should abolish them. It should be noted that Pakistan is the only country included in this study to impose restrictions of this nature.

References

Amjad, Rashid & Kemal, A. R. 1997. Macroeconomic policies and their impact on poverty alleviation in Pakistan. Unpublished.

Hook, Andrew T. 1997. *Savings in Pakistan: Practice and Policy 1981–1996*. State Bank of Pakistan, Karachi.

NGO Resource Centre. 1991. *NGO Registration Study*. NGO Resource Centre, Karachi.

State Bank of Pakistan. 1994. *Rural Financial Market Studies*, Phase 1. State Bank of Pakistan, Karachi.

World Bank. 1995. *Pakistan: Poverty Assessment*. Report no.14397–PAK, World Bank, Washington D.C.

World Bank. 1996. *The Aga Khan Rural Support Program: A Third Evaluation*. World Bank, Washington D.C.

Persons consulted

Mr Azfar Shafqat	Managing Director Small Business Finance Corporation
Mr Ghulam Yasin	Senior Vice President, Recoveries Small Business Finance Corporation
Mr Mohammad Azani Khan	Vice President, Operations Small Business Finance Corporation
Mr Shahzad Ahmad	Assistant Vice President, Accounts Small Business Finance Corporation
Dr A. R. Kemal	Chief Economist/Member Planning Commission
Mr Gunter Walpuski	Resident Representative Friedrich Ebert Stiftung
Dr Sabur Ghayur	Deputy Resident Representative Friedrich Ebert Stiftung

Ms Faiza Effendi	Programme Officer Swiss Agency for Development and Cooperation
Mr Winston Rueben Dudley	Director International Labour Organization
Mr Hamid Rehman	Managing Director Youth Investment Promotion Society
Mr Zahoor A. Malik	Director, Operations and PDD Youth Investment Promotion Society
Mr Masood A. Tahir	Director, Administration and Coordination Youth Investment Promotion Society
Mr Saleem Kassum	Chief Executive Officer Aga Khan Foundation
Mr A. Karim Nayani	Programme Officer, Rural Development Aga Khan Foundation
Mr Paul Greener	Programme Officer, Rural Development Aga Khan Foundation
Mr Asad Azfar	Programme Officer, Institutional Development Aga Khan Foundation
Mr Joe Bolger	Programme Coordinator Aga Khan Foundation
Mr A. H. Qureshi	Consultant World Bank
Mr M. R. Chugtai	Executive Director State Bank of Pakistan
Mr Kazi Abdul Muktadir	Director, Agricultural Credit Department State Bank of Pakistan
Mr Muhammad Mahmood Ahmed	Joint Director Banking Policy & Regulations Department State Bank of Pakistan
Mr Abdul Aziz	Deputy Director Banking Policy & Regulations Department State Bank of Pakistan
Dr Andrew T. Hook	Research Advisor State Bank of Pakistan
Miss Akram Khatoon	President First Women Bank
Ms Zeba Mumtaz	Senior Vice President First Women Bank
Mr Mumtaz Ali Shah	Managing Director Sindh Small Industries Corporation
Mr Mahomed J. Jaffer	Chairman Aga Khan Foundation
Mr Asif B. Fancy	Chairman Aga Khan Rural Support Program
Mr Sultan Allana	Director Aga Khan Rural Support Program

Mr Salim Jiwani	Director, Finance Aga Khan Rural Support Program
Mr William Robinson	Secretariat of His Highness the Aga Khan
Mr Irfan Ahmad Khan	Coordinator, Information Services Unit NGO Resource Centre
Mr Anwar Samad	Senior Executive Vice President Habib Bank Limited
Mr Syed Fazal Mabood	Senior Executive Vice President Habib Bank Limited
Mr Muhammad Rafique	Executive Vice President Habib Bank Limited
Mr Anwar Aziz Jakartawala	Senior Vice President Habib Bank Limited
Mr Mohammad Farhat Khan	Vice President Habib Bank Limited
Mr Anwar Rashid	Chairman Orangi Charitable Trust
Mr Ikramuddin Chahan	Manager Orangi Charitable Trust
Mr Allauddin	Manager Orangi Charitable Trust
Mr Hanif Arian	Manager Orangi Charitable Trust
Ms Qamer Sultana	Manager Orangi Charitable Trust
Mr Mohammad Shabbir	Manager Orangi Charitable Trust
Mr Shahzad Arian	Manager Orangi Charitable Trust

Philippines

1 Introduction and background

1.1 Key demographic and economic data

An archipelagic state, the Philippines has a land mass comprising some 7,000 islands, although 94 per cent of the total area of 300,000 square kilometres is on the eleven largest islands. With a population in 1995 of 68.6 million, the Philippines experiences a population density of around 230 persons per square kilometre, which is substantially higher than that of the other Southeast Asian countries included in this survey, and approaching the densities recorded for Sri Lanka and India in South Asia.

With a population growth rate of 2.2 per cent between 1990 and 1995 and a total fertility rate (births per woman) of 3.7 in 1995, population in the Philippines is growing substantially faster than in either Indonesia or Thailand (although Malaysia's growth in a much less resource-constrained situation is slightly higher at 2.4 per cent). Gross national product (GNP) per capita in 1995 was $1,050, slightly higher than for Indonesia and substantially higher than in the South Asian countries included in this study. However, it was well below the levels of Malaysia ($3,890) and Thailand ($2,740). On a purchasing power parity basis, the Philippines has income per head well below all the other Southeast Asian states in this study, and also below Sri Lanka.

In terms of the structure of production, agriculture (which contributes 22 per cent of GNP) remains relatively more important than in the other Southeast Asian states in this study. Industry (which contributes 32 per cent of output) is weighted substantially less than in the Philippines' Southeast Asian neighbours. This reflects the relative stagnation of the Philippine economy over the past 25 years, with implications for the incidence of poverty which are discussed below. In the decade 1985–1995, income per head increased at only 1.5 per cent annually, sluggish by Southeast Asian standards and below the rate of almost all the countries in this study.

UNDP classifies the Philippines as a 'medium level' country in terms of human development. With a human development index of 0.672 in 1994, the Philippines is at around the same level as Indonesia and substantially higher than most of the South Asian countries (although it ranks below Sri Lanka). The degree of its human development is substantially below that of both Malaysia and Thailand which are ranked in the 'high' category by UNDP. Life expectancy at birth in 1995 was 66 years and the infant mortality rate was 39 per 1,000 live births, close to the average for East Asia as a whole. However, some 95 per cent of adults were literate, the highest proportion among the nine countries in this study.

1.2 Poverty

Estimates of poverty

Poverty continues to be the most important development problem confronting the Philippines. The incidence of poverty is substantially higher than in other market economies of East and Southeast Asia, while Philippine performance in poverty reduction has been relatively disappointing over an extended period. In part, as a recent report notes (World Bank 1996), poor performance in poverty alleviation has been related to disappointing economic growth performance: 'so far, the country has not been able to sustain growth long enough to reduce its incidence of poverty to the levels attained in other East Asian countries'. The World Bank also points to structural distortions in the economy which have acted to prevent the benefits of economic growth flowing through to the poor.

While the incidence of poverty is known to be high, actual measurement is elusive. Official Philippine government measures of poverty incidence are thought to be overstated, because the poverty line is set using a standard food basket unrepresentative of the consumption patterns of the poor. As the World Bank points out, various measures of poverty incidence, depending on definition, showed anything from 37 to 54 per cent of the total population below the poverty line in 1991 (table 3). While the incidence of poverty appears to have fallen over a 30-year period from 1961, the decline has been slow and by no means continuous. The proportion of urban families living in poverty appears to have declined more rapidly than for rural families. However, with urbanisation, the urban poor actually formed a larger proportion of the total population in poverty than was the case thirty years earlier.

A national family income and expenditure survey, conducted in 1994, appears to indicate further modest declines in overall and sectoral measures of poverty. However, the economic setback affecting the East Asian region since mid-1997 (which in the Philippines has resulted in currency depreciation, higher interest rates and a slowdown in economic activity) has probably halted or even reversed this trend for the time being.

Table 3 Poverty incidence, Philippines, 1961–1991

	Poor families			Contribution to total poverty	
Year	Total (%)	Urban (%)	Rural (%)	Urban (%)	Rural (%)
1961	59	51	64	30	70
1965	52	43	55	26	74
1971	52	41	57	24	77
1985	44	37	49	32	68
1988	40	32	46	31	69
1991	39	31	47	39	61
1991 adjusted	37	23	53	35	65

Note Poverty incidence is the head count index for each year using family income — the share of the population with income below the poverty line — the only poverty measure available for all years.

Source World Bank 1996, p.3.

Table 4 Changes in poverty incidence for BWTP countries, Southeast Asia

	Year	Annual reduction (%)	First year (%)	Last year (%)
Philippines	1971–1991	0.7	52	39
Indonesia	1970–1990	2.0	58	19
Malaysia	1973–1987	1.6	37	14
Thailand	1962–1988	1.4	59	22

Note Poverty incidence is the official head count index calculated from family income.
Source World Bank 1996, p.3.

Table 3 adjusts official estimates to show 37 per cent of all families below the poverty line (23 per cent in urban areas and 53 per cent in rural) in 1991. The unadjusted estimate of 39 per for 1991 compares with 35.7 per cent for 1994, based on the family income and expenditure survey. This is the latest national poverty estimate. At that time about 4.7 million Philippine households were classed as poor. The relatively poor performance of the Philippines in reducing poverty, by comparison with the other Southeast Asian states in this study, is shown in table 4.

Other Southeast Asian countries included in this comparative study succeeded in reducing the incidence of poverty by annual rates of between 1.4 and 2.0 percentage points over an extended period of two to three decades. In the Philippines the annual average reduction was considerably less. Moreover, economic growth in the Philippines 'was narrowly based and inequitable, trapping many people in marginal, low paying occupations . . .' (World Bank 1996, p.4). This was a consequence of what the World Bank describes as a 'highly inequitable distribution of incomes and assets'.

By contrast, in Indonesia where per capita income is roughly equivalent to that in the Philippines, the distribution of income was much more even and the incidence of poverty substantially lower. The World Bank notes that 'most other East Asian countries have experienced dramatic improvements in income distribution', whereas income inequality in the Philippines 'has not improved over time' (p.4). The respective Gini Coefficients for Indonesia and the Philippines were 0.317 and 0.407, with the lower figure indicating greater equality. The richest 20 per cent of the population in Indonesia had some five times the income of the poorest fifth: in the Philippines the ratio was ten to one.

Thus, at the beginning of the 1990s more than one third of households in the Philippines still had income below the poverty line and more than a half of the rural population was poor. As against that, despite the relatively high proportion beneath the poverty line, it appeared that the poor were relatively better off, in the sense that the gap between the income of the poor and the poverty line had narrowed. The World Bank noted that a substantial proportion of those below the poverty line could be lifted out by a combination of sustained growth and a more effective poverty alleviation strategy. Here is where appropriate interventions, including microfinance, could make a difference, although recent economic difficulties in the region (even though less severe in the Philippines than elsewhere) have made the task more difficult.

Policies for poverty reduction

After the 'people's power' revolution and the restoration of democracy in 1986, the primary concerns of the Aquino administration were governmental reform and macroeconomic stabilisation. Further progress towards financial sector liberalisation occurred and positive encouragement was given to the development role of NGOs. The advent of the Ramos administration in 1992 saw a number of significant initiatives explicitly directed at poverty as a primary objective. A persistent theme has been the need to rationalise the wide range of government programs directed towards aspects of poverty, and to secure greater effectiveness and better targeting.

The World Bank report of 1996 which commented upon the persistence of poverty in the Philippines referred to the limited success of 'safety net' programs directed to various needs of the poor. A bewildering range of such schemes had come into existence during the 1970s and 1980s. These included employment creation, food subsidies and 'livelihood programs'. Much of this effort had been ineffective and ill-directed (a judgement applying both to the broad range of poverty programs, and to the proliferation of specific 'livelihood' programs offering credit).

With the election of President Fidel Ramos in 1992, the new Administration created the Presidential Commission to Fight Poverty whose head held Cabinet rank. The potential for access to credit to play a role in poverty alleviation was acknowledged in several initiatives. These included the Social Pact on Credit, forged in 1993 between government agencies, government financial institutions, private banks, cooperative rural banks and farmers' groups, and the Social Reform Agenda of 1994. The Social Pact led to the creation of a National Credit Council (NCC), discussed below.

The Presidential Commission to Fight Poverty identified five major strategies to address poverty, which have been endorsed by the Philippines government. These involve a blend of broad-brush macroeconomic measures, microeconomic reform and decentralised, people-centred initiatives with the short-term goal of bringing the incidence of poverty down to 30 per cent by 1998, when the term of the current Administration expires. In summary, these strategies are as follows:

(1) *Promote and sustain economic growth to create employment and livelihood opportunities*: this is to be done by a combination of infrastructure development, taxation reform, financial sector development, microeconomic reform directed at various impediments to growth, and targeted government spending.

(2) *Sustain growth based on people-friendly strategies*: the promotion of labour-intensive technologies, removal of policy biases against agriculture, reform and revival of rural financing facilities, redirection of credit in 'livelihood' programs to the ultra-poor.

(3) *Expand social services to provide minimum basic needs*: primary health care and family planning, elementary education, nutrition, housing, water supply and sanitation.

(4) *Foster sustainable income-generating community projects*: emphasise 'livelihood' programs providing skills training, credit and technical extension; consolidate lending programs for the core poor under the Presidential Commission to Fight Poverty; extend credit at commercial rates and without collateral.

(5) *Build the capabilities of the poor to help themselves*: involve local leadership through implementation of programs through local government, mobilise the private voluntary sector (including NGOs) and facilitate the formation of people's organisations.

Key elements of this program are embodied in the Social Reform Agenda (SRA), approved by the President in 1994. The SRA focuses on the provision of health, nutrition, education, credit and shelter to the target groups. Implementation of the Agenda required the creation of nine 'flagship' programs focusing on basic needs of the poor; one of these is concerned with credit. Various initiatives flowing from this are discussed below.

Since 1993 the National Credit Council (NCC) has been charged with the task of rationalising and coordinating the numerous credit programs operated by agencies of government. It has also conducted a series of studies on aspects of credit policy, with the support of a USAID-funded consultancy. While the articulation of policy guidelines is one thing, and their implementation another, those articulated in the Philippines (most recently, in the National Strategy for Microfinance completed by the NCC in January 1997) are unusually explicit in situating microfinance within the broader financial system, and in according it a key role in poverty alleviation.

The microfinance strategy is set in a framework in which the role of the private sector (including MFIs) is emphasised and an enabling policy environment is to be established. Market interest rates are to apply to loans and deposits, and government line agencies are supposed to withdraw from the implementation of credit and guarantee programs in favour of specialised lending agencies. The institutional framework for microfinance is to be one in which:

(1) MFIs engage in sustainable microfinance intermediation

(2) the government (through the NCC) provides a policy environment supportive of efficient financial markets and private MFI participation in those markets

(3) specialised government financial institutions (in particular, the People's Credit and Finance Corporation) provide wholesale funds and technical assistance to MFIs

(4) commercial banks provide wholesale funds and financial services to MFIs and work with them in mobilising savings

(5) NGOs will provide services of non-financial intermediation between poor households and MFIs

(6) donors will provide assistance for 'social preparation' activities and support the more efficient operation of the microfinance market and microfinance institutions.

Finally, at the time of writing, the Philippines Congress is considering a major piece of legislation for 'An Act institutionalising a national strategy for poverty alleviation'. This Act passed into law in December 1997. The intention was (inter alia) to institutionalise the Social Reform Agenda, strengthen the People's Credit and Finance Corporation, establish a People's Development Fund as a permanent vehicle for providing capacity building for microfinance, and introduce new savings instruments designed for small savers while setting up special new credit windows in government financial institutions for the poor.

1.3 Overview of the financial system

As at end-1996 there were 49 commercial banks in the Philippines, supervised by the central bank, Bangko Sentral ng Pilipinas, and offering the full range of banking services. These banks are represented by an umbrella organisation, the Bankers' Association of the Philippines (BAP). In addition, Bangko Sentral supervises some 108 thrift banks and 805 rural banks, the latter including some 47 cooperative banks. Thrift and rural banks are more restricted in their operations than commercial banks, typically serving a community or limited geographic area, and being more widespread throughout the provinces. They have much lower minimum capital requirements. For 1993, del Rosario (1995) reported that the commercial banks dominated the banking sector. Their assets constituted some 76 per cent of those of the banking system and 56 per cent of those of the whole formal financial sector.

There are also three specialised government banks, the Development Bank of the Philippines, the Land Bank of the Philippines (LandBank) and Al-Amanah Islamic Investment Bank of the Philippines. These banks are governed by their respective charters, and supervised and regulated by Bangko Sentral. Bangko Sentral also regulates various non-bank financial intermediaries, including finance companies, mutual building and loan associations, and non-stock savings and loan associations.

There have been a number of financial reforms since the early 1980s. Interest rate ceilings for banks were removed in 1981 for deposits and in 1983 for loans. Bangko Sentral has considerably relaxed the previous restrictive rules for bank entry. In 1989 the moratorium on the establishment of new commercial banks was lifted. In 1994 the entry of foreign banks was permitted. Restrictions on branching by existing banks were reduced in 1989 and again in 1993. Since 1987 the role of government banks has been reduced, with a shift in emphasis from retail lending to wholesale lending using private banks as conduits. There have also been changes to various prudential requirements, and certain foreign exchange transactions have been liberalised. Bangko Sentral has set up a committee to review the Banking Act of 1935.

Notwithstanding these reforms, the financial system of the Philippines remains relatively undeveloped. As a measure of financial depth, in 1995 the ratio of money and quasi-money to GDP stood at 45.4 per cent. This ratio of money and quasi-money to the value of output is at approximately the same level as in India (with a very much lower per capita income) although higher than in any other of the South Asian countries considered here. It is somewhat higher than in Indonesia, but well below the levels in Malaysia and Thailand (85 and 74 per cent, respectively). Bank deposit rates were virtually zero in real terms, while an interest rate spread of more than 6 per cent between deposit and lending rates in 1995 appeared to reflect a domestic banking environment still somewhat cosseted from market forces.

Reviewing financial sector development in the Philippines soon after the commencement of the current regional financial crisis, Intal and Llanto (1998) credit the financial system with achieving progress in provision of financial services to the broader population over the last few years:

> The robust economic recovery since 1994 in the Philippines has encouraged greater financial deepening. The stable macroeconomy in recent years, with the implicit low inflation expectations, has encouraged expansion of formal financial institutions deeper into the countryside and the urban informal sector, thereby providing stronger competitive pressure vis-a-vis informal financial intermediaries (for example, moneylenders) (p.48).

However, by early 1998, the Philippines was experiencing currency devaluation, higher interest rates and loss of output with higher unemployment. Yet no regulated financial institution had failed and the severity of the crisis appeared much less than elsewhere in Southeast Asia. This was attributed by Intal and Llanto to the country's more robust financial system and its comparatively recent participation in the regional boom in capital inflows. This has meant lower and more favourable composition of external debt, and less speculation in real estate.

1.4 Overview of microfinance

In the Philippines the terms 'microfinance' and 'microenterprise development' are still used in some quarters as though they were synonymous. Many credit programs run by government agencies, and the programs of a range of financial institutions (including rural and thrift banks, credit cooperatives and the bankers' association) may be referred to as 'microfinancing' but are in practice programs for microenterprise development and not directed towards what in the Philippines are termed the ultra poor. Even among the NGOs, many are concerned with the economic activities of persons of limited means and without access to banks. But serving this category of people is not poverty alleviation and the service itself is not microfinance.

In general, the banks do not provide financial services to poor clients. Of all the banks, it is the rural banks that are best placed to engage in microfinance. Rural banks are established to meet the credit needs of borrowers who are often outside the catchment areas of commercial banks and/or who may be considered poor risks by other banks. They are authorised to accept savings and time deposits, and provide short-term loans for productive purposes with minimum collateral requirements. In addition, cooperative banks may be organised to perform banking and credit services for the cooperatives. Most rural and cooperative banks do not have means-tested programs targeted to poor borrowers, and it is understood that most of their clients are people in the rural areas who are slightly better off.

Nevertheless, there are a number of rural banks that are active in providing small loans to poor borrowers, such as the Cooperative Rural Bank of Santa Cruz, the Cooperative Rural Bank of Aklan, the Davao Cooperative Rural Bank, and St Leonardo Rural Bank (which operates a microfinance program based on the Grameen system). The World Bank (1996, p.64) comments that sufficient evidence exists of the profitable provision of savings and credit services to the poor by cooperative rural banks to suggest that '. . . these banks offer an interesting possibility for reaching the poor effectively without setting up alternative institutions'.

The Philippines has a vibrant NGO community, and there are an estimated 500 NGOs providing microfinance services. Most of the larger ones replicate the Grameen approach, with means testing of borrowers, group formation and preparation, and the use of group guarantees. While there is a large number of NGOs, none have particularly large programs and most are very small. It is estimated that as at end-1995, the largest NGO program had only around 3,100 poor borrowers, and the total outreach of the 500 odd programs was only around 30,000. However, this is an area where estimates differ widely.

Most NGO programs are a long way from operating on a sustainable basis. Llanto, Garcia and Callanta (1996) report that fewer than 50 MFIs employ commercial lending and partly cover their costs. Most of the larger NGOs lend at market-based interest rates and seek at least to cover their operating costs. Nevertheless, in their study of six major MFIs and one cooperative rural bank engaged in microfinance, only the cooperative rural bank was financially self-sufficient, and only one of the MFIs was operationally self-sufficient.

There is a large number of government credit programs designed to provide financial services to the poor. The National Credit Council identified 111 government credit programs in 1995, of which no more than 13 are targeted to the ultra poor. Of these, only four have significant outreach: namely the Tulong sa Tao program of the Department of Trade and Industry; the linkage program of the National Livelihood Support Fund; the microfinance program of the Department of Social Welfare and Development; and the

Micro Credit Program for the Bottom Poor, a Grameen Bank replication project implemented by the Agricultural Credit Policy Council and LandBank. Apart from the Department of Social Welfare and Development program, these programs involve lending through NGOs as credit conduits. For instance, the Agricultural Credit Policy Council project involves 23 NGOs and cooperative rural banks. In general, credit programs operated by the government are highly subsidised. Llanto et al. (p.14) comment that:

> . . . Philippine experience has shown the huge inefficiency and high costs of using government non-financial institutions to implement credit programs. Recent research has shown the unsustainability of government supply-led credit programs, the great capacity for leakage of the benefits of government credit programs leading to gross inefficiencies, the distortion of the financial market and weakening of private sector incentive to innovate.

In addition to the banks and specialised microfinance institutions, non-stock savings and loan associations supervised by Bangko Sentral provide savings and credit facilities to members. Membership is confined to a well-defined group of persons, and they are not allowed to provide financial services to the general public. As at end-December 1995, there were 88 non-stock savings and loan associations in the Philippines.

There are also cooperatives and credit unions, supervised by the Cooperative Development Authority. Some 42,000 cooperatives are registered under the Cooperative Code of March 1990 but half of these are considered non-operative. Credit unions and cooperatives offer members fixed deposits which cannot be withdrawn until membership ends, as well as savings and time deposits which are withdrawable. This gives the cooperatives a larger resource base for lending than is available to the NGOs.

Among the cooperatives there are those promoted by the government to implement livelihood programs, most of whose equity is contributed by LandBank. There are also grassroots cooperatives which have national-level federations of their own. There are four such national federations, one of which is NATCCO, the National Confederation of Cooperatives. This has a network of 1,700 affiliated primary cooperatives, a quarter of which are credit cooperatives. NATCCO provides a range of services, including deposit guarantee insurance which is being developed for selected member institutions. It may eventually open the guarantee scheme to other cooperative federations. NATCCO's primary credit cooperatives may be cited here as an example of privately initiated microfinance institutions which, on the evidence of their small loan sizes (Ps5,000 to Ps6,000 or $200 to 240), certainly reach down to the poor even if not serving them exclusively.

A distinctive form of microfinance is provided by the 'lending investor'. Lending investors are basically moneylenders who are licensed by Bangko Sentral and subject to minimal regulatory requirements and supervision. They are permitted to accept deposits from a maximum of 19 individuals, and are permitted to make loans to whomever they wish. There has been a rapid increase in the number of lending investors in recent years, and increased competition has led to reductions in the interest rates they charge. Some 1,400 lending investors typically charge interest of between 3.5 and 4 per cent flat per month. Together with more than 2,000 pawnshops, they deal with segments of the population usually beyond the reach of formal financial institutions and compete with informal financial sector lenders. They are characterised by simple procedures, low transaction costs, rapid response and accessibility, but normally require collateral and probably do not reach the ultra poor.

2 Arrangements for direct support

The government has been heavily involved in directly supporting microfinance, with the multiplicity of government credit programs already discussed above. In some cases, government agencies lend directly to final borrowers. However, the government has increasingly channelled funds through NGOs as a means of providing credit to the poor. For instance, programs such as the Department of Trade and Industry's Microcredit Project and the Grameen Replication Project of the Agricultural Policy Credit Council use NGOs as credit conduits. LandBank uses the National Livelihood Support Fund to channel funds to NGOs and other institutions for relending to the poor. The government credit programs have been criticised for being inefficient, highly politicised, uncoordinated and unsustainable; as described below, the Department of Finance and the National Credit Council are currently working to rationalise them. In their emerging framework, the People's Finance and Credit Cooperation (PCFC) has a major role, also discussed below.

2.1 Support for specialised microfinance institutions

As mentioned previously, the government established the National Credit Council following the 1993 Social Pact on Credit. It has 22 members drawn from government agencies, government financial institutions and the private sector. The council has four major objectives:

(1) to rationalise and optimise government lending programs

(2) to develop a national credit delivery system

(3) to encourage private sector participation

(4) to define and rationalise the role of guarantee and guarantee agencies.

The council's focus has been exclusively on small credit and microcredit; it is concerned with the operations of regulated financial institutions only to the extent that their activities impinge upon these concerns. It has developed a set of guidelines, Policy Guidelines for Credit for the Poor, applying to government agencies undertaking lending programs or programs with a credit component. These guidelines argue that the Philippine banking and financial system is capable of supplying most of the financial requirements for microfinance, and that the role of donor agencies and external funding should be primarily in technical assistance. The NCC guidelines also provide that government line agencies should focus on technical assistance and capacity building for microfinance, and should channel all their lending activities through banks and MFIs, including credit unions, cooperatives and NGOs.

To date, NCC has had limited success in achieving its objectives, as embodied in the National Strategy for Microfinance of January 1997, or the credit policy guidelines described above. This is because it has no authority to require modification or elimination of policies or programs it believes are inconsistent with sound microfinance. The NCC has been relocated from LandBank to the Department of Finance, to eliminate perceptions of conflict of interest (given its aim of stripping lending functions from line agencies). USAID has provided a technical assistance grant to strengthen it, but since the council's efforts at rationalisation confront powerful bureaucratic and political interests, real progress is likely to require sustained political backing at the highest level. The timetable for the NCC calls for its work to be completed by mid-1998, at the end of the term of the current Administration. No continuing role is envisaged for it beyond that date.

In addition to establishing the National Credit Council for policy guidance, the government has taken a number of other program initiatives with respect to microfinance. In 1994, credit was included as one of nine 'flagship' programs under the Social Reform Agenda of the President, mentioned above. Following this, the government created the Task Force on Credit for the Poor, from which flowed the Credit for the Poor Program.

This program has developed a strategy of segmenting the various groups of the poor and encouraging sustainable microfinance provision, with particular emphasis on the Grameen Bank approach for the ultra-poor group. One of the major outcomes of this strategy has been the People's Credit and Finance Corporation (PCFC), a second tier financial institution to serve the credit needs of the poor.

The People's Credit and Finance Corporation

In 1995 LandBank established the People's Credit and Finance Corporation as a government finance company for lending to the poor, and it continues to hold 99 per cent of the share capital. It is incorporated under the Corporations Act and regulated by the Securities and Exchange Commission. Its Articles provide for it to be privatised in due course.

PCFC is the executing agency for a $26.3 million program funded by a loan from the Asian Development Bank (ADB) and the International Fund for Agricultural Development (IFAD). These funds are to be provided exclusively for PCFC to support MFIs replicating the Grameen Bank approach. The loan allocates resources in favour of a particular model, rather than by objective evaluation of the performance of MFIs already active, whatever model they follow.

As this study shows, there is a variety of indigenous institutions exploring various paths to sustainable microfinance provision in the Philippines. Thus, in mid-1997, PCFC was funding 58 conduit institutions from its National Livelihood Support Fund (NLSF) reserves, only 17 of which were Grameen replicators. The World Bank (1996, p.65) notes that:

> The Grameen Bank model is not the only successful approach to microfinance, and the current emphasis on Grameen replication as the only way to reach the ultra-poor may be discouraging the expansion of other successful models in the Philippines.

PCFC should be permitted to be even-handed in its support of MFIs, focusing on their effectiveness and performance, objectively evaluated. Failure to maintain even-handedness is likely, under current conditions of a credit 'squeeze' affecting commercial bank sources of credit for microfinance (discussed in section 2.2 below) to cause the impact of financial sector stringency to fall disproportionatly on non-Grameen Bank MFIs.

PCFC is registered as a finance company, not supervised by the central bank, but reporting to it. More onerous supervision, and adherence to banking ratios and other norms, would be required for it to progress to quasi-bank status. PCFC has given undertakings to the ADB to conform with the quasi-bank guidelines as a preparation for upgrading to that status.

PCFC's issued capital is Ps100 million and will be increased to Ps400 million. The initial capitalisation was provided by NLSF, and the corporation commenced operations by taking over NLSF's loan portfolio. PCFC defines microfinance institutions broadly: it provides funds to NGOs, rural banks, cooperatives and other intermediaries as conduits for on-lending to the poor, and aims to ensure that such intermediaries are replicable, self-sustaining and operationally viable. NCC's strategy for the corporation calls for it gradually to replace many of the other lending programs operated by line agencies of government.

The ADB is requiring PCFC to complete a privatisation plan by mid-1998, with a view to completing the process by end-1999. Its shareholding is envisaged as a mixture of government and public shareholding. In particular, it is hoped that MFIs and other institutions which form the constituency for PCFC will take up stock. In preparation for privatisation, the corporation has been called upon to show a profit. Consequently, for the present PCFC has adopted the policy of extending credit lines only to 'intermediate' and 'advanced' MFIs, where profitability is more assured. For MFIs at the 'start-up' or 'beginner' phase, it plans in due course to mobilise funds from government, UNDP and bilateral sources. It could thus become a force for multiplying the numbers of MFIs, as well as increasing the outreach of established institutions.

At the time of the fieldwork for this study, PCFC's loanable funds were sourced entirely from NLSF. With a cost of funds of 6 per cent, the corporation was lending to intermediaries at 12 per cent on the diminishing balance and required them to charge a market rate (at least 2 per cent per month). The corporation's 'spread' of 6 percentage points was felt adequate for normal operations. However, funds were also loaned to 'conduits' for capacity building. These were soft loans, and although limited to 20 per cent of total outstandings, were a source of concern, given the need for PCFC to show a profit. After privatisation, the government should accept greater responsibility for capacity building.

A further concern, in regard to PCFC's ability to turn a profit, was that the ADB/IFAD funding proposals would allow it a spread of less than 6 percentage points and that the 'pass-on' rate stipulated for these funds was only 10 per cent. This would compare with a cost of funds for non-Grameen intermediaries, as noted above, of 12 per cent. PCFC should be permitted to be even-handed in regard to interest rates for all MFIs, and to avoid the distortions which differential rates would involve. Continuing negotiations over this and other issues appeared to be delaying the disbursement of the loan by the multilaterals. A second ADB/IFAD loan of $157 million has also been signed.

PCFC deserves support as an integral part of the strategy to rationalise the provision of microfinance in the Philippines. Donor agencies should seek so far as possible to channel support for microfinance through PCFC in preference to line agencies of government. They should also avoid supporting unsustainable credit operations mounted through such agencies, which would be better employed offering technical assistance in the areas of their special competence.

Support for capacity building

PCFC is also responsible for providing technical assistance to strengthen NGOs. The soft loans it provides for this purpose are mentioned above in the context of its needs to achieve profitability prior to privatisation. In this respect the corporation is better resourced than PKSF in Bangladesh, which has only loanable funds to offer MFIs. In the 1997 budget, the government allocated Ps100 million for capacity building for MFIs under its national Poverty Alleviation Fund, a 'quick response' fund targeting minimum basic needs, of which the corporation is an implementing agency. The ADB/IFAD loan to PCFC also has a capacity-building component. Soft credits will be available to Grameen replicators for start-up costs, training and self-help group formation and training.

In regard to capacity building for MFIs, the corporation works with the Punla sa Tao Foundation (Punla). A complementary initiative to PCFC, Punla is a non-stock non-profit entity operating as an NGO. It was created at the initiative of the Presidential Commission to Fight Poverty and business interests to build the capacity of institutions to provide financial services to the poor. Punla is represented on the board of PCFC, and on the NCC working group concerned with the ultra-poor, and provides microfinance training services (for example, preparing the training modules for capacity building financed this year under the Poverty Alleviation Fund). It operates on a fee-for-service basis as well as raising funds from the corporate sector and elsewhere. It is an interesting model for an organisation designed to catalyse public and private support for capacity building in microfinance, and will offer management and research as well as training. Punla should be adequately financed and creatively involved by government in the process of equipping MFIs to meet the challenge of greatly expanding their outreach in the Philippines.

2.2 Support through the banking system

Directed credit schemes

Banking institutions are required to allocate at least 25 per cent of loanable funds to agricultural credit, of which at least 10 per cent must be for agrarian reform credit. The 25 per cent allocation can include investments in certain government securities and loans to educational institutions, cooperatives, hospitals, low-cost housing and local government units. However, in 1995 banks were exempted from these requirements so long as a minimum of 5 per cent of their loanable funds were lent to farmers' associations or cooperatives. Under the Magna Carta for Small Enterprises, all lending institutions are required to set aside portion of their loan portfolios for small enterprise credit. The portion mandated is 5 per cent from 31 December 1996, although the requirement may be abolished by 31 December 1997. Such lending has had little relevance to poverty alleviation in any case and the case for retaining it is not strong, given that conditions appear favourable for market forces increasingly to provide the necessary services.

Programs channelled through the banking system

Government agencies also provide support to banks involved in microfinance. Rural banks are able to rediscount eligible papers with Bangko Sentral at preferential rates of interest. In an emergency or financial crisis, Bangko Sentral may give a loan to a rural bank against the security of its assets. Bangko Sentral also provides technical support to rural and cooperative banks. It provides them with free technical assistance both during the process of organisation, and when they are already in operation. It also conducts training programmes for rural bank personnel free of charge.

Linkages between banks and specialised microfinance institutions

Linkages between commercial banks and MFIs are seen as one means by which the resources of domestic financial systems can be marshalled for the benefit of the poor. Such linkages have arisen in the Philippines with the support of external donors, as the result of political pressure, and with the benefit of tax breaks designed to encourage corporate philanthropy. At the time of fieldwork for this study, in mid-1997, there was also increasing evidence of such linkages occurring on a commercial basis.

One such project with official support is the Project Linking Banks with Self-Help Groups, conducted jointly by the LandBank, the Philippine Council for Rural Savings and Finance and the German technical cooperation agency, GTZ. With heavy emphasis on institution-building support from GTZ, this is one of a number of such projects the German government is supporting in Asia. At end-1995, according to APRACA (1996), a total of 16 'conduit' MFIs served by 53 bank branches were dealing with some 670 self-help groups in the Philippines. These groups, with more than 32,000 members, received loan disbursements of almost $8 million and mobilised deposits of some $0.7 million. Not much otherwise is known about the performance or sustainability of these group-based schemes.

There have also been a number of private Philippine initiatives in this field. The Social Pact on Credit, mentioned above, was agreed in 1993. It involved private banks, as well as government agencies and financial institutions and other stakeholders. Among its results was increased awareness among private commercial bankers of the possibilities of microfinance. Subsequently, during 1994 the Bankers' Association of the Philippines (BAP) established its own Credit Guarantee Corporation (CGC) to provide guarantee cover to member banks lending to microfinance institutions. BAP has also supported training courses for NGOs in microfinance management.

A total of Ps784 million ($31.36 million) was reported to have been lent as 'working capital' loans with the facilitation of CGC during the first three years of its operation. The average loan size was Ps264,000 (around $10,500), not a very useful statistic for our purposes, since it seems to relate both to loans made to MFIs and to individual loans. Loans written under CGC auspices cover a very wide range and certainly include small (rather than micro) business borrowers. The borrowers assisted are marginal to the commercial banking system, and unable to qualify for loans under normal criteria. To that degree, the scheme answers a social need and can be seen as a response to the Social Pact on Credit. However, the need addressed does not seem to be poverty alleviation, except perhaps at the bottom end of the range of CGC-guaranteed loans.

Linkages between commercial banks and MFIs are facilitated by tax breaks available to corporations in the Philippines (including private commercial banks) which set up charitable foundations. In a number of cases, banks have been able to conduct exploratory ventures in support of MFIs by channelling the necessary resources via their foundations (and reducing their exposure to losses in the process). One such foundation is the BPI (Bank of the Philippine Islands) Foundation.

The BPI Foundation had resources of about Ps30 million ($1.2 million) in mid-1997, and had extended lines of credit to nine NGOs and three credit cooperatives at a 'soft' interest rate of 8 per cent for on-lending to the poor (as against commercial rates of between 14 and 16 per cent). On average, each of these MFIs had received a line of credit of Ps1 million ($38,000) from the foundation, and on-lent to group members at interest rates ranging from 18 to 30 per cent, which yields a fairly high margin. About 1,600 individual loans had been financed in this manner. The BPI Foundation's dealings with NGOs had been more satisfactory than those with credit cooperatives; the repayment rate from NGOs was 100 per cent and that from cooperatives around 80 per cent. However, total funds made available through this 'window' to NGOs have not been very significant in relation to the foundation's current resources, indicating a very cautious approach to this lending.

MFIs intending to borrow from the BPI Foundation have to meet the following conditions:

(1) a good track record for at least three years

(2) annual audited accounts

(3) repayment rate not less than 90 per cent

(4) loans targeted to the poor (although the foundation does not apply a means test).

The BPI Foundation monitors the continuing compliance of MFIs with these requirements.

A number of other banks, including Solid Bank and Far East Bank, have also set up foundations. Motives for involvement in microfinance in this way are mixed, ranging from tokenism to a genuine interest in trialling microfinancing in an environment of reduced risk. Banks which commenced financing MFIs in this way, notably BPI itself, were in 1997 making the transition to full and profitable commercial financing of MFI operations without benefit of a tax shelter. The study conducted for the BWTP Network in the Philippines by Ms Ruth Goodwin-Groen (forthcoming) provides empirical data relating to the successes of these private commercial initiatives. In India the publication of guidelines in support of bank/MFI linkages by NABARD has been a positive influence. Bangko Sentral could play a similar leadership role in the Philippines.

One powerful motive for the growing interest of commercial banks in microfinance is the potential for savings mobilisation from relatively untapped sections of the national population, allied with the growing competitive pressures to which the industry is becoming subject. They are acquiring small banks and showing increasing interest in agency arrangements with NGOs to tap into the market. The possibility exists for them to assist in the creation of NGOs for this purpose or (as happens in Indonesia) forming self-help groups directly for financial services. These would be positive developments and should be encouraged. Such 'principal/agent' relationships need not be exploitative, and the demand for savings services is in the long run likely to be much greater than the demand for credit, as the experience of Bank Rakyat in Indonesia suggests.

However, effects of the regional financial crisis in the Philippines financial sector since late 1997 have included interest rate increases and the reversion to extremely conservative lending practices by commercial banks. Credit lines available to MFIs, where they are rolled over at all, are renewed at higher rates of interest and with stricter collateral requirements. While the overall impact is not yet clear, current conditions are not conducive to expanded commercial bank engagement with microfinance.

2.3 Direct government programs

Mention has been made at a number of points of the multiplicity of government-administered credit programs which persists in the Philippines, whose rationalisation is the objective of the National Credit Council. The NCC has classified them by sector (table 5).

These government-run credit programs were enumerated in 1995 and involved many agencies of government. Only 13 were said to focus on the 'ultra poor'. More recent information indicates that the actual number of programs is even greater; the latest tally appears to be between 140 and 150, involving around 45 agencies. Lending under these programs is direct as well as through NGO conduits.

Table 5 Government-administered credit programs in the Philippines, 1995

	Agri-credit	Ultra-poor	Salaried & self-employed	Small/medium enterprises	Total
No. of programs	39	13	21	38	111
No. of implementing agencies	19	4	12	9	44
Funds available in billion pesos	> 11.06	n.a.	> 3.2	> 16.7	> 31
Interest p.a. (%)	6–14	0; 6; to market rate	3–18	7–24	

Source World Bank 1996, p. 47

3 Regulation of non-bank microfinance institutions

3.1 The broad regulatory framework

Non-governmental organisations

Non-governmental organisations (NGOs) in the Philippines are classed as 'non-stock, non-profit' organisations, and registered with the Securities and Exchange Commission (SEC). They are not closely supervised by the SEC, but must file audited annual financial statements with it. For an NGO to achieve registration, it must nominate a board of directors (between five and 15 members) a majority of whom should be citizens of the Philippines. Personal information must be provided to determine the standing of persons nominated. The initial capitalisation required is a minimum of Ps50,000 ($2,000). The NGO must provide proof of its financial standing.

After the approval of a name for the organisation, it is necessary to file articles of incorporation and by-laws. The SEC provides a 'pro forma' set of by-laws as a guide. Applications are reviewed in less than a month and are normally approved, following which the business name of the NGO is registered with the Department of Trade and Industry. Registration with the Bureau of Internal Revenue is also required. Finally, it is necessary to obtain approval at the municipal level, and a licence to operate in a particular locality.

In principle, NGOs are liable to tax at the rate of 5 per cent of gross revenue. However, after operating for a minimum of one year, application can be made to the Bureau of Internal Revenue for tax exemption, on the basis that the NGO has shown itself a bona fide charitable organisation. This, however, appears to be an area of some concern to many NGOs. Annual reports must be filed with the SEC, together with a general information statement and audited financials. These are copied to the Bureau of Internal Revenue. The processes of registration and annual reporting are relatively simple, with the exception of proving bona fide status for tax exemption. It is necessary to show that activities are not conducted for benefit of directors.

While NGOs are subject in principle to ongoing supervision, in practice they appear to be examined rarely. NGOs are required to keep all records for a minimum of five years, to observe minimum wage legislation and to register employees with the social security system. Foreign donations must be reported with the annual accounts, but are not subject to any control or supervision.

Guidelines for governance are set out in the pro forma Articles supplied by the SEC. In cases of dispute within an NGO, an appeal can be made to the SEC. Overall, the SEC appears to apply a very light touch with registered NGOs and the regulatory environment appears relatively permissive. On the other hand, ambiguities affecting the tax status of NGOs appear to be of concern to many organisations. For example, rural banks and cooperatives are exempt from income taxation and some NGOs feel that this is discriminatory. The procedures for exempting bona fide NGOs from tax should be clarified and simplified, and such exemptions should not unreasonably be withheld.

NGOs are not permitted to accept deposits from the general public. Moreover, the legal situation with regard to accepting deposits from members is unclear. Many NGOs are reported to have an informal deposit-taking relationship with 'members', using devices such as accepting funds for 'capital buildup'. Llanto, Garcia and Callanta (1996) comment that this is skating on thin ice because of potential legal sanctions against this illegal activity. Under the Banking Act non-stock and non-profit organisations are not permitted to accept savings and deposits in any form. As a consequence, they have to depend on external sources for funding. External funding being uncertain and limited, NGOs' ability to expand their lending outreach has been correspondingly limited.

This has caused some to call for a separate legal framework to be created for NGOs, with their being authorised to collect deposits. The reaction of some NGOs has been to seek registration as formal financial institutions under the laws currently applicable, accepting the regulatory and prudential requirements of Bangko Sentral. Some argue for special arrangements to suit their circumstances, in regard to the capital requirements for small banks, and whether the current requirements for rural banks can be 'stretched' to accommodate NGOs. Others see the value of continuing within the relaxed regulatory environment which has facilitated NGO activity in the Philippines.

These are major issues in the current state of development of NGOs as microfinance institutions in the Philippines, on which there is no consensus as yet. The review of the Banking Act of 1935, mentioned in section 1.3 above, may involve consideration of the range of deposit-taking institutions; for NGOs to gain this capacity would require amendment of the Act. The NCC is also considering the overall regulatory framework for MFIs in the Philippines.

NGOs should be permitted to collect compulsory savings from clients in the course of providing microfinance services. In the same context, they should probably also be permitted to handle voluntary savings while satisfying agreed standards of accounting and reporting. The issue of how such standards might be agreed is discussed below, but it is relevant to note here that most commentators in other countries do not think that MFIs should be subject to official prudential regulation and supervision. This much is clear from the case studies conducted in parallel with this study of the Philippines, and from the wider literature.

Credit unions and cooperatives

Credit unions and cooperatives are registered under the Cooperative Code of 1989, which for the first time brought all types of cooperatives under one law and one government agency. The legislation recognises the role of cooperatives in promoting equity, social justice and economic development. This code also covers credit cooperatives and cooperative banks. The responsible agency is the Cooperative Development Authority (CDA). Apart from its regulatory and supervisory roles, the CDA also has a developmental role with respect to the cooperative movement. There is some suggestion that the developmental role of the CDA is not entirely consistent with its regulatory and supervisory roles.

A primary cooperative may be organised and registered by as few as 15 persons, and with minimum cash reserves of Ps2,000 ($80). To support the application, a simple 'economic survey' justifying the purposes and economic feasibility of the proposed cooperative must be prepared. The encouragement of thrift and savings mobilisation among the members, and the granting of loans to members for productive purposes are among the basic objectives of cooperatives mentioned in the legislation.

A primary cooperative is registered with limited liability and share capital held by the members. It is required to file Articles of Cooperation, as well as by-laws dealing with membership and governance of the cooperative, consistent with the provisions of the Cooperative Code. Applications for registration must be dealt with promptly by the CDA.

The Cooperative Code makes provision for credit cooperatives to mobilise savings among their members and to pool such savings for the purpose of granting loans to members 'for productive or provident purposes'. Credit cooperatives may not, however, accept deposits from the public. All cooperatives are exempt from the payment of taxes for a period of ten years after their formation. Cooperatives which deal with non-members and which accumulate assets beyond Ps10 million ($400,000) may incur some tax liabilities after ten years. The code also provides for the registration of cooperative banks under the supervision of the central bank, but with provision for exemption from some central bank rules and regulations.

3.2 Interest rates

There are no interest rate restrictions applying to MFIs, leaving them free to set their own interest rates. On the other hand, the proliferation of government-sponsored credit schemes introduces substantial subsidy elements into microfinance in the Philippines. The possible discrepancy between interest rates to be charged by the People's Credit and Finance Corporation (PCFC) to MFIs which are Grameen replicators and qualify for ADB/IFAD funding, and other MFIs which do not, has been noted above. Such discrepancies and the battery of subsidies already in existence, introduce damaging distortions into the market for microfinance, discouraging private initiatives. These distortions should not be allowed to continue.

3.3 Prudential regulation and supervision

At present, there is no prudential regulation of NGOs operating microfinance programs. There are no minimum capital requirements, nor are there any requirements concerning capital adequacy, liquidity, reserves or loan loss provisioning. For cooperatives, prudential requirements monitored by the CDA include the filing of annual reports. It appears that the level of compliance with full audit requirements is only around 20 to 30 per cent for all cooperatives. There are no minimum capital or provisioning requirements. As mentioned above, NATCCO (one of the national federations of private cooperatives) is establishing a deposit guarantee scheme for member credit cooperatives. This has regulatory implications since NATCCO is setting performance standards for members to join the scheme, and may also widen membership to other federations in time. This could have beneficial effects by encouraging higher standards more widely throughout the cooperative movement.

Some standards for MFIs would appear appropriate. Llanto et al. found that a number of major MFIs have inadequate financial reporting and monitoring, making it difficult to determine past due loans and the extent of arrears. They also found that the absence of adequate and sound performance standards and a standardised accounting and reporting system makes it difficult to evaluate the relative performance of MFIs. They concluded that:

> In sum, internal financial policies and practices need a lot of improvement, particularly in the installation of sound financial reporting and monitoring systems, portfolio management, assessment and management of risks, product packaging and pricing, management of loan arrears and strategic business planning. Related to these will be the need to upgrade and institutionalise performance standards, particularly in loan repayment, appreciation of loan default and ageing of delinquent accounts, and the installation of appropriate accounting and internal audit systems (p.21).

The National Credit Council will shortly conduct a review of the regulatory environment for NGOs engaged in microfinance. This work is supported by a technical grant from USAID and could lead to the establishment of standards for prudential regulation and supervision, perhaps (as suggested below) in concert with the self-regulatory efforts of MFIs themselves.

3.4 Performance and reporting standards of second tier institutions and other agencies

A number of agencies with some degree of oversight of MFIs are in a position to establish performance and reporting standards for them. In the Philippines, such agencies include the second tier body set up for the industry by government, the People's Credit and Finance Corporation (PCFC). Others which might do so include the National Credit Council and LandBank. The latter has the potential to do so by virtue of its position as a major provider of loanable funds to MFIs (a role which would be strengthened if NCC's goal of stripping lending away from government line agencies is achieved).

PCFC is not a regulator, but rather a funding body which provides lines of credit at concessional interest rates to NGOs and other MFIs. Nevertheless, it imposes certain conditions on MFIs before they can obtain loans from it. Accreditation for NGOs and people's organisations (that is, cooperatives and credit unions) with PCFC is secured on the basis that:

- they are duly registered with the SEC, central bank or Cooperative Development Authority
- they have a three-year track record in lending
- their working capital is at least Ps250,000 ($10,000)
- lending operations are segregated from other activities with appropriate full-time staff
- past due loans are not more than 20 per cent
- no loans are in arrears to PCFC or other agency
- established systems of proven effectiveness are in place.

PCFC has set minimum performance standards for its accredited MFIs in start-up, intermediate and advanced categories. This recognises that institutions progress as their capacities improve, and provides for this progression in the standards. The corporation is critical of the single set of 'ultimate' standards promulgated by CGAP (the Consultative Group to Assist the Poorest, whose secretariat is located in the World Bank), seeing them as out of reach for the great majority of Philippine practitioners at present. Some quantifiable standards are set out below (table 6). In addition, the corporation has set guidelines relating to such qualitative issues as governance, information systems and staffing to benchmark the standards thought necessary at each stage of an institution's development.

Table 6 Minimum performance standards for MFIs

	Beginner	Intermediate	Advanced
Viability (cost recovery)	50%	75%	100%
Outreach	500	1,500	5,000
Collection rate	90%	95%	>98%

Source PCFC

In the case of banks, PCFC requires a 10 per cent ratio of capital to risk-weighted assets; a past due rate not exceeding 15 per cent for commercial banks and 20 per cent for rural financial institutions; no deficiencies in reserve requirements for one year preceding the application; no major deficiencies in the most recent Bangko Sentral audit; and no loan in arrears with any public or private lending institution.

These requirements are not very detailed. Nevertheless, as PCFC expands its role in lending to MFIs and to the extent that other programs are rationalised, there is considerable scope for any standards imposed by PCFC to become more general industry standards. In this connection, the experience of PKSF in Bangladesh is likely to be of value. In developing such standards, it would clearly be desirable to coordinate with the work being done by the National Credit Council and the Microfinance Coalition for Standards as well as ensuring consistency with requirements imposed on MFIs (principally cooperatives) by LandBank. The work of the coalition is discussed below in section 3.5 on self-regulation.

The NCC has developed the Policy Guidelines for Credit for the Poor applying to government agencies undertaking lending programs or programs with a credit component. In some respects, these also provide a basis for a regulatory framework for the industry. For instance, the guidelines provide that credit programs must promote a savings mobilisation or capital build-up program. (In this respect the NCC goes further than PCFC, which does not emphasise savings in its performance standards for MFIs.) The guidelines suggest that such savings be deposited with banks to serve as partial collateral for loans. They also cover such matters as the equity contribution of borrowers, interest rates, and collateral and guarantees. Nevertheless, the relevance of the current guidelines for prudential regulation and supervision of MFIs is limited because of the following:

(1) The guidelines are intended primarily for government agencies, and even here the NCC has not been effective in ensuring compliance.

(2) Some of the guidelines do not seem appropriate in terms of encouraging sustainable microfinance. For instance, the guidelines on interest rates appear confusing and inconsistent. On the one hand, the guidelines state that interest rates should cover the full lending cost, including the cost of funds and transactions, administrative and

monitoring costs. On the other hand, they suggest that in the case of loans to small farmers, the maximum rate of interest should not exceed 75 per cent of the commercial rate inclusive of all charges.

(3) The guidelines do not cover many items relevant to prudential supervision. For instance, they do not cover issues such a minimum capital requirements, capital adequacy, reserve or liquidity requirements, loan loss provisions or reporting standards.

In summary, it is clear that some setting of standards for MFIs would be appropriate. The task will be facilitated if second tier agencies and other strategically placed institutions are involved in the regulatory process. Agencies with oversight of MFIs, notably PCFC, but also the National Credit Council and LandBank, are in a position to exert influence. For the credit cooperatives, the deposit insurance facility being created by NATCCO may also provide the opportunity for setting standards, perhaps leaving the Cooperative Development Authority more free to concentrate on its developmental functions for the great mass of cooperatives.

All these second tier agencies have commenced to set criteria for accreditation for MFIs, and to define performance standards for them. It is important that there be coordination and consistency between the standards set; if the National Credit Council is to have a continuing existence this coordinating function could appropriately rest with it. Otherwise, PCFC should accept responsibility for coordinating standards for MFIs; in this regard the experience of second tier institutions such as PKSF in Bangladesh would prove instructive.

Where initiative exists within the private sector to take the lead in self-regulation, this is usually preferable to the imposition of standards by second tier or other supervisory institutions. This possibility is discussed below.

3.5 Self-regulation

Networks of microfinance institutions

There are two major networks of MFIs in the Philippines. These provide a focal point for coordination and, to a more limited degree, self-regulation among their members. However, both have limited memberships, with each embracing only a small number of MFIs. The two networks are APPEND (the Association of Philippine Partners in Enterprise Development) and PHILNET, a group of MFIs engaged in Grameen replication, affiliated with the international CASHPOR network of Grameen institutions. Reference has also been made in section 3.3 to the efforts of NATCCO to set performance standards for credit cooperatives as a condition for membership of its proposed deposit guarantee scheme. This would provide a mechanism for self-regulation in the cooperative movement, where formal regulation under the Cooperative Code is lacking.

APPEND is an NGO registered on the same basis as its nine member institutions. Its regulatory functions include the examination of the financial statements and operations of member organisations. APPEND acts in a collegial manner to secure adherence to agreed standards by member institutions, with its executive director having responsibility for oversight. In addition, APPEND has a number of other functions:

(1) joint provision of training for member institutions (conducted for boards, chief executives and management staff, loans officers and others)

(2) resource mobilisation on behalf of member institutions (both donor funds and commercially sourced funding)

(3) acting as a project management office for special projects conducted jointly by APPEND members with donor agencies
(4) acting as a lender of last resort to member institutions with liquidity problems
(5) performing an advocacy role on behalf of member institutions.

PHILNET has seven member institutions and is planning to appoint full-time staff to perform administrative and regulatory functions, in particular, the accreditation of potential new members of the network. Regulatory standards within the group are based on the essentials of the Grameen model; member institutions are required to report program and financial data to CASHPOR, and these data serve as the basis for monitoring individual institutions. The Chair of PHILNET intervenes when necessary to assure improvement in performance of member institutions. However, to date, the regulatory capacity has resided more within CASHPOR than in PHILNET itself ('an exercise in transnational self-regulation').

In addition to the two networks described above, a major new initiative in self-regulation, the Developing Standards for Microfinance Project (DSMP) was set up in 1996. Funded by USAID the project has set out to develop and promote standards for microfinance operations. In the process of developing these standards, the project has achieved the following:

(1) It has formed a coalition (the Microfinance Coalition for Standards) that will develop and promote the standards. The coalition has 55 member institutions including leading NGO microfinance practitioners, the central bank, PCFC and other government planning and regulatory bodies, two commercial banks, private foundations, academic and research organisations and donor agencies.
(2) It has begun to build the database necessary for benchmarking and standard setting (this has involved a nationwide inventory of microfinance NGOs and in-depth studies of selected MFIs).
(3) It has commenced the process of documenting best practice among MFIs in the Philippines, with the objective of arriving at benchmarks or standards for good practice.
(4) It has encouraged consultation and consensus building among the members of the coalition.
(5) It has conducted seminars, training activities and conferences (to build awareness of the need for standards and to disseminate standards). These will culminate in a national microfinance summit in 1998).

The DSMP is now working towards these objectives and has developed a conceptual framework for benchmarking the performance of MFIs. Setting these benchmarks and measuring the performance of institutions against them involves the collection of quantitative and qualitative data by institutions themselves and external observation of their performance. Table 7 summarises the 'yardsticks' available for the measurement and evaluation of performance.

The yardsticks draw on the observation of past performance within particular institutions and on the observation of performance of the microfinance 'industry' as a whole. This enables the determination of benchmarks which embody best practice in the industry. Finally, benchmarks are extended into the future with the shaping of budgets, strategic plans and business plans, to guide the future development of institutions. The quality of these plans is an important indicator of the standing of an institution.

Table 7 Standards for performance evaluation for MFIs

Standards	Data source	Evaluation criteria
1. Past performance	Internal to the institution	To determine whether the trend in the institution's performance has been improving or not.
2. Microfinance industry performance	• Inventory of MFIs • National survey (in-depth) of selected MFIs	To determine how the institution has performed relative to the 'average' in the industry.
3. Benchmarks	A priori: set based on documentation of best microfinance practice and experience	To determine whether the institution has overcome the 'hurdle'.
4. Planned performance	Internal and external to the institution. Internal sources include the budget; strategic and business plans. External sources include those based on industry data, such as those gathered in surveys.	To determine whether the targeted performance has been attained.

Source Microfinance Coalition for Standards

The indicators to be observed (which seem to be based quite closely on those of the Donor Working Group, published in 1995) are categorised by the DSMP in its conceptual framework as under:

(1) *Organisational and operational factors*
- organisation structure, culture and capacity
- management information systems
- operational efficiency

(2) *Outreach and services*
- scale and depth of outreach
- microfinance services

(3) *Financial sustainability*
- self-sufficiency
- portfolio quality

Developing performance standards such as those sketched out above is the first step in a process. Further steps include assisting MFIs to adopt the standards, and moving beyond that to assure widespread implementation of them by MFIs. This may involve some regulation of the MFI sector (whether self-regulation or the external imposition of standards upon the industry).

In any case, the DSMP is working towards the development of a 'capacity measurement system' to identify the strengths and weaknesses of individual MFIs. This implies a rating system for MFIs based on the indicators which have been developed. A rating system would be useful to domestic financial institutions which need information to assess the bankability of MFIs. Government and donor agencies would find a rating system for MFIs useful in indicating the need for interventions and support.[1]

Finally, the coalition suggests that a regulatory and supervisory framework will have to be developed for the microfinance industry: 'This may involve establishing a system of accrediting NGOs which have adopted the standards, a system of reporting and validation and a system of rewards or penalties for compliance or non-compliance'. The coalition hopes to arrive at an agreed consensus on standards and to present its recommendations to the Philippines National Microcredit Summit to be held in 1998.

In summary, considerable progress has already been made by the Microfinance Coalition for Standards and the two major microfinance networks, APPEND and PHILNET. The work of the Developing Standards for Microfinance Project is receiving support from USAID. This could lead to the development of systems of 'capacity measurement' for MFIs and a rating system which would be useful to domestic financial institutions and government and donor agencies.

It is appropriate to continue support for the development of a regulatory and supervisory framework by the microfinance industry itself, leading to a system of accrediting NGOs. To the extent this goes beyond self-regulation, close liaison between the microfinance coalition and PCFC, the National Credit Council and other interested agencies should be encouraged.

4 Regulation of banks

4.1 Licensing and minimum capital requirements

All institutions which engage in the lending of funds obtained from the public through the receipt of deposits are required to be approved by the board of Bangko Sentral for licensing as banking institutions. As such, NGOs wishing to expand their sources of funds by accepting deposits from the public need to become licensed as financial institutions. At least two NGOs, in Nueva Ecija and Zambales provinces, have already become rural banks and some other NGOs are considering becoming banks.

As noted above, there are a number of different types of banks, in particular, commercial banks, thrift banks (including savings and mortgage banks, private development banks, and stock savings and loans associations), and rural and cooperative banks.

All of these banks are regulated by Bangko Sentral, but they are licensed under different Acts of Parliament. The General Banking Act defines the scope of activities of each type of bank in broad terms. In addition, the Rural Banks Act 1992 provides for the creation, organisation and operation of rural banks, the Cooperative Code of the Philippines (1989) governs the organisation and operations of cooperative banks, and thrift banks are covered under the Thrift Banks Act 1995.

---

1 At the fifth meeting of its Policy Advisory Group in February 1998, the coalition considered detailed draft performance indicators for MFIs, together with a proposed 'scoring system' which would translate the performance of individual MFIs to an overall rating (from AAA, 'outstanding' to C, 'poor'). The coalition is thus continuing to progress towards its goals (see Microfinance Coalition for Standards 1998).

The most significant difference concerns the minimum capital requirements for banks. The minimum capital required to establish a commercial bank is Ps4.5 billion ($180 million) for expanded commercial banks (which combine the powers of commercial banks and investment houses), and Ps2 billion ($80 million) for ordinary commercial banks. However, capital requirements for other types of banks are much lower. The requirement for a thrift bank is Ps250 million ($10 million) if the head office is in Metro Manila, and Ps40 million ($1.6 million) if the head office is outside Metro Manila. In the case of rural banks, minimum capital varies from Ps20 million ($800,000) down to Ps2 million ($80,000), depending on the location of the head office. There are also minimum capital requirements for establishing bank branches, with higher requirements for commercial banks than for thrift banks and rural banks. A national cooperative bank requires minimum share capital of Ps200 million ($8 million), while a local cooperative bank may have minimum share capital of as little as Ps20 million ($800,000).

The regulatory framework in the Philippines which enables rural banks and local cooperative banks to be established with modest capital requirements is a positive feature of the environment of microfinance in that country. Together with similarly favourable provisions in Indonesia, this provides a model for other countries in the region, since such banks have demonstrated their capacity to access the poor.

For MFIs wishing to expand their operations by accepting deposits from the general public, the requirements for obtaining a banking licence as a rural bank or even a thrift bank would not appear to be too difficult to overcome. At least two NGOs have already obtained licences as rural banks. The largest NGO engaged in microfinance, TSPI Development Corporation, is currently applying for a licence as a thrift bank, and a number of other NGOs are also looking at becoming banks.

4.2 Interest rates

Deregulation of interest rates in the banking sector, with respect to both deposits and advances, is now complete. This has established an environment in which the involvement of regulated financial institutions with microfinance can flourish if other conditions are favourable. Interest rate distortions in the market for microfinance, arising from the activities of government line agencies engaged in a proliferation of subsidised credit programs, are a continuing disincentive to private initiative in the field.

4.3 Prudential regulation and supervision

Regulatory and prudential requirements differ between the different types of banks. Capital adequacy ratios are generally the same for all banks at 10 per cent of risk-weighted assets. However, some large commercial banks are permitted to lend out 12.5 times their capital base with approval from the Monetary Board. Reserve requirements differ between the different types of banks. Since July 1997, the reserve requirement for demand, savings and time deposits and deposit substitutes is in general 13 per cent. However, there are lower requirements in the case of savings and time deposits for thrift banks (11 per cent) and rural banks (5 per cent). In addition to these reserve requirements, all financial intermediaries are required to maintain a liquidity reserve equal to 2 per cent of deposit liabilities and deposit substitutes, in the form of short-term market yielding government securities.

Bangko Sentral does not require that loans by banks be secured, except in the case of loans to directors, officers and stockholders. However, the central bank has issued detailed instructions concerning loan loss provisioning, and loans without collateral are treated differently to secured loans. Loans in arrears are divided into three categories based on a number of criteria, with a required loan loss provision of 25 per cent for the unsecured portion of substandard loans, 50 per cent for doubtful loans and 100 per cent for loss loans. The categorisation of loans depends in part on the security. For instance, an unsecured loan is generally classified as substandard where it is past due for more than ninety days, whereas a secured loan is generally only classified as substandard where it is past due for more than six months.

Reporting requirements are broadly similar for all banks. All banks are required to submit a weekly report to Bangko Sentral on their reserve holdings and capital position. In addition, they are required to submit a consolidated balance sheet on a monthly basis, and a quarterly report on income and expenses. All banks are required to have articles of incorporation and by-laws covering matters such as the stock and stockholders, meetings of stockholders, board of directors and similar matters.

Thrift banks and rural banks are exempted from all taxes and charges, except for income tax and local taxes and charges, for five years from the date they commence operations. Existing rural banks received tax exemption for five years when the Rural Banks Act 1992 was passed, while existing thrift banks also received tax exemption for five years under the Thrift Banks Act 1995.

5 Summary and recommendations

Poverty remains the most important development problem for the Philippines. The incidence of poverty is relatively high, due in part to a disappointing economic growth performance and the inequitable distribution of income. The Presidential Commission to Fight Poverty created by the Philippines government has identified major strategies to overcome poverty in which microfinance is given an explicit role.

The Social Reform Agenda of the government focuses on basic needs of the poor. The 'flagship program on credit' flowing from this agenda has resulted in a number of initiatives, among them the establishment of the People's Credit and Finance Corporation (PCFC), a second tier financial institution. The establishment of the National Credit Council (NCC) has enabled the articulation of a strategy for microfinance in which the role of the private sector (including MFIs) is emphasised, and an enabling policy environment is to be established. The Philippines is unique in the degree to which an explicit role is accorded to microfinance in national poverty strategies, and in the coherence of the policy framework for microfinance (although much remains to be done to reconcile the practice of government agencies with that framework).

The Philippine financial system includes both commercial banks and a number of categories of smaller banks. These serve limited geographic areas and have comparatively low minimum capital requirements. Among the specialised government banks, the Land Bank of the Philippines plays a particularly important role in relation to microfinance and MFIs. A substantial degree of financial sector liberalisation has occurred since the early 1980s. Interest rate ceilings no longer apply for bank deposits or lending. However, the financial system remains relatively undeveloped.

In general, the banks do not provide financial services to poor clients. Small rural banks are best placed to do so and the World Bank has identified cooperative rural banks as capable of providing savings and credit services to the poor on a sustainable basis. The cooperative credit movement includes many grassroots microfinance institutions, some of which succeed in reaching the poor.

The Philippines has a dynamic NGO movement, with some 500 NGOs providing microfinance services, although so far only a small proportion are seriously concerned to operate on a sustainable basis. There is a large number of government credit programs designed to provide financial services to the poor, many of which employ microfinance institutions as conduits to channel credit to the poor. Perhaps as many as 140 such programs exist, involving scores of line agencies of government; these are characterised by inefficiency, unsustainability due to the prevalence of subsidies, leakage of benefits to the non-poor, duplication of services, the distortion of financial markets and the discouragement of private initiative.

Arrangements for direct support

Channel government lending through MFIs

The National Credit Council (NCC) has among its objectives to rationalise government lending programs, develop a national credit delivery system and encourage private sector participation. Rationalisation of government credit activity requires that line agencies should focus their involvement in credit programs on technical assistance and capacity building. Government lending to the very poor should be conducted by specialised government financial institutions (most notably PCFC) and be channelled through microfinance institutions. Donor agencies should also be encouraged to channel support for microfinance through PCFC, and to avoid funding unsustainable credit operations mounted by line agencies. NCC's efforts at rationalisation confront powerful bureaucratic and political interests. These must be overcome. Since the term of the current Administration expires in mid-1998, the time available to the council is limited, and sustained political support at the highest level will be required for it to complete its task.

Allow even-handed support for MFIs

The People's Credit and Finance Corporation (PCFC) is a second tier institution responsible for nurturing and funding sustainable microfinance institutions. It faces the challenge of preparing itself for privatisation while performing these tasks and extending the outreach of the MFIs with which it is dealing. PCFC is currently funding a wide range of MFIs. It funds institutions, not programs or models. However, a major multilateral loan for PCFC has been provided exclusively in support of MFIs replicating the Grameen Bank approach. The World Bank has noted that undue emphasis on Grameen replication as the only way to reach the ultra poor may discourage the expansion of other successful models in the Philippines. PCFC should be permitted to be even-handed in its support of MFIs. This even-handedness should apply also to the 'pass-on' rates of interest applied in PCFC's funding programs. If these are permitted to differ according to the source of the funds, distortions will be introduced into the microfinance market.

PCFC's drive to profitability is necessary to permit privatisation to take place. But the obligation to support capacity building for MFIs places a strain on the corporation's profitability. It will be necessary either to quarantine the costs of capacity building from normal operating costs for the purpose of calculating profit and loss or, alternatively, for the government and donor agencies to make special arrangements to permit the corporation to perform its institutional development role. After privatisation the government will need to accept substantially greater responsibility for capacity building of MFIs. In this regard the Punla sa Tao model of public/private partnership appears to be promising. It should be adequately resourced and be creatively involved in collaboration with PCFC and the microfinance sector.

Directed credit schemes, in the Philippines as elsewhere, are diminishing in importance. This process should continue; direction of credit is not a cost-effective solution, especially in the Philippines where conditions are favourable for market forces increasingly to provide the necessary microfinance services.

Encourage commercial bank involvement with microfinance

Financial linkages between banks and specialised microfinance institutions are one means by which microfinance can be integrated with the formal financial sector. Tax breaks available to the charitable foundations of private commercial banks have permitted them to explore such relationships. A number of banks which commenced financing MFIs in this way are now making the transition to fully commercial financing, although current economic difficulties in the Philippines are retarding this process. The publication of positive guidelines in support of such linkages as has been done in India by NABARD would be helpful in overcoming the conservatism of the commercial banks in relation to such activities. Bangko Sentral would be the appropriate agency to encourage private commercial banks in this regard.

Notwithstanding current economic difficulties, market forces, arising from the progressive impact of financial sector liberalisation, and a growing awareness of the potential for savings mobilisation are factors at work in support of linkages. Mainstream commercial banks are acquiring or setting up small banks for this purpose and display growing interest in agency arrangements with NGOs. This is a positive development and should be encouraged.

Support rationalisation of government credit schemes

A multiplicity of government credit schemes has flourished in the Philippines: up to 150 such schemes involve more than 40 line agencies of government. In general, these supply-led and subsidised government credit programs have proved ineffective in tackling poverty. Moreover, by distorting microfinance markets, subsidies have impeded the advance to sustainability of genuine MFIs. Rationalisation would mean that credit would be administered by financial institutions (principally PCFC) while line agencies would confine themselves to providing technical assistance in the areas of their special competence. This is an appropriate objective and the necessary political leadership should be summoned to achieve it.

Regulation of non-bank microfinance institions

Clarify tax-exemption procedures for NGOs

The broad regulatory framework for NGOs in the Philippines is conducive to their growth by reason of its light touch. However, there appears to be some anomaly in the taxation treatment of NGOs compared with rural banks and cooperatives. The procedures for exempting bona fide NGOs from tax should be clarified and simplified and such exemptions should not unreasonably be withheld.

Allow NGOs to expand handling of savings

NGOs are not permitted to accept deposits from the general public; informal deposit-taking relationships with clients occur in a legal grey area. NGOs should be permitted to collect compulsory savings from clients in connection with the provision of other microfinance services. In the same context, they should probably also be permitted to handle voluntary savings while satisfying agreed standards of accounting and reporting. The review of the Banking Act may provide an opportunity to consider these issues.

With regard to the broader issue of a separate regulatory framework for MFIs, it is relevant to note that most observers in other countries do not think MFIs should be subject to official prudential regulation and supervision. This much is clear from the other country studies conducted in parallel with our work in the Philippines. The answer is more likely to lie in the development of effective mechanisms for self-regulation, perhaps combined with guidance from second tier institutions.

Establish coordinated performance and accreditation standards for MFIs

It is clear that some setting of standards for MFIs would be appropriate. Agencies with oversight of MFIs, notably PCFC, but also the National Credit Council and LandBank, are in a position to exert influence. For the credit cooperatives, the deposit insurance facility being created by NATCCO may also provide the opportunity for setting standards, perhaps leaving the Cooperative Development Authority more free to concentrate on its developmental functions for the great mass of cooperatives.

The National Credit Council is equipped to articulate regulatory standards, although it does not have the working relationship with MFIs enjoyed by PCFC. LandBank (for credit cooperatives implementing government programs) and NATCCO (for private grassroots cooperatives) are also positioned to play a role. All have commenced to set criteria for accreditation for MFIs, and to define performance standards for them.

It is important that there be coordination between the standards set by these agencies; if the National Credit Council is to have a continuing existence this function could rest with it. Otherwise, PCFC should accept responsibility for coordinating standards for MFIs. In this regard, the experience of PKSF in Bangladesh should prove instructive.

Where initiative exists within the private sector to self-regulate, this is usually preferable to having standards imposed. Considerable progress has already been made by the Microfinance Coalition for Standards and the two major microfinance networks, APPEND and PHILNET. The work of the Developing Standards for Microfinance Project is receiving support from USAID. This could lead to the development of systems for capacity measurement for MFIs and a rating system which would be useful to domestic financial institutions and government and donor agencies.

It is appropriate to continue support for the development of a regulatory and supervisory framework by the microfinance industry itself, leading to a system of accrediting NGOs. To the extent that this goes beyond self-regulation, close liaison between the microfinance coalition, PCFC, the National Credit Council and other interested agencies should be encouraged.

Regulation of banks

The present regulatory provisions which make it relatively straightforward for successful MFIs to obtain rural or thrift banking licences should be maintained or even liberalised further. The modest capital requirements for establishing small banks are a positive feature of Philippine legislation.

References

APRACA. 1996. *Regional Performance of Projects Linking Banks and Self-Help Groups.* Asia-Pacific Rural and Agricultural Credit Association, Bangkok.

Center for Community Services.1997. Coop Review: *Profile and Performance of NATCCO Affiliates.* National Confederation of Cooperatives, Quezon City.

Chua, Ronald T. 1996. *Microenterprise Development in the Philippines: A Country Review.* Study prepared for the Asian Development Bank, Manila.

Intal, J. Ponciano & Llanto, Gilberto. 1998. 'Financial reform and development in the Philippines, 1980–1997: Imperatives, performance and challenges'. Discussion paper no.98–02, Philippines Institute for Development Studies, Manila.

LandBank. 1996. *Annual Report* 1995. Land Bank of the Philippines, Manila.

Llanto, Gilberto M., Garcia, Edgardo & Callanta, Ruth. 1996. *'An assessment of the capacity and financial performance of microfinance institutions: The Philippine Case'.* Discussion paper no.96-12, Philippine Institute for Development Studies.

Luang, Eduardo & Vasquez, Malena. 1997. 'Philippines'. In *Regulation and Supervision of Microfinance Systems* ed. Craig Churchill. The Microfinance Network, Washington D.C.

Microfinance Coalition for Standards. 1997. NGO microfinance standards: A conceptual framework. Preliminary draft, September.

Microfinance Coalition for Standards. 1998. Fifth Policy Advisory Group Meeting Workshop. 27 February.

NATCCO. 1990. *The Cooperative Code of the Philippines.* National Confederation of Cooperatives, Manila.

NATCCO. 1996. NATCCO *Annual Report.* National Confederation of Cooperatives, Manila.

Punla Development Trust. *Empowering the Poor to Help Themselves.* Manila (nd).

Republic of the Philippines, House of Representatives. 1997a. Draft bill for an Act institutionalizing a national strategy for poverty alleviation. 5 May.

Republic of the Philippines. 1997b. *Social Reform Agenda: 1997 Poverty Alleviation Fund.* Manila.

del Rosario, Ramon S. 1995. *The Philippine Financial System: An Overview.* Asian Institute of Management, Eugenio Lopez Foundation, Manila.

World Bank. 1996. *A Strategy to Fight Poverty: The Philippines.* World Bank, Washington D.C., March.

Persons consulted

Mr Noel Alcaide	Executive Director Kabalikat para sa Maunlad na Buhay, Inc. (KMBI)
Mr Joselito S. Almario	Fiscal Policy and Planning Office Department of Finance
Ms Cecile del Castillo	Chairperson, Policy Advisory Group Philippine Coalition for Microfinance Standards, and President, PHILNET
Professor Ronald T. Chua	Asian Centre for Entrepreneurship Asian Institute of Management
Mr Jose Zacarias Ejercito	Bank Officer, Supervisory Reports and Studies Office Bangko Sentral ng Pilipinas
Mr Eduardo C. Jimenez	Executive Director Association of Philippine Partners in Enterprise Development (APPEND)
Ms Teresita M. De Leon	General Manager National Federation of Cooperatives
Professor Victor S. Limlingan	Center for Development Management Asian Institute of Management
Mr Ricardo P. Lirio	Managing Director, Supervision and Examination II Bangko Sentral ng Pilipinas
Dr Gilberto M. Llanto	Research Fellow, Monetary Economics and Public Finance, Philippine Institute for Development Studies
Mr Ambrocio U. Mana-Ay	Chief of Operations Presidential Commission to Fight Poverty
Mr Jose Medina	Director People's Credit and Finance Corporation
Ms Lucila S. Nolasco	Bank Officer, Office of the Managing Director, SEII Bangko Sentral ng Pilipinas
Mr Benjamin T. Montemayor	Executive Director TSPI Development Corporation
Ms Emelina M. Santos	Assistant General Manager National Federation of Cooperatives
Mr Glenn Sumido	Special Assistant to the President Land Bank of the Philippines
Ms Marlene G. Tiquia	Bank Officer, Supervisory Reports and Studies Office Bangko Sentral ng Pilipinas
Mr Rolando Victoria	Executive Director Alalay Sa Kaunlaran Sa Gitnang Luzon Inc (ASKI)

Sri Lanka

1 Introduction and background

1.1 Key demographic and economic data

Sri Lanka is an island of some 66,000 square kilometres, located south-east of the Indian subcontinent. The population was 18.1 million in 1995. This equates to a population density of 274 people per square kilometre, below Bangladesh (832) and India (283), but higher than for the other six countries included in this study. Between 1990 and 1995 the population grew by a modest 1.3 per cent per annum, with a total fertility rate of 2.3 births per woman in 1995. These figures suggest that Sri Lanka has proceeded further along the demographic transition than any other country in this study apart from Thailand.

With a per capita income of $700 in 1995, average incomes in Sri Lanka are much higher than those of any other country in South Asia, but below those of the four Southeast Asian countries included in the study. GNP per capita increased by a reasonably healthy 2.6 per cent per year between 1985 and 1995, above the growth rate for most countries in South Asia, but slightly below India and well below the dynamic Southeast Asian economies of Thailand, Indonesia and Malaysia.

The sectoral allocation of GDP also suggests that, in terms of economic development, Sri Lanka is between the other countries of South Asia on the one hand, and the Southeast Asian countries on the other. In 1995 agriculture contributed 23 per cent of GDP, the lowest in South Asia but higher than for any of the Southeast Asian countries included in the study. Industry contributed 25 per cent, while the remaining 52 per cent came from services. On the other hand only 22 per cent of the population lived in urban areas, lower than for all countries in the study except Bangladesh and Nepal.

The picture regarding human development is noteworthy. Sri Lanka has long emphasised human development, and it is widely recognised that social indicators here are generally much better than for other countries with similar income levels. For instance, Sri Lanka achieved a score of 0.711 on the UNDP human development index for 1994, higher than for all countries in this study except Thailand and Malaysia. While GDP per capita was lower than in Indonesia and the Philippines, human development was higher. In 1995 Sri Lanka had the highest life expectancy at birth of any of the nine countries included in the study (72 years), the second lowest infant mortality rate (16 per 1,000 live births), and the third highest adult literacy rate (90 per cent).

1.2 Poverty

Estimates of poverty

Official poverty statistics in Sri Lanka have been derived using broad rules of thumb, rather than rigorously derived estimates of the poverty line, and do not necessarily provide a clear indication of the incidence of poverty. World Bank (1995) estimates suggest that the incidence of poverty in Sri Lanka is considerably lower than in any other country in South

Asia but slightly higher than in three of the four countries in Southeast Asia included in this study.

The official poverty line in Sri Lanka is based on monthly household income. In 1977 it was set at Rs300 ($5.40) per month per household. It remained at this level until 1989, when it was increased to Rs700 ($12.70) per month per household. Based on the official poverty line, the government estimates that the percentage of households below the poverty line has fallen from 62 per cent in 1979 to 37 per cent in 1991 and 39 per cent in 1994.

The poverty line has been adjusted infrequently, and has therefore tended to become out of date between adjustments. Partly for this reason, the official poverty line has not always been used in targeting households under the government's anti-poverty programs. For instance, in the second round of the Janasaviya program beginning in 1991, poor households were selected on the basis of a set of qualitative criteria determined at the sub-district level. The National Development Trust Fund (NDTF) defines the poor as those with a household income of less than Rs1,500 ($27.20) per month, more than double the official poverty line.

The World Bank (1995) has conducted a more rigorous study of poverty in Sri Lanka. It notes that in the post-independence period and especially since 1965, Sri Lanka has made good progress in reducing poverty. Between 1965 and 1985 there was a rapid decline in poverty, propelled by rapid growth in per capita income and consumption, and a stable and egalitarian distribution of household income. Between 1985 and 1990, poverty continued to decline as a result of an improvement in the distribution of consumption.

The World Bank study derived estimates of the incidence of poverty for 1985–86 and 1990–91 from socioeconomic surveys undertaken by the Department of Census and Statistics. Based on a poverty line of Rs471.20 ($8.50) per person per month, the incidence of poverty declined from 27.3 per cent of the population in 1985–86 to 22.4 per cent in 1990–91. Using 1995 population data, this equates to around 4.1 million people. The incidence of poverty was 24.4 per cent in the rural areas, 18.3 per cent in the urban areas, and 12.6 per cent in the estates (around 7 per cent of the population, predominantly Sri Lankan Tamils, live on estates in the plantation sector). These estimates are significantly lower than the official estimates. Using a higher poverty line of Rs565.44 ($10.20) per person per month, the incidence of poverty declined from 40.6 per cent in 1985–86 to 35.3 per cent in 1990–91.

The data also enabled some conclusions about the distribution of poverty. Poverty was lower in the western region than in other parts of the country. Surprisingly, female-headed households did not have a significantly higher incidence of poverty than male-headed households. The incidence of poverty among Sinhalese and Sri Lankan Tamils was also about the same. However, it should be stressed that because of lack of data as a result of the civil war, the calculations exclude the north and east provinces. Given the civil war it is likely that the incidence of poverty is higher in these regions than in the rest of the country, and poverty in these regions is likely to have increased between the two surveys.

Policies for poverty reduction

Clearly, the level of poverty is affected by the full range of the government's policies, including macroeconomic, investment and human development policies, as well as policies specifically directed at reducing poverty. As noted above, the government has placed a great deal of emphasis on education and health policies in particular, and there is considerable evidence that these have been very effective in reducing poverty. This discussion, however, focuses on those government policies that are specifically targeted to the poor.

The central component of the government's anti-poverty policies is the Samurdhi program, with a budget of Rs10 billion ($180 million) in 1997. The program commenced in 1995, but incorporated elements from a series of earlier government programs such as the Janasaviya program, which operated from 1989 to 1994.

One component of the Samurdhi program provides direct welfare payments to an estimated 1.2 million families at the bottom of the income scale. Direct welfare payments to poor households, whether in the form of food stamps or cash, have existed since 1979 and are far more prevalent in Sri Lanka than in any other country included in this study. The poorest of the poor, around 45,000 families with incomes of around Rs500 ($9.10) per month, receive a direct income transfer of Rs1,000 ($18.10) per month. Around 760,000 poor families, with incomes of around Rs1,000 ($18.10) per month, receive an income transfer of Rs500 ($9.10) per month. Another 220,000 families who are slightly better off receive a transfer of Rs200 ($3.60) per month, while another 180,000 receive a transfer of Rs100 ($1.80) per month.

In addition, government-appointed 'animators' establish a Samurdhi Task Force in each village. These task forces undertake five activities. First, they conduct a family profile survey to determine the number of poor families for the provision of welfare. Second, based on the information gathered, they identify community works to benefit the village and provide employment. Third, they encourage small savings and credit activities within the village (this Samurdhi microfinance program is described in more detail below). Fourth, they encourage and assist persons to undertake self-employment projects. And fifth, they implement nutrition programs for vulnerable groups.

1.3 Overview of the financial system

The formal financial system in Sri Lanka includes eight domestic commercial banks and 18 foreign commercial banks, with a total of 1,060 branches between them as at December 1996. The two state commercial banks, the Bank of Ceylon and the People's Bank, have by far the largest branch networks. There are also a number of specialised financial institutions, including the National Savings Bank, two development banking institutions and a number of non-bank financial institutions. In addition, there are 17 regional rural development banks (RRDBs). The above institutions are all supervised by the Central Bank of Sri Lanka.

In the past, the two state commercial banks, the Bank of Ceylon and the People's Bank, have lent heavily in the rural areas. While they still have extensive outreach in the rural areas, their lending to agriculture has declined in real terms in recent years as they have been forced to become more competitive. They operate a number of loan schemes designed for small entrepreneurs, and act as conduits for some of the government's microfinance programs. Except for these government microfinance programs, however, they have not tended to reach the poor. Moreover, repayment rates on small loans have tended to be low. A more successful program is the small microfinance program of a private commercial bank, Hatton National Bank, discussed in more detail below.

The RRDBs were established by the central bank in 1985 as specialist institutions for lending for rural development. With some exceptions, they have tended to lend primarily to borrowers in the rural areas who are better off. Some commentators suggested that they have been subject to political interference, and their repayment performance has been poor. The government has recently passed legislation to amalgamate the existing RRDBs into larger rural development banks at the provincial level. It is understood that it has also given some consideration to floating shares in some or all of the new rural development banks, to expand their capital base and enable them to operate more independently.

Additional to the banks discussed above are the cooperative rural banks (CRBs), which are supervised by the Department of Cooperative Development. They have extensive branch networks, with a total of some 1,250 branches and 4 million depositors at end-1995. These are operated by the state-dominated multi-purpose cooperative societies, and are quite separate from the thrift and credit cooperative movement. Their main activity is to mobilise savings, which are deposited primarily with the People's Bank and used in its lending operations. Their own lending accounts for only around 40 per cent of their deposits, and around half of this is related to their pawnbroking operations. Moreover, it is understood that they lend mainly to people in rural areas who are better off. Hence, CRBs provide only very limited microfinance services.

Since 1990, there has been considerable deregulation of the banking system under a series of reforms sponsored by the World Bank and the International Monetary Fund. While in the past the central bank was heavily involved in refinancing loans by commercial banks to priority sectors, this has been withdrawn. There has also been a series of reforms aimed at strengthening regulation and supervision of banks, and bringing banking supervision into line with international practices. Areas that have been strengthened include classification and provisioning of non-performing loans and advances, capital adequacy requirements, and accounting and auditing standards. Most exchange controls have also been removed.

Surprisingly, macroeconomic data suggest a lack of depth in the banking system, with a ratio of money and quasi money to GDP of only 31.8 per cent in 1995. This is lower than for any other country in the study for which data are available, including much poorer countries such as Bangladesh and Nepal. While the reasons for this are not clear, it may reflect a reliance on thrift and credit cooperative societies instead of banks. Unlike bank deposits, deposits with thrift and credit cooperative societies are not included in the definition of quasi money.

There are no restrictions applying to interest rates for banks or other financial institutions, either for deposits or loans. According to the World Bank's World Development Report for 1997, in 1995 bank interest rates for both deposits (16.1 per cent) and loans (14.7 per cent) were considerably higher than the inflation rate (7.7 per cent). While these data suggest that interest rates on deposits were higher than those applying to loans, data from the central bank suggest that the prime lending rate charged by commercial banks was actually 20.1 per cent. There are no longer any requirements on banks to lend to particular priority sectors of the economy. However, there is an incentive for them to lend for agriculture, with the government paying an interest subsidy of 7.5 per cent on short-term crop lending. To be eligible for the subsidy, banks must lend at an interest rate of 16 per cent. This subsidy was to be reviewed at the end of 1997.

1.4 Overview of microfinance

Since 1989, microfinance has been a central element of the government's poverty reduction programs. The Presidential Commission on Finance and Banking (1992) considered the appropriate policy for credit to the poor. It concluded that:

> . . . a pluralistic approach which provides scope for the involvement of a wide array of financial institutions, cooperatives, NGOs and a range of governmental and informal agencies, each employing different techniques and strategies based on their different credit cultures, together with market based interest rates and adequate support services, would be the appropriate policy to adopt in order to improve the access of the rural population to formal credit institutions (p.122).

The Janasaviya program, which operated from 1989 to 1994, included a microcredit scheme where loans were disbursed to poor beneficiaries for income-generating projects. Loans were made on the referral of village-level support teams, and were disbursed through the state commercial banks, RRDBs and CRBs. In addition, the Janasaviya Trust Fund (JTF) was established in 1991, one of its main functions being to manage a credit fund for disbursing credit to partner organisations, for on-lending to beneficiaries for income-generating self-employment projects. The JTF, now known as the National Development Trust Fund (NDTF), is still in operation. However, recent attention has shifted to the Samurdhi program, which replaced the Janasaviya program in 1995. Under the Samurdhi program, village task forces select poor borrowers to receive loans from a fund managed by the two state banks.

As noted above and with some exceptions, the commercial banks and RRDBs do not engage in microfinance to any significant extent except as a conduit for government programs. While the CRBs are active in mobilising savings in the rural areas, they do not provide microfinance loans to any significant extent. Other than the direct government programs, the major institutions engaged in microfinance in Sri Lanka are the thrift and credit cooperative societies (TCCSs), and a small number of non-governmental organisations (NGOs).

TCCSs operate throughout Sri Lanka, although their coverage and strength varies between regions. As at end-1996 there were 8,340 primary societies with a total membership of 772,000. Given that the total population is only around 18.1 million, this clearly represents a significant proportion of households in Sri Lanka. Around 55 per cent of members are women. The societies collect savings from their members, and provide loans for income-generating activities and consumption. The credit cooperative movement in Sri Lanka has been far more successful than in most other countries in the region. For instance, Hulme, Montgomery and Bhattacharya (1996, p.177) argue that:

> Cooperatives in developing countries have a weak record for helping poor people to improve their living standards and for assisting microentrepreneurs. The experience of thrift and credit cooperative societies in Sri Lanka stands in marked contrast to this general situation and supports the case for a reconsideration of the role of credit cooperatives in rural finance. Since 1978 the thrift and credit movement has pursued a strategy of rapidly expanding its membership and activities, and of shifting from an orientation towards middle income households to a greater focus on poorer rural people.

Membership of the TCCSs is open to anyone and is not confined to the poor, and it is understood that most members are not poor. Nevertheless, the movement has served as a vehicle for various targeted poverty lending programs operated by the government and donor agencies. Moreover, it has also had its own projects for lending a portion of its funds to low-income groups.

There are also a number of NGOs involved in microfinance. In 1986 Sarvodaya, the largest NGO in Sri Lanka, established a microfinance division called Sarvodaya Economic Enterprises Development Services (SEEDS). It provides microfinance services through some 2,000 independent primary societies, with a combined membership of around 150,000 households. Other well-regarded NGOs involved in microfinance include Women's Development Foundation, People's Rural Development Association and Janashakti Banku Sangam. It should be noted that a large number of credit NGOs have sprung up in recent years as a result of government programs such as NDTF, but it is understood that most of these are not operating on a very sound basis.

One innovative microfinance program is the Gami Pubuduwa Upadeshaka (GPU) scheme operated by Hatton National Bank, a private commercial bank. The program was introduced in 1989, and is aimed at rural and semi-urban unemployed youth. It is based on the concept of 'barefoot banking'. Essentially, the GPU officers function as a linkage between the bank and the rural community, with most banking transactions carried out in the village, rather than at a bank branch. At present there are around 7,000 borrowers under the program, and the program has also been very successful in terms of savings mobilisation. In addition, the bank has a linkage program for lending to the poor, involving around fifteen NGOs. The bank's microfinance program has recently been considered in detail by the World Bank (Gallardo, Randhawa & Sacay 1997).

One concern expressed about microfinance in Sri Lanka is the lack of targeting. The TCCSs and most of the NGOs discussed above do not specifically target the poor, and no data on the number of borrowers who are poor are available. The major government programs, such as NDTF, the Small Farmers and Landless Credit (SFLC) project and the Samurdhi program are, in principle, targeted to the poor. Where TCCSs and NGOs have received funds under NDTF and the SFLC project, they have been required to establish targeted cells within their overall lending programs. However, it is understood that the targeting guidelines in the government programs have often not been followed by either NGOs or government agencies, and there has been little if any monitoring of the extent to which these projects have reached the poor.

The government microfinance programs, most particularly the Samurdhi program, do not operate on a sustainable basis. Government has provided the loan capital, and this is lent through the state commercial banks to final borrowers at highly concessional interest rates (for example, 10 per cent under the Samurdhi program). Moreover, administrative costs associated with the village task forces are borne by the budget. On the other hand, the TCCSs and some of the major NGOs, such as SEEDS and the People's Rural Development Association, are more concerned about sustainability. While they still rely on donor funds to a considerable extent, these programs meet most of their operational costs from interest earnings. Few data on the smaller NGOs are available, but it is understood that they rely much more heavily on donor funds and cheap loan capital, and are not operating on a sustainable basis.

2 Arrangements for direct support

2.1 Support for specialised microfinance institutions

National Development Trust Fund

In the past, the government and World Bank have provided extensive support for microfinance through the National Development Trust Fund (NDTF), previously known as the Janasaviya Trust Fund (JTF). In addition, many donor agencies have provided direct support to particular microfinance institutions (MFIs).

NDTF was established in 1991 as a second tier microfinance institution, similar in functions to the Palli Karma Sahayak Foundation (PKSF) in Bangladesh and second tier institutions in other countries. It was incorporated under the Trusts Ordinance, and is governed by a 20-member board of trustees, selected by the government and comprising around half public-sector and half private-sector representatives. Its main function is to manage a credit fund for disbursing credit to partner organisations, whereby funds are channelled through various microfinance institutions — including NGOs, RRDBs, commercial banks and cooperative rural banks — to final borrowers for income-generating self-employment projects. In addition, it manages a human resources development fund for providing skills training to beneficiaries, a rural works fund, and a nutrition fund.

A credit fund of $35 million was established, with support from the World Bank ($20 million), the government of the Federal Republic of Germany ($10 million) and the government of Sri Lanka ($5 million), and NDTF commenced operations in 1992. By March 1997, it had provided funds totalling Rs1.188 billion ($21.5 million) to 157 partner organisations, including commercial banks, RRDBs, thrift and credit cooperative societies (TCCSs) and NGOs. Of these, around 130 are currently active. NDTF resources are available to partner organisations at an interest rate of 7 per cent, and are on-lent to final borrowers at a minimum interest rate of 19 per cent. Interest rates on loans to final borrowers range between 19 and 36 per cent.

NDTF also provides assistance to partner organisations for institutional development. For instance, it provides funds to small partner organisations for the purchase of equipment. It also employs a number of accounting technicians who are available for secondment to partner organisations to develop their financial management capacity. Nevertheless, a World Bank mission in November 1996 found that NDTF had not focused sufficiently on capacity building among its partner organisations.

NDTF has achieved a solid repayment rate of 90 to 95 per cent on its loans to partner organisations. However, while in some respects the operation of the fund has been reasonable there have been a number of problems, to the extent that the mid-term project review by the World Bank in May 1995 classified the project as a 'problem' project. Difficulties included the following:

(1) There were inadequate processes for selecting partner organisations, with loans given to many organisations without prior experience in managing credit and savings programs. In fact, many were set up specifically to obtain a loan under the program.

(2) There was inadequate monitoring and supervision by NDTF, with many partners having flawed lending programs and maintaining poor accounting records.

(3) There were concerns about the targeting of the program, and guidelines to ensure that the project reached the poor were not always being followed.

These failures appear to reflect a number of factors. Some commentators stated that NDTF was under pressure to disburse funds too quickly, and that there were not enough sound MFIs available to use as partner organisations. It would also appear that it did not have sufficient staff with the technical skills to properly implement the program. Finally, some commentators pointed to politicisation of the organisation. It was reported that the problems experienced under NDTF have done considerable damage to the NGO movement as a whole, and have led to doubts within the government about the capacity of NGOs to engage in microfinance.

More recently, some measures have been implemented to try to overcome these problems, and there appears to have been a marked improvement in the performance of NDTF. It has now adopted more detailed guidelines for the selection of partner organisations, and is taking steps to ensure that these are implemented more rigorously than in the past. A World Bank mission in November 1996 found that the main recommendations of the mid-term project review had been satisfactorily implemented, and advised that the project's problem status should be lifted with immediate effect. Nevertheless, uncertainty as to the future role of NDTF continues to affect its performance. For instance, the World Bank mission found that staff were demotivated because the government has not given clear signals about NDTF's future. Hence, staff turnover was high and it was difficult to recruit good professionals.

The project was originally scheduled to terminate at the end of 1996, but the closing date was extended to the end of 1997. It is intended that there will be a second World Bank project after the first project terminates, and the board of NDTF has recently prepared a concept paper with some ideas for a project design. However, the final shape of any second project is not clear at this stage.

Second tier microfinance institutions such as NDTF offer a number of advantages over the traditional arrangements, whereby donor agencies and governments have provided largely ad hoc support to individual MFIs. They can ensure that different forms of support to a particular MFI are complementary and directed to the same objectives. They can ensure that all MFIs face a level playing field, with support available to all MFIs meeting predetermined standards. And they can require that MFIs face one set of performance and reporting standards, rather than a number of different standards or no standards at all. By lending to MFIs, such institutions also harness the strengths of non-government microfinance programs, which have generally been much more successful than programs involving direct lending by government agencies or commercial banks. It would be appropriate for the government to renew its commitment to NDTF as the primary vehicle for channelling direct support to microfinance in Sri Lanka. This in itself would improve the operating environment for the fund and make it easier to recruit and retain high-quality staff.

NDTF also needs to continue to improve its performance. One critical issue is to ensure that it is not politicised. In practice, this may be difficult to achieve. However, it may be possible to secure greater autonomy by altering the trust deed to:

(1) strengthen the independence of the board of trustees — for instance, by reducing the number of public sector representatives, making fixed-term appointments for a period of five years, and enabling various private and non-government bodies to appoint representatives to the board directly

(2) spell out clearly the objectives of the fund, and allow the board of trustees maximum independence to meet these objectives as they see fit.

It will also be necessary for the fund to set and, more importantly, to enforce appropriate performance and reporting standards for the MFIs that it funds. This will mean striking an appropriate balance between the need to increase outreach and the need to strengthen the capabilities of existing MFIs. On the one hand, given that there is currently only a relatively small number of strong MFIs, it may not be possible to impose standards as rigorous, for instance, as PKSF is able to impose in Bangladesh. On the other hand, it would clearly be counter-productive to provide large loans to small and inexperienced MFIs that do not have the institutional capacity to handle them. It would be appropriate to require all partner organisations to meet a set of minimum standards, and to increase these gradually over time. NDTF is already moving in this direction.

2.2 Support through the banking system

Directed credit schemes

As noted above, there are no longer any requirements on banks to lend to particular priority sectors of the economy. Sri Lanka is slightly unusual in this regard, with Sri Lanka and Bangladesh the only two countries in this study to have abolished all such directed credit schemes.

Small Farmers and Landless Credit Project

There are, however, two major microfinance programs which are channelled through the banking system. One is the Small Farmers and Landless Credit (SFLC) project. This project is executed by the central bank, with the funds channelled through RRDBs to NGOs and other partner organisations. It is funded by the International Fund for Agricultural Development (IFAD), \$6.7 million; the Canadian International Development Agency (CIDA), \$6.6 million; and the government of Sri Lanka (\$4.1 million). The project has operated in four districts since 1990.

A key objective of the project is to establish a cost-effective and sustainable microcredit delivery system for the poorest of the poor. The project has a tighter poverty focus than other programs in Sri Lanka, with borrowers required to have an annual per capita income of less than Rs5600 (\$101), the income necessary to obtain at least 2240 calories per day. This requirement has meant that participating agencies which do not normally means-test their clients, such as the TCCSs and Sarvodaya, have had to establish means-tested components within their broader operations. Another objective is to inculcate savings habits and thrift among the rural poor. Loans are granted only after clients have demonstrated regularity in savings for a period of three to six months.

The central bank lends to the RRDBs at an interest rate of 3 per cent, and they in turn on-lend to partner organisations at 9 to 11 per cent. Partner organisations on-lend to final borrowers at interest rates of between 16 and 20 per cent. A number of NGOs, including the district TCCSs and Sarvodaya, have been involved in the project. They are required to lend using a Grameen-style methodology, although some flexibility is allowed. By end-December 1996, 35,480 loans had been disbursed under the project, with an average loan size of Rs8,560 (\$155) and a recovery rate of 91 per cent. Some 65 per cent of borrowers were women. The project appears to have been reasonably successful, and more successful than most government programs in other countries channelled through the banking system. This may reflect the involvement in many cases of NGOs as conduits between the RRDBs and the final borrowers. However, relatively few data are available, and the project does not appear to have been evaluated rigorously.

The project was scheduled to be completed in December 1997, at which time the central bank would hand over the revolving funds to the participating RRDBs for them to continue the project. The government has applied to IFAD for a second loan, and initial indications are reported to be favourable.

Until now, the project has been executed by the central bank. As with other projects where funds are channelled through the central bank, the central bank lends only to banks under its supervision, in this case RRDBs. It does not lend directly to NGOs or other institutions.

Indeed, this is one factor motivating the federation of TCCSs to apply for a banking licence, to enable it to borrow directly from the central bank under such projects. Where RRDBs on-lend to NGOs, this restriction appears to impose an unnecessary layer between the central bank and the final borrower. To the extent that the central bank continues to be involved in this and other microfinance projects, it would be appropriate for it to lend directly to NGOs rather than through RRDBs.

In any case, the central bank was scheduled to withdraw from the project at the end of 1997 and hand it over to individual RRDBs. This is perhaps symptomatic of a change in the attitude of the central bank towards microfinance. In the past, the central bank has played an important role in rural credit and microfinance by providing refinancing, managing funds such as under the SFLC project, and providing technical support to RRDBs and other MFIs. However, some commentators suggested that the central bank was withdrawing from this kind of development work and concentrating on more traditional central banking functions.

It is not clear that the RRDBs are well placed to take over the project. As noted above, their repayment performance has generally been poor, and some commentators suggested that they have been subject to political interference. Moreover, they are currently being restructured, with the government recently passing legislation to amalgamate the existing RRDBs into larger rural development banks at the provincial level. As such, it is not clear that they have the capacity to undertake effective supervision and monitoring of either loans to final borrowers or loans to NGOs for on-lending. With regard to loans to NGOs, the RRDBs are in any case acting as quasi-second tier institutions and duplicating the role of NDTF. One option would be to consolidate these functions with NDTF, which could continue to lend to both RRDBs and specialist MFIs for on-lending to final borrowers. It may perhaps be appropriate for the government to consider transferring the central bank's loan portfolio under the project to NDTF at the end of the project period.

Samurdhi Development Credit Scheme

The government has introduced two major microfinance programs in recent years:

(1) The Samurdhi Development Credit Scheme is targeted at Samurdhi beneficiaries (that is, those who qualify for welfare payments), and is implemented by the Ministry of Youth Affairs, Sports and Rural Development in collaboration with the People's Bank and Bank of Ceylon.

(2) The Surathura Diriya Programme is designed for the not-so-poor, and is implemented by the central bank in collaboration with the Ministry of Youth Affairs, Sports and Rural Development.

Both schemes commenced operations in 1996. In the case of the Samurdhi program, the government provided Rs500 million ($9.1 million) to the two participating banks for 1997. The program is intended to operate in 12,141 villages. Each village has a Samurdhi task force, and will be allocated credit of Rs41,500 ($750). Additional funds come from the compulsory savings from welfare payments provided to poor households under another arm of the Samurdhi program. The task force selects people to receive loans of between Rs2,500 ($45.30) and Rs10,000 ($181.20). The loans are then released by the relevant bank. The interest rate is 10 per cent, repayable over 6 to 24 months.

The program is targeted to Samurdhi beneficiaries, although it was suggested that in some cases people who are better off have benefited. Village task forces are required to prepare monthly reports on the progress of the schemes. These are provided to the divisions, districts, and ultimately to the head office of the ministry. Because of the newness of the scheme, no data are yet available on repayment rates or other aspects of performance.

Nevertheless, there are some causes for concern in the design of the scheme. The scheme involves state commercial banks lending directly to individual borrowers on the recommendation of village task forces. Commercial banks are generally not geared up to lend directly to poor borrowers in a cost-effective manner. Moreover, the funds for the scheme have been provided to the banks by government, reducing the incentive for the banks to ensure high repayment rates. The village task forces are effectively government-sponsored agencies, albeit at the local level, also with a limited incentive to ensure high repayment rates.

The scheme does not envisage any explicit role for NGOs or other specialist MFIs, either in identifying and motivating borrowers or as direct financial intermediaries. Community-based NGOs generally have a comparative advantage over commercial banks and government agencies in reaching the poor, reflecting factors such as proximity, trust, commitment, flexibility and responsiveness. While the reasons for this lack of involvement by NGOs are not entirely clear, it was suggested that not many NGOs operate in the poorer and more remote villages, and that some of the problems experienced under NDTF have contributed to a suspicion of NGOs in official circles.

A number of commentators suggested that, given its design, it is unlikely that the scheme will achieve high repayment rates. Moreover, the scheme does not appear to use the most cost-effective lending technologies for reaching poor borrowers. It would appear appropriate to provide a role for NGOs and other specialist MFIs, either in identifying and motivating borrowers or as direct financial intermediaries. One alternative would simply be to merge the scheme into NDTF, subject to measures being taken to ensure that NDTF continues to improve its performance.

Moreover, the scheme is not designed to be sustainable. Loanable funds have been provided to the participating banks from the budget. The banks are charging an interest rate of 10 per cent, which would clearly not be sufficient for them to operate the scheme on a commercial basis if they were using their own funds. The cost of administering the village task forces is also being met by the government. Clearly, outreach could be increased significantly, for the same resource cost, if the scheme was redesigned to operate on a more self-sufficient basis. There is also a danger that the availability of cheap credit will crowd out existing NGOs and other specialist MFIs, which do not have access to large subsidies and generally lend at interest rates between 19 and 36 per cent. Regardless of any other changes that might be desirable, it would be appropriate to redesign the scheme to require it to be more self-sufficient.

Linkages between banks and specialised MFIs

As noted above, one highly innovative program in Sri Lanka is the microfinance program operated by Hatton National Bank. The bank involves around fifteen NGOs in the program as a means of reducing costs. In some cases the NGOs operate as non-financial intermediaries, identifying and training borrowers, but the loan contract remains between the bank and the final borrower. In other cases, NGOs deposit members' savings with the bank, and the bank extends a loan to the NGO based on a multiple of the savings. The bank is careful in selecting NGO partners, looking in particular at their management, field structure, the sustainability of their operations and their legal status, but there are no written guidelines about the selection of NGOs.

While there do not appear to be any regulatory impediments to other commercial banks establishing such programs, they have been very reluctant to do so. It would therefore be appropriate for the central bank to take a more active role in encouraging linkages, by documenting and publicising the experience of Hatton National Bank, and issuing clear guidelines that other banks could follow. In this regard, the guidelines issued by the National Bank for Agriculture and Rural Development (NABARD) in India may be a useful starting point (see the India country study), although they would need to be adapted to suit the institutional framework in Sri Lanka.

2.3 Other issues

Some commentators noted that the government had waived loan repayments for small loans by state commercial banks and under some of its own microfinance programs from time to time, and that this had negatively affected the environment for microfinance. The most recent debt forgiveness took place in 1995. The government should avoid debt forgiveness for small loans in the future.

3 Regulation of non-bank microfinance institutions

3.1 The broad regulatory framework

Thrift and credit cooperative societies

The operations of thrift and credit cooperative societies (TCCSs), along with other cooperatives, are governed by the Cooperative Societies Law of 1972. Cooperatives are required to be registered with the Registrar of Cooperative Societies. To be registered, a society must have as its object the promotion of the economic, social or cultural interests of its members in accordance with cooperative principles. It must have at least ten members owning shares with a value of at least Rs100 ($1.80) each, and must have its own by-laws (to a large extent, these are based on a standard model). Moreover, officers from the Department of Cooperative Development supervise the operations of a pre-cooperative for around six months before it is registered, to ensure its economic and organisational viability. Every society is required to have a monthly meeting of the membership. It is also required to have an annual general meeting, and to table an annual report and financial statements. The executive committee is elected from the general body at the annual meeting. Societies are exempt from stamp duties but are liable for all other taxes, including company income tax.

The federation of TCCSs commented that it found the provisions of the Cooperative Societies Law of 1972 and associated regulations restrictive in a number of ways. In particular, the law gives considerable discretion to the departmental minister and to the Registrar of Cooperative Societies, and requires their approval for numerous activities undertaken by the societies. For instance, various staffing decisions, relatively small capital purchases, and even large loans to borrowers require approval from the registrar. The federation stated that it found these requirements cumbersome and inefficient. It would be appropriate to review the regulatory requirements facing cooperatives, with a view to streamlining them and removing unnecessary requirements.

The law specifically permits TCCSs to receive deposits from persons who are not members. Many societies are now actively seeking deposits from non-members by offering competitive interest rates, and deposits by non-members account for around 15 per cent of total deposits. Given the lack of prudential requirements, it is perhaps surprising that societies should be permitted to receive deposits from non-members. Indeed, the federation itself commented that the lack of prudential requirements reduces the credibility of societies as deposit-taking institutions, making it difficult for them to attract deposits on a large scale. This is a major reason for the federation's proposal to establish a bank, which would be subject to more rigorous prudential requirements and would be able to attract a greater volume of deposits. It does not seem appropriate for institutions other than banks, such as TCCSs, to accept deposits from the general public in their own right. When the federation establishes a bank, however, there is no reason why the primary societies should not serve as agents, accepting deposits and offering withdrawals on behalf of the bank.

Non-governmental organisations

Non-governmental organisations (NGOs) engaged in microfinance are subject to a different regulatory regime to cooperatives. There are three avenues for registration. First, some large NGOs, such as Sarvodaya and Lanka Mahila Samiti, have been incorporated under their own Acts of Parliament. This is probably the most complicated method. The NGO will need to arrange for a bill to be introduced into Parliament (generally as a private member's bill), and publish notices in the government gazette and in the newspapers in case anyone objects to their establishment. While the requirements may vary from one Act to another, such NGOs generally need to have a constitution, and to produce an annual report and audited financial statements.

Second, some NGOs are registered as non-profit companies under the Companies Act of 1982. The registration procedure is essentially the same as for companies, except that there is no minimum capital requirement. Non-profit companies are required to have a memorandum and articles of association covering matters such as their objectives, governance and management structure. They are also required to prepare an annual report, to have their annual accounts audited, and to lodge these with the Registrar of Companies. However, it is understood that not all non-profit companies meet these conditions, and that the conditions are not systematically enforced.

Third, some NGOs are registered under the Societies Ordinance of 1891. This is the simplest method, and has been adopted by most of the smaller NGOs. Broadly, the requirements are similar to those for non-profit companies. Registrations are approved by the Registrar of Companies. To be registered, a society must have at least seven members and a subscribed capital of at least Rs10,000 ($180), and must provide two copies of its rules to the registrar. The rules must cover the objects of the society, the operation of the management committee, internal governance and the keeping of accounts. In addition, societies are required to provide an annual report to the registrar, and to have the annual accounts audited. Again, however, these requirements are not strictly enforced.

Even though these various provisions for registration are not particularly onerous, it is possible for an NGO to operate without being registered. However, unregistered NGOs may have difficulty in attracting external funds.

International NGOs operating in Sri Lanka do not need to be registered. They generally sign a memorandum of understanding with the Ministry of Policy Planning and Implementation (as at May 1997, 53 international NGOs had signed such a memorandum), or at least an agreement with the Director of External Resources, before they commence operations. However, there is no legal requirement for them to do so. NGOs are also allowed to receive funds from foreign donors without any restrictions, control or supervision by the government.

Hence, while most NGOs involved in microfinance are registered, it is quite possible to operate as a microfinance institution (MFI) without any legal backing whatsoever. It would appear that this unstructured regime has led to some problems, with some NGOs reportedly engaging in activities of a controversial nature. On the other hand, the environment for NGOs has at times been highly politicised, with NGOs subject to considerable uncertainty. In the early 1990s, a presidential commission was established to examine and report on alleged irregularities in the operations of some NGOs. However, to date, there have not been any changes to the registration procedures. It would be appropriate to tighten up the procedures, to require NGOs to be registered and to monitor their activities to ensure they are properly accountable to their members and third parties. At the same time, NGOs meeting the necessary requirements should be permitted to operate with maximum flexibility and certainty.

According to the law, NGOs are not allowed to provide savings facilities. Under the Banking Act of 1988 and the Finance Companies Act of 1988, an institution must be licensed as a bank or finance company in order to collect deposits. This applies to all deposits, whether from members or non-members, and includes compulsory savings that may be a pre-condition for obtaining a microfinance loan. Any such savings must be invested in a bank account, and cannot be used for re-lending by the NGO. (As noted above, these provisions do not apply to cooperatives, which are specifically permitted under the Cooperative Societies Law of 1972 to raise deposits. Moreover, the Samurdhi task forces are specifically exempted from the restriction on mobilising savings by virtue of the Samurdhi Authority Act.)

In practice, the prohibition on mobilising savings has generally not been applied strictly. Indeed, major government programs such as the National Development Trust Fund (NDTF) and the Small Farmers and Landless Credit (SFLC) project have required NGOs borrowing from them to establish savings programs, and have encouraged them to use these savings in their credit programs. On the other hand, in 1992 the largest NGO, Sarvodaya, was prosecuted for mobilising savings and required to return all savings to members. It now mobilises savings only through independent primary societies, and these are not remitted to Sarvodaya itself. Amendments to the Finance Companies Act that would give NGOs more flexibility in accessing savings have been mooted, but have not been introduced.

Clearly, the current situation leads to uncertainty, and if the law were interpreted strictly, would severely impede if not effectively prohibit NGOs from engaging in microfinance. Savings represent a stable source of funds for MFIs in many Asian countries. Moreover, saving can be important in ensuring borrower discipline, and 'savings first, credit later' has been the working guideline of many successful MFIs. Therefore, it is important that MFIs should at least be permitted to accept members' savings. There is a need to amend the law to give NGOs greater certainty in this area.

3.2 Interest rates

There are few regulations governing interest rates. In the case of the TCCSs, societies are free to set their own interest rates for both deposits and loans. However, where societies receive outside funds for on-lending to members, they are not permitted to charge a margin of more than 4 per cent. While this may seem restrictive, the margin has been set in consultation with the federation, and the federation commented that it is sufficient to enable societies to cover their transaction costs. There are no restrictions on the interest rates that NGOs engaged in microfinance can charge.

3.3 Prudential regulation and supervision

There is virtually no prudential regulation and supervision of MFIs in Sri Lanka, whether TCCSs or NGOs. In the case of TCCSs, the registrar advises them that they should maintain a minimum of 15 per cent of their deposits in the form of liquid assets, but this does not appear to be binding and is not enforced. Other than this, there are no capital adequacy requirements, reserve requirements, or requirements relating to loan loss provisioning, loan documentation or collateral applying to either TCCSs or NGOs.

In terms of reporting and supervision, TCCSs are required to prepare an annual statement of accounts, including a statement of income and expenditures and balance sheet, and to submit this to the registrar within three months of the end of the financial year. They are also required to prepare an annual budget, setting out projections of revenue and expenditure, and provide it to the registrar. In addition, officers from the Department of Cooperative Development visit societies from time to time and carry out inspections. The department is required to conduct an annual audit of every society, although it is understood that the department is constrained by a lack of resources, and that such audits are not always timely nor very thorough.

In the case of NGOs, there are no requirements for the maintenance or provision of portfolio or other accounting data, beyond the general requirements concerning annual accounts that apply where NGOs are registered. These do not apply to all NGOs, and are not strictly enforced even where they do apply.

There does not appear to be a strong case for requiring a government agency to monitor and supervise TCCSs on a day-to-day basis. The performance of the TCCSs has generally been good. It is understood that several societies become dormant each year as a result of inadequate financial management, but this is only a very small proportion of the more than 8,000 societies in operation. Given the large number of societies, it would require a considerable input of resources for the Department of Cooperative Development or another government agency to monitor and supervise them in a rigorous manner. Moreover, any such effort would largely duplicate the monitoring and supervision already undertaken by the district unions and the federation. It may therefore be more cost-effective for the Department of Cooperative Development to monitor the activities of the federation and perhaps conduct spot checks on individual primary societies, rather than establishing a parallel system for monitoring all primary societies.

The situation regarding NGOs involved in microfinance is somewhat different. There are far fewer NGOs than there are TCCSs, with maybe 200 in total. There is also no apex body responsible for monitoring or supervising them. And, as noted above, many of them have not operated on a very sound basis. Hence, it would appear that some more intensive monitoring and supervision is necessary. On the other hand, it is generally accepted that it is unnecessary and inappropriate to subject MFIs which do not accept deposits from the general public to full prudential regulation and supervision. It would therefore be appropriate to consider other approaches to ensuring that MFIs maintain high standards in their operations.

3.4 Performance and reporting standards of the National Development Trust Fund

In some countries, de facto standards for self-regulation are being established based on the policies of second tier institutions which lend to MFIs. Where such second tier institutions lay down standards for MFIs wishing to borrow from them, there is a major incentive for MFIs to meet them, and a tendency for them to become industry standards. It would appear that NDTF has the potential to play a similar role.

NDTF has laid down operational procedures for partner organisations which borrow from it. According to the guidelines, an organisation must have legal status, and must have at least two years' experience in lending to the poor, with a recovery rate of at least 90 per cent over the last year and at least 70 per cent over the last two years, to qualify as a partner organisation. In addition, it must meet the following criteria:

(1) It must demonstrate financial viability or the potential for viability.

(2) It must have a well-developed and active savings mobilisation component, with loans from NDTF limited to the balance of members' savings and shares.

(3) It must demonstrate sound, well-organised management, and acceptable accounting systems and credit monitoring facilities.

(4) It must have the capacity to make small short-term loans at commercial rates of interest without collateral, and use a group lending approach.

In the past, these conditions were not enforced. Many partner organisations with little or no previous experience in microfinance were given loans. An external audit of partner organisations completed in August 1996 found that a significant number had not maintained proper accounting records and did not follow generally accepted accounting principles. More than 60 per cent did not have a recovery rate of 90 per cent or above (although as noted previously, the repayment rate for partner organisations to NDTF has remained solid), and a fair number did not mobilise savings. It is understood, however, that since 1995 the requirements in terms of experience and repayment rates have been enforced more rigorously.

NDTF has also introduced a number of more specific prudential requirements. In particular, partner organisations are required to:

(1) Maintain a group contingency fund, established by deducting 5 per cent of the principal of all loans, and subject to certain conditions.

(2) Establish a loan loss reserve as a provision against defaults. A minimum of 20 per cent of interest earned on sub-loans must be retained in the reserve, which must be invested in an interest-earning bank account.

(3) Maintain a minimum of 35 per cent of members' savings in reserve at all times.

There are also a number of criteria for the selection of borrowers. They must have a household income of less than Rs1,500 ($27) a month, with priority given to women and people under 35. They must participate in social mobilisation and training activities for a minimum of three months before obtaining the loan, and be organised in mutual support groups. They must participate in an individual savings program, and should not have defaulted on previous loans. Moreover, sub-loans are only to be given for income-generating activities, with a maximum of Rs10,000 ($181) for the initial loan. NDTF does not generally monitor these conditions. Some commentators suggested that many loans were, in fact, going to borrowers with higher incomes.

In terms of financial reporting, NDTF requires partner organisations to have their accounts audited by a qualified auditor, and partners are eligible to have the cost of the audit reimbursed by NDTF. Nevertheless, not all partners have had their accounts audited. In 1993 less than half had their accounts audited, but by 1995 the proportion with audited accounts had risen to around 80 per cent. NDTF has decided that from 1997 only those with audited accounts will be eligible to receive loans.

Partner organisations are also required to provide a quarterly report to NDTF. The report covers loan balances and arrears with respect to loans from NDTF to the partner, and statistics on the group contingency fund. In addition, partners are required to provide single line data on the number of members, value of members' shares and savings, other savings, value of loans from savings, number of loans, average loan size and cumulative recovery rate. While these data are not particularly onerous, it is understood that many partners do not provide the necessary data, and need to be reminded to do so.

Hence, while NDTF has laid down detailed operational procedures for partner organisations borrowing from it, in the past most of these procedures have not been enforced and many, if not most, partner organisations have failed to meet them. It may be possible to develop the standards adopted by NDTF, with appropriate modifications and in consultation with MFIs, into more general standards for MFIs operating in Sri Lanka. For this to happen, however, it would be necessary for the standards to be enforced more rigorously than they have been in the past. Moreover, there is currently considerable uncertainty as to the future role of NDTF, and a need for it to improve its performance further. These issues would need to resolved before it could operate as an effective apex institution for MFIs in Sri Lanka.

3.5 Self-regulation

Federation of Thrift and Credit Cooperative Societies

The Federation of Thrift and Credit Cooperative Societies is the apex body for the credit cooperative movement. Below the federation are 33 district unions which in turn are responsible for some 8,340 primary societies. The apex body provides a range of services to the movement. It provides training to staff from the district unions and more specialised training to staff from some of the larger primary societies. The district unions in turn provide training and support to the primary societies. The apex body also plays a coordination role, and acts as a focal point for policy dialogue and discussions with donor agencies. It also coordinates guidelines and procedures for the operation of primary societies. For instance, it has introduced standard loan documentation and other forms for all primary societies.

Primary societies deposit excess funds with district unions, which are then able to give loans to other primary societies. District unions also deposit funds with the federation, which makes loans to other district unions. The federation also acts as a conduit for funds from other sources, such as government programs and donor agencies. Individual district unions and primary societies are free to set their own interest rates for deposits and loans.

The district unions supervise the activities of the primary societies. The primary societies are required to provide monthly financial statements covering portfolio data, income and expenses, and balance sheet data to the district union. Officers from the district union monitor this information and conduct visits to the primary societies. If primary societies do not provide the necessary information, or if their statements reveal problems, they are not able to obtain loans from the district union.

Hence, there is a well-developed structure for coordination and self-regulation, with the federation and district unions providing a range of services to the primary societies. These structures have contributed importantly to the overall strength of the movement, which is much more successful than in most other countries in the region. It may be appropriate for other countries to study the operations of the credit cooperative movement in Sri Lanka, to see what lessons there may be for their own operations.

Forum of microfinance NGOs

Networks of MFIs have an important role in a number of areas, including information exchange, training, research, policy dialogue with government and donor agencies, and establishing standards for self-regulation. An informal forum for microfinance NGOs has recently been established under the UNDP Civil Society Organisations Development project. The forum follows and builds on previous efforts to establish an apex body for microfinance NGOs. An earlier grouping was convened by the federation of TCCSs following the Sri Lanka national workshop on Banking with the Poor, organised by The Foundation for Development Cooperation in January 1994, and met on several occasions during that year.

The current forum was established in early 1995, and is coordinated by UNDP. Originally, it met once a month, but it now meets once every two months. There are around 55 members, with about 35 attending meetings regularly. Around ten to twelve of the participants are local NGOs, including the major NGOs such as the federation of TCCSs and Sarvodaya. Other participants include donor agencies, the central bank, the Bank of Ceylon and international NGOs working in Sri Lanka. It is understood that a sub-group consisting solely of NGOs has also been formed under the auspices of the Sri Lanka Business Development Centre, and has been meeting since late 1996.

The forum has three main activities. First, it is collecting and disseminating information on training in credit and savings operations. At this stage, it is not planning to conduct its own training courses. Second, it is coordinating research and documentation on microfinance. So far, it has mainly been gathering information, but it has developed draft terms of reference for a study to evaluate the relative strengths and best practice of microfinance programs in Sri Lanka. To date, it has not obtained funding to carry out this study. Third, it provides a focal point for liaison and policy dialogue with government bodies. The forum has held discussions with government about restrictions on MFIs in collecting savings from members, and about problems caused by debt write-offs under government programs. It has not yet looked at issues related to self-regulation of the microfinance sector. Nevertheless, the proposed study of best practice microfinance in Sri Lanka will provide a basis for starting to consider such issues.

The forum is a very positive initiative, with the potential to play a significant role in areas such as training, coordination, policy dialogue and establishing standards for self-regulation. It is important that it continues to develop and expand its membership and range of activities.

4 Regulation of banks

4.1 Licensing and minimum capital requirements

As noted above, MFIs other than cooperatives and Samurdhi task forces are not permitted to raise deposits from the general public. Indeed, strictly speaking, most MFIs are not even allowed to accept savings from their own members. Generally, only institutions licensed as banks can accept deposits from the general public.

The minimum capital requirement for a commercial bank is Rs500 million ($9.1 million). This is likely to be too high for MFIs wishing to establish banks, or bodies wishing to establish small banks operating at the local level. Following amendments to the Banking Act of 1995, it would be easier for such institutions to seek licensing as a specialised bank. The minimum capital requirement for specialised banks is only Rs100 million ($1.8 million). On the other hand, they are not permitted to accept demand deposits (they can accept savings and time deposits only), and cannot offer chequeing facilities. While there is a network of regional rural development banks (RRDBs) operating in the rural areas, these are owned by the government and there would not appear to be any scope for private investors to use this institutional form to establish a new bank. In any case, the government is currently seeking to amalgamate them into larger units.

The federation of TCCSs has recently applied for a banking licence under the new provisions. It intends to create a separate bank to mobilise deposits for on-lending to the TCCSs (while the TCCSs already have the right to raise deposits from the public, the federation considers that establishing a bank would increase its credibility with the public and the protection that it can offer depositors). In addition, a new bank, Pramuka Bank, has recently been licensed and intends to include microfinance in its overall operations. Pramuka Bank intends to develop a number of innovative approaches to reaching poor borrowers in the villages, including through the establishment of agencies at the village level and the use of incentive payments for agents. Nevertheless, the scope for other institutions wishing to establish small microfinance banks to make use of the new provisions may be limited, as the minimum capital requirement is still quite high and may be difficult to meet.

Experience in other countries suggest that small banks are much more likely to become involved in microfinance than large banks. If banks are to play an active role in microfinance it is necessary to have some mechanism to enable small banks to be licensed. It would be appropriate to establish a framework for licensing small banks, setting realistic minimum capital requirements and removing any other restrictions which may prevent their establishment. In this regard, the experiences of countries such as Indonesia and the Philippines may be instructive (see the Indonesia and Philippines country studies).

4.2 Interest rates

As noted above, there are no restrictions on the interest rates that commercial banks can charge. Hence, interest rate regulation is not a factor impeding regulated banks from becoming involved in microfinance.

4.3 Prudential regulation and supervision

Prudential standards for commercial banks generally follow the Basle Accord. The required capital adequacy ratio is 8 per cent of risk-weighted assets, there is a liquidity requirement of 20 per cent of deposit liabilities, and loan provisioning requirements are 25 per cent for sub-standard loans, 50 per cent for non-performing loans and 100 per cent for loss loans. Commercial banks are also subject to frequent reporting requirements. Prudential requirements for specialised banks have not yet been developed, but are expected in broad terms to follow those applying to commercial banks. These requirements would not appear to impose any undue restrictions on small banks or banks engaged in microfinance, although it would be appropriate to review them if special provisions for licensing small banks were introduced.

5 Summary and recommendations

The World Bank estimates that 22.4 per cent of the population were in poverty in 1990–91. This is considerably lower than in other countries in South Asia, but slightly higher than in Malaysia, Thailand and Indonesia. Sri Lanka has long emphasised human development, with social indicators such as life expectancy, infant mortality and literacy generally much better than for other countries with similar income levels.

The major institutions engaged in microfinance in Sri Lanka are the thrift and credit cooperative societies (TCCSs) and a small number of non-governmental organisations (NGOs). The credit cooperative movement in Sri Lanka has been far more successful than in most other countries in the region. Whilst most members are not poor, the movement has sought to increase its outreach at the village level and has served as a vehicle for various targeted poverty lending programs. There are also a number of NGOs involved in microfinance.

Arrangements for direct support

Government and donor agencies have provided support for microfinance through a variety of channels. Recently, there has been some shift away from the use of NGOs and back to schemes more directly involving government agencies.

Affirm NDTF as primary vehicle for microfinance

The National Development Trust Fund (NDTF) operates essentially as a conduit for donor and government funds, channelling them to microfinance institutions (MFIs) for on-lending to final borrowers. While there have been a number of problems in its operations, this model has worked well in other countries and NDTF has recently improved its operations. The government should renew its commitment to NDTF as the primary vehicle for channelling direct support to microfinance in Sri Lanka.

Strengthen independence and clarify objectives of NDTF

At the same time, NDTF needs to continue to improve its performance. One critical issue is to ensure that it is not politicised. This may be achieved by strengthening the independence of the board of trustees, and spelling out more clearly the fund's objectives. The fund should continue to set and, more importantly, enforce minimum standards for partner organisations, and gradually raise these over time.

Consider transferring SFLC project to NDTF

The Small Farmers and Landless Credit (SFLC) project appears to have been reasonably successful. It is now entering a transition period, with responsibility being handed over from the central bank to the regional rural development banks (RRDBs). To the extent that the central bank continues to be involved in this and other microfinance projects, it would be appropriate for it to lend directly to NGOs rather than lending to NGOs through RRDBs. It is not clear that the RRDBs are well placed to take over the project. The government should perhaps consider transferring the project to NDTF instead.

Redesign Samurdhi scheme to include NGO role and achieve more self-sufficiency
The Samurdhi Development Credit Scheme is very new, and hence no data are yet available on repayment rates or other indicators of performance. Nevertheless, there are some causes for concern in the design of the scheme. The scheme does not envisage any explicit role for NGOs or other specialist MFIs. It should be redesigned to provide a role for NGOs and other specialist MFIs, either in identifying and motivating borrowers or as direct financial intermediaries. It should also be redesigned to make it more self-sufficient, and to reduce the possibility of its undermining more sustainable microfinance programs.

Publicise Hatton National Bank linkage program success
One highly innovative program is the program operated by Hatton National Bank for linking to NGOs and poor borrowers. The central bank should take a more active role in encouraging linkages, by documenting and publicising the experience of Hatton National Bank, and issuing clear guidelines that other banks could follow. The government should also avoid debt forgiveness for small loans in the future.

Regulation of non-bank microfinance institutions

Review and streamline regulations for cooperatives
Regulations facing TCCSs are restrictive in a number of ways, with the registrar and relevant departmental minister having considerable discretion. The government should review the regulatory requirements facing cooperatives, with a view to streamlining them and removing unnecessary requirements.

Ensure NGO standards and accountability
By contrast, it is possible for NGOs involved in microfinance to operate without any legal backing whatsoever. It would appear that this unstructured regime has led to some problems. On the other hand, it is also clear that the environment for NGOs has at times been highly politicised, and that NGOs have been subject to considerable uncertainty. The government should tighten up the procedures, requiring NGOs to be registered and monitoring their activities to ensure they are properly accountable to their members and third parties. At the same time, the government should ensure that NGOs meeting the necessary requirements are permitted to operate with maximum flexibility and certainty.

Restrict the acceptance of general deposits to banks only
The law specifically permits TCCSs to receive deposits from persons who are not members, and many societies are now actively seeking deposits from non-members. Given the lack of prudential requirements, it is surprising that societies should be permitted to receive deposits from non-members. The government should not permit TCCSs to accept deposits from the general public in their own right. However, when the federation establishes a bank, there is no reason why the primary societies should not act as agents.

Allow MFIs to accept members' savings
According to the law, NGOs are not allowed to provide savings facilities, even to members. In practice, the prohibition on mobilising savings has generally not been applied strictly.

However, one NGO has been prosecuted for mobilising savings, and the current situation leads to considerable uncertainty. MFIs should at least be permitted to accept members' savings. The government should amend the law to give NGOs greater certainty in this area.

TCCSs are free to set their own interest rates for both deposits and loans. However, where societies receive outside funds for on-lending to members, they are not permitted to charge a margin of more than 4 per cent. While this may seem restrictive, the margin has been set in consultation with the federation. There are no restrictions on the interest rates that NGOs engaged in microfinance can charge.

Establish reasonable monitoring of federation activities

There is virtually no prudential regulation and supervision of MFIs in Sri Lanka, whether TCCSs or NGOs. Reporting requirements are also minimal. In the case of the TCCSs there is a well-developed structure for coordination and self-regulation, with the federation and district unions monitoring and supervising the primary societies. These structures have contributed importantly to the overall strength of the movement. The Department of Cooperative Development should monitor the activities of the federation and perhaps conduct spot checks on individual primary societies, rather than establishing a parallel system for monitoring all primary societies.

Establish appropriate monitoring for NGOs and MFIs

In the case of NGOs, more intensive monitoring and supervision is necessary. On the other hand, it is generally accepted that it is unnecessary and inappropriate to subject MFIs which do not accept deposits from the general public to full prudential regulation and supervision.

NDTF has laid down operational procedures for partner organisations which borrow from it. It may be possible to develop the standards adopted by NDTF, with appropriate modifications and in consultation with MFIs, into more general standards for MFIs operating in Sri Lanka. For this to happen, however, it would be necessary for the standards to be enforced more rigorously than they have been in the past. Moreover, there is currently considerable uncertainty as to the future role of NDTF, and a need for it to improve its performance further.

Encourage MFI networks

Networks of MFIs have an important role in a number of areas, including information exchange, training, research, policy dialogue with government and donor agencies, and establishing standards for self-regulation. The new forum of microfinance NGOs is a very positive initiative. Leading MFIs should continue to develop and expand its membership and range of activities, with support from UNDP.

Regulation of banks

The minimum capital requirement to establish a commercial bank is too high for MFIs wishing to establish banks, or bodies wishing to establish small banks operating at the local level. The minimum capital requirement for specialised banks is lower at Rs100 million ($1.8 million), but is still likely to be too high. If banks are to play an active role in microfinance it is necessary to have some mechanism to enable small banks to be licensed. The government should establish a framework for licensing small banks, with realistic minimum capital requirements. It should also remove any other restrictions which may prevent the establishment of small banks.

References

De Silva, G. M. P. 1996. *Grassroots Financial Systems in Sri Lanka*. APRACA–GTZ Publication 1996/2, Asia Pacific Rural and Agricultural Credit Association, Bangkok.

Fernando, Sunimal. 1996. *Microfinance Capacity Assessment: Sri Lanka*. Asian Pacific Development Centre, Kuala Lumpur.

Gallardo, Joselito S., Randhawa, Bikki K., & Sacay, Orlando J. 1997. 'A commercial bank's microfinance program: The case of Hatton National Bank in Sri Lanka'. Discussion paper no.369, World Bank, Washington D.C.

Hulme, David, Montgomery, Richard & Bhattacharya, Debapriya. 1996. 'A study of the Federation of Thrift and Credit Cooperatives (SANASA) in Sri Lanka'. In *Finance against Poverty*, vol.2, eds David Hulme & Paul Mosley, Routledge, London.

Jayasundere, Ramani. 1996. Laws and regulations governing non-government organisations in Sri Lanka. Paper prepared for the South Asian Conference on Laws, Rules and Regulations for the Voluntary Sector, March.

Kiriwandeniya, P. A. 1997. 'SANASA: The savings and credit cooperative movement in Sri Lanka'. In *Reasons for Hope: Instructive Experiences in Rural Development*, eds Anirudh Krishna, Norman Uphiff & Milton J. Esman. Kumarian Press, West Hartford.

Presidential Commission on Finance and Banking. 1992. *Final Report*. Presidential Commission on Finance and Banking, Department of Government Printing, Colombo.

Ratnayake, R. M. K. 1997. Paper presented to a Meeting of Officials concerned with Poverty Eradication and Social Development in SAARC Countries, Islamabad, April.

World Bank 1995, *Sri Lanka Poverty Assessment*, Report no.13431-CE, World Bank, Washington D.C.

Persons consulted

Mr R. T. Wijetilleke	Managing Director & Chief Executive Hatton National Bank
Mr N. Hapuarachchy	Assistant General Manager, Domestic Credit Hatton National Bank
Mr Victor M. Fernando	Senior Manager, Rural Credit Hatton National Bank
Mr Gamini Swarnapala	Manager, Rural Credit Hatton National Bank
Mr G. M. P. D. De Silva	Executive Director Central Bank of Sri Lanka
Mr W. A. Wijewardena	Director, Rural Credit Department Central Bank of Sri Lanka
Mr Y. A. De Silva	Deputy Director, Rural Credit Department Central Bank of Sri Lanka
Mr C. J. Fernando	Project Manager, Small Farmers & Landless Credit Project Central Bank of Sri Lanka
Ms Savitri Jayasinghe	General Manager Bank of Ceylon

Mr Thilak S. Ranasinghe	Assistant General Manager, Developmental Banking Bank of Ceylon
Mr G. Hettiarachchi	Registrar of Cooperative Societies Department of Cooperative Development
Ms Sriyani Hulugalle	Industrial Economist The World Bank
Dr Naresha Duraiswamy	Institutional Development Specialist The World Bank
Dr M. U. A. Tennakoon	Executive Director (retired) Central Bank of Sri Lanka
Mr Tapan K. Barman	Project Manager United Nations Development Programme
Mr Alex Perera	Executive Director National NGO Council of Sri Lanka
Dr S. G. Samarasinghe	National NGO Council of Sri Lanka
Mr L. M. Samarasinghe, JP	National NGO Council of Sri Lanka
Mr Deepthi de Mel	National NGO Council of Sri Lanka
Mr C. R. Ekanayake	National NGO Council of Sri Lanka
Mr P. A. Kiriwandeniya	President Federation of Thrift and Credit Cooperative Societies
Mr Rohan Perera	Chairman, President and CEO Pramuka Bank
Mr A. H. A. Mendis	Managing Director Pramuka Bank
Mr Sunil A. Mendis	General Manager Pramuka Bank
Mr Bandula Ranasinghe	Deputy General Manager, Credit Pramuka Bank
Mr Asoka Fernando	Regional Manager, Development Banking Pramuka Bank
Mr Prabhath Vidanagamage	Manager, Rural Credit Pramuka Bank
Mr S. H. Piyasiri	Director, Credit and Microenterprise Development National Development Trust Fund
Dr K. M. Ratnayake	Secretary Ministry of Youth Affairs, Sports and Rural Development
Mr Sunimal Fernando	Founder and Honorary Vice Chairman Initiative in Research and Education for Develoment in Asia
Dr Susil Liyanarachchi	General Manager People's Rural Development Association
Dr Sunil Jayantha Nawaratne	Director-General & Chairman National Youth Services Council
Mr B. B. A. E. Mediwake	Director, Development National Youth Services Council

Ms Ramani Gunatilaka	Research Economist Institute of Policy Studies
Mr David Henry	Section Head, Development Cooperation Australian Agency for International Development
Mr Dunstan J. Fernando	Projects Coordinator Australian Agency for International Development
Mr J. Charitha Ratwatte	Managing Director Sri Lanka Business Development Centre
Mr Saliya J. Ranasinghe	Chief Executive Sarvodaya Economic Enterprises Development Services

Thailand

1 Introduction and background

1.1 Key demographic and economic data

Thailand is located in mainland Southeast Asia, opening on to the South China Sea and Indian Ocean, and sharing land borders with Malaysia, Myanmar, Laos and Cambodia. In 1995 it had a population of 58.2 million people occupying an area of some 513,000 square kilometres, with a density of 113 people per square kilometre. Population growth over the period 1990 to 1995 averaged only 0.9 per cent per year, the lowest for any of the nine countries in the study. In 1995 the total fertility rate stood below replacement level at 1.8 births per woman. Thailand has proceeded much further along the demographic transition than the other countries.

Thailand is at a very different stage of development to most of the other countries in the region, and is now classified as a middle-income country by the World Bank. In 1995, income per capita was $2,740, less than Malaysia but well over double that of any other country included in this study. This reflects rapid economic growth over an extended period. Over the period 1985 to 1995 per capita income grew at an exceptional rate of 8.4 per cent per year, much higher than for any other country included in this study. However, since mid-1997 Thailand has experienced a financial crisis, requiring an emergency loan from the International Monetary Fund. Little economic growth is expected over the next two to three years.

Very rapid economic growth has been accompanied by significant changes in the structure of output. Between 1980 and 1995, the share of agriculture in GDP declined from 23 to 11 per cent, the lowest for any country in this study. This decline was matched by an increase in the share of industry, from 29 per cent of GDP to 40 per cent, while the share of services remained broadly unchanged at just under 50 per cent. These changes have had significant effects on settlement patterns, with the proportion of the population living in urban areas more than doubling, from 17 per cent in 1980 to 36 per cent in 1995. Fifty (50) per cent of the urban population live in Bangkok, a higher concentration in the largest city than for any other country in the study.

Human development is also relatively high compared with most other countries in the region. Thailand scores highest of the nine countries in this study in the UNDP human development index for 1994, and scores in the top three in terms of life expectancy at birth, the infant mortality rate, and adult literacy. Nevertheless, on some indicators Thailand's performance is disappointing given its per capita income. For instance, life expectancy at birth at 69 years is less than Malaysia (71), and three years less than Sri Lanka (72), despite the fact that per capita income is nearly four times that of Sri Lanka. Similarly, the infant mortality rate (35 per 1,000 live births) is more than double Malaysia (12) and Sri Lanka (16), and only slightly lower than the Philippines (39).

1.2 Poverty

Estimates of poverty

Reflecting the high per capita income, the incidence of poverty is lower than in most other countries in the region. The official poverty line in Thailand is based on an estimate of nutritional adequacy. In 1976, the recommended daily per capita consumption was set at 1,978 calories but in 1981 it was revised to 2,016 calories, based on changes in the population structure. This recommended daily consumption is then converted into typical 'food consumption baskets', consisting of representative samples of food items consumed in rural and urban environments. These baskets are then costed, based on average retail prices in rural and urban areas. Finally, a component is allowed for non-food items, based on the ratios of food to total expenditure for the lowest quintiles of the rural and urban populations in the socioeconomic survey of 1975–76.

Based on official estimates, the incidence of poverty stood at 30.0 per cent in 1975–76. While the incidence of poverty fell to 23.0 per cent in 1981, it rose sharply to 29.5 per cent in 1986, reflecting large drops in commodity prices in that year. Since then it has fallen significantly, to 22.2 per cent in 1988, 18.0 per cent in 1990 and 13.1 per cent in 1992. Estimates of the depth and severity of poverty have also fallen. The incidence of poverty differs significantly between regions, ranging from 1.1 per cent in Bangkok to 22.3 per cent in the north-east. In 1992, around 58 per cent of the poor lived in the north-east, almost 85 per cent lived in rural areas, and 98 per cent had household heads with primary school education or less.

Much of the data on which the official poverty line is based are now somewhat dated. The estimates of nutritional adequacy are based on daily dietary allowances obtained from the Ministry of Public Health in the mid-1970s. While the minimum calorie intake was revised in 1981 to take account of changes in the population structure, it has not been revised since then. The allowance for non-food items is based on expenditure patterns from 1975 to 1976.

In recent years Dr Medhi Krongkaew of the National Economic and Social Development Board (NESDB) has undertaken considerable research on the poverty line (see, for example, Medhi 1997), and has proposed a number of changes to revise and update it. His estimates suggest a much higher poverty line than official estimates. Using Medhi's methodology, the poverty line in 1990 was equivalent to annual per capita expenditure of B12,764 ($505) for urban areas and B8,366 ($331) for rural areas, compared with the official poverty lines of B7,632 ($302) and B4,968 ($196) respectively. Not surprisingly, his estimates of the incidence of poverty are much higher than the official estimates. Medhi estimates the incidence of poverty in 1992 at 36.5 per cent, more than double the official estimate, with poverty incidence ranging from 5.0 per cent in Bangkok to 55.0 per cent in the north-east. Deloitte and Touche Management Consultants (1996) have also derived estimates of poverty, based on daily calorie intake. Their estimates of the incidence of poverty in 1992 are slightly higher than the official estimates, but significantly lower than the Medhi estimates.

In summary, poverty in Thailand has reduced considerably in recent years, and the official estimates suggest that the incidence of poverty has now fallen to around 10 to 15 per cent of the population. On the other hand there is considerable regional variation, and analysis by Medhi suggests that poverty remains a pervasive problem.

Moreover, it is clear that there has been a long-term trend, dating from at least the mid-1970s, towards greater income inequality. Between 1988 and 1992 alone, the income share of the top 20 per cent of households rose from 54.9 to 59.4 per cent of GDP, while the share of the bottom 20 per cent of households fell from 4.5 to 3.8 per cent. In this respect, Thailand's experience is quite different from that of other countries in East Asia, which have experienced reduced income inequality over the last twenty years. While income inequality in Thailand was substantially lower than in the Philippines and Malaysia in the mid-1970s, it is now substantially higher, with Thailand now having the most unequal distribution of income in East Asia. The World Bank (1996) suggests that reasons for the increase in inequality include structural change in the economy, the fact that formal sector jobs have not been distributed equitably across households, and the lack of access by the poor to secondary education.

Policies for poverty reduction

Poverty reduction has been a central objective of development planning in Thailand since the Third Plan (1972–1976). However, it has not consistently been a top priority. Thailand has adopted policies which have emphasised high economic growth and led to very rapid growth in GDP and per capita incomes. This has contributed to significant reductions in the proportion of people in poverty. However, as noted above, the trickle down to the poorest segments of the population has been slow, and there has been a significant increase in income inequality.

Clearly, a wide range of government policies, including macroeconomic, investment and human development policies affect poverty, both positively and negatively. However, there are several programs in Thailand that are specifically designed to reduce poverty. These are described by the World Bank (1996).

First, there are a number of programs that provide cash transfers and in-kind transfers to the poor. The Department of Public Welfare provides a monthly allowance to the elderly without other means of support. It has also established village community funds, administered by village welfare committees, to be used in assisting poor residents. The Ministry of Public Health provides low-income cards to around 20 per cent of the population, entitling them to free medical services. Another in-kind transfer program is the school lunch program operated by the Ministry of Education, which provides a free meal each school day to children from poor families at the preschool and primary levels.

Second, there are some programs directed at income generation by the poor. The most significant of these is the poverty alleviation project, a microfinance program operated by the Community Development Department, and discussed in more detail below. Another major program is the Tambon Development Program (the tambon is the administrative unit at the sub-district level) administered by the Office of the Prime Minister, which includes a public works component aimed at providing rural infrastructure and employment generation.

The World Bank notes that expenditure on these anti-poverty programs is modest, accounting for only 1.6 per cent of government expenditures in 1995. Moreover, the share has fallen in recent years, although it was budgeted to rise to 2 per cent in 1996. The World Bank argues that better targeted policies are needed to reach the hard-core rural and urban poor. It argues that the government should identify the major schemes by which the poor are to be assisted, and define clear poverty-oriented goals for these.

The Eighth Plan, to cover the period 1997–2001, signals some changes in development policy. It advocates a shift to 'people-centred development', intended to support human development, improve quality of life and promote increasing community participation.

Among the targets are to:

(1) narrow the gap in income between the richest and poorest households, focusing on the middle to lower income group

(2) reduce the number of people living in poverty to no more than 10 per cent of the population by 2001.

Nevertheless, this plan was developed on the assumption of continued rapid economic growth, prior to the current financial crisis. Clearly, much slower economic growth and the need for significant reductions in government spending will make it harder to reduce poverty. It is likely that a major reorientation of government spending will be necessary if the poor are to be protected from the effects of the downturn and inequality is to be reduced.

1.3 Overview of the financial system

The formal financial sector in Thailand consists primarily of commercial banks, non-bank financial institutions, specialised financial institutions established by the government, and cooperatives. As at the end of 1996, there were 15 domestic commercial banks and 14 foreign commercial banks, with a total of 3,138 branches throughout the country. There were also a number of credit foncier companies, finance companies, and finance and securities companies. The above institutions are supervised by the Bank of Thailand. In addition, there were seven specialised financial institutions supervised by the Ministry of Finance. Most notable among these are the Bank for Agriculture and Agricultural Cooperatives (BAAC), 628 branches and sub-branches; the Government Savings Bank (GSB), 543 branches; and the Government Housing Bank with 169 branches. Finally, there were 1,127 thrift and savings cooperatives and 2,832 agricultural cooperatives, supervised by the Ministry of Agriculture and Cooperatives. Some, but not all, of the agricultural cooperatives provide financial services to their members.

The financial system in Thailand is reasonably well developed. In 1995 bank interest rates on both loans and deposits were significantly positive in real terms (that is, well above the inflation rate), encouraging financial development. There is a general ceiling on interest rates applying to loans of 15 per cent, but since 1992 all financial institutions regulated by the Bank of Thailand, including commercial banks, have been exempted from this provision, and are free to charge interest rates based on market conditions. The ratio of money and quasi-money (currency outside banks, demand deposits, time and savings deposits, and similar bank accounts) to GDP stood at 73.8 per cent in 1995, slightly lower than for Malaysia but much higher than for any other country included in this study. This ratio tends to increase with the development of the economy and the financial sector, because deposits tend to increase as monetisation accelerates and banking facilities increase. On the other hand, it can fluctuate widely in the short term depending on the macroeconomic situation.

The Bank of Thailand has carried out two financial development plans since 1990, designed to identify obstacles to financial development and implement measures to overcome them. The measures taken relate to regulation reform and the establishment of financial infrastructure. Important measures include relaxing exchange controls, abolishing interest rate ceilings for financial institutions, introducing greater competition, and modernising the payments system. Nevertheless, the current crisis suggests that there has been insufficient attention to prudential regulation and supervision. The crisis at least partly reflects financial factors, with banks incurring significant losses after lending large amounts on the basis of unsustainable property values. While it remains to be seen what longer term effects this will have on the financial system, it is clear that there has been a considerable erosion of confidence in the short term. The crisis has led the Bank of Thailand to increase its focus on prudential regulation and supervision, and it is unlikely that the bank will issue any new banking licences in the short term.

Bank for Agriculture and Agricultural Cooperatives

The Bank for Agriculture and Agricultural Cooperatives is by far the largest lender in rural areas. In 1995–96, BAAC provided credit of B112 billion ($4.4 billion) to farmers and farmer institutions. It reached 4.65 million farm families, or 82 per cent of all farm families in Thailand. This consisted of 3.33 million individual farmers, 855 agricultural cooperatives with a total membership of 1.28 million, and 323 farmers' associations with a total membership of 43,000. BAAC also provides extensive deposit services, with the value of deposits totalling B91 billion ($3.6 billion) at end-1995.

Interest rates for small loans are maintained at below market rates, with interest rates for loans to individual farmers set at 9 per cent for loans below B60,000 ($2,370) and 11.25 to 12.25 per cent for loans between B60,000 ($2,370) and B1 million ($39,530). These loans are cross-subsidised by the bank's other operations. Overall repayment rates are satisfactory and BAAC operates profitably, although this in part reflects its access to soft loans from the Bank of Thailand, the Asian Development Bank and other sources.

As noted above, BAAC also lends to agricultural cooperatives, and has a small program for lending to farmers' associations. Farmers are organised in joint liability groups of five or more members who guarantee each other's loans. Loans to cooperatives and associations attract interest rates of 6 per cent where the amounts on-lent to individual farmers are below B60,000 ($2,370), and 9.25 per cent where the amounts on-lent are between B60,000 ($2,370) and B1 million ($39,530). For loans up to B50,000 ($1,980), no collateral is required. Hence, BAAC uses some lending techniques similar to those used by microfinance institutions (MFIs).

However, BAAC does not specifically target the poor, and some commentators suggested that it may not reach the poorest farm families. Moreover, the poorest people are often without land and therefore are not farmers. These people are not eligible to receive loans from BAAC, by virtue of its mandate as stipulated in its charter (it is understood that the government is considering amending the charter to enable BAAC to be a rural development bank). Therefore, while BAAC has huge outreach in the rural areas, it may not reach the poorest rural households. It should also be noted that repayment rates by members to cooperatives and farmers' associations, and by the cooperatives and farmers' associations to BAAC, are relatively low. In 1995–96, the repayment rate by members to cooperatives was 70.2 per cent, and the repayment rate by members to farmers' associations was 67.9 per cent. BAAC has commented that the farmers' associations lack knowledge, understanding and true cooperation, and BAAC has found it difficult to expand lending through them.

Historically, the BAAC charter only permitted it to provide loans to farmers for on-farm activities. In 1992 the charter was amended to allow a fixed percentage of lending for agriculture-related activities, but only if operated by farmers. In 1995, the Asian Development Bank provided a soft loan of $50 million to facilitate this lending. This amount has already been drawn down, and the Asian Development Bank is considering a further loan of $100 million. There is also some discussion of amending the charter to enable BAAC to lend for non-agricultural projects in rural areas. However, it is unlikely that the bank will increase its poverty lending. While there is some pressure for it to do so, its cost structure and interest rate structure mean that it is unlikely that it could engage in poverty lending on a commercial basis.

The German agency for technical cooperation (GTZ) is currently in the process of establishing a small revolving fund to enable BAAC to develop lending procedures and products which cater to the financial needs of non-farm enterprises, and to develop the capacity and skills of credit officers in an experimental stage. The experience from this pilot test will be used for replication if and when BAAC obtains approval from government for lending to the non-farm sector.

1.4 Overview of microfinance

The government's main policy thrusts for reducing poverty appear to be promoting community participation in general, and increasing employment opportunities, especially wage employment, in rural areas. Nevertheless, the Eighth Plan contains some references to the role of microfinance and financial services. It calls for the extension of the scope of the operations of the rural development fund managed by GSB, to encourage savings at the community level and give wide-ranging support to local and community development activities. It also calls for the extension of financial services by formal financial institutions, especially commercial banks, BAAC and GSB, to lower income and less capitalised customers in regional and rural areas.

There are a number of government programs which support microfinance. The largest is the poverty alleviation project operated by the Community Development Department (CDD). This project provides for the establishment of a fund at the village level, for on-lending to poor households. By 1995 loans outstanding were nearly B1 billion ($40 million), benefiting up to 200,000 households.

The other two major programs are the rural development fund operated by GSB, and the program operated by the Urban Community Development Office (UCDO) within the National Housing Authority. These two programs operate by providing loans to community organisations (sometimes referred to as savings and credit organisations), which then on-lend to individual members. Between them they have provided loans to nearly 1,500 community organisations with a combined membership of around 200,000 households. There are also a number of smaller government programs. Of the three major programs, the CDD program and UCDO program generally reach poor borrowers, whereas the GSB program reaches both poor and non-poor borrowers.

The community organisations financed under the GSB and UCDO programs may take a variety of forms. Some are registered as cooperatives, but most are not registered. Such community organisations obtain funds from a variety of sources, including the savings of members. The performance of different community organisations in reaching the poor also differs. There are a number of types of cooperatives, with both agricultural cooperatives and thrift and credit cooperatives providing savings and credit services. It is understood that the agricultural cooperatives generally do not reach the poorest borrowers. Moreover, many of the thrift and credit cooperatives cater for groups of wage and salary earners rather than the poor. However, is understood that the credit union cooperatives, that subset of thrift and credit cooperatives based on locality rather than employment, generally reach poor borrowers. There are 236 credit union cooperatives, with a total membership of around 93,000 members. The Credit Union Federation of Thailand serves as an apex body for these credit union cooperatives. Generally, the community organisations lend on an individual basis, but UCDO in particular has been trying to encourage them to adopt a group lending approach.

There is also a small number of private bodies and NGOs involved in microfinance. Of these, the Small Enterprise Development Company, based in Surin in the north-east, is perhaps the only one that is involved exclusively in microfinance. In addition, some multi-purpose NGOs such as the Local Development Institute and the Population and Community Development Association, also operate microfinance programs. Nevertheless, NGOs have a much more limited role in microfinance than in most other countries in the region.

The demand for microfinance

Before analysing the policy and regulatory environment, it is useful to consider the demand for microfinance. A number of commentators suggested that the demand for microfinance in Thailand is much less than in most other countries in the region. If this is the case, the imperative to increase outreach may not be as great as in some other countries.

The size of the potential market is clearly more limited than in many other countries. As noted above, the incidence of poverty in Thailand is much lower than in all other countries included in the study except for Malaysia. Moreover, the population tends to be highly mobile, and growth in wage employment has been very rapid, with very low rates of unemployment. A number of commentators noted that in most cases poor people have access to wage employment. While wages for unskilled workers are low, the returns may still be higher than from self-employment in the informal sector of the economy, especially for people with few business skills. Again, the availability of wage employment sets Thailand and Malaysia apart from the other countries included in the study.

Notwithstanding these points, the distribution of resources in Thailand is heavily skewed. Opportunities for wage employment are heavily concentrated in Bangkok and the other major urban centres while the vast majority of the poor live in rural areas. While there has been substantial migration from rural to urban areas, this causes considerable social dislocation and places additional demands on urban infrastructure which is already stretched. Moreover, much migration is 'circular migration', where one family member works in Bangkok for part of the year because of the lack of opportunities in rural areas. As well as causing disruption to family life, the income generated may not be sufficient to support family members remaining in the rural areas. There are also increasing pockets of poverty in the main urban centres. The government's policy is therefore to encourage development in the rural areas.

These problems are likely to increase with the economic downturn. Growth in wage employment is likely to slow considerably, forcing the unskilled and new labour market entrants to rely more heavily on self-employment in the informal sector. There has also been a significant reversal of migration patterns, with large numbers of urban workers who have been laid off returning to rural areas. Hence, it appears that there is a significant demand for microfinance, and this may well increase, at least in the medium term.

To what extent has this demand already been satisfied? To date, the CDD program has provided loans to perhaps 200,000 households. The GSB program has provided loans to

1,360 organisations with a total membership of 188,000 households. And the UCDO program has provided loans to 103 organisations with a total membership of maybe 20,000 households. In addition, there are a number of other government and NGO schemes. Hence, on the face of it, outreach is already quite high.

Nevertheless, outreach is still relatively low compared to the some 1.5 million households in poverty. While few data on the CDD program are available, it would appear that it essentially provides a one-off loan (or grant) to beneficiary households, rather than any ongoing access to financial services. In the case of GSB and UCDO, the data relate to the total membership of the organisations that have received loans. It is not known how many individual members have received loans. The size of the loans, and whether they were large enough to support income-generating activities, is also not known. Further, it is likely that there has been considerable leakage to the non-poor under some schemes. It would therefore appear likely that there is still a substantial need for microfinance programs to increase their outreach to poor borrowers.

2 Arrangements for direct support

2.1 Support for specialised microfinance institutions

There are two major government programs which provide support to cooperatives and community organisations involved in microfinance. These are the rural development fund operated by the Government Savings Bank (GSB), and the program operated by the Urban Community Development Office (UCDO).

The credit program for rural development, administered by GSB, was originally administered by the Office of the Prime Minister and later by the National Economic and Social Development Board (NESDB). However, it suffered from low repayment rates. Responsibility for administering the program was assigned to GSB in 1995. The government has provided a total of B546 million ($21.6 million) to the bank as loanable funds for the program. In addition, the bank took over a loan portfolio of around B103 million ($4.0 million) when it took on the program, although much of this was in the form of bad debts. The program provides loans to savings and credit organisations in rural areas at an interest rate of 7 per cent, either for on-lending to their members or for investment projects undertaken by the groups themselves. Currently, 2,600 savings and credit organisations, with a total membership of 367,000, are affiliated with the program. Of these, 1,360 organisations, with a total membership of 188,000, have obtained loans. The program is not means tested, and the savings and credit organisations include members from a range of income levels. Repayment rates are reported to be high since the bank took over the program. While there are some arrears, no loans to savings and credit organisations have been written off.

The other major program is the urban poor development program operated by UCDO. This started in 1992 with a budget grant of $50 million. UCDO offers loans to community organisations in low-income urban settlements for income generation, housing and land, and small-scale community activities. Interest rates vary from 3 to 10 per cent, but the interest rate for income generation projects is 8 per cent. While UCDO is a government agency, it is governed by a nine-person board with three representatives from government (Bank of Thailand, Ministry of Finance and NESDB), three elected by the member community organisations, two from NGOs and one from the private sector. There are currently 616 member organisations, with a total membership of 53,000. Of these organisations, 385 have savings activities, and 103 have received loans from UCDO for income generation activities. The recovery rate for loans from UCDO to member organisations, measured as repayments collected as a percentage of repayments due on a monthly basis, is around 90 per cent.

As well as providing loans to savings and credit organisations, both GSB and UCDO provide them with technical support. For instance, GSB provides training in leadership and management and some skills training to the organisations. It also assists organisations to develop simple accounting and reporting systems, and visits them from time to time to follow up and keep track of the performance of its investments, exchange information and provide assistance. UCDO plays an even more active role in this regard. It has a number of activities to support the formation of savings groups, including advising people on how to structure their savings groups and financial systems, training in finance and accounting systems for savings groups, training in business skills such as accounting, marketing, planning and investment, and training in community development techniques such as participatory techniques. To date, UCDO has organised 168 training courses on these and similar matters, with a total of 6,200 participants. UCDO also makes frequent visits to member organisations to offer advice and assistance.

Both programs rely heavily on funds from the government, and neither of them is close to self-sufficiency. The GSB scheme relies on grant money from the budget for its loanable funds. The bank receives a margin of 4 per cent for managing the scheme, which is not sufficient to cover its costs, and the program is cross-subsidised by its other operations. Similarly, in the case of the UCDO program, loanable funds come from a grant from the government. Interest from loans to community organisations covers only about 30 per cent of administrative expenses.

The government is planning to establish the Community Organisation Development Institute (CODI) to organise microfinance on a more systematic basis. The proposal is being developed by the Prosperity Decentralisation Policy Committee, chaired by the Ministry of Finance and with representatives from the Community Development Department (CDD), NESDB, Bank of Thailand, GSB, and NGOs.

In effect, the new institute will take over the overall policy responsibility for the programs operated by GSB and UCDO with respect to microfinance. It is expected that, at least initially, GSB and UCDO will continue to administer the schemes. CODI will be overseen by a committee similar to the Prosperity Decentralisation Policy Committee. Moreover, it is envisaged that GSB and UCDO will on-lend funds to individual corporations at the district level. These district corporations will be managed by a board with representatives from government, NGOs and the local community, and will in turn on-lend to cooperatives and community organisations in their districts. The district corporations will also provide training to cooperatives and community organisations. Detailed lending guidelines, such as loan terms and conditions, targeting/means testing, lending methodologies, and accounting and reporting standards, have not yet been developed.

The relatively few non-government and private schemes in existence have tended to rely on outside funds, primarily from external agencies. For instance, the Small Enterprise Development Company has been supported by Catholic Relief Services.

Comment

GSB and UCDO have much better repayment rates than the CDD program and most other government programs, although the available data suggest that repayment rates are well below those achieved by second tier microfinance institutions in other countries such as Bangladesh, India and Sri Lanka. It is likely that their reasonably good performance reflects their independent boards and high degree of autonomy, and the fact that they lend to non-government cooperatives and community organisations. In establishing CODI, care should be taken to ensure that it is managed by an independent board and is free from political and bureaucratic interference. It is also important that CODI develop rigorous performance and reporting standards for the organisations that it lends to, to ensure that they operate on a sound basis and that they maintain repayment rates of at least 95 to 98 per cent on their loans to CODI.

As noted above, neither the GSB program nor UCDO is close to self-sufficiency. Clearly, if the two programs could increase their self-sufficiency, they could increase their outreach to poor clients for any given outlay of government funds. In setting up CODI, it would be appropriate for the government to establish explicit targets and timetables in terms of outreach and self-sufficiency. This would provide an incentive for CODI to improve its cost-effectiveness over time. It should be possible for CODI to cover all of its operational costs, and a portion of its notional financial costs, through its interest earnings on loans to community organisations.

To maximise outreach to the poor, it is also important to minimise leakages to the non-poor. Neither the UCDO program nor the GSB program has an explicit means test. It would be appropriate for CODI to adopt an explicit means test to ensure that it reaches the poor. Given the difficulty of measuring income in the informal and subsistence economy, means tests should be based on a range of indicators in addition to income, including housing quality.

2.2 Support through the banking system

The commercial banks are required to lend 20 per cent of their total deposits from the previous year to the rural sector. Fourteen (14) per cent is allocated for lending to agriculture and the remaining 6 per cent for lending to agricultural business. If they do not meet this target they are required to deposit the balance with the Bank for Agriculture and Agricultural Cooperatives (BAAC), but in practice most commercial banks meet the 20 per cent target. However, there are no requirements concerning lending to the poverty sector. Given the extensive outreach of BAAC in the rural areas, the commercial banks tend to serve only large borrowers in rural areas and leave the small and medium borrowers for BAAC. For instance, until the mid-1970s, Bangkok Bank provided a significant number of small loans in the rural areas, but it now concentrates almost exclusively on large borrowers.

The only significant microfinance program channelled through the banking system is the rural development fund administered by GSB and discussed above. GSB is a specialised financial institution supervised by the Ministry of Finance. It operates as a second tier microfinance institution, lending to savings and credit organisations which on-lend to final borrowers. Hence, under this program, GSB does not lend to final borrowers in its own right. The program has been much more successful than most microfinance programs channelled through the banking system in other countries, which have generally involved banks lending direct to final borrowers.

2.3 Government microfinance programs

The largest microfinance program in Thailand is the poverty alleviation project operated by CDD, which provides loans in poor sub-districts. The program operates only in villages that are identified as poor, with a revolving fund of B280,000 ($11,070) established in each village. Individual borrowers are required to have household incomes of less than B5,000 ($200) per person per year, although it is not known how rigorously this is enforced. Borrowers are identified by local government authorities using basic minimum needs data collected by the village, and loans are provided for income-generating activities. Loans to individual borrowers are interest free, with administrative costs met through the budget. By 1995, around B2.8 billion ($110 million) had been advanced to village welfare committees in around 10,000 villages, and nearly B1 billion ($40 million) had been on-lent to final borrowers. The World Bank (1996) noted that the repayment record in 1994 and 1995, for loans advanced in 1993, appeared to be extremely low, varying from 0.02 to 3.1 per cent of loans in different villages.

There appears to be little hard data available on the CDD program. Nevertheless, the data that are available suggest that repayment rates are very low, and that the program is operating more as a grant scheme than as a genuine microfinance program. The program is consuming a large volume of government funds, and does not appear to provide an ongoing stream of financial services to borrowers. If the government intends to persist with the scheme, it should be comprehensively reviewed as a matter of priority. More fundamentally, a scheme operated by a government department through local government authorities is unlikely to be the most cost-effective way to maximise outreach, and it would appear necessary to review the basic design of the scheme.

There are also a number of other government programs for microfinance. For instance, the Cooperative Promotion Department provides soft loans to cooperatives, including for on-lending to their members. Many other departments have also provided funds for microfinance. Most of these programs are quite small. They are generally not means tested, and it is understood that repayment performance has generally been poor.

Establishing CODI presents an excellent opportunity for rationalising existing government programs, especially those operated directly by government departments. It would appear desirable to consolidate the CDD program and other government microfinance programs under CODI.

3 Regulation of non-bank microfinance institutions

3.1 The broad regulatory framework

Cooperatives, including those involved in savings and credit activities, are registered under the Cooperative Societies Act 1968. While there are a number of types of cooperatives, it is mainly the agricultural cooperatives and thrift and credit cooperatives (including the credit union cooperatives) which are involved in savings and credit activities. To be registered, a cooperative must have at least ten members with a common interest, and regulations covering the name, type and objectives of the cooperative, and details of membership. Cooperatives are required to have a board of directors, elected annually by the members at an annual general meeting. The board is responsible for the overall management of the cooperative. Agricultural and thrift and credit cooperatives are exempt from most forms of taxation, including income tax and dividend tax.

While some community organisations engaged in microfinance are registered as cooperatives, most are unregistered and operate informally. For instance, figures from the Urban Community Development Office (UCDO) show that of the 385 members with savings activities, only 66 are legally registered as cooperatives. The other 319 are not registered and operate informally.

There is also a small number of private and non-governmental organisation (NGO) microfinance programs operating in Thailand. These institutions are not owned by their members, and hence they cannot register as cooperatives. There is no specific provision for such organisations to register as NGOs and obtain a legal identity. Most of them are registered as associations or foundations, and provide a range of services of which microfinance is just one. Associations and foundations are not liable for taxation, but are not permitted to undertake business activities. Hence, it is not clear if these organisations are strictly entitled to provide savings and credit services. These organisational forms would not appear to be appropriate for specialist microfinance institutions (MFIs) which provide only financial services.

The Small Enterprise Development Company is one of very few specialist MFIs. It found that the simplest way to obtain a legal identity was to register as a company under the Civil and Commercial Code. To register as a company, it is necessary to meet a minimum capital requirement of B500,000 ($19,760). This may be prohibitive for a small NGO wishing to engage in microfinance. It is also necessary to have a memorandum and articles of association providing details of the name of the company, objectives, election of board of directors, and similar matters. If an MFI registers as a company, it is liable for company income tax if it makes a profit.

Clearly, the company registration procedures are not designed with the needs of NGOs providing microfinance in mind, and some of the requirements may be difficult for NGOs — in particular, smaller NGOs — to comply with. It would be appropriate to establish a simple registration procedure for NGOs wishing to engage in microfinance. To some extent, the lack of such provisions may explain the paucity of microfinance NGOs in Thailand.

3.2 Interest rates

There is a general ceiling of 15 per cent on interest rates applying to loans. This ceiling is spelled out in the Civil and Commercial Code, and applies to all bodies and transactions unless they are specifically excluded. Examples of exclusions are as follows:

(1) Since 1992, all financial institutions regulated by the Bank of Thailand, including commercial banks, have been exempted from this provision, and are free to charge interest rates based on market conditions.

(2) The Bank of Thailand has also excluded thrift and credit cooperatives from this ceiling, but they are subject to an interest rate ceiling of 19 per cent.

Agricultural cooperatives, informal organisations, private and NGO microfinance programs and private transactions are still subject to the 15 per cent ceiling. It is understood that registered cooperatives generally stay within the relevant ceilings. However, this is not the case for unregistered community organisations. In theory, unregistered community organisations are subject to the general 15 per cent interest rate ceiling which applies to all bodies and transactions that are not specifically excluded. However, it is understood that many, if not most, charge higher interest rates. It was reported that most community organisations funded by the Government Savings Bank (GSB) and UCDO charge around 2 per cent interest flat per month to their members.

These interest rate ceilings affect different institutions differently, and are a constraint to the development of microfinance on a sustainable basis. Both the 15 and 19 per cent ceilings are low compared to the interest rates charged by most successful MFIs in other countries. Given the relatively high unit costs associated with microfinance, it is unlikely that programs operating within these ceilings could achieve self-sufficiency. This is implicitly recognised in that the ceilings are not strictly enforced, and even community organisations funded by government agencies such as GSB and UCDO are in practice not prevented from charging higher interest rates. Nevertheless, the ceilings mean that such organisations are currently operating on an illegal basis, and could be subject to challenge or political pressure. Moreover, the ceilings appear to apply more strictly to some organisations than to others. Given the above, it would seem appropriate to remove all of the interest rate ceilings applying to cooperatives, community organisations and other MFIs.

3.3 Prudential regulation and supervision

MFIs in Thailand, whether in the form of credit union cooperatives, unregistered community organisations or NGOs, are subject to few requirements of a prudential nature. Cooperatives are required to have capital divided into shares of equal value. However, there is no specific minimum capital requirement. Nor are there any capital adequacy requirements, liquidity or reserve requirements, or loan loss provisioning requirements on cooperatives engaged in savings and credit activities. Because private and NGO microfinance programs are registered under laws that are not designed with MFIs in mind, they too are not subject to any such prudential requirements.

Reporting requirements are also limited. Registered cooperatives are required to provide a monthly trial balance to the provincial office of the Cooperative Promotion Department. In addition, they are required to provide an annual report, audited financial statements and forward program to the departmental headquarters on an annual basis. It was reported that these requirements are not always fulfilled or rigorously enforced, and that some cooperatives may not have their accounts audited for two or three years at a time. They are not required to provide specific portfolio data on their savings and credit operations. In practice, credit unions are much more accountable to their apex body, the Credit Union League of Thailand, than they are to government regulators. Unregistered community organisations, which make up the majority of MFIs, are not subject to any reporting requirements.

Private and NGO microfinance programs are also not subject to any reporting requirements of a prudential nature. Programs registering as companies are required to provide an annual report and audited financial statements to the Commercial Registration Department within the Ministry of Commerce. However, they are not required to provide regular portfolio reports as is generally required of financial institutions. The situation for programs registered as associations or foundations is similar.

It is generally agreed that it is not appropriate to subject MFIs which do not accept deposits from the public to full prudential regulation and supervision. Moreover, such an approach would be impractical in the case of Thailand. Microfinance in Thailand is dominated by a large number of cooperatives and community organisations owned by their members. There are more than 3,200 such organisations affiliated with GSB and UCDO, and it is not known how many others are in operation. Given the large number of small cooperatives and community organisations, it is unlikely that a government agency could monitor and supervise them in a cost-effective manner. In any case, existing bodies such as the Credit Union League of Thailand, GSB and UCDO are already involved in monitoring many of these organisations. It would therefore be more cost-effective to strengthen the role of existing bodies in monitoring and supervising cooperatives and community organisations, rather than creating a new regulatory structure. This is discussed below.

3.4 Performance and reporting standards of second tier institutions

Where community organisations obtain funds from second tier institutions such as GSB and UCDO, they are subject to various requirements. While there is no legal obligation on organisations to meet these requirements, there is a strong incentive for them to do so if they wish to obtain external funding. Moreover, especially in the case of UCDO, these standards are developed largely through a process of consultation with community organisations.

To become a member of the GSB program, a community organisation is required to provide detailed information about the activities to be implemented and a list of members. Generally, organisations must have at least 25 members, a management committee selected by group members, and an adequate management system. Organisations are also required to have operated a savings program for at least six months before they can obtain a loan from the bank. When applying for a loan, they are required to provide a financial statement and details of the group's operating performance during the past six months. Moreover, every month, organisations are requested to provide a trial balance and some basic portfolio data to the bank. It was reported that some community organisations find it difficult to meet this requirement. In these cases, the bank tries to assist them to improve their accounting procedures.

The requirements for members of the UCDO program are broadly similar. However, there are some slight differences. Unlike the GSB program, there is no minimum size for groups to become members of the program. In addition to having operated a savings program for six months, organisations are encouraged to operate a loans program from their own funds for three months before they obtain a loan from UCDO. Individual members may repay their loans to community organisations daily, weekly, fortnightly or monthly, but not less frequently than monthly. The requirements in terms of management and reporting are similar to the GSB program. UCDO intends to strengthen these guidelines progressively in the future. For instance, UCDO has been giving some thought to developing standards for loan loss provisioning, in consultation with its community organisations.

As well, both programs impose limits on the amount that they will lend to a community organisation. GSB tailors the amount of the loan to the particular circumstances of the group, but with a maximum of five times the group's own funds. Under the UCDO program the maximum loan amount is set at ten times the value of the group's own savings, reflecting the fact that loans are also given for housing. However, it is preferred that groups build up gradually to this amount. These limits are of a quasi-prudential nature in that, to some extent, they restrict the degree to which organisations can leverage members' savings to obtain external resources. However, the limits apply only to loans from GSB and UCDO, and do not prevent organisations from obtaining loans from other sources.

As noted above, it may be more cost-effective to strengthen the role of these bodies in setting standards for and monitoring community organisations, rather than creating a new regulatory structure. The establishment of the Community Organisation Development Institute (CODI) should provide scope for consolidating these guidelines as well as requiring more rigorous reporting on the part of community organisations. It is also expected that guidelines will be strengthened in the future. For instance, there are currently no guidelines covering loan loss provisioning, but UCDO has been giving some thought to developing standards in this area.

Over time, it would be appropriate for CODI to develop standards covering prudential matters such as loan classification and provisioning, savings facilities, accounting and audit standards, etc. These are all critical areas. CODI should consult widely with community organisations in developing such standards, to ensure that they are appropriate to their needs. These standards should also be applied by the Community Development Department (CDD) and other government programs which lend to community organisations, if these are to continue as separate programs.

It would also be appropriate to establish more rigorous reporting standards for community organisations, for example, to ensure that monthly balance sheets and portfolio reports are provided as a matter of course, based on standard formats including for loan loss provisioning. It would then be possible to monitor indicators such as the net asset position, the ratio of savings to loans, and the ratio of liquid assets to savings liabilities, and to initiate remedial action where appropriate.

3.5 Self-regulation

There are no overall institutions involved in the coordination or self-regulation of microfinance in Thailand. In the case of the credit union cooperatives, the Credit Union League of Thailand serves as the apex body. The league has around 50 staff at its headquarters in Bangkok, and a number of field staff throughout the country. It assists in the establishment of credit unions, and provides training to credit unions. The league also requires affiliated credit unions to provide monthly reports on their loan portfolios and annual financial statements. As such, it requires considerably more information than the Cooperative Promotion Department, and monitors credit unions more closely. There is some liaison between the league and the Cooperative Promotion Department. Representatives from the department attend the monthly meetings of the board of the league as observers. The league also advises the department when new credit unions have been trained to the point where they are ready to be registered as credit union cooperatives.

Over time, it would be appropriate to establish national networks for all types of MFIs operating in Thailand, including community organisations and NGO programs. CODI could take the initiative in facilitating networks, although it is important that they operate independently. Such networks could perform a number of important roles, including information exchange, training, research, policy dialogue with government and donor agencies, and establishing standards for self-regulation.

4 Regulation of banks

4.1 Licensing and minimum capital requirements

Cooperatives and other microfinance programs are generally permitted to mobilise savings from their members. However, they are not permitted to raise deposits from the general public. Only institutions with a banking licence are permitted to raise deposits from the general public.

Banking licences are issued by the Minister of Finance under the Commercial Banks Act, following screening by the Bank of Thailand. There is a minimum capital requirement of B750 million ($29.6 million) to establish a commercial bank and, unlike the situation in many other countries, there is no network of small retail banks operating at the local level. The number of licences is restricted, and even institutions meeting all the regulatory requirements may not be able to obtain one. The Bank of Thailand is likely to be very cautious in issuing any new licences in the wake of the current financial crisis. Hence, there would not appear to be any scope for MFIs to establish banks, or for the establishment of small microfinance banks operating at the local level.

While the current cautious approach by the Bank of Thailand is understandable, experience in other countries suggest that small banks are much more likely to become involved in microfinance than large banks. If banks are to play an active role in microfinance, it is important that there be some mechanism to enable small banks to be licensed. It would therefore be appropriate to consider establishing a framework for licensing small banks. There would need to be a realistic minimum capital requirement, and other unnecessary restrictions would need to be removed. In this regard, the experiences of countries such as Indonesia and the Philippines may be instructive (see the Indonesia and Philippines country studies).

4.2 Interest rates

As noted above, there are no longer any restrictions on the interest rates that commercial banks can charge. Hence, interest rate regulation is not a factor impeding regulated banks from becoming involved in microfinance.

4.3 Prudential regulation and supervision

Banks must maintain a capital adequacy ratio of 8.5 per cent of risk-weighted assets. This is higher than the Basle Accord standard of 8 per cent, although the current financial crisis may indicate some lack of attention to appropriate risk weighting. In addition, they must maintain a liquidity reserve of at least 7 per cent of domestic deposits plus short-term offshore borrowing. This reserve must be in the form of deposits at the Bank of Thailand. In terms of reporting requirements, commercial banks are required to provide detailed monthly reports on their portfolio and balance sheet, and six-monthly reports on income and expenses. These requirements appear to be quite standard, and would not impose any undue burden on small banks or banks engaged in microfinance.

The Bank of Thailand also requires that commercial banks classify non-performing assets into three categories:

(1) Sub-standard loans are those where the borrower is unable to repay interest on schedule, but where the loan is still fully collateralised. For these loans, loss provisioning is not required.

(2) Doubtful loans are those where the borrower fails to pay interest for 12 months or more. In these cases, the outstanding debt exceeds collateral value, and a provision of 100 per cent of the unsecured loan value is required.

(3) Bad loans are those that the commercial bank cannot recover, and the whole amount must be written off as a loss.

Hence, while there is no specific requirement for loans by commercial banks to be collateralised, the loan loss provisions treat loans with collateral more favourably than those without. These provisions should not pose any undue difficulties for any commercial banks making unsecured loans, whether to MFIs through linkage arrangements or to final borrowers, so long as they maintain high repayment rates. On the other hand, recent events are likely to make the banks much more cautious in their lending policies and discourage any loans seen as more risky, even if for small amounts.

5 Summary and recommendations

Thailand is at a very different stage of development to most of the other countries in the region, with an annual per capita income of $2,740 in 1995. Reflecting this relatively high per capita income, the incidence of poverty is lower than in most other countries in the region, with an estimated 13.1 per cent of the population below the poverty line in 1992. Nevertheless, the distribution of expenditures is the most unequal of any country included in this study. While the demand for microfinance in Thailand may be less than in most other countries in the region, there is still a need to increase outreach considerably.

Microfinance in Thailand is a mixture of government and non-government activity. The three main programs, those of the Community Development Department (CDD), the Government Savings Bank (GSB) and the Urban Community Development Office (UCDO), are operated through government agencies. The CDD program is very much government driven, with a government department establishing revolving funds at the village level to be managed by local government authorities. On the other hand, the programs of GSB and UCDO are managed by independent boards and operate by extending loans to cooperatives and community organisations, which are mainly non-government bodies owned by their members. There is also a very small number of non-governmental organisations (NGOs) and other private bodies engaged in microfinance. It is not clear why there is so little involvement by NGOs other than organisations owned by their members, but this is an issue that warrants further investigation.

Arrangements for direct support

Ensure independence of overall policy body

The GSB and UCDO programs provide support to community organisations engaged in microfinance, in the form of loanable funds and technical assistance. The government is currently planning to establish the Community Organisation Development Institute (CODI), which will take over the overall policy responsibility for the programs operated by GSB and UCDO. In establishing CODI, the government should ensure that it is managed by an independent board and is free from political and bureaucratic interference.

Establish specific targets and parameters

Neither the GSB program nor UCDO is close to self-sufficiency. Clearly, if the two programs could increase their self-sufficiency, they could increase their outreach to poor clients for any given outlay of government funds. In setting up CODI, the government should establish explicit targets and timetables in terms of outreach and self-sufficiency. Moreover, neither the UCDO program nor the GSB program has an explicit means test. The CODI should adopt an explicit means tests to ensure that it reaches the poor.

Consolidate microfinance under central organisation

The largest microfinance program in Thailand is the poverty alleviation project operated by the CDD, which provides loans in poor sub-districts. There appears to be little hard data available on the CDD program. Nevertheless, the data that are available suggest that repayment rates are very low, and that the program is operating more as a grant scheme than as a genuine microfinance program. There are also a number of other government programs for microfinance, but it is understood that repayment performance has generally been poor. The government should consolidate the CDD program and other government microfinance programs under CODI.

Regulation of non-bank microfinance institutions

Register NGOs engaging with microfinance

Cooperatives, including those involved in savings and credit activities, are registered under the Cooperative Societies Act 1968. While some community organisations engaged in microfinance are registered as cooperatives, most are unregistered and operate informally.

There is also a small number of private and NGO microfinance programs operating in Thailand. There is no specific provision for such organisations to register as NGOs and obtain a legal identity. Most of them are registered as associations or foundations, but these organisational forms are not appropriate for specialist microfinance institutions (MFIs) which provide solely financial services. Nor are company registration procedures designed with the needs of NGOs providing microfinance in mind. The government should establish a simple registration procedure for NGOs wishing to engage in microfinance.

Remove interest rate ceilings

There is a general ceiling on interest rates applying to loans of 15 per cent, which applies to all bodies and transactions unless they are specifically excluded. The ceiling applies to agricultural cooperatives, unregistered community organisations, and private and NGO microfinance programs. Thrift and credit cooperatives are subject to a separate interest rate ceiling of 19 per cent.

It is understood that registered cooperatives generally stay within the relevant ceilings. However, many if not most unregistered community organisations charge higher interest rates. Nevertheless, the ceilings mean that such organisations are currently operating on an illegal basis, and could be subject to challenge or political pressure. Moreover, the ceilings appear to be applied more strictly to some organisations than to others. The government should remove all of the interest rate ceilings applying to cooperatives, community organisations and other MFIs.

Develop prudential and reporting requirements

MFIs in Thailand, whether in the form of credit union cooperatives, unregistered community organisations or NGOs, are subject to few requirements of a prudential nature.

Reporting requirements are also limited, and do not cover the regular portfolio reports generally required of financial institutions. Nevertheless, it is generally agreed that it is not appropriate to subject MFIs which do not accept deposits from the public to full prudential regulation and supervision. Moreover, such an approach would be impractical in the case of Thailand.

Where community organisations obtain funds from second tier institutions such as GSB and UCDO, they are subject to various requirements. While there is no legal obligation on organisations to meet these requirements, there is a strong incentive for them to do so if they wish to obtain external funding. The establishment of CODI provides scope for consolidating these guidelines, and requiring more rigorous reporting on the part of community organisations.

CODI should develop standards covering prudential matters such as loan classification and provisioning, savings facilities, accounting and audit standards through consultation with community organisations. It should also establish more rigorous reporting standards for community organisations.

Establish national MFO networks

There are no overall institutions involved in the coordination or self-regulation of microfinance. It would be appropriate to establish national networks for all types of MFIs operating in Thailand, including community organisations and NGO programs. Such networks could perform a number of important roles, including information exchange, training, research, policy dialogue with government and donor agencies, and establishing standards for self-regulation.

Regulation of banks

Establish a framework for licensing small MFI banks

Cooperatives and other microfinance programs are not permitted to raise deposits from the general public. Only institutions with a banking licence are permitted to raise deposits from the general public. There is a minimum capital requirement of B750 million ($29.6 million) to establish a commercial bank, and unlike the situation in many other countries, there is no network of small retail banks operating at the local level. The number of licences is also restricted. There is therefore little if any scope for MFIs to establish banks or for the establishment of small microfinance banks operating at the local level.

If banks are to play an active role in microfinance, it is important that there be some mechanism to enable small banks to be licensed. The government should consider establishing a framework for licensing small banks. In this regard, the experiences of countries such as Indonesia and the Philippines may be instructive.

References

Deloitte and Touche Management Consultants. 1996. Strengthening poverty reduction and income distribution policy analysis and planning: Poverty analysis component: Final report. Prepared in association with Agrodev Canada, Inc. for the Asian Development Bank and the Royal Thai Government, unpublished.

Medhi Krongkaew. 1997. Macroeconomic policies and poverty: The Thai experience. Background paper for the Asian Regional Policy Workshop on Macro Policies and Micro Interventions for Poverty Alleviation, Bangkok, 5–7 February.

NESDB. 1997. The Eighth National Economic and Social Development Plan. National Economic and Social Development Board, Bangkok.

Paiboon Wattanasiritham, Orajitt Bamrungsakulsawat & Muller, Larissa. 1996. Effective participatory urban management in Thailand: A case study of the Urban Community Development Office. Paper prepared for the Policy Seminar on Effective Participatory Urban Management, Shanghai, 7–9 November.

Pittayapol Nattadarol. 1997. Agricultural finance policy in the context of Thailand's changing economic structure. Paper prepared for the Seventh Technical Consultation on the Scheme for Agricultural Credit Development, Teheran, 4–5 May.

Somsuk Boonyabancha. 1995 'The emergence of community savings and credit activities'. *Trialog*, vol.47, pp.20–24.

Somsuk Boonyabancha. 1996. Case study of the Urban Community Development Office, Thailand. Mimeo.

World Bank. 1996. *Thailand: Growth, Poverty and Income Distribution: An Economic Report.* Report no.15689-TH, World Bank, Washington D.C.

Persons consulted

Mr Paiboon Wattanasiritham	Managing Director Urban Community Development Office
Ms Pam Tansanguanwong	Program Manager The Asia Foundation
Ms Marie Luise Haberberger	Senior Rural Banking Advisor Thai-German Technical Cooperation Project
Mr Supachai Sathakarn	Vice President Bank for Agriculture and Agricultural Cooperatives
Mr Robert Moreland	Consulting Economist
Mr Chamnan Rungsaeng	Director, Rural Development Coordination Division National Economic and Social Development Board
Mr Suparat Manmin	Assistant Director Rural Development Coordination Division National Economic and Social Development Board
Mr Chitti Chuenyong	Chief of Monitoring and Evaluation Section, RDCD National Economic and Social Development Board
Mr Montri Ramana	Chief, Credit Refinancing and Appraisal Division Bank of Thailand
Ms Sunet Ratanavanich	Chief, Information and Analysis Division Financial Institutions Supervision and Development Department Bank of Thailand
Ms Ruchukorn Sangsubhan	Chief, Financial System and Development Section Economic Research Department, Bank of Thailand
Mr Yongkiat Jaranasaksakul	Chief Analyst, Financial Institutions Supervision and Development Department Bank of Thailand

Ms Primsara Poonyathawon	Economist, Economic Research Department Bank of Thailand
Ms Mala Kholuckchai	Economist, Economic Research Department Bank of Thailand
Dr Charles Myers	Senior Coordinator, SHD Resource Facility United Nations Development Programme
Ms Nipa Krupaisarn	Manager, Income Generation and Urban Development Unit United Nations Development Programme
Mr Colin White	Project Manager, Highland Peoples Programme United Nations Development Programme
Ms Juri Oka	Junior Professional Officer United Nations Development Programme
Mr Montri Taworn	Chief, Agricultural Cooperative Promotion Section Cooperative Promotion Department
Mrs Dusanee Danapong	Cooperative Technician Cooperative Promotion Department
Mrs Kwanchai Watanachuwakul	Cooperative Technician Cooperative Promotion Department
Mr Cherdahai Phromkaen	Cooperative Technician Cooperative Promotion Department
Ms Sunee Karndee	Cooperative Technician Cooperative Promotion Department
Mr Bantorn Ondam	Chairman Small Enterprise Development Company
Ms Yupaporn Boontid	Manager Small Enterprise Development Company
Mr Terdsak Jittimit	Assistant Vice President Agricultural and Rural Credits Department Bangkok Bank
Mr Thiraboon Buasri	Section Chief Agricultural and Rural Credits Department Bangkok Bank
Ms Ubonvan Keesiri	Senior Loans Officer Agricultural and Rural Credits Department Bangkok Bank
Dr Nipon Poapongsakorn	Vice President Thailand Development Research Institute Foundation
Mr Sunai Saubhayana	Deputy Director-General Government Savings Bank
Mr Vicheal Nititham	Assistant Director-General Government Savings Bank

The Foundation For Development Cooperation

Publications on Microfinance

Publication	Prices Australia (incl P&H)	Prices Overseas excluding Europe (incl P&H)	Prices Europe (incl P&H)
Best Practice of Banking with the Poor, 1995, x + 117 pp	$18.00	$23.00	£12.00
Banking with the Poor, 1992, xiv + 223 pp.	$18.00	$23.00	£12.00
Access to credit: Creating income and jobs for the world's poor, 1993, 16 pp., full colour. An introduction to the ideas of *Banking with the Poor.*	$6.50	$10.00	£5.00
How to build self help groups for successful banking with the poor: A rural model, revised 1995, 16 pp.	$2.00	$3.00	£1.00
How to build self help groups for successful banking with the poor: An urban model, 1995, 20 pp.	$2.00	$3.00	£1.00
V. Puhazhendhi, *Transaction Costs of Lending to the Rural Poor* (India), 1995, xiii + 98 pp.	$15.00	$20.00	£9.00
Gilberto M. Llanto & Ronald T. Chua, *Transaction Costs of Lending to the Poor,* 1996, xiv + 72 pp. A case study of Philippine NGOs.	$15.00	$20.00	£9.00
Banking with the Poor in the South Pacific, 1996, iv + 25 pp.	$8.50	$12.00	£5.50
Paul B. McGuire, *Accounting and Reporting Standards for Microfinance Institutions,* 1996, 28 pp.	$6.50	$10.00	£5.50
Paul B. McGuire & John D. Conroy, *Bank-NGO Linkages and Transaction Costs of Lending to the Poor through Groups: Evidence from India and the Philippines,* 1996, ii + 18 pp.	$6.50	$10.00	£5.50
Paul B. McGuire, *Microfinance in the Pacific Island Countries,* 1997, viii + 127 pp.	$23.00	$28.00	£15.00
Getting the Framework Right: Policy and Regulation for Microfinance in Asia, 1998, xx + 307pp.	$32.00	$39.00	£20.00

Please send your order to:

The Foundation for Development Cooperation
PO Box 10445 Adelaide Street
Brisbane QLD 4000 Australia
Tel:+ 61 7 3236 4633
Fax: +61 7 3236 4696
E.mail: fdc@ozemail.com.au

Note

For UK and European customers, Sterling cheques drawn on a UK bank are acceptable.
USA customers can send personal cheques and should add $7.00 to total to cover collection charges.